The *Act*
Of *Writing*

The Act Of Writing

Canadian Essays for Composition

Ronald Conrad

Ryerson Polytechnical Institute

McGraw-Hill Ryerson Limited

Toronto   Montréal   New York   St. Louis   San Francisco
Auckland   Bogotá   Guatemala   Hamburg   Lisbon   London
Madrid   Mexico   New Delhi   Panama   Paris   San Juan
São Paulo   Singapore   Sydney   Tokyo

THE ACT OF WRITING: Canadian Essays for Composition

Copyright © McGraw-Hill Ryerson Limited, 1983. All rights reserved. No part of this publication may be reproduced, stored in a retrieval system, or transmitted, in any form or by any means, electronic, mechanical, photocopying, recording, or otherwise, without prior written permission of McGraw-Hill Ryerson Limited.

6 7 8 9 0 WC 2 1 0 9 8 7 6

Printed and bound in Canada

Cover Photo: © Miller Services. Photo from *Camerique,* Blue Bell, PA.

Canadian Cataloguing in Publication Data

Conrad, Ronald, date
  The act of writing: Canadian essays for composition

Includes index.
ISBN 0-07-549067-6

1. English language - Rhetoric.   2. Canadian essays (English).*   I. Title.

PE1429.C66   808'.0427   C82-095201-X

TABLE OF CONTENTS

AND THEN. . . .

Chapter 1: NARRATION   15

WRITING ABOUT MYSELF

GEORGE GABORI, Coming of Age in Putnok   **17**
"There were cheers and laughter as Tivadar hit me in the nose before I got my jacket off. It was not the first time I had tasted my own blood, but it was the first time a Christian had made it flow."

WRITING ABOUT OTHERS

FOR EXAMPLE. . . .

Chapter 2: Example   55

IT'S LARGE AND YELLOW AND. . . .

Chapter 3: DESCRIPTION   81

HERE'S WHY. . . .

Chapter 4:   CAUSE AND EFFECT   113

IT'S JUST THE OPPOSITE OF. . . .

Chapter 5: COMPARISON AND CONTRAST 155

IN A WAY, IT'S LIKE. . . .

Chapter 6: ANALOGY and related devices   189

THERE ARE THREE KINDS OF THEM. . . .

Chapter 7: CLASSIFICATION 219

HERE'S HOW IT'S DONE. . . .

Chapter 8: PROCESS ANALYSIS 255

HERE'S EXACTLY WHAT IT IS. . . .

Chapter 9: EXTENDED DEFINITION 301

TABLE OF CONTENTS BY SUBJECT

OUTSIDERS

THE CITY

WORK

LEISURE

VIOLENCE IN SOCIETY

SCIENCE AND TECHNOLOGY

THE ARTS

LAUGHS

PEOPLES AND PLACES

ACKNOWLEDGEMENTS

Ian Adams: "Living With Automation in Winnipeg" from *The Poverty Wall* by Ian Adams. Reprinted by permission of the Canadian Publishers, McClelland and Stewart Limited, Toronto.

Robert Thomas Allen: "Who Is Your Skinny Friend, Mary?" from *We Gave You the Electric Toothbrush* by Robert Thomas Allen. Copyright © 1971 by Robert Thomas Allen. Reprinted by permission of Doubleday & Company Inc.

Doris Anderson: "The 51-Per-Cent Minority," Doris Anderson, *Maclean's* January 1980. Reprinted by permission of Doris Anderson, novelist.

Margaret Atwood: "Canadians: What Do They Want?" by Margaret Atwood from *Mother Jones,* January 1982. Used by permission of *Mother Jones.*

Pierre Berton: "The Dirtiest Job in the World" from *The Smug Minority* by Pierre Berton. Reprinted by permission of The Canadian Publishers, McClelland and Stewart Limited, Toronto.

Harry Bruce: "Johnny Canuck is a Yuk," Harry Bruce, *Saturday Night,* November 1976. Used by permission of the author.

Emily Carr: "D'Sonoqua" from *Klee Wyck* by Emily Carr. © 1941 by Clarke, Irwin & Company Limited. Used by permission.

Gregory Clark: "The Cat" by Gregory Clark, used by permission of Montreal Standard Inc.

Austin Clarke: Excerpt from *Growing Up Stupid Under the Union Jack* by Austin Clarke. Reprinted by permission of the Canadian Publishers, McClelland and Stewart Limited, Toronto.

Susan Cole: "Jesse James and the New Frontier," by Susan G. Cole, *The Globe and Mail,* February 6, 1982. Permission granted by the author and *The Globe and Mail,* Toronto.

Mary Conrad and Jean-Paul Chavy: Translation of letter by Edgar Roussel to The Honourable Mark MacGuigan in *Le Devoir.* Permission granted by the translator and by The Honourable Mark MacGuigan.

Donald Creighton: excerpt from *Canada: The Heroic Beginnings,* 1974. Reproduced by permission of the Minister, Supply and Services Canada from the publication *Canada: The Heroic Beginnings,* published by Macmillan of Canada in cooperation with Indian and Northern Affairs Canada, Parks Canada and the Canadian Government Publishing Centre, Supply and Services Canada.

Robertson Davies: "The Decorums of Stupidity" from *A Voice from the Attic* by Robertson Davies. Reprinted by permission of the Canadian Publishers, McClelland and Stewart Limited, Toronto.

Barry Dickie: "The Only Lesson I Still Remember" by Barry Dickie, *The Globe and Mail,* November 8, 1980. Used by permission of the author.

Kildare Dobbs: "The Scar" from *Reading The Time,* 1968, Macmillan of Canada. © copyright Kildare Dobbs.

John Fraser: "Strangers" from *The Chinese: Portrait of a People,* John Fraser. Copyright © 1980 by John Fraser.

Robert Fulford: "Where, Exactly, Are This Book's Readers?" from *Crisis at the Victory Burlesk,* Robert Fulford, 1968.

George Gabori: "Coming of Age in Putnok" from *When Evils Were Most Free,* George Gabori, Deneau Publishers. Used by permission of the publishers.

Dave Godfrey: "No More Teacher's Dirty Looks," from *Gutenberg Two,* Dave Godfrey et al, 1979. By permission of Press Porcépic.

Martin Allerdale Grainger: "In Vancouver" from *Woodsmen of the West* by Martin Allerdale Grainger, 1908. Courtesy of The Canadian Kinetoscope Company Limited.

Ray Guy: "Outharbor Menu" from *That Far Greater Bay,* Ray Guy, 1976. First published by Breakwater Books Ltd., St. John's Newfoundland.

Roderick Haig-Brown: "Articles of Faith for Good Anglers" from *The Master and His Fish* by Roderick Haig-Brown. Reprinted by permission of The Canadian Publishers, McClelland and Stewart Limited, Toronto.

Charles Yale Harrison: from *Generals Die in Bed* by Charles Yale Harrison (Potlatch Publications Limited, Hamilton Ontario).

Joy Kogawa: Selection reprinted from the novel *Obasan* by Joy Kogawa, published by Lester & Orpen Dennys. © Joy Kogawa, 1981.

Bruce Hutchinson: "Cowboy from Holland" from *Canada: Tomorrow's Giant,* Bruce Hutchinson, 1957. Permission granted by the author.

Maryon Kantaroff: Excerpt reprinted from Maryon Kantaroff, "Breaking Out of the Female Mould," in *Women in the Canadian Mosaic*, ed. Gwen Matheson (Toronto, 1976), by permission of PMA Books.

W.P. Kinsella: "Junk Mail Junkie" by W.P. Kinsella in *Weekend Magazine*, June 9, 1979. Used by permission of Montreal Standard Inc.

Myrna Kostash: "Profile of the Rapist as an Ordinary Man" by Myrna Kostash, *Maclean's*, April 1975. Used by permission of the author.

Gary Lautens: "Man, You're a Great Player!" from *Laughing with Lautens* by Gary Lautens. Reprinted by permission of McGraw-Hill Ryerson Limited.

Stephen Leacock: "How to Live to be 200" from *Literary Lapses* by Stephen Leacock. Reprinted by permission of the Canadian Publishers, McClelland and Stewart Limited, Toronto.

Félix Leclerc: Excerpt from *Pieds nus dans l'aube*. Coll. "Bibliothèque canadienne-francaise." Montréal, Fides 1978. Permission to reprint Philip Stratford's English translation of the excerpt granted by Nelson Canada Limited.

David Macfarlane: "Skin Trade" by David Macfarlane in *Weekend Magazine*, May 19, 1979. Used by permission of Montreal Standard Inc.

Hugh MacLennan: Selection from *Barometer Rising* by Hugh MacLennan. Reprinted by permission of the author and his agent, Blanche C. Gregory, Inc. Copyright © 1941 by Hugh MacLennan.

Thierry Mallet: Extract from "Glimpses of the Barren Lands" by Captain Thierry Mallet, one of the Canada fur trading post settlers of REVILLON FRERES, pioneer fur company since 1723. Permission also granted by The Atlantic Monthly.

Philip Marchand: "Learning to Love the Big City" from *Just Looking, Thank You* by Philip Marchand. Copyright © 1976 by Philip Marchand.

Janice McEwen: "Thunderstrokes and Firebolts." Reprinted with the permission of Janice Burchell McEwen and *Harrowsmith Magazine*. Copyright © 1978 by Camden House Publishing Ltd.

Christie McLaren: "Suitcase Lady Holds a Package of Dreams," from *The Globe and Mail*, January 24, 1981. Permission granted by *The Globe and Mail*.

Kenneth Mews: "You Dirty Rat!" by Kenneth Mews, reprinted from *Audio Scene Canada* magazine, June 1981.

Farley Mowat: Excerpt from *People of the Deer* by Farley Mowat © 1952. Used by permission of the author.

Richard J. Needham: "A Sound of Deviltry by Night" from *The Hypodermic Needham*, 1970. Used by permission of Richard J. Needham and *The Globe and Mail*, Toronto.

Andrew Osler: "Warily into a Wired-up World," Andrew Osler from *Maclean's*, November 16, 1981. Used by permission of the author.

Al Pittman: "The Day I Became a Canadian" by Al Pittman in *Weekend Magazine*, March 31, 1979. Used by permission of Montreal Standard Inc.

Al Purdy: "The Iron Road" from *No Other Country,* Al Purdy. Reprinted by permission of the Canadian Publishers, McClelland & Stewart Limited, Toronto.

Alan Stewart: "Cars Make The Man a Boy" by Alan Stewart, *The Globe and Mail,* May 9, 1981. Used by permission of the author.

Judy Stoffman: "The Way of All Flesh," by Judy Stoffman, *Weekend Magazine,* September 15, 1979. Reprinted by permission of the author.

Cindy Titus: Essay entitled "The Debate" by Cindy Titus. Used by permission of the author.

Catherine Parr Traill: Excerpt from *The Female Emigrant's Guide* and *Hints on Canadian Housekeeping* by Mrs. C.P. Traill, Toronto, 1854.

Marvin A. Zuker and June Callwood: "You are a Child" from *The Law is Not For Women,* Zuker & Callwood, © 1976 Pitman Publishing. Reproduced with permission from the publisher.

TO THE STUDENT

This book is designed to help you develop a skill: your writing. But it is designed for you on another level as well: If you love or hate computers, if the small town bores you or the big city excites you, if cars remind you of sex, if you like being young and fear growing old, if you work with factory machines and feel like one yourself, if you think Americans help us or harm us, if you have suffered because of your race or language or religion or sex, if you like hockey because it's a rough game, if you love or hate work — then read the essays in this book. Hear what some of our most provocative Canadian writers say about life. You will agree sometimes and disagree other times. But since most of these writers discuss things that in some way you have experienced or will experience, let them make their argument. You may learn something. And if you sometimes disagree, you may still learn something as your reaction helps you to realize what you believe.

The essays in this book vary greatly. Some are short and some are long; some are easy and some are challenging; some are funny and some are serious. But they all have two important things in common:

    1. They are models of good writing — writing that is entertaining,

graceful in style, and clearly focused on a message. Just as hearing good models of speech helps us to speak, reading good models of writing helps us to write.

2. They illustrate the most common ways of organizing information. Each chapter contains four to six essays that all use the same underlying pattern of development. As you begin a chapter, you will probably read two or three of the essays, then discuss their message and their underlying form in class. (Key terms that appear in SMALL CAPITALS in the discussion questions are explained in a glossary at the end of the book.) Finally, you will practice the form that you have discussed in an essay of your own.

The essay topics are carefully chosen for their significance. Writing about things that matter increases our interest in the writing. And research has demonstrated what many students and teachers have experienced: it is motivation, more than any other factor, that leads to improvement in writing. It is my hope, then, that you will enjoy not only these readings but also the act of writing that follows them.

R. C.

TO THE TEACHER

This book is the first composition anthology to combine all these features: an introduction to the process of writing essays, a sizable collection of essays that are all Canadian, an arrangement of essays according to their basic form, an introduction to the form exemplified in each chapter, an introduction to each author, discussion questions and assignments after each selection, a very wide selection of essay topics at the end of each chapter, and a glossary.

The introduction to writing essays puts to rest some widespread misconceptions that plague students in the classroom, then attempts to describe what it is that an essayist actually does. It emphasizes the individuality of the writer, the importance of motivation, and a balance of spontaneity and craftsmanship.

The essays are all by Canadians or by persons with Canadian experience, but the scope ranges widely: some essays are about Canada, some are about other countries, and most are concerned with such universal themes as childhood, aging, work, technology, sport and war. The use of Canadian essays is not a statement of nationalism. In fact, it is an attempt to bring to Canada the kind of anthology that is taken for granted in other countries: a collection of works that are mostly universal in theme but that, naturally, draw a good part of their content from the country in which the book will be used.

The selections are chosen first of all for their quality, so that they will serve as enjoyable reading and as models of good writing. The other main considerations are clarity of organization; variety and significance of subject matter; variety of style, tone, length and difficulty; and representation of women and minorities.

Composition anthologies produced in this country have tended to group essays by subject matter or by function, neglecting the more basic and useful matter of form. The Table of Contents by Subject does group the essays of this book by the first method, but their main grouping in chapters is by underlying form — on the theory that patterns of organization, once learned, can support whatever subject matter is at hand and whatever purpose is required.

Narration starts the book off because no approach is easier or more motivating for a first assignment than writing a story, in chronological order, about oneself. Example and Description follow, because these methods of development are used to some degree in almost all writing. Cause and Effect and the following chapter, Comparison and Contrast, are the heart of the book: these are probably the most effective patterns to know. Analogy and Classification follow Comparison and Contrast, for they are both varieties of comparison. Process Analysis and Extended Definition end the book. Although they are well-used devices of organization, one or both might be omitted from a busy course without doing major damage.

In nine chapters this book offers 48 selections. Most are essays. A few are carefully selected popular journalism, and a few are self-contained passages of fiction or autobiography. Most chapters contain five or six selections and no chapter less than four, on the theory that a large choice enables a teacher to pick works whose subject, approach and level of difficulty best fit the needs of the class.

Each of the nine chapters begins with a discussion of how and why to use the form at hand, and ends with a selection of 25 to 30 essay topics chosen to fit that form. Some of these topics came from a survey that asked students what they would most like to write about; others were originated by students in journal writing or in open-ended class essays; still others have been newly devised to tap some of the students' deepest concerns and channel them into motivation for writing. The reason for this attention to topics is that no one problem is more destructive to the performance of both student and teacher than dull or superficial subject matter. How can writing be important if its content is not? And how can a teacher enjoy or even tolerate marking without an interest in *what* the students are saying? Further topics for writing appear *within* the chapter, one or more at the end of each selection. If class members have had a good discussion about the selection, their motivation and writing performance may be greatest if they explore these topics which draw upon both the subject and underlying form of the essay that precedes them.

About half the writers represented in this book are nationally known. Others are younger or newer writers, regional writers, unjustly forgotten writers, and in a few cases not professional writers at all (two are students, one is a sculptor, one is a judge and one is a convict). On the theory that writings do not exist in a vacuum, each author is introduced in a short biography that appears before his or her essay. And after each essay appear questions and topics for class discussion, divided into three categories: Structure, Style and Ideas. A *teacher's manual,* gratis upon request, gives answers to all those questions that are not obviously open-ended. It also lists vocabulary that may need attention, ranks each selection by level of difficulty, and gives suggestions for teaching the material.

Finally, a glossary at the end defines literary terms often used in the discussion questions; when one of these terms is a key part of a passage, it appears in SMALL CAPITALS.

I would like to thank the people who helped me in planning and writing this book: students, colleagues, writers and editors. I would particularly like to thank Christie McLaren, Andrew Osler, Philip Marchand, Cindy Titus, Barry Dickie, Alan Stewart, Susan Cole, Judy Stoffman, Kenneth Mews, Marvin Zuker and Janice McEwen, who gave me information that has appeared in the introductions to essays, and Doris Anderson who updated "The 51-Per-Cent Minority" for this book. Thanks also to Robert Nielson of Potlatch Press, to Paule Deneau of Deneau Publishers & Company, to Richard Brown of York Memorial Collegiate Institute in Toronto, and to Karen Mulhallen, John Cook and Bill Emery of the English Department and Jean-Paul Chavy of the French Department at Ryerson Polytechnical Institute. This is as good a place as any to express appreciation to Don Strickland, whose love of good writing, whose endless stories about the writers he has known — including his own great-great aunt Catherine Parr Traill, who appears in this book — and whose interest in this project have encouraged me greatly. Thanks also to the person who said that in Canada this book could not be written, because that's why I wrote it. Finally and especially, I'd like to thank Mary, Suzanne, Charles and Katherine.

R. C.

THE ACT OF WRITING

Writing is one of the most widely misunderstood of human activities. It is odd that after all the years we have spent in school, after all the hours we have spent reading other peoples' writing and producing our own, most of us cannot say what really happens when we write. We can describe other complicated tasks — driving a car, baking bread, building a radio or programming a computer. But to most people the act of writing is a mystery. Not that we don't have theories, either those told us in school or those we have arrived at ourselves. But many of these theories are misconceptions that actually hinder our efforts to write. Let's look at some of them.

MISCONCEPTION: *Writing is like following a blueprint: I figure it all out in advance and then just fill in the details.*
Of course an outline, used sensibly, will help. But too many of us were taught in school that our best thinking goes into a logical and detailed outline — and that the writing itself is secondary. Thus we are reduced to carpenters or plumbers of the written word, who merely saw, cut and fit the pieces in place once the master plan has been established. The problem with this reassuringly logical approach is that it views writing as a science, not as the art that all our practical experience tells us it is. How many of us have given up on a required outline, done our thinking mostly as we wrote the essay itself, then produced an outline by seeing what we just wrote? Or how many of us have painfully constructed a detailed outline in advance, only to find while writing the essay that our real message does not fit the plan?

Writing is exploring! We know the direction in which we will go and the main landmarks we hope to pass, but not every twist and turn of the path. What a dull trip it would be if we did! Let's leave room for discovery, because some of our best ideas occur in the act of writing. But while avoiding the rigor mortis of overplanning, let's not go to the opposite extreme, like Stephen Leacock's famous horseman who "rode madly off in all directions." We do work best with an outline, five or ten or fifteen lines that define the main point and how we will support it. But our outline should be a brief one — a compass on a journey, not a blueprint for a construction project.

MISCONCEPTION: *If I don't hit it right the first time, I've failed.*
It's not hard to see where this idea came from: in school we write so many essays and tests within the limits of one class period that writing in a hurry begins to seem normal. But merely completing such an assignment is difficult; seriously revising it is impossible. Few people, under these circumstances, can "hit it right the first time." Professional writers

1

know this; most of them take longer to write than do the rest of us. They tinker with words and sentences, they cross out and replace sections, they go through two or three or even five or ten drafts — and sometimes they throw the whole thing out and start over. These writers know by experience that writing is not a hit-or-miss affair with only one try allowed, but a process. They know that careful polishing can yield astonishing results.

Unfortunately, little can be done to polish an in-class essay. Your other writing, though, deserves better. Scrutinize it. Hear it read aloud. Replace weak words with strong ones, and vague words with exact ones. Revise awkward sentences. Make sure that what you mean is what you say. Of course the process is work, but that work brings with it the pleasure of craftsmanship.

MISCONCEPTION: When I write, I am speaking on paper.
If you have heard yourself speaking on tape, you were no doubt surprised at the number of filler words you used. "Uh," "um," "well" and "hmmm" are good to fill in the gaps between your thoughts, but hardly help to carry the message. And if you listened closely, you may have been surprised at the number of incomplete statements — fragments that by themselves made little or no sense. Fillers and fragments are tolerated in speech because, after all, we are making up our message on the spot. There is no chance to plan, revise, proofread or polish.

But in writing there is, and this fact increases the expectations of your reader far beyond those of your listener. Language in written form is planned. It is complete. It is precise and concise. It uses standard words. It is punctuated. It follows all the rules. In short, it is a product of the time that its written form allows you to give it, not a spur-of-the-moment hope-for-the-best effort like the speech that comes so easily from your mouth.

MISCONCEPTION: The best words are the biggest words.
Variations on this theme are *If my writing looks scholarly it will impress the reader,* and even *If I make my essay so difficult that no one knows what I'm saying, everyone will believe me.* At the roots of these widespread ideas is a totally false notion that writing is a kind of competition between writer and reader. If the writer is obscure enough he will make the reader feel like a dummy and will thus win the game.

Avoiding the game altogether is difficult when so many leaders in business, education and government play it. The first step toward open communication, though, is to think of your reader not as an opponent but as an ally. You are both working toward the same goal, which is the reader's clear understanding of your ideas. Another step is to admit that words small in size can be large in meaning. The best-loved writings in our language show a strong preference for short words. Writing made of them is more concise, more vivid and usually more understandable than writing made of the elephantine words that some of us ransack the dictionary for. When a long word conveys your meaning best — perhaps like "elephantine" above — by all means use it. But all too often the writer, like the architect, finds that *more is less.*

MISCONCEPTION: *I don't like to write.*
For some unfortunate people this statement is true. For most who say it, though, the truth is really "I don't like to *begin* writing." Who does? Staring at that blank page is like staring from a diving board at the cold water below. But a swimmer and a writer both work up their courage to plunge in, and soon they both experience a new sensation: they don't want to come out. Teachers whose students write journals in class see the process at work every day. As class begins, the writers are filled with stress: they chew their pens and frown as they stare at the page to be filled. But a few minutes later they are scribbling furiously away, recording in an almost trance-like state their latest experiences, feelings and insights. And when the teacher asks them to stop, in order to begin the next activity, they are annoyed: they sigh and *keep on writing* until asked a second or third time to stop.

Let's admit that most writers — and that includes professionals — dread the beginning. Let's also admit that most writers enjoy the rest of it, hard work though it may be.

With some of the most widespread misconceptions behind us, let's take a fresh look at the act of writing. First, let's allow for personal differences. *Know yourself!* If you are the kind of person whose desk is piled a foot high with papers and books, whose closet is an avalanche waiting to happen and whose shoes have not been shined in two years, you may write best by planning little and emphasizing your spontaneity. If you are the kind of person who plans an August holiday in January, who keeps a budget right down to the penny, and who washes the car every Wednesday and Saturday whether it needs it or not, you may write best by planning extensively. On the other hand, your natural tendencies may have caused you problems and may therefore need to be fought. If your spontaneity has produced writings that can't stay on topic, plan more: make a careful outline. If overorganizing has sucked the life out of your writing, free yourself up: leave more room for discovery as you write. Whatever the case, use the approach that works for *you.*

Let's allow also for differences in assignments. If you are dashing off a short personal sketch, your planning may be no more than an idea and a few moments of thought. If you are writing a 30-page research essay, the product of weeks in the library, you may need an outline two pages long. No one approach works for every person and for every assignment. Keep in mind, then, that the process we are about to examine is a *starting point,* a basis but not a blueprint for your own writing.

The beginnings of an essay can be found in the answering of several questions:

1. *Why am I writing?* This most basic of questions too often goes unasked. If the answer is "to fill up five pages," "to impress" or "to get an 'A'," you are beginning with a severe handicap. The immediate reason to write may be a class assignment, but the real reason must be to communicate something of value. Otherwise your motivation is lost and so is your performance. Therefore, choose from a list of topics the one that is most significant to you. If no topic seems significant, devise a way to *make* one significant. Look at it from a new viewpoint or approach it in some unusual way. If that fails, and if your teacher is approachable, voice your concern and suggest an alternative topic. One teacher always made his first-year university students analyze the relative merits of chocolate and vanilla ice cream, on the theory that a dull subject will not distract a writer from the real goals: grammar and style. He was wrong. Research demonstrates that motivation is the prime cause of improvement in writing — and motivation comes largely from writing about things that matter.

When you write on your own, as in a private journal, you may still need to answer the question *Why am I writing?* Simply recording events can be dull. Record also your feelings, your perceptions and your conclusions about those events. If you have personal problems, as most people do, confront them on the page. The more you discover yourself and your world through writing, the more important the writing becomes.

2. *How big is my topic?* Classroom essays are shorter than most people realize. A book may contain 100,000 words; a magazine article 2000 or 5000; a classroom essay as few as 500 or even 250. Therefore narrowing the essay topic is more important than most people realize.

One student, who had been a political prisoner, decided to write about economic systems. He knew the subject well and was committed to it. But what he attempted was an analysis of communism, socialism and capitalism— all in two pages! A lack of focus spread his very short essay so thin that it approached the state of saying nothing about everything. It was the barest scratching of the surface, a summary of basic facts that everyone already knows.

If the same person had described his arrest and imprisonment — or even one day in his cell — he might have said far more about the system he had fought against. It is in specifics that we best learn generalities. Think of writing as photography. Putting aside the wide-angle lens that includes too much at a distance, look through the telephoto lens that brings you up close to a small part of the subject. Select the part most meaningful to you, perhaps the part most characteristic of the whole, and then take the picture.

Nearly all of the essays in this book are closeups: they tend to explore one situation, one incident, one person or one process. Yet most of them are longer than the essays you will write, especially in class. Therefore when you choose a topic, judge its size before you write. And if you have to, *change* its size.

3. *What message am I sending?* You may know your topic well. But unless you send a message concerning it, your reader will think *what's the point?* A message is often a value judgment: are robots dangerous? Will they take away our jobs or someday even rule over us? Or do they help us? Will they free us at last from the dehumanizing tyranny of manual labour? Most of the essays in this book take such a stance, either pro or con, toward their subject. Some avoid judging their subjects but send other messages: one shows that aging is a continual, life-long process; one shows that lightning is an immensely powerful force; another shows that a childhood event can shape us as adults.

If you have chosen a topic because it seems meaningful, you will no doubt have a message to send. What do you most feel like saying about the topic? Once you know, get it down in writing. This THESIS STATE-MENT, as it is often called, normally comes at or near the beginning of an essay. It is an introductory sentence or passage that does more than just tell what the topic is; it clearly states, as well, what you are saying *about* the topic. It lets your reader know what is coming — and, in the process, it commits you to a purpose that all the rest of the essay must in one way or another support. It is your guide as you write.

4. *Who is my reader?* Do you talk the same way to a friend and a stranger? To an old person and a child? To a clergyman and a bartender? Probably not. Neither should you write the same way to all readers. In a private journal you can write as freely as you think, for you are the reader: omissions and excesses of all kinds will be understood and forgiven. In letters to a close friend you are nearly as free, for the reader knows you well enough to supply missing explanations or interpret remarks in the light of your personality. But your freedom shrinks when you write for others: a business person, a public official, a teacher. Now you must fight a misconception shared by many people: *everyone is like me.*

This idea is seldom articulated but may lurk as a natural assumption in the backs of our minds. It is a form of egotism. If you assume that everyone is like you, many readers will not accept or even understand your message — because they are *not* like you. They did not grow up in your family, neighbourhood or even country. They are older or younger, or of the opposite sex. They have had different life experiences, and as a result have different knowledge and temperaments and values.

Keep these differences in mind as you write. You will not prove your point by quoting Marx to a capitalist, the Bible to an atheist, or Germaine Greer to a male supremicist. Any argument built on a partisan foundation will collapse if the reader does not accept that foundation. Instead, build from facts or ideas that your reader probably does accept: killing is bad, government is necessary, women are human beings, and so on. Is your topic controversial? Then avoid an open display of bias. Calling intellectuals "Commies" or abortionists "hired killers" will appeal only to those who shared your view in the first place.

Does the reader know what you know? If you write about statistics for a statistics teacher, use any technical terms customary to the field, and avoid the insult of explaining elementary points. But if you write on the same subject for a class exercise in English or a letter to the editor, your reader will be very different: avoid most technical terms, define those you do use, and explain more fully each step of your argument.

The more open you become to the individuality of your reader, the more open your reader becomes to your message. It is a matter of mutual respect.

THE FIRST WORDS

As the philosopher Lao-Tze put it, "A journey of a thousand miles begins with the first step." And as we have seen, writers may dread that first step. Some begin with their environment by finding a quiet spot in front of a blank wall, a particularly soft or hard chair, good lighting and a favourite pen. Others fortify themselves with a good night's sleep, food or a cup of coffee. And still others loosen up through exercise or music.

Tricks such as these will help, but of course the real act of writing begins with those first words on that blank page. In a very short essay your thesis statement may serve also as the first words. It is worth polishing, because if it is good enough the rest may grow from it like a plant from a seed. In many longer essays it comes at the end of an introduction. Only about one-fourth of the selections in this book start right off with what could be called a thesis statement. What do the others start with?

Background information: About half the essays in this book lead off by relating the circumstances in which the topic is set. For examples, see the beginnings of our essays by Berton (p. 181), Dobbs (p. 43), Gabori (p. 17) and Roussel (p. 227).

ANECDOTE: A brief story, usually of a humorous or dramatic incident, can lead into the topic. See Atwood (p. 132), Kostash (p. 313), Leacock (p. 257) and Pittman (p. 120).

QUOTATION or ALLUSION: The words of a philosopher, of a news report, of a recognized specialist in the subject or of anyone with close experience of it can be used to break the ice. See Bruce (p. 307), Godfrey (p. 241) and Kogawa (p. 62).

SENSE IMAGES: Vivid description can attract a reader's interest to the topic. See Adams (p. 83), Clarke (p. 177), Grainger (p. 280) and Mallet (p. 87).

A striking comparison or contrast: Showing how things are like or unlike each other is a dramatic way to introduce a topic. See Haig-Brown (p. 221), Marchand (p. 165) and Mews (p. 270).

A poem: See Purdy (p. 20).

Narrative: Nearly a fourth of the selections in this book start right off telling a story upon which the essay is based. See Carr (p. 95), Harrison (p. 27) and MacLennan (p. 103).

Unusual or puzzling statement: Such an opening appeals to the reader's curiosity. See Fulford (p. 58) and Pittman (p. 120).

FIGURES OF SPEECH: A striking METAPHOR, SIMILE or PERSONIFICATION can spark the opening. See Leclerc (p. 212), Osler (p. 128), Stewart (p. 198) and Stoffman (p. 261).

Most of these introductions are short: a couple of sentences or a paragraph or two at the most. And almost all of them are designed to *interest* the reader, for an apathetic reader may not even finish the essay, let alone like or understand it. Writing is fishing: You throw in the line. Your reader tastes the bait (your introduction). If it is good, he bites. Once your fish is hooked, you pull him through the waters of your argument and, if the line doesn't break, land him in your net.

You, too, may be like the fish. Once you have hit upon a strong introduction, one that shows off the drama or importance of your topic, the beginning may carry you along with it. And once you get going, the idea embodied in your thesis statement may pull you through the essay, enabling you to write freely as one passage leads to another. You may become less and less aware of your surroundings as you become more and more immersed in your subject. With a good beginning, you may experience the act of writing the way one student described it: "At first I couldn't start, but then I couldn't stop."

THE BODY

By itself, an introduction is a head without a body. A head gives direction, but without a body it goes nowhere. The "body" of your essay has the main work to do: following the direction set by your introduction, and especially by your thesis statement, it explains, illustrates, and sometimes attempts to prove your point. But if it ever ignores the direction set by the head, it ceases to do its job. Even the best of explanations, without a sense of direction, is like one of those unfortunate football players we sometimes hear about who complete a ninety-yard run to the wrong goal.

The most obvious way to keep a direction is to base your essay on a particular form — and that is what most of this book is about. As you read and discuss the essays that follow, and as you write your own essays using the forms upon which other writers have based their organization, you will develop a range of choices:

Narration: In simple time order, from the first event to the last event, tell a story that illustrates the point.

Example: Give one in-depth example or a number of shorter examples that explain the point.

Description: Recreate for your reader, through the most vivid language possible, your own or someone else's experience with the subject.

Cause and effect: Explain by showing how one situation or event causes another.

Comparison and contrast: Explain by showing how two things are like or unlike each other.

Analogy: In comparing two things, use the one to explain the other.

Classification: Make a point by fitting the parts of your subject into categories.

Process analysis: Show how something happens or how something is done.

Extended definition: Explain your subject by showing in detail what it is.

Seldom does one of these forms appear alone. A *process analysis*, for example, is usually told as a *narrative*. Here and there it may use *examples, description* or any of the other patterns to help make its point. But these combinations occur naturally, often without the writer's knowing it. In most cases the only form deliberately chosen by the writer is the main one upon which the whole essay is structured.

How do you choose the right form? Let the subject be your guide. In architecture, form follows function. Rather than cram an office into a pre-selected structure, a designer likes to begin with the *function* of that office. How much space best serves its needs? What shape? What barriers and passageways between one section and another? What front to present to the world?

An essay is much the same: the needs of its subject, if you are sensitive to them, will in most cases suggest a form. If the main point is to show your reader what something is like, you may naturally use examples and description. If the subject is unusual or little known, you may use a comparison or contrast, or an analogy to something that the reader does know. If its parts seem important, you may discuss them one by one in a classification. And when some other need is greater, you may use still another form. If you stay open to the subject, whatever it is, this process can be so natural that you often seem to *recognize* rather than *choose* a form.

If the process is natural, then why study the forms in this book? Think of the architect again: why does he or she study design in school? For one thing, knowing how each form is constructed assures that the building will not collapse. For another, in those cases when the choice is *not* easy, a conscious knowledge of all the possibilities will help.

Consider the longer essay — perhaps a report or research paper. A stack of notes sits on your desk. They are in chaos. Even knowing your purpose, having the facts and completing a thesis statement, you can't think of how to coordinate all those facts. First give the natural process its best chance: sort all your notes into groups of related material, using a pair of scissors if necessary to divide unrelated points. When everything is in two stacks, or five stacks or ten, let your mind work freely. How do these groups relate to each other? Does one come before another in time? Does one cause another? Does one contradict another? Are they all steps in a process or parts of a whole? Now add your conscious knowledge of the forms: do you see narration, example, description, cause and effect, comparison and contrast, analogy, classification, process analysis or extended definition? It is the rare case when one of these forms will not supply the basic structure to best support your argument.

If you use the essay topics at the end of each chapter in this book, your choice of form will already be made. This process may seem to bypass the ideal method of letting form follow function. The topics, though, are selected to go well with the form studied in their chapter. And just as the architect practices the standard designs in school to learn their forms and functions, so can the writer deliberately practice the standard essay designs to learn *their* forms and functions. Both architect and writer will then be ready when the choice is truly open.

TRANSITIONS

We have mentioned the passageways inside a building. Without them an office would be useless: no one could move from one room to another or pass business from one stage to another. Yet some essays are built without passageways. One point ends where another begins, without even a "then" or "therefore" or "however" or "finally" to join them. Readers have to spend a great deal of effort breaking through the walls in order to follow the writer's train of thought from one room to the next.

Help your readers. *You* know why one point follows another, but do *they?* Make sure by supplying transitions: say "although" or "but" or "on the other hand"; say "because" or "as a result" or "since"; say "first" or "next" or "last"; say "for example" or "in conclusion." And when moving readers from one major division of your essay to the next, devote a full sentence or even a paragraph to the job (one good example is paragraph 10 of Doris Anderson's essay).

Your plan may be the right one, setting your points in their most logical order. But let that logic show: give your readers a transition between every room.

THE CLOSING

We've discussed the beginning, the middle, and transitions between parts. What remains is of course the ending. Every essay has one — the point at which the words stop. But not all endings are closings. A closing is deliberate. In some clear way it tells the reader that you have not just run out of time, ink or ideas — but that you have *chosen* to stop here. If you end at just any convenient spot, without engineering an effect to fit your ending, the essay may trail off or even fall flat. But as preachers, composers, playwrights and film directors know, a good closing can be even stronger than a good opening. How do the essays in this book come to a close? They use a variety of devices:

Reference to the opening: Repeating or restating something from the opening gives a sense of culmination, of having come full circle. See the openings and closings by Atwood (pp. 132 and 135), Berton (pp. 181 and 185), Kogawa (pp. 62 and 65) and Stoffman (pp. 261 and 268).

Contrast or reversal: This ironic device exploits the dramatic potential of the closing. See the openings and closings by Fulford (pp. 58 and 60), Purdy (pp. 20 and 25) and Stoffman (pp. 261 and 268).

Question: A question and its answer, or a question calling for the reader's answer, is a common means of closing. See Bruce (p. 307), Davies (p. 191), Leacock (p. 257) and Stewart (p. 198).

Quotation: A good quotation, either of prose or poetry, can add authority and interest to a closing. See Haig-Brown (p. 221), Pittman (p. 120) and McEwen (p. 321).

Transition signals: Words, phrases or sentences of transition commonly signal the closing. See Gabori (p. 17), Marchand (p. 165) and Zuker and Callwood (p. 303).

Revealing the significance: Showing the implications or importance of the subject makes for a strong closing. See Bruce (p. 307), Clark (p. 115) and Gabori (p. 17).

Summary: About a fourth of the essays in this book give a summary, either alone or in combination with other closing techniques, but one that is always *short.* See Allen (p. 137), Berton (p. 181), Haig-Brown (p. 221) and Mallet (p. 87).

Conclusion: Although "conclusion" is often a label for the closing in general, more accurately it is only one of many techniques — the drawing of a conclusion from the discussion in the essay. See Fraser (p. 286), Kostash (p. 313), Osler (p. 128) and Traill (p. 161).

Prediction: A short look at the subject's future can very logically close a discussion of that subject's past or present. See Godfrey (p. 241), Kantaroff (p. 143) and Marchand (p. 165). Sometimes discussing the future takes the form of a call to action (see Osler, p. 128).

You have probably noticed that some of these authors are named twice; like openings, closings can exploit more than one technique. In fact the more, the better. Stay open to techniques that appear while you write, even as you construct a closing on the one technique you have deliberately chosen. Any of these choices will be stronger, though, when used with the most fundamental technique of all: building your whole essay toward a high point or climax. Put your points in order from least important to most important, from least useful to most useful or from least dramatic to most dramatic. Then you will have made possible a closing that applies all the dramatic power of the final position.

When you get there, apply the force of that closing to a real message. Techniques used just for their own sake are cheap tricks. Do not waste them. Instead, use them to underline your basic message, to impress upon your reader one last and most convincing time that what you have to say is significant. Your closing, more than any other part of your essay, can send the reader away disappointed — or moved.

AFTER THE WRITING

We have discussed the misconception that an essayist must "hit it right the first time." It is unlikely that even one of the essays in this book is a first draft — an act of writing that is unchanged, unedited, unpolished by its writer. Many are no doubt in their third, fourth or fifth draft. Few students have that much time to spend on an essay, but everyone who cares about quality will know that once through is not enough. At the least — say, for an in-class essay — a slow and careful proofreading should follow the writing. When you write at home, you will have time for much greater improvements: the careful deletion of words that do not contribute, the substitution of short and strong words for long and flabby ones, sometimes the relocation of parts (using scissors and tape), perhaps the dropping or adding of whole sections, and the writing or typing of a good copy after the changes are made. As you rewrite and proofread, try these suggestions:

1. If you suspect that a passage is bad, you are probably right. Change it or throw it out.
2. If your best efforts will not improve a stubborn passage, scrap it and begin again.
3. If something that you wrote made you highly emotional, be suspicious. It may later fall apart when examined in the light of reason.
4. Read your first draft aloud to catch clumsy repetition and other violations of good style.
5. Proofread *slowly,* word by word, because when you go fast the brain supplies what the eye misses. And if you do not proofread at all, you may hand in work like this sentence from a student essay:
   > With modern technology, we can sent massages to other parts of the world as fast as we can sent them to some office in downtorn Toronto, if not fast.
6. Most importantly, leave time between the writing, rewriting and proofreading. The mind works in marvellous ways that we have hardly begun to understand: while you are "thinking" about other things or even sleeping, it may be processing the thoughts you wrote yesterday or last week. When you get back to your first draft, you may suddenly detect faults in logic or see new relationships or discover new examples or envision a whole new way to make your point.*

---

*These suggestions first appeared, in slightly different form, in my *Canadian Writing Workbook* (McGraw-Hill Ryerson, 1980).

The act of writing does not end with the last words of your first draft. Writing is craftsmanship as well as inspiration. The polishing of language and the polishing of thought are sometimes considered little things, but their effect is not little. The greatest of your rewards as a writer comes after all the fine-tuning is done: it is the act of reading your own response to a significant topic, in a form so exact and forceful that at last you know exactly what you think. It is clear that you were writing for others, but at that moment it is even clearer that you were writing for yourself.

Ontario Ministry of Industry and Tourism

"'Take that play where I skate up to the referee and stand nose-to-nose with my face turning red. It was my old junior coach who taught me that.'"
Gary Lautens, "Man, You're a Great Player!"

And then. . . .

NARRATION

Telling a story, or narrating, is one of the most appealing and natural ways to convey information. Every time you tell a joke, trade gossip, invent a ghost story or tell a friend what you did on the weekend, you are narrating. In both speech and writing, telling a story can be the most direct way to make a point. If your idea or opinion was formed by your experience, a clear account of that experience will often help people to understand and even to accept your point.

How could a soldier explain the terrors of a shelling attack better than by narrating his own experience of it? Charles Yale Harrison narrates the third selection of this chapter, "In the Trenches." He might have constructed a logical argument to make his point. But instead he tells us how the blast threw him into the air, how the ground heaved, how he breathed the smoke and tasted his own blood. As his readers, we tend to identify with him, share his experience, and, most important of all, understand his point.

In some ways narrating is easy. The only research Harrison required was his own experience. And his basic plan of organization was no more complicated than the chronological order in which the events occurred.

(A flashback to the past or a glance at the future may intervene, but basically a narrative is the easiest of all writing to organize.) Yet a narrative, like any other form of writing, is built on choices:

Scope: Time stretches infinitely toward both the past and future — but where does your narrative most logically begin and end? In "The Iron Road," Al Purdy narrates a journey, telling how at age seventeen he rode the rails to Vancouver. He also rode the rails back, but does *not* include that part: instead he chooses to end on a high point, the sudden self-perception that made him start back the very day he arrived. Include only the section of your story that best illustrates your point. If facts about the past or future are needed, sketch them in, as Purdy does, with a few words of explanation.

Details: Which details will contribute to the main point? Reject the trivial ones and seek those that represent your dominant impression or idea. Which details are most vivid? Reject the weak ones and select those that help the reader to see, hear, feel, smell or taste — in other words, those that most encourage the reader to *experience* the events.

Connections: Readers like to be "swept along" by a narrative. How is this effect achieved? Partly by an economical use of words, and partly by the use of time signals. Like road signs for the motorist, the words "at first," "next," "then," "immediately," "suddenly," "later," "finally" and "at last" show the way and encourage progress. Use these words, and others like them, wherever they fit. Choose carefully, making the right signals help to build your effect.

So far we have discussed only the first-person narrative. There are many advantages to writing about yourself. You know your subject well (in fact, is there any subject that you know better?), yet in writing about yourself you may come to new understandings of your ideas and actions. You are vitally interested in your subject, and thus will be motivated to do your best in writing about it. And finally, your reader may appreciate the authenticity of a story told by the very person who experienced the event.

But it is not always possible or even desirable to limit the subject to oneself. In choosing the third-person narrative, which tells the actions of others, the writer opens up a vast area of possibilities. Only through writing about others can one discuss past eras, places one has never visited and events one has never experienced. In the second half of this chapter, Donald Creighton uses archaeological and historical evidence to write about the Vikings, Kildare Dobbs uses an interview to write about the first victims of nuclear war, and Gary Lautens consults his imagination to produce a narrative in its freest form, fiction.

George Gabori

Coming of Age in Putnok

Translated from the Hungarian by Eric Johnson with George Faludy

George Gabori (pronounced Gábori) is a taxi driver in Toronto. But like many immigrants to Canada, he has a past that he will not soon forget. Gabori was born in 1924 to a Jewish family in the village of Putnok, Hungary. His childhood was happy but short, for when the Germans occupied Hungary and threatened the existence of the Jews, he joined the resistance. He led daring sabotage raids on railyards and docks until the Gestapo sent him, still a teenager, to a concentration camp. Things did not improve when the Russians drove out the Germans; soon after his release from a Nazi camp, he found himself breaking rocks in a notorious Soviet labour camp. Always outspoken, Gabori played a part in the 1956 Revolution, then escaped from Hungary and eventually wrote his memoirs in Hungarian. Eric Johnson condensed and translated the work. When it appeared in 1981, the critics were moved. Our selection, "Coming of Age in Putnok," is the opening passage of George Gabori's story in When Evils Were Most Free.

When I was nine years old my father, victorious after a long argument with my grandfather, took me out of our town's only *cheder* and enrolled me in its only public school. Overnight I was transported from the world of Hebrew letters and monotonously repeated texts to the still stranger world of Hungarian letters, patriotic slogans and walls covered with maps.

Grandfather rolled his eyes and predicted trouble, but it seemed he was wrong. I sat beside a boy my own age named Tivadar, a gentile — everybody was a gentile in that school except me. Tivadar and I got along famously until, after two or three weeks, he approached me in the schoolyard one day and asked me if it was true what the others were saying, that "we" had murdered Jesus.

Strange to tell — for this was 1933 and we were in Hungary — I had never heard about this historical episode, and I left Tivadar amicably enough, promising to ask my father about it. We met again the next morning and I told him what I had learned: that the Romans had killed Jesus, and that anyway Jesus had been a Jew, like me, so what did it matter to the Christians?

"That's not true," said Tivadar menacingly.

"My father does not lie," I replied.

By now a crowd had gathered around us and there was nothing for it but to fight it out. There were cheers and laughter as Tivadar hit me in the nose before I got my jacket off. It was not the first time I had tasted my own blood, but it was the first time a Christian had made it flow. Tivadar was flushed with pleasure and excitement at the applause and not at all expecting it when I lashed out with my fist and sent him sprawling backward on the cobbles. The crowd of boys groaned and shouted to Tivadar to get up and kill the Jew, but poor Tivadar did not move. Frightened, I grabbed my jacket and shoved my way through the crowd stunned into silence by this overturning of the laws of nature.

7 They were silent at home too when I told them what had happened. My father sent for me from his office in the afternoon, and I entered cap in hand. He always wore a braided Slovak jacket at work and looked more like a peasant than a Jewish wine merchant.

8 "Well, who started it?" asked my father, wearing an expression I had never seen on his face before. I was not at all frightened.

9 "He did. I told him what you said about Jesus and he challenged me."

10 My father clamped his teeth on his cigar and nodded, looking right through me.

11 "Jews don't fight," he finally said.

12 "Then why did you put me in a Christian school?" I asked in a loud, outraged whine.

13 "That's why I put you there, my son," he said at last, then swept me up and kissed me on the forehead. "You're learning fast; only next time don't hit him quite so hard."

14 Then he sent me out quickly and I stopped on the landing, startled to hear loud, whooping, solitary laughter coming out of my father's office.

STRUCTURE:
1. What is the most basic pattern by which this selection is organized?
2. Point out at least ten words or phrases that signal the flow of time in this narrative.
3. Reread the first paragraph carefully. Has Gabori given us a good background to the selection? Name every fact that this introduction reveals about the setting and about the author.

STYLE:
1. How economical or wasteful of words is this opening passage of George Gabori's autobiography? After reading it, how well do you think you know the author and his times? Could you predict with confidence anything of his character or fate as an adult? Does this opening selection make you feel like reading the rest of the book? Why or why not?

2. Gabori's book, *When Evils Were Most Free,* is a translated and condensed version of the Hungarian original. To what extent does this fact separate us from the author's thoughts? How exact can a translation be? If you yourself speak two languages, how precisely can you express sayings from one in the other? To what extent can Gabori's translator, Eric Johnson, be thought of as the author of this selection?

3. Gabori states in paragraph 6, "It was not the first time I had tasted my own blood. . . ." Is this image effective? If so, why?

4. When Gabori refers to "poor Tivadar" (par. 6), is the word "poor" used in a special sense? What is Gabori really saying?

IDEAS:

1. What is the "overturning of the laws of nature" to which Gabori refers at the end of paragraph 6?

2. Was Gabori's father right in moving the boy from a Hebrew *cheder* to a public school? In disproving the idea that "Jews don't fight" (par. 11), has the boy learned a worthwhile lesson? Or has he merely imitated the worst traits of his opponents, thereby becoming like them?

3. Every ethnic group in Canada — including the English Canadians — is a minority. Has your minority suffered any form of persecution in Canada? If you have been a victim, narrate an actual incident and your reaction to it. Give plentiful details, as Gabori does.

4. What are autobiographies for? What do you think writing your own life story would do for you? What might it do for others?

5. Write a chapter of your own autobiography. Select *one* incident that taught you something about yourself or about life in general, and narrate it in chronological order. Following the example of Gabori, use words economically and vividly.

(NOTE: See also the Topics for **Writing** at the end of this chapter.)

Al Purdy

The Iron Road

Al Purdy is one of Canada's most prolific and best-known poets. Born in 1918 in Wooler, Ontario, Purdy has had a wide range of experiences that have been reflected in the unusual variety of his writings. He rode the rails during the Depression, spent six years with the RCAF during World War II, ran a taxi business, helped organize a union in a Vancouver mattress factory, and has travelled widely both in Canada and abroad. He now lives in Ameliasburg, Ontario. Purdy has written more than a hundred plays for radio and television, and since 1944 has published and edited over twenty-five books, mostly of poetry. Among his best-known are The Cariboo Horses *(winner of the Governor General's Award, 1965),* Wild Grape Wine *(1968),* Love in a Burning Building *(1970),* Sex and Death *(1973) and* In Search of Owen Roblin *(1974). He has also written many articles for magazines. Our selection was first published in* Canada Month *in 1963, then in 1977 was collected in a book of Purdy's essays,* No Other Country. *It illustrates both Purdy's love of concrete experience and his ability to convey that experience in words.*

Riding the boxcars out of Winnipeg in a
morning after rain so close to
the violent sway of fields it's
like running and running
naked with summer in your mouth
being a boy scarcely a moment and you
hear the rumbling iron roadbed singing
under the wheels at night and a door jerking open
mile after dusty mile riding into Regina with
the dust storm crowding behind you
night and morning over the clicking rails

1   The year was 1937, and I was seventeen. I rode the freight trains to Vancouver, along with thousands of other Canadians during the Great Depression. In the Hungry Thirties it seemed that half the population was on the move. The unemployed workmen of Toronto and Montreal and all the other big cities swarmed over the boxcars, moving west to the Prairies, west to Vancouver, wherever there might be hope of finding work.

2   There were also the professional hoboes, who always went in the opposite direction from where there was any rumour of employment. They lived in hobo jungles beside rivers and near the towns, never far from the railway yards. There they lit campfires, cooked food, washed clothing — if it was absolutely necessary — and told tales of the steel highways while

standing over the fires at night. Of towns where housewives always invited you inside for dinner when you asked for a handout, and never handed you an axe while pointing sternly at the woodpile. Of towns where you never had to work, there was always plenty of beer. . . . But after a day or two in the jungle they got restless again, and boarded the train to Anywhere.

It was a dark night in early June when I caught my first train at the railway yards in Trenton, Ontario. It had chuffed in from the east an hour earlier, and was about to pull out for Toronto. The yards were full of shunting switch engines bustling back and forth in the night, red and green signal lights gleaming like the eyes of stationary cats, and every now and then you heard a hoarse, impatient scream from the whistles of the westbound train.

I'll never know how I had the nerve to board that train, for I was scared to death of it. I'd quit school a couple of years before, and there was no work at all in Trenton. But that wasn't the reason why I was heading west. The reason was boredom. I wanted adventure. That was why I crouched in some bushes beside the tracks, almost too nervous to breathe, wondering how I'd ever manage to climb onto that boxcar. Was it something like getting on a bicycle or a horse? And where were the railway police hiding?

Suddenly the westbound train made a peculiar "toot-toot" that signaled departure — a sound I've heard many times since. Hoboes call it "the highball." Then a great metallic crash came from the couplings, and the train grunted away into the night. I broke from cover and ran alongside, grabbing at the steel ladder of a passing boxcar, and climbed up onto the roof — collapsing on the swaying catwalk while all the vertebrae of the wriggling wooden serpent beneath me thundered west.

A few days later and miles from home, I received my first instructions from a professional bum about the proper method of boarding a moving train. A lean little man with a dark stubble of beard, he'd seen me swing onto a train by the rear ladder of a boxcar.

"That's the way guys get killed," he said. "Ya gotta do it the right way." He spat tobacco on the boxcar floor and gestured. "I seen guys lose a leg or arm falling under them wheels. Ya always go for the ladder at the front end of the car, never the one at the back end. If ya miss yer hold on the rear ladder ya fall between the cars and yer a gone goose. Always the front ladder. An remember that, kid."

There were other famous bums who wrote their names and deeds on boxcar walls or on the supports of watertanks with knife and pencil — Regina Sam Jones, Montana Slim, Midnight Frank. I've often wondered: why should a man call himself "Midnight Frank"? There was also the immortal Kilroy, who wrote "Kilroy was here" the length and breadth of the continent.

9   Farther west, at Broadview, Saskatchewan, the Mounties had a reputation for being very tough on bums. The stories about their toughness alarmed me so much that I crawled down the trap door of a threshing machine mounted on a flatcar before going through town. I crouched in the darkness of that monster, nervously waiting to be discovered and hauled off to jail. I heard the police tramping around outside, making a tremendous racket, but they didn't find me. When the train pulled out on its way west, I was the only illicit passenger left of the three score or so who had ridden with me into Broadview.

10   When I first started out for Vancouver I had some money in my pockets. But it was soon spent. I had to forsake the aristocratic habit of eating in restaurants and join the other bums knocking on doors to ask for handouts. It was embarrassing, but I got used to it. You nerved yourself, knocked on a door, and waited, wondering what might happen. The dignity of man was, of course, a lesser consideration than being hungry.

11   You might get a sandwich from a housewife, perhaps even a full meal, a "sitdown" we used to call it; but you might also be given an axe and directed to the woodpile; or a man in shirtsleeves might come to the door and tell you to "Beat it, bum!" It was all part of the game, and you didn't really hold any grudges for a harsh reception. You just kept on trying.

12   Sometimes you went to the bakery of whatever small town you happened to be passing through, asking the baker if he had any stale bread or buns. Most of the time you got something to eat, but occasionally there were long stretches on the train where it wasn't possible to ask for a handout. At such times you stayed hungry.

13   On my first trip west I hitchhiked north from Sault Ste. Marie, and was disheartened to find that the road ended at a little village called Searchmont (at that time the Trans-Canada Highway was not yet completed through Northern Ontario). Near midnight I boarded a freight travelling north and west, riding in an open-air gondola used to transport coal. After an hour it began to rain, and the coaldust made things worse. My face and hands were streaked with it. We stopped around 5 AM and it was still dark. I had no idea where I was, but the rain and coaldust were too miserable to be borne. I ripped the seal off a boxcar with my hunting knife and tried to get inside. But the door was too big and heavy for me to move, so I went back to my gondola and huddled under the rain in silent misery.

14   A railway cop materialized out of the greyness not long after I got settled. He'd seen the broken seal, and knew I was responsible. He told me that the settlement was named Hawk Junction, then locked me up in a caboose with barred windows and padlocked door. And I thought: how would my mother feel now about her darling boy? At noon the railway cop took me to his house for dinner with his wife and children, gave me

some *Ladies Home Journals* to read, and casually mentioned that I could get two years for breaking the boxcar seal.

When returned to my prison-on-wheels I felt panicstricken. I was only [15] seventeen, and this was the first time I'd ventured far away from home. I examined the caboose-prison closely, thinking: two years! Why, I'd be nineteen when I got out, an old man! And of course it was hopeless to think of escape. Other prisoners had tried without success, and windows were broken where they'd tried to wrench out the bars. And the door: it was wood, locked on the outside with a padlock, opening inward. It was a very springy door though: I could squeeze my fingertips between sill and door, one hand at the top and the other a foot below. That gave me hope, blessed hope, for the first time. My six-foot-three body was suspended in air by my hands, doubled up like a coiled spring, and I pulled. Lord, how I pulled! The door bent inward until I could see a couple of daylight inches between door and sill. Then, Snap! and screws pulled out of the steel hasp outside. I fell flat on my back.

Peering cautiously outside, right and left, I jumped to the ground, [16] walking as slowly and sedately as I could make myself — toward freedom. The urge to run was hard to resist, especially when crossing a bridge over a wide river along the tracks, and continuing steadily in the direction of Sault Ste. Marie, 165 miles south of the railway divisional point. But that cop would be looking for me, and so would other blue uniforms! Two years! Walking the tracks would make me far too obvious, much too easy to find. So how about making the journey twenty or thirty feet into the heavy forest lining both sides of the right of way? That way I could see if anyone came after me, and duck back among the trees. Brilliant, positively brilliant.

But the trees went uphill and down, turned leftways and rightways, [17] without landmarks or anything to orient me with the tracks. I began to feel uneasy: better stay close to the railway. Too late. I was deep into the woods, not knowing in which direction to turn. I was lost — and didn't even feel stupid, just terrified. My heart began to pump hard, and I ran, with branches and leaves slapping my face, blundering into trees, splashing through little streams.

Finally I stopped, knowing panic was useless but feeling it anyway. [18] The possibility of dangerous animals occurred to me: what about bears? — bears must live in these woods. I had no defense against them; the railway cop had confiscated my hunting knife. Besides, what good would such a feeble weapon be against an angry black bear? And the brown shape that flitted between the trees, not so much seen as realized, what was that?

I slept on the side of a hill, huddled around a mother-tree, and it was [19] cold, cold. Morning was grey with a light rain falling, more mist than rain. By this time I'd thought of the sun as some kind of directional reference, but there was no sun. And just a couple of miles away I could hear engines shunting and butting back and forth in the railway yard, the sound seeming to come from all directions among the trees. Old logging trails meandered through the forest, but they were so old that when I tried to follow them they vanished in the vague greyness. Once I stumbled on an old hunting camp, so ancient that the lean-to logs were rotten. Later in the day, during my stumbling, lurching progress, I came on that hunting camp twice more, each time increasingly terrified about walking in circles.

20   At age seventeen I didn't believe in God, at least I told myself I didn't. But this was no time to take chances one way or the other. I prayed. Fervently, passionately, and with no reservations, I prayed to get out of that forest. And remembered the forty-some Sundays I'd attended church two years before, without listening to the preacher's sermon but in order to receive a prize for attendance. Since then I'd become a non-believer in that fire-and-brimstone God, but now for reasons of expediency I pretended to myself and to a possible Him that my backsliding was over — at least for as long as I was lost in this northern forest.

21   And maybe it worked: I still don't know. That railway bridge I'd crossed when leaving Hawk Junction popped into my head. Adolescent high school logic took over. The river and railway tracks would make two sides of a very large isosceles triangle. And carry it a step farther: if I could finally walk in something close to a straight line, which hadn't happened thus far, then I must finally locate either river or tracks. And the sun, now becoming a pale spot in the overhead grey, gave me some small direction. I walked and walked, and two hours later nearly fell head-first down an embankment into that blessed blessed river.

22   That same evening I boarded a passenger train just behind the engine, and rode south to the Soo in style, careless of legal consequences. But no cops appeared on the smoky, cindered horizon of fear. At the steel town I dived into a Scandinavian steambath to stop the shivering chill that I'd picked up from two days in the woods. And sleeping that night in a cheap flophouse, I was still shuddering a little, in slow motion.

23   I think my first sight of the mountains was worth all the hardships — waking early in the morning inside an empty boxcar and gazing down into a lake surrounded by forest stretching for miles and miles — cupped and cradled by the white peaks. And myself crawling round the side of a mountain like a fly on a sugar bowl. For the first time I realized how big this country was. And, naively, because I was only seventeen years old, I felt a tremendous exaltation at the sight. How marvelous to be alive and to ride a barebacked train through such a country. And, naively, forty years later, I've not changed my mind.

24   Vancouver was a sprawling, dingy, beautiful giant of a waterfront city even in 1937. I walked down Water Street, over the puddles and wet grey

concrete in the early morning. An old Indian woman on an iron balcony called down for me to come up and see her daughter, mentioning explicitly certain delights that could be expected. Rather prudishly, I declined. I spent the afternoon at a movie, paying fifteen cents for the privilege of watching Dorothy Lamour disport herself in a sarong. But I'm not sure if the Indian girl wouldn't have been a better bargain.

After the movie I was seized with a realization of the immense distance I had come from home. Originally I had meant to get a job fishing on a purse seiner at Vancouver, but the smelly old harbour depressed me. The Lions Gate Bridge, stretching spider-like across First Narrows, seemed alien; the streets themselves were unfriendly and peopled by strangers. I was homesick.   25

On the same day that I had arrived I slipped under the barrier at a level crossing and boarded a freight train moving east. And all the immense width of a continent was before me again, all the lakes and rivers and mountains — and the green country of childhood lay behind.   26

> *Riding into the Crowsnest mountains with*
> *your first beard itching and a*
> *hundred hungry guys fanning out thru*
> *the shabby whistlestops for handouts and*
> *not even a sandwich for two hundred miles*
> *only the high mountains and knowing*
> *what it's like to be not quite a child*
> *any more and listening to the tough men*
> *talk of women and talk of the way things are*
> *in 1937 —*

STRUCTURE:
1. What do the lines of poetry at the beginning and end contribute to this essay?
2. What do paragraphs 1 and 2 achieve?
3. Which paragraph begins the actual narrative and which paragraph ends it?
4. Does the narrative move steadily in chronological order or does it stop for explanations or flashbacks?
5. In addition to chronological order, what other order helps to organize this essay?
6. If you think paragraph 26 is effective, explain why.

STYLE:
1. Apart from the actual poems at beginning and end, a number of passages in this essay seem to reflect the fact that Al Purdy is a poet.

Point out some especially poetic passages that are rich in SENSE IMAGES or in FIGURES OF SPEECH.

2. In paragraph 3 Purdy writes, ". . . and every now and then you heard a hoarse, impatient scream from the whistles of the westbound train." What is the effect of the word "you," which Purdy uses here and elsewhere in the essay?
3. Is "The Iron Road" a good title for this essay? What feelings do the words convey and how do they fit what follows?

IDEAS:

1. Like this nonfiction essay, a great many novels are stories of growing up. Why do you think this theme has been popular in literature?
2. The journey is another of this essay's themes that commonly appears in literature. Why do you think it does?
3. In what ways do you think Purdy's journey would be different if it were undertaken today instead of in 1937?
4. In what ways is poverty presented in this essay?
5. How is Purdy's poverty different from that of the others?

(NOTE: See also the Topics for Writing at the end of this chapter.)

Charles Yale Harrison

In the Trenches

Charles Yale Harrison (1898-1954) was born in Philadelphia and grew up in Montreal. His independent spirit revealed itself early: in grade four he condemned The Merchant of Venice *as anti-semitic, and when his teacher beat him he quit school. At sixteen he went to work for the* Montreal Star *and at eighteen joined the Canadian army. As a machine gunner in France and Belgium during 1917 and 1918, Harrison witnessed the gruesome front-line scenes he was later to describe in fiction. He was wounded at Amiens and decorated for bravery in action. After the war Harrison returned to Montreal but soon left for New York, where he began a career in public relations for the labour movement and for numerous humanitarian causes. He also wrote several books, both nonfiction and fiction. By far the best is* Generals Die in Bed, *an account of trench warfare that shocked the public and became the best seller of 1930. Spare in style, biting and vivid, this autobiographical novel was described by the* New York Evening Post *as "the best of the war books." From it comes our selection, "In the Trenches."*

We leave the piles of rubble that was once a little Flemish peasant town and wind our way, in Indian file, up through the muddy communication trench. In the dark we stumble against the sides of the trench and tear our hands and clothing on the bits of embedded barbed wire that runs through the earth here as though it were a geological deposit. 1

Fry, who is suffering with his feet, keeps slipping into holes and crawling out, all the way up. I can hear him coughing and panting behind me. 2

I hear him slither into a water-filled hole. It has a green scum on it. Brown and I fish him out. 3

"I can't go any farther," he wheezes. "Let me lie here, I'll come on later." 4

We block the narrow trench and the oncoming men stumble on us, banging their equipment and mess tins on the sides of the ditch. Some trip over us. They curse under their breaths. 5

Our captain, Clark, pushes his way through the mess. He is an Imperial, an Englishman, and glories in his authority. 6

"So it's you again," he shouts. "Come on, get up. Cold feet, eh, getting near the line?" 7

Fry mumbles something indistinctly. I, too, offer an explanation. Clark ignores me. 8

"Get up, you're holding up the line," he says to Fry. 9

Fry does not move. 10

11   "No wonder we're losing the bloody war," Clark says loudly. The men standing near-by laugh. Encouraged by his success, the captain continues:

12   "Here, sergeant, stick a bayonet up his behind — that'll make him move." A few of us help Fry to his feet, and somehow we manage to keep him going.

13   We proceed cautiously, heeding the warnings of those ahead of us. At last we reach our positions.

    •   •   •   •   •   •

14   It is midnight when we arrive at our positions. The men we are relieving give us a few instructions and leave quickly, glad to get out.

15   It is September and the night is warm. Not a sound disturbs the quiet. Somewhere away far to our right we hear the faint sound of continuous thunder. The exertion of the trip up the line has made us sweaty and tired. We slip most of our accouterments off and lean against the parados. We have been warned that the enemy is but a few hundred yards off, so we speak in whispers. It is perfectly still. I remember nights like this in the Laurentians. The harvest moon rides overhead.

16   Our sergeant, Johnson, appears around the corner of the bay, stealthily like a ghost. He gives us instructions:

17   "One man up on sentry duty! Keep your gun covered with the rubber sheet! No smoking!"

18   He hurries on to the next bay. Fry mounts the step and peers into No Man's Land. He is rested now and says that if he can only get a good pair of boots he will be happy. He has taken his boots off and stands in his stockinged feet. He shows us where his heel is cut. His boots do not fit. The sock is wet with blood. He wants to take his turn at sentry duty first so that he can rest later on. We agree.

19   Cleary and I sit on the firing-step and talk quietly.

20   "So this is war."

21   "Quiet."

22   "Yes, just like the country back home, eh?"

23   We talk of the trench; how we can make it more comfortable.

24   We light cigarettes against orders and cup our hands around them to hide the glow. We sit thinking. Fry stands motionless with his steel helmet shoved down almost over his eyes. He leans against the parapet motionless. There is a quiet dignity about his posture. I remember what we were told at the base about falling asleep on sentry duty. I nudge his leg. He grunts.

25   "Asleep?" I whisper.

26   "No," he answers, "I'm all right."

27   "What do you see?"

28   "Nothing. Wire and posts."

29   "Tired?"

"I'm all right."   30

The sergeant reappears after a while. We squinch our cigarettes.   31

"Everything O.K. here?"   32

I nod.   33

"Look out over there. They got the range on us. Watch out."   34

We light another cigarette. We continue our aimless talk.   35

"I wonder what St. Catherine Street looks like—"   36

"Same old thing, I suppose — stores, whores, theaters—"   37

"Like to be there just the same—"   38

"Me too."   39

We sit and puff our fags for half a minute or so.   40

I try to imagine what Montreal looks like. The images are murky. All   41
that is unreality. The trench, Cleary, Fry, the moon overhead — this is
real.

In his corner of the bay Fry is beginning to move from one foot to   42
another. It is time to relieve him. He steps down and I take his place. I
look into the wilderness of posts and wire in front of me.

After a while my eyes begin to water. I see the whole army of wire   43
posts begin to move like a silent host towards me.

I blink my eyes and they halt.   44

I doze a little and come to with a jerk.   45

So this is war, I say to myself again for the hundredth time. Down on   46
the firing-step the boys are sitting like dead men. The thunder to the right
has died down. There is absolutely no sound.

I try to imagine how an action would start. I try to fancy the prelim-   47
inary bombardment. I remember all the precautions one has to take to
protect one's life. Fall flat on your belly, we had been told time and time
again. The shriek of the shell, the instructor in trench warfare said, was
no warning because the shell traveled faster than its sound. First, he had
said, came the explosion of the shell — then came the shriek and then
you hear the firing of the gun. . . .

From the stories I heard from veterans and from newspaper reports I   48
conjure up a picture of an imaginary action. I see myself getting the
Lewis gun in position. I see it spurting darts of flame into the night. I
hear the roar of battle. I feel elated. Then I try to fancy the horrors of the
battle. I see Cleary, Fry and Brown stretched out on the firing-step. They
are stiff and their faces are white and set in the stillness of death. Only I
remain alive.

An inaudible movement in front of me pulls me out of the dream. I   49
look down and see Fry massaging his feet. All is still. The moon sets
slowly and everything becomes dark.

The sergeant comes into the bay again and whispers to me: 50

"Keep your eyes open now — they might come over on a raid now that   51
it's dark. The wire's cut over there—" He points a little to my right.

52   I stand staring into the darkness. Everything moves rapidly again as I stare. I look away for a moment and the illusion ceases.

53   Something leaps towards my face.

54   I jerk back, afraid.

55   Instinctively I feel for my rifle in the corner of the bay.

56   It is a rat.

57   It is as large as a tom-cat. It is three feet away from my face and it looks steadily at me with its two staring, beady eyes. It is fat. Its long tapering tail curves away from its padded hindquarters. There is still a little light from the stars and this light shines faintly on its sleek skin. With a darting movement it disappears. I remember with a cold feeling that it was fat, and why.

58   Cleary taps my shoulder. It is time to be relieved.

•   •   •   •   •   •

59   Over in the German lines I hear quick, sharp reports. Then the red-tailed comets of the *minenwerfer** sail high in the air, making parabolas of red light as they come towards us. They look pretty, like the fireworks when we left Montreal. The sergeant rushes into the bay of the trench, breathless. ''Minnies,'' he shouts, and dashes on.

60   In that instant there is a terrific roar directly behind us.

61   The night whistles and flashes red.

62   The trench rocks and sways.

63   Mud and earth leap into the air, come down upon us in heaps.

64   We throw ourselves upon our faces, clawing our nails into the soft earth in the bottom of the trench.

65   Another!

66   This one crashes to splinters about twenty feet in front of the bay.

67   Part of the parapet caves in.

68   We try to burrow into the ground like frightened rats.

69   The shattering explosions splinter the air in a million fragments. I taste salty liquid on my lips. My nose is bleeding from the force of the detonations.

70   SOS flares go up along our front calling for help from our artillery. The signals sail into the air and explode, giving forth showers of red, white and blue lights held aloft by a silken parachute.

71   The sky is lit by hundreds of fancy fireworks like a night carnival.

72   The air shrieks and cat-calls.

73   Still they come.

74   I am terrified. I hug the earth, digging my fingers into every crevice, every hole.

**minenwerfer:* mine-throwing trench mortars

A blinding flash and an exploding howl a few feet in front of the   75
trench.

My bowels liquefy.   76

Acrid smoke bites the throat, parches the mouth. I am beyond mere   77
fright. I am frozen with an insane fear that keeps me cowering in the bottom of the trench. I lie flat on my belly, waiting. . . .

Suddenly it stops.   78

The fire lifts and passes over us to the trenches in the rear.   79

We lie still, unable to move. Fear has robbed us of the power to act. I   80
hear Fry whimpering near me. I crawl over to him with great effort. He is
half covered with earth and débris. We begin to dig him out.

To our right they have started to shell the front lines. It is about half a   81
mile away. We do not care. *We* are safe.

Without warning it starts again.   82

The air screams and howls like an insane woman.   83

We are getting it in earnest now. Again we throw ourselves face   84
downward on the bottom of the trench and grovel like savages before
this demoniac frenzy.

The concussion of the explosions batters against us.   85

I am knocked breathless.   86

I recover and hear the roar of the bombardment.   87

It screams and rages and boils like an angry sea. I feel a prickly sensa-   88
tion behind my eyeballs.

A shell lands with a monster shriek in the next bay. The concussion   89
rolls me over on my back. I see the stars shining serenely above us.
Another lands in the same place. Suddenly the stars revolve. I land on my
shoulder. I have been tossed into the air.

I begin to pray.   90

"God — God — please . . ."   91

I remember that I do not believe in God. Insane thoughts race through   92
my brain. I want to catch hold of something, something that will explain
this mad fury, this maniacal congealed hatred that pours down on our
heads. I can find nothing to console me, nothing to appease my terror. I
know that hundreds of men are standing a mile or two from me pulling
gun-lanyards, blowing us to smithereens. l know that and nothing else.

I begin to cough. The smoke is thick. It rolls in heavy clouds over the   93
trench, blurring the stabbing lights of the explosions.

A shell bursts near the parapet.   94

Fragments smack the sandbags like a merciless shower of steel hail.   95

A piece of mud flies into my mouth. It is cool and refreshing. It tastes   96
earthy.

Suddenly it stops again.   97

I bury my face in the cool, damp earth. I want to weep. But I am too   98
weak and shaken for tears.

99   We lie still, waiting. . . .

STRUCTURE:

1. Does this narrative ever deviate from chronological order? If so, where and how?
2. This selection contains a great many short paragraphs, some only a word or two long. Examine paragraphs 25-30, 53-56 and 60-68, determining in each passage why the paragraphs are so short.
3. This account of an artillery attack ends with the words "We lie still, waiting. . . ." Is the ending effective, and if so, how?

STYLE:

1. What degree of CONCISENESS has Harrison achieved in this selection?
2. Discuss the horror of this statement about the rat, and how Harrison achieves such horror in so few words: "I remember with a cold feeling that it was fat, and why" (par. 57).
3. An apparently simple account of events can sometimes carry great power. Discuss the sources of power in paragraph 89: "A shell lands with a monster shriek in the next bay. The concussion rolls me over on my back. I see the stars shining serenely above us. Another lands in the same place. Suddenly the stars revolve. I land on my shoulder. I have been tossed into the air."
4. One way in which Harrison makes war come alive for us is by attacking our five senses. Find at least one example each of a strong appeal to our senses of sight, hearing, touch, taste and smell.
5. This narrative is filled with FIGURES OF SPEECH. Point out at least one good SIMILE and one good METAPHOR.
6. All the other narratives in this chapter are in the past tense. Why is "In the Trenches" in the present tense, even though the book in which it appeared was published years after the war?

IDEAS:

1. Our narrator relates his first experience of war. Has it taught him anything?
2. Have you read books or seen films that show war in a positive light? Name them. In what ways does "In the Trenches" differ from those accounts?
3. "In the Trenches" is part of a book entitled *Generals Die in Bed*. Discuss the implications of this title.
4. In paragraph 48, our narrator imagines what the attack will be like: "I see Cleary, Fry and Brown stretched out on the firing-step. They are

stiff and their faces are white and set in the stillness of death. Only I remain alive.'' Do many people think this way, expecting to survive though others may not? Do we secretly feel immortal, despite knowing intellectually that we are not? If so, can you think of reasons why?

5. If you have read "Coming of Age in Putnok," compare the conflict described by George Gabori with that described by Harrison. Does hostility between individuals in any way contribute to hostility between nations?

6. If you have not been to war, as our narrator has, have you been through another dangerous or frightening experience that taught you something? Tell the story in a narrative, using chronological order, the present tense and vivid details, as Harrison does.

(NOTE: See also the Topics for Writing at the end of this chapter.)

Donald Creighton

The Western Way[*]

*Donald Creighton (1902-1979) has been one of Canada's most widely read histor-
ians. He was born in Toronto, held numerous degrees both earned and honorary,
had a distinguished career as history professor at the University of Toronto from
1927 to 1970, and wrote numerous and varied works of history that brought him
both scholarly and popular acclaim. The most important of these are* The Commercial Empire of the St. Lawrence *(1937); his massive biography in two volumes*
John A. Macdonald: the Young Politician *(1952) and* John A. Macdonald: the
Old Chieftain *(1955); and* The Forked Road: Canada 1939-1957 *(1976). In his
later years Creighton was seen by some as overly conservative, writing history
that favoured the powerful and slighted the weak, while he was seen by others as
anti-American, anti-Quebec and overly nationalistic. But if his interpretation was
at times controversial, his research was massive and solid. Others criticized him
for his style, often so vivid and dramatic that it seemed more typical of fiction
than of history. But it is this very style that enabled the general public, as well as
specialists, to read and appreciate his work. Creighton's colourful and at times
even racy prose is nowhere better displayed than in our selection, "The Western
Way," which appeared in a book aimed at the general public,* Canada: The
Heroic Beginnings *(1974).*

1   It was the Norsemen who first fought their way westward
across the North Atlantic and gained the earliest footholds
on the shore of what is now Canada. Their precarious
lodgement at the edge of the New World was the ultimate
achievement of a vast expansion of the Scandinavian peoples. Driven
forth by the pressure of over-population and the hope of spacious lands
and easy riches, the Vikings of Norway and Denmark first burst out of
their restricted homelands towards the end of the eighth century. Their
assault on western Europe and the islands beyond, maintained for more
than 200 years of raids, pillage, conquest, and colonization, was the
greatest movement of people that the West had known since the
Germanic barbarians had overwhelmed the Roman Empire five centuries
earlier. The Franks and the Goths had travelled westward by land; but
the Vikings, "the dark red seabirds," came by sea, and a large part of the
surprise and terror of their coming lay in the swift mobility of their ships.

2   Their typical warship, the Viking "long-ship", was a long, low, graceful vessel, clinker-built with overlapping planks of oak, a single, square,
brightly coloured sail, and carved and ornamented dragon prows. Sixty
or seventy warriors, their shields hung on the bulwarks of the vessels,
their barbaric costumes adorned with brooches and bracelets, would man

[*]Editor's title

the long-ship, sail or row it across the North Sea or down the Channel, beach it on some shore or drive it up an estuary or river, and then, with bow and sword and battle-axe, descend upon the countryside and its helpless villages.

These savage pirates and marauders followed two main routes. One ran north-westward to Scotland, to the Orkney, Shetland, and Faroe Islands, and beyond to Iceland. The other led south-westward towards England, the Netherlands, France, Spain, and Portugal and into the Mediterranean. The second route, which was soon distinguished by such Viking triumphs as the founding of the Danelaw in England and the conquest of Normandy in France, became the more frequented and the more famous of the two; but the north-west route, the "western way" as it was called, which swept in a great arc across the North Atlantic and ended in North America, had its own special interest and importance.

Although almost everything the Vikings did was marred by violence and stained with blood, the advance along the "western way" was marked, not so much by warfare and conquest, as by discovery and colonization. The Norwegians had found and peacefully settled the Orkney, Shetland, and Faroe Islands before the violent Viking onslaught on western Europe began; and during the latter part of the ninth century, they discovered and occupied Iceland, a volcanic island, much of it a desolate wilderness of lava and glacier. Like the long-ships, the ships of these Norwegian colonists were clinker-built, but in other respects they differed radically from the Viking war vessels; they were cargo boats, decked fore and aft, with a wide beam and a deep draft, and roomy enough to carry passengers, animals, and cargo, as well as crew. Unlike the ornately garbed warriors who terrorized England and Europe, the mariners of the "western way" wore plain hooded gowns made of a coarse woollen cloth called wadmal, and carried sleeping bags of sheepskin or cowhide.

On good days, as one looked out from the west coast of Iceland, a faint line of mountains could be seen in the remote distance; and to Eric the Red, the violent son of a savage father, they offered both a way of escape and a promise of adventure. Thorwaldr, the father, outlawed from Norway for manslaughter, had fled to Iceland; Eric, outlawed in his turn for homicide, determined to find his refuge in the unknown country to the west. In 982 he sailed west, discovered a huge ice-covered island, and wintered on its farther coast. He could not return home for good, nor did he want to: instead, he decided to found a colony on the land of his discovery. He called it Greenland, a boldly fraudulent advertisement intended to attract prospective immigrants; and in 986, triumphantly leading a fleet of twenty-four ships, he set sail again, reached the west coast of his island once more in safety, and laid the bases of two settlements.

6   Even yet the westward urge had not spent itself. The drive that had brought Thorwaldr to Iceland and Eric to Greenland was still strong and insistent enough to carry Leif, Eric's son, to the end of the "western way" and to the New World. About 1000, he captained a planned expedition to the west and south. He found first a barren land of flat rock and glacier, which he called Helluland (Flagstone Land), and then a very different country, heavily forested, with white sandy beaches, which he named Markland (Forestland). A strong north-east wind drove the ship on for two days; and finally, on the bright morning of the third, it brought the voyagers to a beautiful land, with ample pasture, and grape vines, and the biggest salmon they had ever seen. Leif called their discovery Vinland (Wineland), and there he and his men built houses and started a permanent settlement. The good reports they brought home stimulated the interest of the Greenlanders, and during the next fifteen years, there were several voyages to Vinland, two by Leif's brothers and one by his illegitimate daughter, Freydis, as ferocious a murderess as any in Viking history. There was at least an attempt at large-scale colonization, but in fact the settlement did not endure.

7   Helluland was probably the southern shore of Baffin Island, and there can be little doubt that Markland formed part of the Labrador coast. The location of Vinland is much more uncertain. The topographical indications in the Norse Sagas are confused and at times seemingly contradictory. Vinland, the beautiful land of the Greenlanders, has been located all the way from Newfoundland to New England; but until 1960, no archaeological evidence had been found to prove the truth of any of these conjectures. In that year, a Norwegian, Helge Ingstad, discovered the buried foundations of a number of pre-Columbian houses at L'Anse aux Meadows, on Epaves Bay, part of Sacred Bay, a much larger body of water, at the northern tip of Newfoundland.

8   Epaves Bay is a broad, gently curving bay facing the entrance to the Strait of Belle Isle and so shallow that at low tide it is dry a long way out from the shore. A wide, green, grassy plain, level or slightly undulating, springy to the step with peat turf, stretches away inland on every side. A rich variety of small bushes, plants, and grasses — mountain ash, prostrate juniper, iris, angelica, Labrador tea, blueberries, and partridge and bakeapple berries — covers the plain with a dense shaggy coat; and through it, ending in the bay, winds a tumultuous little river, picturesquely named the Black Duck Brook. A little way in from the shore, the land rises slightly in an ancient marine terrace; and along it, in a straggling line, lie the foundations, made of layers of turf, of eight houses of different sizes, and the remnants of boat sheds and of cooking and charcoal pits. Most of these sites, including the largest, where a structure of six rooms once stood, are north of Black Duck Brook; but one, which was evidently a smithy, is situated on the south side of the little river; and

since bog iron is available near by, a Norse smith may have smelted ore here as well as worked iron. A Norse woman must have sat spinning in one of the rooms in the largest house, for a soapstone spindle whorl, of characteristic Norse design, was found there, as well as a bronze pin with a ring in its head and several iron rivets.

The Norse sagas date the discovery and occupation of Vinland at the   9 beginning of the eleventh century, and radio carbon tests place the ruins at L'Anse aux Meadows in approximately the same period. The L'Anse aux Meadows site may not be Vinland; but there can be no doubt that the Norse men and women who built and inhabited these houses were among the first Europeans who ever lived in North America.

STRUCTURE:

1. Why does Creighton discuss the violence of Viking expansion to the east before he describes in detail Viking expansion to the west?
2. To what extent does this selection analyze the *causes* of Norse exploration and settlement along the "Western Way"? Name all the major causes identified by Creighton.
3. In what sense are paragraphs 1-4 a narrative? What is the story being narrated?
4. What is the main difference between the opening narrative and the narrative found in paragraphs 5 and 6?
5. In what sense do paragraphs 7-9 form a narrative?
6. What similarity do you find between the opening and closing of this selection?

STYLE:

1. Our selection is typical of historical writing in its narrative form, but certainly not in its STYLE. Point out at least five passages which, in their vivid or even racy style, seem more typical of FICTION than of history.
2. Reread carefully the opening paragraph of this selection, then point out all the ways in which it appeals to the reader's interest.
3. In what way does the beginning of paragraph 5 appeal to the reader?
4. What effect is sought in the words "Leif, Eric's son" (par. 6)?
5. How long would Creighton's paragraphs be if you wrote them out? Do you ever write paragraphs as long as his? Should his be shorter? Why or why not?

IDEAS:

1. Name as many reasons as you can for the study of history.
2. Napoleon defined history as "a set of lies agreed upon." Oscar Wilde defined it as "gossip" and Henry Ford as "bunk." What motives do

you think might lead some historians to falsify history? If falsification occurs, is it deliberate or unconscious? Can you think of an example of history as ' 'bunk''?

3. Why do historians pay more attention to the "discovery" of the New World by Europeans than to the original discovery of the New World by Asians who crossed the Bering Strait to Alaska?

4. Both the Scandinavians and the French had colonized what is now Canada long before the British arrived. In what major ways can you imagine your present life to be different if the Vikings had established the dominant culture of our country? If the French had established it?

5. Write a narrative about one branch of your family, beginning with your earliest known ancestor. Show, as fully as you can, how the actions of these ancestors resulted in your being where you are and in your being what you are.

(NOTE: See also the Topics for Writing at the end of this chapter.)

Gary Lautens

Man, You're a Great Player!

"An old English teacher of mine," writes Gary Lautens, "once said she'd drop dead if I ever made a living as a writer. Now, if she's a good sport, she'll keep her end of the bargain." In fact Lautens, now executive managing editor of the Toronto Star, has for quite some time made his living as a writer. His father, who worked for Canadian Press, set the example. After graduating from McMaster in 1950 with a B.A. in history, Gary Lautens spent thirteen years with the Hamilton Spectator as a sports columnist. He then moved to the Toronto Star where he began the column of humour for which he is best known by Toronto readers. Lautens' experience both as a sports writer and as a humorist is evident in our selection, "Man, You're a Great Player!" It is from his book Laughing with Lautens (1964).

O ccasionally I run into sports figures at cocktail parties, on the street, or on their way to the bank.   1

"Nice game the other night," I said to an old hockey-player pal.   2

"Think so?" he replied.   3

"You've come a long way since I knew you as a junior."   4

"How's that?"   5

"Well, you high-stick better for one thing — and I think the way you clutch sweaters is really superb. You may be the best in the league."   6

He blushed modestly. "For a time," I confessed, "I never thought you'd get the hang of it."   7

"It wasn't easy," he confided. "It took practice and encouragement. You know something like spearing doesn't come naturally. It has to be developed."   8

"I'm not inclined to flattery but, in my book, you've got it made. You're a dirty player."   9

"Stop kidding."   10

"No, no," I insisted. "I'm not trying to butter you up. I mean it. When you broke in there were flashes of dirty play — but you weren't consistent. That's the difference between a dirty player and merely a colourful one."   11

"I wish my father were alive to hear you say that," he said quietly. "He would have been proud."   12

"Well, it's true. There isn't a player in the league who knows as many obscene gestures."   13

"I admit I have been given a few increases in pay in recent years. Management seems to be treating me with new respect."   14

15   "You're selling tickets," I said. "You're a gate attraction now — not some bum who only can skate and shoot and the rest of it. Your profanity is beautiful."

16   "C'mon."

17   "No, I'm serious. I don't think anyone in the league can incite a riot the way you can."

18   "I've had a lot of help along the way. You can't make it alone," he stated generously.

19   "No one does," I said.

20   "Take that play where I skate up to the referee and stand nose-to-nose with my face turning red. It was my old junior coach who taught me that. He was the one who used to toss all the sticks on the ice and throw his hat into the stands and pound his fist on the boards."

21   "You were lucky to get that sort of training. A lot of players never learn the fundamentals."

22   "I think there are a few boys in the league who can spit better than me."

23   "Farther, perhaps, but not more accurately," I corrected.

24   "Well, thanks anyway. I've always considered it one of my weaknesses."

25   "That last brawl of yours was perfectly executed. Your sweater was torn off, you taunted the crowd, you smashed your stick across the goal posts. Really a picture Donnybrook."

26   "The papers gave me a break. The coverage was outstanding."

27   "Do you ever look back to the days when you couldn't cut a forehead or puff a lip or insult an official?"

28   "Everyone gets nostalgic," he confessed. "It's a good thing I got away from home by the time I was fifteen. I might never have been any more than a ham-and-egger, you know, a twenty-goal man who drifts through life unnoticed."

29   "What was the turning point?"

30   "I had heard prominent sportsmen say that nice guys finish last, and that you have to beat them in the alley if you hope to beat them in the rink. But it didn't sink in."

31   "Nobody learns overnight."

32   "I wasted a few years learning to play my wing and to check without using the butt of the stick. But I noticed I was being passed by. I skated summers to keep in shape, exercised, kept curfew."

33   "Don't tell me. They said you were dull."

34   "Worse than that. They said I was clean. It's tough to live down that sort of reputation."

35   I nodded.

36   "Anyway, during a game in the sticks, I was skating off the ice — we

had won five-one and I had scored three goals. The home crowd was
pretty listless and there was some booing. Then it happened."

"What?" 37

"My big break. My mother was in the stands and she shouted to me. I 38
turned to wave at her with my hockey stick and I accidentally caught the
referee across the face. He bled a lot — took ten stitches later."

"Is that all?" 39

"Well someone pushed me and I lost my balance and fell on the poor 40
man. A real brawl started. Luckily, I got credit for the whole thing —
went to jail overnight, got a suspension. And, talk about fate! A big
league scout was in the arena. He offered me a contract right away."

"It's quite a success story," I said. 41

"You've got to get the breaks," he replied, humbly. 42

STRUCTURE:

1. What proportion of this selection do you estimate is DIALOGUE? And
   what function is served by the parts that are not dialogue?
2. What is the most basic way in which the dialogue is organized? Are
   there major divisions within it? If so, where, and how do the parts
   differ?
3. Should this selection be labelled ESSAY or FICTION? In what senses
   might it be both?

STYLE:

1. Why are there so many paragraph breaks in this short selection?
2. In paragraph 9 the narrator tells his friend, "'I'm not inclined to
   flattery but, in my book, you've got it made. You're a dirty player.'"
   Discuss the IRONY that underlies this comment. How important is
   Lautens' ironic TONE to the humour and the message of this selection
   as a whole? In particular, examine the use of irony in the title and in
   paragraphs 1, 8, 12, 15, 20, 21, 34 and 40.
3. Do you think the humorous approach chosen by Lautens has made the
   point strongly? Would a serious approach, like that of the other narratives in this chapter, have worked as well?
4. Point out at least five COLLOQUIAL or SLANG terms that seem more at
   home in the dialogue of this selection than they would in a typical
   essay.

IDEAS:

1. As the saying puts it, "I went to the fights and a hockey game broke
   out." To what extent do people watch hockey for the fights and to

what extent do they watch it for the traditional skills of the game? Is violence necessary to attract fans? How could hockey be made more interesting without resorting to fights?

2. In this selection that criticizes violence in hockey, where does Lautens blame parents? Fans? Coaches? Management? Sports writers?

3. It is said that soccer originated in warfare: villagers would kick the severed head of an enemy, like a ball, from one end of the village to the other. Think of the sports you play. What resemblances, if any, do you see between competition on the playing field and competition on the battlefield?

4. Must a sport be based on conflict, as in two teams each moving a puck or ball in the opposite direction? Name or devise a sport that is free of conflict. Can such a sport be interesting?

5. Compare the conflict examined in "Man, You're a Great Player!" with that examined in Gabori's "Coming of Age in Putnok," Harrison's "In the Trenches" or Dobbs' "The Scar."

6. Write a detailed narrative of a violent incident that you witnessed at a sports event.

(NOTE: See also the Topics for Writing at the end of this chapter.)

Kildare Dobbs

*The Scar**

Kildare Dobbs was born in Meerut, India, in 1923, was educated in Ireland, then during World War II spent five years in the Royal Navy. After the war he worked in the British Colonial Service in Tanganyika, and after earning an M.A. at Cambridge, came in 1952 to Canada. Dobbs has been a teacher, editor for Macmillan's, staff writer for the Toronto Star Weekly, and book editor for the Toronto Star. He is also the author of three books. Running to Paradise (1962, winner of the Governor General's Award) and Reading the Time (1968) are collections of his essays, while The Great Fur Opera (1970) is a light history of the Hudson's Bay Company. Our selection is from Reading the Time: "The Scar" is about an event that Dobbs did not witness, yet its vivid style recreates all too clearly what that event was like.

This is the story I was told in 1963 by Emiko Okamoto, a young Japanese woman who had come to live in Toronto. She spoke through an interpreter, since at that time she knew no English. It is Emiko's story, although I have had to complete it from other sources.

But why am I telling it? Everyone knows how terrible this story is. Everyone knows the truth of what von Clausewitz said: "Force to meet force arms itself with the inventions of art and science." First the bow-and-arrow, then Greek fire, gunpowder, poison-gas — and so on up the lethal scale. These things, we're told, should be considered calmly. No sweat — we should think about the unthinkable, or so Herman Kahn suggests, dispassionately. And he writes: "We do not expect illustrations in a book of surgery to be captioned 'Good health is preferable to this kind of cancer'. Excessive comments such as 'And now there is a lot of blood' or 'This particular cut really hurts' are out of place. . . . To dwell on such things is morbid." Perhaps the answer to Herman Kahn is that if surgeons hadn't dwelt on those things we wouldn't now have anaesthetics, or artery forceps either, for that matter.

To think about thermonuclear war in the abstract is obscene. To think about any kind of warfare with less than the whole of our mind and imagination is obscene. This is the worst treason.

Before that morning in 1945 only a few conventional bombs, none of which did any great damage, had fallen on the city. Fleets of U.S. bombers had, however, devastated many cities round about, and Hiroshima had begun a program of evacuation which had reduced its popula-

*Editor's title

43

tion from 380,000 to some 245,000. Among the evacuees were Emiko and her family.

5   "We were moved out to Otake, a town about an hour's train-ride out of the city," Emiko told me. She had been a fifteen-year-old student in 1945. Fragile and vivacious, versed in the gentle traditions of the tea ceremony and flower arrangement, Emiko still had an air of the frail school-child when I talked with her. Every day, she and her sister Hideko used to commute into Hiroshima to school. Hideko was thirteen. Their father was an antique-dealer and he owned a house in the city, although it was empty now. Tetsuro, Emiko's thirteen-year-old brother, was at the Manchurian front with the Imperial Army. Her mother was kept busy looking after the children, for her youngest daughter Eiko was sick with heart trouble, and rations were scarce. All of them were undernourished.

6   The night of August 5, 1945, little Eiko was dangerously ill. She was not expected to live. Everybody took turns watching by her bed, soothing her by massaging her arms and legs. Emiko retired at 8.30 (most Japanese people go to bed early) and at midnight was roused to take her turn with the sick girl. At 2 a.m. she went back to sleep.

7   While Emiko slept, the *Enola Gay,* a U.S. B-29 carrying the world's first operational atom bomb, was already in the air. She had taken off from the Pacific island of Iwo Jima at 1.45 a.m., and now Captain William Parsons, U.S.N. ordnance expert, was busy in her bomb-hold with the final assembly of Little Boy. Little Boy looked much like an out-size T.N.T. block-buster but the crew knew there was something different about him. Only Parsons and the pilot, Colonel Paul Tibbets, knew exactly in what manner Little Boy was different. Course was set for Hiroshima.

8   Emiko slept.

9   On board the *Enola Gay* co-pilot Captain Robert Lewis was writing up his personal log. "After leaving Iwo," he recorded, "we began to pick up some low stratus and before very long we were flying on top of an under-cast. Outside of a thin, high cirrus and the low stuff, it's a very beautiful day."

10   Emiko and Hideko were up at six in the morning. They dressed in the uniform of their women's college — white blouse, quilted hat, and black skirt — breakfasted and packed their aluminum lunch-boxes with white rice and eggs. These they stuffed into their shoulder bags as they hurried for the seven-o'clock train to Hiroshima. Today there would be no classes. Along with many women's groups, high school students, and others, the sisters were going to work on demolition. The city had begun a project of clearance to make fire-breaks in its downtown huddle of wood and paper buildings.

11   It was a lovely morning.

12   While the two young girls were at breakfast, Captain Lewis, over the

Pacific, had made an entry in his log. "We are loaded. The bomb is now alive, and it's a funny feeling knowing it's right in back of you. Knock wood!"

In the train Hideko suddenly said she was hungry. She wanted to eat   13
her lunch. Emiko dissuaded her: she'd be much hungrier later on. The two sisters argued, but Hideko at last agreed to keep her lunch till later. They decided to meet at the main station that afternoon and catch the five-o'clock train home. By now they had arrived at the first of Hiroshima's three stations. This was where Hideko got off, for she was to work in a different area from her sister. "Sayonara!" she called. "Goodbye." Emiko never saw her again.

There had been an air-raid at 7 a.m., but before Emiko arrived at   14
Hiroshima's main station, two stops farther on, the sirens had sounded the all-clear. Just after eight, Emiko stepped off the train, walked through the station, and waited in the morning sunshine for her street-car.

At about the same moment Lewis was writing in his log. "There'll be a   15
short intermission while we bomb our target."

It was hot in the sun. Emiko saw a class-mate and greeted her. To-   16
gether they moved back into the shade of a high concrete wall to chat. Emiko looked up at the sky and saw, far up in the cloudless blue, a single B-29.

It was exactly 8.10 a.m. The other people waiting for the streetcar saw   17
it too and began to discuss it anxiously. Emiko felt scared. She felt that at all costs she must go on talking to her friend. Just as she was thinking this, there was a tremendous greenish-white flash in the sky. It was far brighter than the sun. Emiko afterwards remembered vaguely that there was a roaring or a rushing sound as well, but she was not sure, for just at that moment she lost consciousness.

"About 15 seconds after the flash," noted Lewis, 30,000 feet high and   18
several miles away, "there were two very distinct slaps on the ship from the blast and the shock wave. That was all the physical effect we felt. We turned the ship so that we could observe the results."

When Emiko came to, she was lying on her face about forty feet away   19
from where she had been standing. She was not aware of any pain. Her first thought was: "I'm alive!" She lifted her head slowly and looked about her. It was growing dark. The air was seething with dust and black smoke. There was a smell of burning. Emiko felt something trickle into her eyes, tasted it in her mouth. Gingerly she put a hand to her head, then looked at it. She saw with a shock that it was covered with blood.

She did not give a thought to Hideko. It did not occur to her that her   20
sister who was in another part of the city could possibly have been in danger. Like most of the survivors, Emiko assumed she had been close to a direct hit by a conventional bomb. She thought it had fallen on the

post-office next to the station. With a hurt child's panic, Emiko, streaming with blood from gashes in her scalp, ran blindly in search of her mother and father.

21 The people standing in front of the station had been burned to death instantly (a shadow had saved Emiko from the flash). The people inside the station had been crushed by falling masonry. Emiko heard their faint cries, saw hands scrabbling weakly from under the collapsed platform. All around her the maimed survivors were running and stumbling away from the roaring furnace that had been a city. She ran with them toward the mountains that ring the landward side of Hiroshima.

22 From the *Enola Gay*, the strangers from North America looked down at their handiwork. "There, in front of our eyes," wrote Lewis, "was without a doubt the greatest explosion man had ever witnessed. The city was nine-tenths covered with smoke of a boiling nature, which seemed to indicate buildings blowing up, and a large white cloud which in less than three minutes reached 30,000 feet, then went to at least 50,000 feet."

23 Far below, on the edge of this cauldron of smoke, at a distance of some 2,500 yards from the blast's epicentre, Emiko ran with the rest of the living. Some who could not run limped or dragged themselves along. Others were carried. Many, hideously burned, were screaming with pain; when they tripped they lay where they had fallen. There was a man whose face had been ripped open from mouth to ear, another whose forehead was a gaping wound. A young soldier was running with a foot-long splinter of bamboo protruding from one eye. But these, like Emiko, were the lightly wounded.

24 Some of the burned people had been literally roasted. Skin hung from their flesh like sodden tissue paper. They did not bleed but plasma dripped from their seared limbs.

25 The *Enola Gay*, mission completed, was returning to base. Lewis sought words to express his feelings, the feelings of all the crew. "I might say," he wrote, "I might say 'My God! What have we done?'"

26 Emiko ran. When she had reached the safety of the mountain she remembered that she still had her shoulder bag. There was a small first-aid kit in it and she applied ointment to her wounds and to a small cut in her left hand. She bandaged her head.

27 Emiko looked back at the city. It was a lake of fire. All around her the burned fugitives cried out in pain. Some were scorched on one side only. Others, naked and flayed, were burned all over. They were too many to help and most of them were dying. Emiko followed the walking wounded along a back road, still delirious, expecting suddenly to meet her father and mother.

28 The thousands dying by the roadside called feebly for help or water. Some of the more lightly injured were already walking in the other direction, back towards the flames. Others, with hardly any visible wounds,

stopped, turned ashy pale, and died within minutes. No one knew then that they were victims of radiation.

Emiko reached the suburb of Nakayama. 29

Far off in the *Enola Gay*, Lewis, who had seen none of this, had been 30 writing, "If I live a hundred years, I'll never get those few minutes out of my mind. Looking at Captain Parsons, why he is as confounded as the rest, and he is supposed to have known everything and expected this to happen. . . ."

At Nakayama, Emiko stood in line at a depot where riceballs were be- 31 ing distributed. Though it distressed her that the badly maimed could hardly feed themselves, the child found she was hungry. It was about 6 p.m. now. A little farther on, at Gion, a farmer called her by name. She did not recognize him, but it seemed he came monthly to her home to collect manure. The farmer took Emiko by the hand, led her to his own house, where his wife bathed her and fed her a meal of white rice. Then the child continued on her way. She passed another town where there were hundreds of injured. The dead were being hauled away in trucks. Among the injured a woman of about forty-five was waving frantically and muttering to herself. Emiko brought this woman a little water in a pumpkin leaf. She felt guilty about it; the schoolgirls had been warned not to give water to the seriously wounded. Emiko comforted herself with the thought that the woman would die soon anyway.

At Koi, she found standing-room in a train. It was heading for Otake 32 with a full load of wounded. Many were put off at Ono, where there was a hospital; and two hours later the train rolled into Otake station. It was around 10 p.m.

A great crowd had gathered to look for their relations. It was a night- 33 mare, Emiko remembered years afterwards; people were calling their dear kinfolk by name, searching frantically. It was necessary to call them by name, since most were so disfigured as to be unrecognizable. Doctors in the town council offices stitched Emiko's head-wounds. The place was crowded with casualties lying on the floor. Many died as Emiko watched.

The town council authorities made a strange announcement. They said 34 a new and mysterious kind of bomb had fallen in Hiroshima. People were advised to stay away from the ruins.

Home at midnight, Emiko found her parents so happy to see her that 35 they could not even cry. They could only give thanks that she was safe. Then they asked, "Where is your sister?"

For ten long days, while Emiko walked daily one and a half miles to 36 have her wounds dressed with fresh gauze, her father searched the rubble of Hiroshima for his lost child. He could not have hoped to find her alive. All, as far as the eye could see, was a desolation of charred ashes and wreckage, relieved only by a few jagged ruins and by the seven estuarial rivers that flowed through the waste delta. The banks of these rivers were covered with the dead and in the rising tidal waters floated thousands of corpses. On one broad street in the Hakushima district the crowds who had been thronging there were all naked and scorched cadavers. Of thousands of others there was no trace at all. A fire several times hotter than the surface of the sun had turned them instantly to vapour.

37   On August 11 came the news that Nagasaki had suffered the same fate as Hiroshima; it was whispered that Japan had attacked the United States mainland with similar mysterious weapons. With the lavish circumstantiality of rumour, it was said that two out of a fleet of six- engined trans-Pacific bombers had failed to return. But on August 15, speaking for the first time over the radio to his people, the Emperor Hirohito announced his country's surrender. Emiko heard him. No more bombs! she thought. No more fear! The family did not learn till June the following year that this very day young Tetsuro had been killed in action in Manchuria.

38   Emiko's wounds healed slowly. In mid-September they had closed with a thin layer of pinkish skin. There had been a shortage of antiseptics and Emiko was happy to be getting well. Her satisfaction was short- lived. Mysteriously she came down with diarrhoea and high fever. The fever continued for a month. Then one day she started to bleed from the gums, her mouth and throat became acutely inflamed, and her hair started to fall out. Through her delirium the child heard the doctors whisper by her pillow that she could not live. By now the doctors must have known that ionizing radiation caused such destruction of the blood's white cells that victims were left with little or no resistance against infection.

39   Yet Emiko recovered.

40   The wound on her hand, however, was particularly troublesome and did not heal for a long time.

41   As she got better, Emiko began to acquire some notion of the fearful scale of the disaster. Few of her friends and acquaintances were still alive. But no one knew precisely how many had died in Hiroshima. To this day the claims of various agencies conflict.

42   According to General Douglas MacArthur's headquarters, there were 78,150 dead and 13,083 missing. The United States Atomic Bomb Casualty Commission claims there were 79,000 dead. Both sets of figures are probably far too low. There's reason to believe that at the time of the surrender Japanese authorities lied about the number of survivors, exaggerating it to get extra medical supplies. The Japanese welfare ministry's figures of 260,000 dead and 163,263 missing may well be too high. But the very order of such discrepancies speaks volumes about the scale of the catastrophe. The dead were literally uncountable.

43   This appalling toll of human life had been exacted from a city that had been prepared for air attack in a state of full wartime readiness. All civil-

defence services had been overwhelmed from the first moment and it was many hours before any sort of organized rescue and relief could be put into effect.

It's true that single raids using so-called conventional weapons on other cities such as Tokyo and Dresden inflicted far greater casualties. And that it could not matter much to a victim whether he was burnt alive by a fire-storm caused by phosphorus, or by napalm or by nuclear fission. Yet in the whole of human history so savage a massacre had never before been inflicted with a single blow. And modern thermonuclear weapons are upwards of 1,000 times more powerful and deadly than the Hiroshima bomb.

The white scar I saw on Emiko's small, fine-boned hand was a tiny metaphor, a faint but eloquent reminder of the scar on humanity's conscience.

STRUCTURE:

1. What is Dobbs' THESIS STATEMENT? And what is the most important way in which his narrative supports it?
2. In "The Scar," two narratives are combined. Compare and contrast them. How does each help to explain nuclear war? And in the process, how does the one complement the other?
3. Kildare Dobbs did not witness the nuclear blast that, on August 6, 1945, levelled Hiroshima — yet he wrote an account of the event that may seem only too real. How did he know what it was like? Name the sources of information which he mentions. What other kinds of sources do you think he may have used? Do you think any of this narrative is the product of his imagination? If so, would that be a weakness or a strength?

STYLE:

1. In his log, Captain Lewis writes ". . . it's a very beautiful day" (par. 9), and in paragraph 11 Dobbs writes "It was a lovely morning." What effect do these pleasant words have in the context of the situation? What literary device underlies their power?
2. Captain Lewis writes in his log, "There'll be a short intermission while we bomb our target" (par. 15). Do these words seem peculiar? If so, why?
3. In referring to the first operational nuclear bomb as "Little Boy" (par. 7), what does Dobbs add to the force of his narrative?
4. Paragraphs 23, 24, 27 and 36 are filled with gruesome details that illustrate the effects of "Little Boy." Do these details help or hurt the purpose of the narrative? Do they encourage in the reader an opposi-

tion to nuclear weapons? Or, in their dreadfulness, do they encourage the reader merely to drop the subject and think of other things?

5. In paragraphs 42-44, why does Dobbs leave the narrative and turn instead to statistics and generalizations?

6. In what sense is the scar on Emiko's hand a METAPHOR, and what qualifies this metaphor to end our selection?

IDEAS:

1. According to the estimates quoted by Dobbs, between 78,150 and 260,000 people were killed by the one bomb that hit Hiroshima. And according to Jonathan Schell, 1,600,000 times the firepower of that bomb now exists in the nuclear arsenals of the world (*The Fate of the Earth,* Knopf, 1982). What is your response to these statistics?

2. It has been estimated that the Soviet Union has enough nuclear warheads to destroy the United States twenty-five times over, and that the United States has enough nuclear warheads to destroy the Soviet Union fifty times over. In view of these figures, how do you interpret the fact that in recent years both East and West have greatly increased the production of nuclear warheads and their delivery systems?

3. Robert Falls, the Canadian head of NATO's military committee in Europe, said, "NATO strategy is to use nuclear weapons *first* if we are faced with overwhelming conventional odds and if retreat or surrender are the only alternatives" (*Maclean's,* February 15, 1982). Do you believe that NATO's concept of a "limited" nuclear war such as this is valid? Or do you believe that any nuclear first strike would result in a global conflict?

4. Do you think that civilians around the world should be trained in civil defence against a nuclear attack? Would it save lives? Or on the other hand, would it make such an attack more acceptable to military leaders and thus more likely?

5. What do you believe Canada's role should be in limiting or contributing to the arms race? For example, Litton Systems, Ltd., of Toronto, makes the guidance system that leads the American Cruise missile to its target. Do you approve or disapprove? Explain your reasons.

6. In a letter to the prime minister, the minister of national defence, your M.P. or the editor of your local newspaper, argue for or against Canada's participation in the arms race. Explain your reasons clearly. If this is a required assignment let your teacher see your letter, then mail it.

7. Write, in either first person or third person, a vivid narrative telling in detail what you imagine one of the following events would be like:

The council of war at which a national leader decides to launch or not to launch a nuclear attack

A nuclear attack on your own city

A nuclear attack on your own country, experienced from the relative safety of a bomb shelter or a remote location

A day in the life of a survivor ten years after a global nuclear war

The visit of a Martian, one thousand years from now, and his report to his chief about what he sees on earth

(NOTE: See also the Topics for Writing at the end of this chapter.)

Topics for Writing

Chapter 1: Narration

Writing About Myself

(Note also the topics for writing that appear after each selection in this chapter.)

Choose one of these topics as the basis of a narrative about yourself. Tell a good story: give colourful details and all the facts needed to help your reader understand and appreciate the event.

1. The day I was born (interview one or both parents first)
2. My earliest memory
3. The most important event of my childhood
4. The day I learned to know myself
5. The day I learned to appreciate my parents
6. The day I first met my husband, wife or friend
7. An event that changed my life
8. The day I began my first job
9. The day I conquered a fear
10. The day I broke the law
11. My most serious accident or illness
12. The best day of my life
13. \
14. My { most frightening / proudest / most heroic } moment
15. /

Narration:

Writing About Others

From this list of events, choose one that you witnessed in person (or, in the case of numbers 9 and 10, that you learned about by interviewing). Narrate it, giving colourful details and all the facts needed to help your reader understand and appreciate the event.

1. The birth of a brother, sister, son or daughter
2. The wedding of a friend or relative
3. The death of a family member or friend
4. The day a friend or relative suddenly became rich or poor
5. The day a friend or relative experienced a religious conversion or a loss of faith

6. The day a friend or relative surprised everyone by revealing his or her true self
7. An event that was a major success or failure in the life of a friend or relative
8. The day that a friend or relative experienced a major change of attitude about life
9. The most important event in the life of an elderly relative (interview the person before writing the narrative)
10. The day your parents first met (interview one or both before writing the narrative)
11. An accident in the neighbourhood
12. A fire in the neighbourhood
13. A crime in the neighbourhood
14. A major confrontation between two or more people
15. An event that symbolizes the spirit of the town, city, province or country in which it occurred

"What feeds we used to have. Not way back in the pod auger days, mind you. That was before my time. I mean not long ago, just before the tinned stuff and the packages and the baker's bread started to trickle into the outports."

Ray Guy, "Outharbor Menu"

For example . . . .

EXAMPLE

Many an audience, after trying in vain to understand a speaker's message, has been saved from boredom or even sleep by those powerful words, "FOR EXAMPLE. . . ." Heads lift up, eyes return to the front, and suddenly the message is clear to everyone. Writers, as well as speakers, need to use examples. Pages of abstract reasoning, of generalizations, of theory without application, will only confuse, bore and finally alienate your reader. But the same ideas supported by well-chosen examples will much more easily interest and even convince your reader. Examples take many forms:

Personal experience: To illustrate your point, narrate an incident that you experienced. Did an earthquake or tornado or flood show you the power of nature? Did an accident illustrate the dangers of drinking and driving, or did a fire illustrate the dangers of smoking in bed? Did a major success or failure demonstrate the importance of work or planning or persistence?

The experience of others: To illustrate your point, narrate an incident that you have seen yourself or heard about from other sources. Did your neighbour's unloved child run away from home or rob a milk store or get married at age sixteen? Did your uncle lose his job because of automation or recession or imports? Did a famous person succeed despite a physical handicap or a deprived childhood?

Hypothetical examples: In a future-oriented society like ours, many arguments speculate about what might happen *if*. . . . Since the event or situation has not yet come to pass, use your best judgment to imagine the results. What would happen if children had the vote? If street drugs were legalized? If shopping were done by computer? If gasoline were five dollars a litre? If a woman became prime minister? If a world government were adopted?

Quotations: If the words of a poet, politician, scientist or other prominent person illustrate your point clearly and authoritatively, quote them and of course state who said them. What did Aristotle, Shakespeare, Machiavelli, Freud, Marx or John Diefenbaker say about love or power or sex or money or old age or war? Start with the index of *Bartlett's Quotations* or *Colombo's Canadian Quotatations* to find an apt statement on almost any important topic.

Statistics: These numerical examples lend a scientific, objective quality to your argument. Tell what percentage of marriages will end in divorce, or how many minutes each cigarette takes off your life, or how much energy a person consumes travelling by car as opposed to train, bus or airplane. Five good sources of statistics are *Information Please Almanac, The World Almanac and Book of Facts, The Corpus Almanac of Canada, Canada Year Book,* and any good atlas. Be scrupulously honest, because almost everyone knows how statistics are sometimes made to lie (remember the statistician who drowned in the river that averaged two feet deep!).

Other devices: Later chapters in this book discuss cause and effect, comparison and contrast, and analogy. These devices may be used not only to plan the structure of an entire essay, but also to construct short and vivid examples within the essay.

Almost all good writing contains examples, but some writing contains so many that it uses examples as a means of organizing as well as a means of illustrating. Ray Guy's essay "Outharbor Menu" has a brief introduction, a one-sentence closing, and a body made of nothing but examples. Such a collection could be a mere list of trivia, but Ray Guy — like anyone who writes well — has chosen his examples carefully for their colour and for the support which they give to his point.

Another technique is to use one long, well-developed example — in effect, a narrative. Bruce Hutchison does so in "Cowboy from Holland":

EXAMPLE **57**

focussing almost totally on the little Dutch boy, he gives us one long example to represent the millions of other immigrants who have become Canadians. Of course one example — or twenty — will prove nothing. Statistics come close to it, especially when based on a large and carefully designed study. But in general an example is not a device of proof; it is a device of illustration, and therefore an aid to both understanding and enjoyment.

Robert Fulford

Where, Exactly, Are This Book's Readers?

Robert Fulford is one of Canada's most respected journalists and editors. Born in Ottawa in 1932, he grew up in Toronto where in 1949 he began his career in journalism as a copy boy for the Globe and Mail. *Soon after, he became a reporter. In 1957 Fulford was named editor of* Canadian Homes and Gardens, *and since then has held editorial positions at* Maclean's, Mayfair, The Canadian Forum *and, since 1968,* Saturday Night. *Fulford's greatest achievement, through his editorial abilities and his own penetrating and well-written columns, has been to secure the position of* Saturday Night *as Canada's best magazine of culture and public affairs. Fulford has also been a columnist for the Toronto* Star, *a radio and television broadcaster, and the author of several books. "Where, Exactly, Are this Book's Readers?" appeared first in the Toronto* Star, *then in a 1968 collection of Fulford's essays,* Crisis at the Victory Burlesk: Culture, Politics & Other Diversions.

1 There's always the possibility, of course, that the world already has enough books; may, in fact, have *too many* books. This thought has never occurred to a publisher; it has probably occurred to only a minority of authors; but certainly it has occurred at one time or another to every book reviewer in the world.

2 For the fact is that book reviewers spend their lives surrounded by piles of books they will never read and they can't imagine anyone else reading. Every morning a young man comes into my office with a pile of half a dozen books, and on the average three of them fall into this category.

3 Take one that turned up yesterday: *They Gave Royal Assent*, subtitled *The Lieutenant-Governors of British Columbia*. Imagine it. Not just a book on lieutenant-governors — a subject with truly monumental possibilities for producing boredom — but a book on *British Columbia* lieutenant-governors.

4 Now the thing about lieutenant-governors is that, in general, they don't do anything. They just sort of *preside*. Their lives lack, not to put too fine a point on it, drama. So who will read this book? If you were lieutenant-governor of British Columbia you might well want to read it, and if you aspired to that office you would almost certainly be anxious to obtain a copy. But surely that makes a limited market. In addition there are descendants and other connections of lieutenant-governors; but this, too, must be a comparatively small group. Will the author, D.A. McGregor ('veteran journalist, editor and history-researcher,' the jacket

says) meet friends who have read his book and who will congratulate him on it? 'Nice job on the lieutenant-governors, old man,' one imagines them saying. But who would they be?

The publishers, Mitchell Press of Vancouver, have dutifully sent out review copies. Why? Because publishers do this — they operate automatically on the I-shot-an-arrow-into-the-air theory of publicity. They just send out books at random, whether anybody wants them or not. It gives them some queer sense of satisfaction. They feel they are playing their part.

So here are all these books floating around in the mails and then ending up on the desks of people who view them with apathy if not distaste. Any book reviewer can at any moment, and to his horror, look around his office and instantly spot three books on the Quebec crisis, four histories of Ontario counties, five books on how to diet, two authorized biographies of Teilhard de Chardin, and one book by a man who lived six months with a colony of apes and didn't find out anything.

Right now I have here, in front of me: *The Bahamas Handbook* (547 pages, would you believe it?); *One of Our Brains is Draining*, a novel by someone named Max Wilk; *The Nation Keepers*, a book of essays by the likes of Wallace McCutcheon and John Robarts; *Brant County, A History, 1784-1945; Success at the Harness Races*, by Barry Meadow, 'a practical guide for handicapping winners'; *Churchill, His Paintings*, a gift book priced at only $12.50 and worth, anyway, a nickel; *Vigor for Men Over 30*, as depressing a title as any I've encountered this season, by Warren Guild, M.D., Stuart D. Cowan, and Samm Sinclair Baker (a slim book, but it took three men to write it); *A History of Peel County, 1867-1967; Nineteenth Century Pottery and Porcelain in Canada;* and *Great True Hunts*, a $17.95 picture book all about how various famous men — such as the Shah of Iran, Tito, and Roy Rogers — go out and kill beautiful animals for fun.

I can't get a copy of the new John O'Hara novel, no matter how hard I try, but I have all these other books around me, and they're piling up, piling up. A man came to my office yesterday and claimed he couldn't find me. I was there all the time, but hidden. The situation, as it often does in December, is reaching a critical phase.

But what about those Vancouver publishers? What exactly did they have in mind when they sent out those review copies of their lieutenant-governor book? Did they think people would *read* it, and then *write* something about it? Did they anticipate that soon they would begin receiving clippings, full of praise for their courage, imagination, and resourcefulness in publishing this significant volume? One can imagine the quotes:

'*A stimulating and indeed an engrossing account of . . . in places thrilling, in others richly analytical . . . abrasive, tough, probing . . pro-*

found and moving in its depiction of . . . a very badly needed contribution to the history of . . . . full of those insights we have come to expect from . . .'

11   Or did they, retaining some grasp on reality, know all the time what would happen — that one book editor after another across the country would silently pass the book along to his paper's library, hoping that someday someone on the staff — for some unthinkable reason — would want to know something about the lieutenant-governors of British Columbia?

12   The notion that perhaps there may be too many books in the world, that perhaps it is more creative *not* to write a book than to write one, occurred to me when I returned the other day from two weeks of leave and began wading through a pile of books on Christian revival, books on space exploration, and books on nineteenth-century Canada. . . . But I immediately set that whole subversive idea aside. Because after all I'd just spent the previous two weeks, uh, writing a book.

STRUCTURE:
1. Where is Fulford's main point first stated?
2. What effect is achieved in the final sentence where Fulford confesses that he himself has just written a book?
3. Why do you think Fulford devotes six paragraphs to *They Gave Royal Assent: The Lieutenant-Governors of British Columbia,* but only a few words to each of the many other books he names?
4. How convincing are Fulford's examples? Would you want to read any of the books that he makes fun of?

STYLE
1. When did you first realize that this is a humorous essay?
2. People say "uh" but hardly ever write it. Why does Fulford use it in his final sentence? Point out other places where he uses INFORMAL, conversational language and discuss the effects he achieves in doing so.
3. In paragraph 7, Fulford tells us that *Vigor for Men over 30* is "a slim book, but it took three men to write it." Point out other examples of IRONY, in which we hear the opposite of what we might have expected.
4. Why do you think Fulford wrote paragraph 7 as one long sentence?
5. What do Fulford's imagined book review quotations in paragraph 10 make fun of?

IDEAS:

1. Fulford begins his essay by stating, "There's always the possibility, of course, that the world already has enough books; may, in fact, have *too many* books." Do you agree? How do you feel in a large library with thousands of books around you? Can you think of reasons why a library might collect the books Fulford criticizes?
2. What kinds of books do you own? Name your favourites. How do you choose a book to buy?
3. Why do people write books: What are some bad reasons? What are some good reasons?
4. Suppose you decide to become an author. Write an essay describing your first book: its subject, its approach to that subject, the most important points or scenes it would contain, and the identity of its intended readers. Do you think a reviewer like Robert Fulford would consider it a book to read or avoid? Use frequent examples to explain all these points.

(NOTE: See also the Topics for Writing at the end of this chapter.)

Joy Kogawa
*Grinning and Happy**

With three published books of poetry to her credit — The Splintered Moon (1967), A Choice of Dreams (1974) and Jericho Road (1977) — Joy Kogawa had become a respected minor poet. But in 1981 she created a sensation with her first novel. Obasan *represents a new step for Kogawa as a writer and as a person: in it she explores her own past and one of the most dubious events of Canadian history. Born in 1935, Kogawa was a child during World War II when the federal government classified Japanese Canadians as "enemy aliens." Her parents' house in Vancouver was seized, and the family was moved first to a relocation camp in Slocan, B.C., then to the sugar beet fields of southern Alberta, which are the setting of our selection from the novel. Our narrator is modelled after Kogawa herself, Stephen is the narrator's brother, Obasan is the narrator's silent and suffering aunt, and "Aunt Emily" is modelled after Muriel Kitagawa, a Japanese-Canadian activist whose letters Kogawa studied in the National Archives in Ottawa. Kogawa now lives in Toronto.*

1   There is a folder in Aunt Emily's package containing only one newspaper clipping and an index card with the words "Facts about evacuees in Alberta." The newspaper clipping has a photograph of one family, all smiles, standing around a pile of beets. The caption reads: "Grinning and Happy."

2   Find Jap Evacuees Best Beet Workers
Lethbridge, Alberta, Jan. 22.

3   Japanese evacuees from British Columbia supplied the labour for 65% of Alberta's sugar beet acreage last year, Phil Baker, of Lethbridge, president of the Alberta Sugar Beet Growers' Association, stated today.

4   "They played an important part in producing our all-time record crop of 363,000 tons of beets in 1945," he added.

5   Mr. Baker explained Japanese evacuees worked 19,500 acres of beets and German prisoners of war worked 5,000 acres. The labour for the remaining 5,500 acres of Alberta's 30,000 acres of sugar beets was provided by farmers and their families. Some of the heaviest beet yields last year came from farms employing Japanese evacuees.

6   Generally speaking, Japanese evacuees have developed into most efficient beet workers, many of them being better than the transient workers who cared for beets in southern Alberta before Pearl Harbor. . . .

7   Facts about evacuees in Alberta? The fact is I never got used to it and I
*Editor's title

62

cannot, I cannot bear the memory. There are some nightmares from which there is no waking, only deeper and deeper sleep.

There is a word for it. Hardship. The hardship is so pervasive, so inescapable, so thorough it's a noose around my chest and I cannot move any more. All the oil in my joints has drained out and I have been invaded by dust and grit from the fields and mud is in my bone marrow. I can't move any more. My fingernails are black from scratching the scorching day and there is no escape. 8

Aunt Emily, are you a surgeon cutting at my scalp with your folders and your filing cards and your insistence on knowing all? The memory drains down the sides of my face, but it isn't enough, is it? It's your hands in my abdomen, pulling the growth from the lining of my walls, but bring back the anaesthetist turn on the ether clamp down the gas mask bring on the chloroform when will this operation be over Aunt Em? 9

Is it so bad? 10

Yes. 11

Do I really mind? 12

Yes, I mind. I mind everything. Even the flies. The flies and flies and flies from the cows in the barn and the manure pile — all the black flies that curtain the windows, and Obasan with a wad of toilet paper, spish, then with her bare hands as well, grabbing them and their shocking white eggs and the mosquitoes mixed there with the other insect corpses around the base of the gas lamp. 13

It's the chicken coop "house" we live in that I mind. The uninsulated unbelievable thin-as-a-cotton-dress hovel never before inhabited in winter by human beings. In summer it's a heat trap, an incubator, a dry sauna from which there is no relief. In winter the icicles drip down the inside of the windows and the ice is thicker than bricks at the ledge. The only place that is warm is by the coal stove where we rotate like chickens on a spit and the feet are so cold they stop registering. We eat cloves of roasted garlic on winter nights to warm up. 14

It's the bedbugs and my having to sleep on the table to escape the nightly attack, and the welts over our bodies. And all the swamp bugs and the dust. It's Obasan uselessly packing all the cracks with rags. And the muddy water from the irrigation ditch which we strain and settle and boil, and the tiny carcasses of water creatures at the bottom of the cup. It's walking in winter to the reservoir and keeping the hole open with the axe and dragging up the water in pails and lugging it back and sometimes the water spills down your boots and your feet are red and itchy for days. And it's everybody taking a bath in the round galvanized tub, then Obasan washing clothes in the water after and standing outside hanging the clothes in the freezing weather where everything instantly stiffens on the line. 15

16   Or it's standing in the beet field under the maddening sun, standing with my black head a sun-trap even though it's covered, and lying down in the ditch, faint, and the nausea in waves and the cold sweat, and getting up and tackling the next row. The whole field is an oven and there's not a tree within walking distance. We are tiny as insects crawling along the grill and there is no protection anywhere. The eyes are lidded against the dust and the air cracks the skin, the lips crack, Stephen's flutes crack and there is no energy to sing any more anyway.

17   It's standing in the field and staring out at the heat waves that waver and shimmer like see-through curtains over the brown clods and over the tiny distant bodies of Stephen and Uncle and Obasan miles away across the field day after day and not even wondering how this has come about.

18   There she is, Obasan, wearing Uncle's shirt over a pair of dark baggy trousers, her head covered by a straw hat that is held on by a white cloth tied under her chin. She is moving like a tiny earth cloud over the hard clay clods. Her hoe moves rhythmically up down up down, tiny as a toothpick. And over there, Uncle pauses to straighten his back, his hands on his hips. And Stephen farther behind, so tiny I can barely see him.

19   It's hard, Aunt Emily, with my hoe, the blade getting dull and mud-caked as I slash out the Canada thistle, dandelions, crab grass, and other nameless non-beet plants, then on my knees, pulling out the extra beets from the cluster, leaving just one to mature, then three hand spans to the next plant, whack whack, and down on my knees again, pull, flick flick, and on to the end of the long long row and the next and the next and it will never be done thinning and weeding and weeding and weeding. It's so hard and so hot that my tear glands burn out.

20   And then it's cold. The lumps of clay mud stick on my gumboots and weight my legs and the skin under the boots beneath the knees at the level of the calves grows red and hard and itchy from the flap flap of the boots and the fine hairs on my legs grow coarse there and ugly.

21   I mind growing ugly.

22   I mind the harvest time and the hands and the wrists bound in rags to keep the wrists from breaking open. I lift the heavy mud-clotted beets out of the ground with the hook like an eagle's beak, thick and heavy as a nail attached to the top of the sugar-beet knife. Thwack. Into the beet and yank from the shoulder till it's out of the ground dragging the surrounding mud with it. Then crack two beets together till most of the mud drops off and splat, the knife slices into the beet scalp and the green top is tossed into one pile, the beet heaved onto another, one more one more one more down the icy line. I cannot tell about this time, Aunt Emily. The body will not tell.

23   We are surrounded by a horizon of denim-blue sky with clouds clear as spilled milk that turn pink at sunset. Pink I hear is the colour of llama's

milk. I wouldn't know. The clouds are the shape of our new prison walls — untouchable, impersonal, random.

There are no other people in the entire world. We work together all 24 day. At night we eat and sleep. We hardly talk any more. The boxes we brought from Slocan are not unpacked. The King George/Queen Elizabeth mugs stay muffled in the *Vancouver Daily Province*. The cameraphone does not sing. Obasan wraps layers of cloth around her feet and her torn sweater hangs unmended over her sagging dress.

Down the miles we are obedient as machines in this odd ballet without 25 accompaniment of flute or song.

"Grinning and happy" and all smiles standing around a pile of beets? 26 That is one telling. It's not how it was.

STRUCTURE:
1. Where is the main point of this selection first stated?
2. What percentage of this selection would you estimate consists of examples that illustrate the main point?
3. In what way does "Grinning and Happy" use contrast as a structural device?
4. To what extent is this selection based on description?
5. What qualifies paragraph 26 to end this selection?

STYLE:
1. Until the publication of *Obasan*, Joy Kogawa was best known as a poet. What poetical qualities do you find in this selection of her PROSE?
2. To what extent has Kogawa used SENSE IMAGES to make this selection vivid? Give one example each of appeals to sight, hearing, touch, taste and smell.
3. A SIMILE states that one thing is like another, while a METAPHOR states poetically that one thing is another. Which of the following are similes and which are metaphors?
   A. "The hardship is so pervasive, so inescapable, so thorough it's a noose around my chest . . . ." (par. 8)
   B. ". . . all the black flies that curtain the windows . . . ." (par. 13)
   C. "In summer it's a heat trap, an incubator, a dry sauna from which there is no relief." (par. 14)
   D. "The only place that is warm is by the coal stove where we rotate like chickens on a spit . . . ." (par. 14)
   E. "The whole field is an oven . . . ." (par. 16)
   F. "We are tiny as insects crawling along the grill . . . ." (par. 16)

G. ". . . heat waves that waver and shimmer like see-through curtains . . . ." (par. 17)

H. ". . . the hook like an eagle's beak, thick and heavy as a nail attached to the top of the sugar-beet knife." (par. 22)

I. ". . . the knife slices into the beet scalp . . . ." (par. 22)

J. "The clouds are the shape of our new prison walls — untouchable, impersonal, random." (par. 23)

4. In paragraphs 14 through 17, how many times do you find the contraction "it's" at or near the beginning of a sentence? Is this repetition accidental or deliberate? What is its effect?

5. How many words long is the first sentence of paragraph 19? How many times does it use the word "and"? Is this run-on sentence accidental or deliberate? What is its effect?

IDEAS:

1. The narrator of "Grinning and Happy" and her immediate family are Canadian citizens of Japanese descent, removed by the federal government from the coast of British Columbia during World War II for fear they would betray Canada to enemy Japan. They were separated from other family members and their property was taken, never to be returned. Discuss the wisdom of our government's action against the Japanese-Canadians, who are accurately represented by this fictitious family. Did anything like it happen before World War II? Has anything like it happened since? Under what circumstances can you imagine it happening again, and to what group or groups?

2. Have you personally or have any of your ancestors faced persecution based on race, nationality or religion? If so explain how and why, giving examples.

3. How much racial prejudice, if any, do you see in the area where you live? What do you think may be its causes? Against whom is it directed? Give examples that you have personally witnessed.

4. If you have read "Coming of Age in Putnok," compare prejudice and its effects as they are described by George Gabori and by Kogawa.

5. The American black comedian Dick Gregory once said, "A lot of people tell me: 'We just have a small racial problem in Canada.' What I want to know is how do you say that a woman is a little bit pregnant?" He added, "I think the acid test to the problem here in Canada will be if every white person would go to bed and imagine waking up tomorrow morning black. I think then they would be aware that there are problems" (*Scan*, November 1965). Following Gregory's suggestion, imagine that you wake up one morning as a member of another race. Write an essay that describes that day in your life, showing through numerous examples how your life might have changed.

(NOTE: See also the Topics for Writing at the end of this chapter.)

Richard Needham
A Sound of Deviltry by Night

Richard Needham is a newspaperman who since 1964 has written a column of aphorisms, puzzles, riddles and satire for the Toronto Globe and Mail. *He has been described as one of our few genuine cynics, a writer who delights in attacking sacred cows — and who, for this reason, tends to provoke either love or hatred among his readers. Needham was born in 1912 in Gibraltar, grew up in India, Ireland and England, and at age sixteen left home to come to Canada. After working as a farm hand, he found his first writing job at the Toronto* Star. *Through the years he has worked also at the Hamilton* Herald, *the Sudbury* Star, *the Calgary* Herald *and — for most of the time since 1951 — the* Globe and Mail. *His short satires have been collected in* Needham's Inferno *(1966), which won the Stephen Leacock Award for Humour,* The Garden of Needham *(1968),* A Friend in Needham *(1969) and* The Wit & Wisdom of Richard Needham *(1977). Our selection typifies Needham's ironical tone, his love of puns and his extraordinarily concise style. It appears in* The Hypodermic Needham *(1970), in slightly different form.*

I n the city, you can go broke on $20,000 a year; but in the suburbs, you can do it on $30,000. Suburbanites accomplish this in some measure by staging lavish cocktail parties at which matrons gobble pizza as they discuss their weight problem, and men get smashed out of their skulls while they boast how they gave up smoking. 1

What function these parties serve (outside of plunging the host and hostess further into debt) has long baffled sociologists. My theory — true for myself, at least — is that the cocktail party is a form of shock treatment comparable to the snake pit of earlier times. So great is the horror of it, so keen the sense of relief at escaping, that all one's other sufferings and problems are reduced to triviality. 2

Finding myself beset by fortune's slings and arrows not long ago, I subjected myself to the ordeal by guzzle, gabble and gorge at a home so far north of the city that several of the guests greeted each other by rubbing noses. The usual cocktail-party types were on hand — languid immigrants, inferior decorators, insulting engineers, gloomy dames, misplaced trustees, impractical nurses, a dean of women who had been fired for having men in her room at all hours of the day and night, a marriage counsellor who announced that his third wife had just left him for the fifth time, and a psychiatrist who kept getting down on his hands and knees and frisking about the place, nipping at the women's heels. 3

It is customary at these gatherings to have the phonograph on at full blast; this forces people to shout and scream at each other, which in turn dries out their throats, which in turn causes them to get bagged more quickly, which is why they went to the party in the first place. Having no 4 opinions or information worth bellowing, I customarily listen to those of others. Standing near a group of women, I caught the following fragments:

'The only thing I have against men is me . . . *The Naked Ape* is disgusting, I stayed up all night reading it . . . I don't know how old she is exactly, but she does enjoy a nice hot cup of tea . . . Even a newspaperman is better than no man at all . . . We eventually had to leave Picton; the pace was too fast . . . I keep having this awful nightmare; a big brute of a man is chasing me, and I escape . . . I found out early on Bay Street that all men are married, but some are less married than others . . . I didn't mind Jack's cruelty and extravagance; what finished it off was the way he kept clearing his throat every five minutes.'

Going out in the garden, I found a young man who told me, 'I hate university but I have to stay there so I can graduate and get a good job, and pay back the money I borrowed to go to university.' The young woman with him said she had a different problem. 'It's my parents. They're so good and kind and trusting, and I'm so rotten. When I come home drunk at two in the morning with my clothes torn, and tell them I was in a car accident, they believe me. This makes me feel guilty, and so I become twice as rotten. I wish I had parents like Jill; her father drinks his pay, and her mother runs around with every man on the block, so she doesn't have to feel guilty about being even more rotten than I am.'

Going back into the house, I listened in on a group of men: 'I've always thought of Highway 7 as the square route . . . When the postal strike ends, how will people be able to tell? . . . I've at last figured it out, Doris Day is her own grandmother . . . I know beer's the drink of moderation, that's why I hate it . . . When your plane lands in Toronto, you have to set your watch back thirty years . . . Liquor at the C.N.E.? It's enough to make Judge Robb turn over in his grave . . . I'm still looking for a woman who measures down to my standards . . . I didn't mind Marge's boozing and infidelity; what drove me out was that she never changed the blade after shaving her legs with my razor.'

It seemed at this point I'd had enough, so I finished the Scotch-and-tonic someone had pressed on me, said farewell to the hostess, and made an inglorious exit by tripping over the dachshund. Still, I was safely out; I wouldn't need to do it again for a long time; and I walked steadily south until the crumbling tenements, polluted air, garbage-littered streets, and screams of hold-up victims informed me I was back in civilization.

STRUCTURE:
1. Which paragraph states the main point of this essay?

2. Does the fact that the main point is satirical (see SATIRE) detract from its importance as the focus of this essay?
3. Where does the introduction end and what does it accomplish?
4. Which paragraphs are devoted to examples that illustrate the main point, and how are these paragraphs developed?
5. What effect is achieved by the use of a great many very short examples?
6. Paragraph 5 consists of comments by women, paragraph 6 of comments by one couple, and paragraph 7 of comments by men. Do these groupings serve any purpose?
7. What basic form of development, other than example, helps to structure this essay?

STYLE:

1. Richard Needham is a journalist. Do you see ways in which this essay resembles or differs from a news article?
2. Needham uses words playfully. In paragraph 3, what is he doing when he refers to "languid immigrants," "inferior decorators" and "insulting engineers"?
3. Pick out examples of COLLOQUAL or SLANG words used by Needham, and discuss the effects of this very informal language. What kinds of writing would you not use such words in?
4. Needham is known for his ability to condense an idea or a characterization into a one-sentence EPIGRAM. In paragraph 7, a guest says, "I know beer's the drink of moderation, that's why I hate it." How many more epigrams do you find?
5. When in paragraph 7 a guest says, "I've always thought of Highway 7 as the square route," what device of humour is Needham using?
6. Do you think that Needham's devices of light humour trivialize the argument? Or do they enhance the argument by making it entertaining?
7. In the phrase "beset by fortune's slings and arrows" (par. 3), Needham is alluding to Hamlet's famous speech:

> To be, or not to be: that is the question:
> Whether 'tis nobler in the mind to suffer
> The slings and arrows of outrageous fortune,
> Or to take arms against a sea of troubles,
> And by opposing end them?

Is the ALLUSION appropriate? Should we be thinking of Hamlet's serious problems and his contemplation of suicide in a sentence that continues with Needham's "ordeal by guzzle, gabble and gorge"?

IDEAS:

1. Is Needham's only aim to amuse us, or is he at least partly serious in portraying a cocktail party as "a form of shock treatment"?

2. Are there topics so serious that they cannot be developed through SATIRE?
3. Why do people go to parties? Give some good reasons. Give some bad reasons.
4. What STEREOTYPES do you recognize in Needham's thumbnail portraits of the guests?
5. Does the narrator hate only cocktail parties or does he seem cynical about humanity in general?
6. Write an essay describing the best or worst party you have ever attended. Supply frequent and colourful examples, as Needham has.

(NOTE: See also the Topics for Writing at the end of this chapter.)

Ray Guy
Outharbor Menu

Although Ray Guy has been Newfoundland's favourite writer for some years, he is only now being discovered by the rest of Canada. Guy was born in 1939 at Arnold's Cove, an outport on Placentia Bay, and as a child learned to value the self-reliance of traditional Newfoundland life. After two years at Memorial University he went to Toronto, where in 1963 he earned a diploma in journalism at Ryerson Polytechnical Institute. Upon his return to Newfoundland he began reporting for the St. John's Evening Telegram, *but found that reporting was not enough. His distaste for the Liberal government of Joey Smallwood, and especially for its policy of closing down the outports where for centuries Newfoundlanders had lived as fishermen, led Guy to become a political columnist. His satirical attacks on Smallwood were so devastating that some people credit him with Smallwood's defeat in the provincial election of 1971. Guy no longer works for the* Evening Telegram, *but writes a column that appears in several newspapers. His humorous essays about many aspects of life in Newfoundland have been collected in* You May Know Them as Sea Urchins, Ma'am *(1975) and in* That Far Greater Bay *(1976), which won the Leacock Award for Humour. Our selection first appeared in the latter.*

What feeds we used to have. Not way back in the pod auger days*, mind you. That was before my time. I mean not long ago, just before the tinned stuff and the packages and the baker's bread started to trickle into the outports. 1

Out where I come from the trickle started when I was about six or seven years old. One day I went next door to Aunt Winnie's (that's Uncle John's Aunt Winnie) and she had a package of puffed rice someone sent down from Canada*. 2

She gave us youngsters a small handful each. We spent a long time admiring this new exotic stuff and remarking on how much it looked like emmets' eggs. We ate it one grain at a time as if it were candy, and because of the novelty didn't notice the remarkable lack of taste. 3

"Now here's a five cent piece and don't spend it all in sweets, mind." You never got a nickel without this caution attached. 4

Peppermint knobs. White capsules ringed around with flannelette pink stripes. Strong! You'd think you were breathing icewater. They're not near as strong today. 5

Chocolate mice shaped like a crouching rat, chocolate on the outside and tough pink sponge inside. Goodbye teeth. Bullseyes made from molasses. And union squares — pastel blocks of marshmallow. 6

*the pod auger days: a common Newfoundland expression meaning "the old days." Literally a pod auger is an auger with a lengthwise groove.
*from Canada: Newfoundland did not join Confederation until 1949, after the time Ray Guy describes.

71

7   Those mysterious black balls that were harder than forged steel, had about 2,537 different layers of color and a funny tasting seed at the centre of the mini-universe.

8   Soft drinks came packed in barrels of straw in bottles of different sizes and shapes and no labels. Birch beer, root beer, chocolate, lemonade, and orange.

9   Spruce beer, which I could never stomach, but the twigs boiling on the stove smelled good. Home brew made from "Blue Ribbon" malt and which always exploded like hand grenades in the bottles behind the stove.

10   Rum puncheons. Empty barrels purchased from the liquor control in St. John's. You poured in a few gallons of water, rolled the barrel around, and the result was a stronger product than you put down $7.50 a bottle for today.

11   Ice cream made in a hand-cranked freezer, the milk and sugar and vanilla in the can in the middle surrounded by ice and coarse salt. I won't say it was better than the store-bought stuff today but it tasted different and I like the difference.

12   Rounders (dried tom cods) for Sunday breakfast without fail. Cods heads, boiled sometimes, but mostly stewed with onions and bits of salt pork.

13   Fried cod tongues with pork scruncheons.* Outport soul food. Salt codfish, fish cakes, boiled codfish and drawn butter, baked cod with savoury stuffing, stewed cod, fried cod.

14   Lobsters. We always got the bodies and the thumbs from the canning factories. When eating lobster bodies you must be careful to stay away from the "old woman," a lump of bitter black stuff up near the head which is said to be poisonous.

15   I was always partial to that bit of red stuff in lobster bodies but never went much on the pea green stuff although some did.

16   We ate turrs* (impaled on a sharpened broomstick and held over the damper hole to singe off the fuzz), some people ate tickleaces* and gulls but I never saw it done.

17   We ate "a meal of trouts," seal, rabbits that were skinned out like a sock, puffin' pig (a sort of porpoise that had black meat), mussels and cocks and hens, otherwise known as clams, that squirt at you through air holes in the mud flats.

18   Potatoes and turnips were the most commonly grown vegetables although there was some cabbage and carrot. The potatoes were kept in cellars made of mounds of earth lined with sawdust or goosegrass. With the hay growing on them they looked like hairy green igloos.

---

*pork scruncheons: crisp slices of fried pork fat.
*turr: a term applied to both the razor-billed auk and the murre, in this case probably the auk.
*tickleace: the kittiwake, a kind of gull.

A lot was got from a cow. Milk, certainly, and cream and butter made   19
into pats and stamped with a wooden print of a cow or a clover leaf, and
buttermilk, cream cheese. And I seem to remember a sort of jellied sour
milk. I forget the name but perhaps the stuff was equivalent to yogurt.

There was no fresh meat in summer because it wouldn't keep. If you   20
asked for a piece of meat at the store you got salt beef. If you wanted
fresh beef you had to ask for "fresh meat."

Biscuits came packed in three-foot long wooden boxes and were   21
weighed out by the pound in paper bags. Sultanas, dad's cookies, jam
jams, lemon creams with carroway seeds, and soda biscuits.

Molasses was a big thing. It was used to sweeten tea, in gingerbread,   22
on rolled oats porridge, with sulphur in the spring to clean the blood
(eeeccchhhh), in bread, in baked beans, in 'lassie bread.'

It came in barrels and when the molasses was gone, there was a layer of   23
molasses sugar at the bottom.

Glasses of lemon crystals or strawberry syrup or limejuice. Rolled   24
oats, farina, Indian meal. Home made bread, pork buns, figgy duff*,
partridgeberry tarts, blanc mange, ginger wine, damper cakes*.

Cold mutton, salt beef, peas pudding, boiled cabbage, tinned bully   25
beef for lunch on Sunday, tinned peaches, brown eggs, corned caplin*.

And thank God I was twelve years old before ever a slice of baker's   26
bread passed my lips.

STRUCTURE:

1. Point out everything that Ray Guy's first sentence tells us about the
   essay which will follow.
2. In his last sentence Ray Guy exclaims, "And thank God I was twelve
   years old before ever a slice of baker's bread passed my lips." What
   does this sentence achieve that qualifies it to conclude the essay?
3. What percentage of this essay do you estimate consists of examples?
   Are there enough to illustrate the point? Are there too many?
4. Why does Ray Guy relate the incident of the puffed wheat (pars. 2 and
   3)?

STYLE:

1. How wastefully or economically does Ray Guy use words in this
   essay?
2. Point out sentence fragments in this essay. Why do you think Guy
   uses them?

*figgy duff: boiled raisin pudding.
*damper cakes: a kind of bannock made on the damper (upper surface) of a cookstove.
*caplin: a small and edible ocean fish often used by cod fishermen as bait.

3. Point out the expressions that most strongly give "Outharbor Menu" a TONE that is folksy and COLLOQUIAL. Is this tone appropriate to the topic?
4. In paragraph 18 Guy describes the root cellars: "With the hay growing on them they looked like hairy green igloos." Where else has he used SIMILES — comparisons that describe one thing in terms of another?

IDEAS:

1. How nostalgic is Ray Guy about his topic? To what extent do you think he exaggerates or presents a one-sided picture because he is writing about his childhood? Is nostalgia desirable in our lives? Can it ever work against us?
2. In his newspaper columns, Ray Guy strongly opposed governmental measures to move people from Newfoundland's outports — such as the one described in this essay — to centralized locations where they would work in factories instead of fish. To what extent do you think the traditional life of a culture should be preserved? Is a government ever justified in deliberately changing it? If so, under what conditions?
3. In the last decade or two, fast-food chains such as McDonald's have been standardizing the eating habits not only of North America but also of many other parts of the world. What are we gaining in this process? What are we losing in this process?
4. Describe the worst or best meal you have ever had in a fast-food restaurant, using numerous examples to support your main idea.
5. In paragraph 13, Guy uses the expression "outport soul food." What does "soul food" usually refer to? Do we all prefer a kind of "soul food" that we experienced while growing up? In an essay, describe the "soul food" of your own childhood. Give plentiful examples, as Ray Guy does in "Outharbor Menu."

(NOTE: See also the Topics for Writing at the end of this chapter.)

Bruce Hutchison
Cowboy from Holland

Bruce Hutchison, born in 1901 in Prescott, Ontario, has had a very long and full career as a journalist. Considered the dean of political commentators in Canada, Hutchison has written a dozen books, won three National Newspaper Awards and four Governor General's literary awards. He began reporting in Ottawa, was associate editor of the Winnipeg Free Press *from 1944 to 1950, editor of the Victoria* Daily Times *from 1950 to 1963, and from 1963 until his retirement in 1979 was editorial director of the* Vancouver Sun. *With a writing schedule that at times has reached 10,000 words a day, Hutchison has not stopped at newspaper work: he has also produced books of history, fiction, biography, geography and politics. His best-known are* The Unknown Country *(1942) and* Canada: Tomorrow's Giant *(1957). "Cowboy from Holland," our selection from the latter book, exemplifies the colourful and even impassioned nature of Hutchison's prose.*

T he great myth of Canada and the essential ingredient of the nation recently hurtled into my garden on a tricycle. It was ridden by a golden-haired boy of five years just out from Holland. I do not know his name. He has yet to master the English language. But he has learned the first word of the myth. The word, of course, is "cowboy." He shouted it through my gate, brandished two toy pistols, and whipped his three-wheeled horse over my flower beds. 1

Though my young friend knows little about Canada, he has hit unerringly on its true content and oldest instinct. He has joined that long procession which started out of Europe in the first days of the seventeenth century, crossed an ocean and a continent, and marched westward to another ocean. He has grasped, by the deep wisdom of childhood, the primal force forever driving the Canadian westward against the wilderness. After the trim postage stamp of Holland he has seen the limitless space of a new land. He has breathed the west and become a cowboy. We are witnessing in our neighborhood the birth of a Canadian. 2

The other day the carefree cowboy got down to the serious business of Canada. He became, by hereditary impulse, a farmer. His father, who had long cultivated the soil of Holland and acquired a Canadian farm only a month ago, gave the boy a set of tools, a little tin spade, rake, and hoe. Immediately the horse and pistols were laid aside. 3

As I drove down our country lane, the boy was digging up the roadside, smoothing it with his rake, and preparing to sow his first crop. There, in that small figure, was the genius of an ancient farm people transplanted across ocean and continent. 4

5   He shouted at me, in his own tongue, to observe his labors. They didn't amount to much beside his father's long spring furrows near by, but they were a beginning. The seeds of Holland would germinate in the Canadian soil, and the seeds of Canada in the boy.

6   Soon, I suppose, he will forget his native land and his father's language. Within a year or so of entering a Canadian school he will be indistinguishable from other young Canadians in appearance, speech, and mind. Yes, but he, and other boys from foreign lands, carry with them certain invisible baggage that no customs inspector will discern. They carry, like the first French Canadians, the English, the Scots, the Irish, and the rest of us, a fraction of the old world. It is of such fractions, mixed together and smoothed by environment, that Canada is made.

7   Yesterday some boys born in Canada jeered at the Dutch immigrant and trampled his new seed bed. When he sought refuge in my garden, I tried to tell him that the Canadians were only demonstrating, by a perverse method, their pride in Canada. They acted, I said, like boys everywhere and much like the world's statesmen.

8   I tried to tell the immigrant about another boy of his own age who reached Upper Canada in 1820, the son of a Scots storekeeper with a habit of unprofitable speculation and an addiction to strong drink. That boy seemed to have less chance in life than the boy from Holland. Yet he died as the first prime minister of Canada and the idol of his people.

9   John Alexander Macdonald, as I attempted to explain, was an immigrant. So were the French before him and the Indians before them. All Canadians were immigrants a few generations back, and so diverse in blood that no racial stock could now claim to be a national majority. We are a nation of immigrants and minorities, slowly combining and issuing in what we call the Canadian breed.

10   The Dutch boy listened, but he didn't understand. Repeating the only Canadian word in his vocabulary, he said he was a cowboy. Well, that would serve well enough for a start. He had begun to get to the root of the matter. And today I observed the next chapter in an old story — the native Canadian boys were teaching an immigrant the art of baseball, the secret of a robin's nest in an apple tree, the green mysteries of a swamp.

STRUCTURE:

1. In what way and to what degree does this extended example of one immigrant develop the topic of immigration to Canada?
2. To what extent does this essay use short examples, in addition to the one long example of the Dutch boy?

3. Is the last sentence effective as a conclusion? What does it accomplish?

STYLE:

1. The "three-wheeled horse" mentioned in paragraph 1 is of course not a horse but a tricycle. Point out at least three more METAPHORS, figures of speech that are literally false but poetically true.
2. Is Hutchison's approach to his topic mainly OBJECTIVE or SUBJECTIVE? Give reasons for your answer. In what ways might his essay be different if he had used the opposite approach?

IDEAS:

1. In 1957 this selection first appeared as a part of Bruce Hutchison's book *Canada: Tomorrow's Giant.* Has the author's prophecy come true? In the years since 1957 has Canada become a "giant"? Might it be a "giant" in some ways but not in others? Give examples to support your answer.
2. The Dutch immigrant "has grasped, by the deep wisdom of childhood, the primal force forever driving the Canadian westward against the wilderness" (par. 2). Are Canadians still being driven westward, and if so, why?
3. Hutchison states in paragraph 3 that farming is "the serious business of Canada." If he had written his essay today, what do you think the immigrant boy would learn as "the serious business of Canada"?
4. To what extent is the myth of the cowboy still with us in Canada? Does it affect our lives in any concrete way? Do you view its influence, if any, as positive or negative? Give examples to support your answers.
5. If you have read "Grinning and Happy," compare the treatment given by Canada to Joy Kogawa's minority group with that given by the Canadian boys to the "cowboy from Holland."
6. If you have immigrated to Canada, write the story of your own first days in the country, illustrating the opportunities and/or pitfalls of the process. If you are a native-born Canadian, write a similar essay about moving to a new neighbourhood, school, town, city or province. Develop your story through examples.

(NOTE: See also the Topics for Writing at the end of this chapter.)

Topics for Writing

Chapter 2: Example

(Note also the topics for writing that appear after each selection in this chapter.)

Write an essay that develops one of the following ideas either through a number of short examples or through one more fully developed example.

1. Dreams express our lives
2. Superstition is widespread even today
3. Games imitate life
4. Professional sports teach violence
5. We learn best from our mistakes
6. Children learn best from their parents' example
7. Travel is the best education
8. Hitchhiking is dangerous
9. First impressions can mislead
10. Opposites attract
11. Short
12. Intelligent
13. Ugly
14. Illegitimate ⎬ people are discriminated against in our society
15. Adopted
16. Lefthanded
17. Disabled
18. Men have the power in our society
19. Information is power
20. Computers can make mistakes
21. Books are friends
22. Automation causes unemployment
23. Some products are built to fall apart
24. The more people get, the more they want
25. You are what you eat

Photo by Christie McLaren.

"'I bum on the street. I don't like it, but I have to. I have to survive. The only pleasure I got is my cigaret . . . . It's not a life.'"

Christie McLaren, "Suitcase Lady"

It's large and yellow and . . . .

DESCRIPTION

Consider the writer's tools: words in rows on the page. The writer cannot use gestures, facial expression or voice as the public speaker does. The writer cannot use colour, shape, motion or sound, as the filmmaker does. Yet words on the page can be powerful. We have all seen readers so involved in a book that they forget where they are; they will fail to hear their own name called or they will pass their own stop on the bus or subway. These readers have passed into another world, living at second hand what the writer has lived or at least imagined at first hand. How does writing convey experience so vividly? One way is through description.

In simulating direct experience, description makes frequent appeals to our senses:

sight

sound

touch

smell

taste

How many senses does Ian Adams appeal to in the opening of our first selection, "Living with Automation in Winnipeg"?

Hear it! The crunching smash of twenty-four bottles of beer, all splintering against each other as I misdeal on the packing machine. Smell the stink of the warm beer pouring over my clothes, washing over the sour sweat of my body. I can feel the unheard curse as I toss the wet, mangled carton down the rollers for some poor bastard to sort out.

Not all words are equal. Adams prefers the short and strong ones to the long and flabby ones. He does not write "perspiration" but "sweat," and he does not write "imprecation" but "curse." He seeks words that convey exact feelings as well as exact meanings. In a negative passage like this, could he have written "damaged" for "mangled," or "aroma" for "stink"? Choosing words carefully takes time, more time than was spent by one student who ended a pretty description of the ocean by saying that the water was "as still as a pan full of oil." The image of water as oil may imply stillness, but this water is not exactly something we would want to swim in or even watch at sunset — we'd be too busy thinking of pollution! Spend the time, then, to sense the emotional as well as logical meanings of your words. Search your first draft for weak or inexact or inappropriate words, and replace them. If the right word doesn't come, find it in a thesaurus or dictionary of synonyms.

Figures of speech — like the similes and metaphors discussed in Chapter 6 — are powerful tools of description. When Emily Carr writes in "D'Sonoqua" that a man's face is "greeny-brown and wrinkled like a baked apple," or when Thierry Mallet writes in "The Firewood Gatherers" that a woman's throat, "thin and bare as a vulture's neck, showed the muscles like cords," the idea of old age is swiftly and powerfully conveyed. Onomatopoetic language — words like "scuttled," "slithered," "grated," or "ooze" — describes by sounding like what it means. Emily Carr enriches her description with these and many others.

The basic strategy behind all descriptive techniques is a preference for concrete language. In a description, avoid generalizations except where they are needed to make the point clear. In helping us to experience the great Halifax explosion, Hugh MacLennan *tells* us very little of theory; instead, he *shows* us houses swept off their foundations, trees and lamp posts snapped off, and red-hot steel raining down from the skies. In fact, a good summation of how to describe is *show, don't tell.*

Ian Adams
Living with Automation
in Winnipeg

Ian Adams was born in 1937 to missionary parents in Tanzania, and came to Canada at age 16. In the mid-sixties, after several years of work and travel in other countries, Adams joined Maclean's *as a staff writer. For four years he covered Canadian events, Latin American revolutions and the Vietnam War. Two books of pointed social criticism followed:* The Poverty Wall *(1970) and* The Real Poverty Report *(co-authored in 1971). But since then Adams has said, "I used to have this idea that people could change their ideas . . . if you gave them information . . . but it really doesn't work that way." Now Adams clothes his social criticism in fiction, which "can have a much more powerful effect" (*Maclean's, *January 28, 1980). His novel* The Trudeau Papers *appeared in 1971,* S, Portrait of a Spy *in 1977 and* Endgame in Paris *in 1979. Adams' new strategy may be effective, but when the* Toronto Sun *claimed that the main character of* S, Portrait of a Spy *(a double agent for the KGB and RCMP) was a thinly disguised version of an actual RCMP officer now retired in Australia, a sensational libel suit followed. Although the case was settled out of court, it cast some doubt upon the freedom of novelists to base fictional characters on actual persons. In its style our selection resembles fiction, but "Living with Automation in Winnipeg" is from Adams' nonfiction book* The Poverty Wall.*

Hear it! The crunching smash of twenty-four bottles of beer, all splintering against each other as I misdeal on the packing machine. Smell the stink of the warm beer pouring over my clothes, washing over the sour sweat of my body. I can feel the unheard curse as I toss the wet, mangled carton down the rollers for some poor bastard to sort out. And back to the mother-eating machine where the bottles are already starting to pile up on the conveyor belt. The ten-second delay bell starts ringing. The jangling vibrations echo in my skull, and the foreman comes running over, screaming incoherently. How the hell can I hear him over the roar of four acres of machinery and the teeth-jarring rattle of 25,000 bottles, all clinking against each other as they ride down the hundred yards of clanking metal conveyor belts.

But don't try to figure out what the foreman's yelling, you'll only lose more time. The bottles will back up all the way to the pasteurizer, the thirty-second delay hooter will start whooping like an air-raid siren, then they'll pull you off this job for sure and send you down to the washers, so forget him and just keep moving. With your left hand crush the right hand corner of the next empty carton and ram it on the hydraulic lift. Kick your heel down on the pedal to send the drawer up. The bottles

1

2

83

drop through the metal leaves this time with a nice *thonk*, thank God! And even as they are hitting the bottom of the box, stab the pedal with your toe to bring the drawer back down. Before it stops, spin off the loaded carton with your right hand to send it in the direction of the sealing machine. Don't wait for it to clear the drawer, reach for the next empty carton with your left hand. But you have to waste time, reaching in to push the "filler" down flat. And without even looking at him, you scream at the filler-man, "Look what you're doing, you son-of-a-bitch! Can't you even put these lousy pieces of cardboard in straight?" He, seeing only your lips curling, snarls obscenely back. Never mind him either. He's been here fourteen years, paying his union dues, kissing the foreman's ass. Look at the zombie, pot-bellied on all the free beer, draggy-eyed from a lifetime of night shifts, skin like a corpse, embrace your fellow industrial worker!

3 A group of tourists are coming through the brewery. Cowed by the noise, they shy away from the machines, cringing behind the protective eyeglasses issued at the front office. They stop to wonder at the frantic activity around the packing machine. And we, the sweat running down our faces, our shirts soaked, our hands and feet doing five different things at once, turn smiling and scream the crudest of obscenities at the women. And they, unhearing, smile and mouth thank you, then walk on with another uncertain smile for the monkeys in the freak show.

4 All this ten hours a day. Surrounded by four or five other workers who endlessly fold cardboard cartons in a bored blur of hand movements. Their hands turn flat shapes into square boxes, insert handles and fillers that will keep the bottles separated from each other. Behind them on scores of wooden platforms await thousands of unfolded cardboard cartons. They are literally unfolding a forest of trees between their hands. Other men tend the monotonous machines. One feeds thousands of bright little labels into slots; each label costs one cent, but that's more than the beer inside the bottle is worth. "Everything else is taxes and profit," that's what the brewmaster said. Another man sits dreamily beside a lighted yellow panel. In hypnotic progression, each bottle passes briefly in front of this panel before being filled with beer. The man tries to catch the ones that are still jammed with trapped mice, cigarette butts, and old safes, even after going through the washers.

5 All the men are wearing the same dingy uniforms, green workpants and shirts. They are my brotherhood, and we are men of our time, working in feverish, mute activity, unable to communicate, drowned out by the roar of our age, the ass-end of this industrial epoch. Run this packing machine, you slob. Pack twenty-four bottles of beer every six seconds. Ten cases every minute, six hundred in an hour, six thousand in a ten-hour shift. Fill all those empty bottles full of beer so all the leisure- programmed people in this country can drink their beer in creepy bars and

dirty, men-only beer parlours. Pack so the whores on Main Street can tease their fancy men over a couple, so the businessmen can pull on a three-o'clock beer and ease a contented fart. And you, you sad bastard, work! Work to fill up those empty boxes with bottles of beer so that all those beautiful people out there can piss it away.

Don't waste time thinking about the absurdity of this effort. Just pack and think about the $125 a week you're clearing. Pack and forget about the bills you can't pay. Pack and don't look at the man going around giving out pink slips. Just keep packing, you dummy. Because while you're sitting there running that machine, with the sweat running down into your eyes, with your hands and feet going like an epileptic's, they're already building a machine to do your job. And brother, nobody can hear a word you're screaming.

6

STRUCTURE:

1. To begin his description, Ian Adams boldly demands our attention with the words "Hear it!" What does he do in the rest of the opening paragraph?
2. What is the basic message of this selection and where is it most openly stated?
3. Later in this book we will examine process analysis — telling how a process is performed. Which paragraphs has Adams devoted to process analysis?

STYLE:

1. Why has Adams used racy language? Do the COLLOQUIAL and even vulgar expressions have a purpose? If so, what?
2. "Clinking" and "clanking" (par. 1) are examples of ONOMATOPOEIA — words that sound like what they mean. Point out other sound- effect words in this selection and discuss their contribution to the total effect.
3. Look up "thonk" (par. 2) in your dictionary. Is it a word? Can you imagine "thonk" appearing in a business letter? In the Bible? In a scientific report? In the comics? Why does Adams use it?
4. Adams says "Run this packing machine, you slob" (par. 5) and "Just keep packing, you dummy" (par. 6). What is the effect of these and other passages that seem addressed to the reader? Is use of the word "you" a good technique in essays?
5. Why is paragraph 2 so long? How long can a paragraph be?

IDEAS:

1. Did this description make you feel as though you were in the brewery yourself? Why or why not?

2. What purposes can be served by reproducing for your reader an experience that you yourself had?

3. Is industrial work as sordid as Adams makes it seem? Have you had experiences that confirm or contradict Adams' view? If so, describe them.

4. If you have read "Grinning and Happy," compare work as described by both Joy Kogawa and Adams. If you had to perform one of these jobs, which would you choose and why?

5. In paragraph 5, Adams writes of his co-workers: "They are my brotherhood, and we are men of our time, working in feverish, mute activity, unable to communicate, drowned out by the roar of our age, the ass-end of this industrial epoch." Where else in Adams' description do you find evidence of isolation among the workers? Do you agree with Adams that workers are "drowned out by the roar of our age"?

6. Do you think automation helps or harms society? Should we allow further automation to eliminate jobs like the already automated ones Adams describes, or is unemployment a worse evil? Does automation necessarily mean unemployment?

7. Using vivid appeals to the senses, as Adams does, write a description of the best or worst job you have ever held. Choose your details carefully to support the dominant impression.

(NOTE: See also the Topics for Writing at the end of this chapter.)

Thierry Mallet

The Firewood Gatherers*

Thierry Mallet joined the French fur company Revillon Frères as an apprentice trader, and went on to establish and oversee a large group of trading posts in the Barrens of the Canadian arctic. Through each of the twenty years before our selection was published, Mallet had travelled through the region, sometimes at great risk, inspecting those posts. His intimate knowledge of the land and of the people who lived on it led him to write a small book, Plain Tales of the North. *Then in 1930 appeared his second small volume,* Glimpses of the Barren Lands. *From it comes our selection "The Firewood Gatherers." Both books were published in New York by Revillon Frères. As if to reflect the arctic itself, Mallet's style is spare but powerful.*

Our camp had been pitched at the foot of a great, bleak, ragged hill, a few feet from the swirling waters of the Kazan River. The two small green tents, pegged down tight with heavy rocks, shivered and rippled under the faint touch of the northern breeze. A thin wisp of smoke rose from the embers of the fire.

Eleven o'clock, and the sun had just set under a threatening bank of clouds far away to the northwest. It was the last day of June and daylight still. But the whole country seemed bathed in gray, boulders, moss, sand, even the few willow shrubs scattered far apart in the hollows of the hills. Half a mile away, upstream, the caribou-skin topeks of an Eskimo settlement, fading away amid the background, were hardly visible to the eye.

Three small gray specks could be seen moving slowly above our camp. Human shapes, but so puny, so insignificant-looking against the wild rocky side of that immense hill! Bending down, then straightening up, they seemed to totter aimlessly through the chaos of stone, searching for some hidden treasure.

Curiosity, or perhaps a touch of loneliness, suddenly moved me to leave camp and join those three forlorn figures so far away above me near the sky line.

Slowly I made my way along the steep incline, following at first the bed of a dried-up stream. Little by little the river sank beneath me, while the breeze, increasing in strength, whistled past, lashing and stinging my face and hands. I had lost sight momentarily of the three diminutive figures which had lured me on to these heights. After a while a reindeer trail enabled me to leave the coulee and led me again in the right direction, through a gigantic mass of granite which the frost of thousands of

*Editor's title

87

years had plucked from the summit of the hill and hurled hundreds of feet below.

6   At last I was able to reach the other side of the avalanche of rocks and suddenly emerged comparatively in the open, on the brim of a slight depression at the bottom of which a few dead willow bushes showed their bleached branches above the stones and the gray moss. There I found the three silent figures huddled close together, gathering, one by one, the twigs of the precious wood. Two little girls, nine or ten years old, so small, so helpless, and an aged woman, so old, so frail, that my first thought was to marvel at the idea of their being able to climb so far from their camp to that lonely spot.

7   An Eskimo great-grandmother and her two great-granddaughters, all three contributing their share to the support of the tribe. Intent on their work, or most probably too shy to look up at the strange white man whom, until then, they had only seen at a distance, they gave me full opportunity to watch them.

8   All were dressed alike, in boots, trousers, and coats of caribou skin. The children wore little round leather caps reaching far over their ears, the crown decorated with beadwork designs. One of them carried on the wrist, as a bracelet, a narrow strip of bright red flannel. Their faces were round and healthy, the skin sunburned to a dark copper color, but their cheeks showed a tinge of blood which gave them, under the tan, a peculiar complexion like the color of a ripe plum. Their little hands were bare and black, the scratches caused by the dead twigs showing plainly in white, while their fingers seemed cramped with the cold.

9   The old woman was bareheaded, quite bald at the top of the head, with long wisps of gray hair waving in the wind. The skin of her neck and face had turned black, dried up like an old piece of parchment. Her cheeks were sunken and her cheek bones protruded horribly. Her open mouth showed bare gums, for her teeth were all gone, and her throat, thin and bare as a vulture's neck, showed the muscles like cords. Her hands were as thin as the hands of a skeleton, the tip of each finger curved in like a claw. Her eyes, once black, now light gray, remained half closed, deep down in their sockets.

10   She was stone blind.

11   Squatting on her heels, she held, spread in front of her, a small reindeer skin. As soon as the children dropped a branch beside her, she felt for it gropingly; then, her hands closing on it greedily, like talons, she would break it into small pieces, a few inches long, which she carefully placed on the mat at her feet.

12   Both little girls, while searching diligently through the clumps of dead willows for what they could break off and carry away, kept absolutely silent. Not only did they never call to one another when one of them needed help, but they seemed to watch each other intently whenever they

could. Now and then, one of them would hit the ground two or three times with the flat of her hand. If the other had her head turned away at the time, she appeared to be startled and always wheeled round to look. Then both children would make funny little motions with their hands at one another.

The little girls were deaf and dumb. 13

After a while they had gathered all the wood the reindeer skin could 14
contain. Then the children went up to the old woman and conveyed to her the idea that it was time to go home. One of them took her hands in hers and guided them to two corners of the mat, while the other tapped her gently on the shoulder.

The old, old woman understood. Slowly and carefully she tied up the 15
four corners of the caribou skin over the twigs, silently watched by the little girls. Groaning, she rose to her feet, tottering with weakness and old age, and with a great effort swung the small bundle over her back. Then one little girl took her by the hand, while the other, standing behind, grasped the tail of her caribou coat. Slowly, very slowly, step by step they went their way, following a reindeer trail around rocks, over stones, down, down the hill, straight toward their camp, the old woman carrying painfully for the young, the deaf and dumb leading and steering safely the blind.

STRUCTURE:

1. "The Firewood Gatherers" is narrated in chronological order. Point out at least fifteen words or phrases that signal the flow of time.
2. Which paragraphs are devoted so fully to description that they interrupt completely or almost completely the flow of time?
3. To what extent is the effect of "The Firewood Gatherers" based upon comparisons and contrasts?
4. In what way does the last sentence summarize the entire selection?

STYLE:

1. How CONCRETE or ABSTRACT is the language of this selection? Point out three or four passages that illustrate your answer.
2. How economical or wasteful is Mallet's use of words? Does the large amount of description cause this passage to be wordy? Why or why not?
3. Mallet's description of the old woman, in paragraph 9, makes extensive use of SIMILE. For example, her throat is "thin and bare as a vulture's neck." Point out all the other similes in this paragraph.
4. In paragraph 5, Mallet writes of "a gigantic mass of granite which the

frost of thousands of years had plucked from the summit of the hill and hurled hundreds of feet below.'' Where else in this selection does he use the device of PERSONIFICATION, in which inanimate things are described in human terms?

IDEAS:

1. How often do we take the time to fully observe our surroundings, as Mallet has observed his? What prevents us from doing so? What are the rewards of such observation?

2. Judging by the evidence in "The Firewood Gatherers," how do this traditional society and our modern society differ in their views of the old and the handicapped? What do you imagine the old blind woman and her deaf and dumb great-granddaughters would be doing if they lived today in your town or city?

3. Does compulsory retirement at age 65 help or harm our society? Does it help or harm the people who have reached that age? What are the alternatives? When would you retire if you had the choice? And what will you do in retirement to retain a sense of your own worth?

4. What are some advantages and disadvantages of the extended family? If you live in the same house as your grandparents, describe what they do for you that your parents cannot do. Describe also the problems, if any, that their presence creates. When you grow old will you prefer to live with your descendants or in a home for the aged? Why?

5. If you have read "Suitcase Lady," by Christie McLaren, compare the two women: If you had to be one or the other, would you choose to be the Eskimo great-grandmother of the barrens or the homeless "suitcase lady" of Toronto? Why?

6. Describe the oldest person you know or the youngest person you know. Use concrete details, as Mallet has done, and if possible write from life rather than from memory.

(NOTE: See also the Topics for Writing at the end of this chapter.)

Christie McLaren
*Suitcase Lady**

When she wrote "Suitcase Lady," Christie McLaren was reporting for the Tor-onto Globe and Mail as part of the work experience required in her co-op English program at the University of Waterloo. McLaren was born in 1958 in Kitchener, Ontario. She has hitchhiked over much of western Canada, has been a helicopter hiking guide in the Cariboo Mountains of British Columbia, has reported on the mentally ill and mental health care in Ontario, and hopes to report on native issues and resources in the Yukon or Northwest Territories. Among her other in-terests are photography (she took the portrait accompanying her article), skiing and canoeing. Although she looks forward to a career of reporting, she says, "Writing . . . is nothing but pain while you're doing it and nothing but relief when it's done. Any joy or satisfaction, I think, is a bit of fleeting luck." McLar-en spent several nights with "the Vicomtesse" before hearing the story she reports in "Suitcase Lady." The article and photograph (see p. 80) appeared in 1981 in the Toronto Globe and Mail.

Night after night, the woman with the red hair and the pur-   1
ple dress sits in the harsh light of a 24-hour doughnut shop
on Queen Street West.

Somewhere in her bleary eyes and in the deep lines of her   2
face is a story that probably no one will ever really know. She is taking
pains to write something on a notepad and crying steadily.

She calls herself Vicomtesse Antonia The Linds'ays. She's the suitcase   3
lady of Queen Street.

No one knows how many women there are like her in Toronto. They   4
carry their belongings in shopping bags and spend their days and nights
scrounging for food. They have no one and nowhere to go.

This night, in a warm corner with a pot of tea and a pack of Player's,   5
the Vicomtesse is in a mood to talk.

Out of her past come a few scraps: a mother named Savaria; the child   6
of a poor family in Montreal; a brief marriage when she was 20; a son in
Toronto who is now 40. "We never got along well because I didn't bring
him up. I was too poor. He never call me mama."

She looks out the window. She's 60 years old.   7

With her words she spins herself a cocoon. She talks about drapes and   8
carpets, castles and kings. She often lapses into French. She lets her tea
get cold. Her hands are big, rough, farmer's hands. How she ended up in
the doughnut shop remains a mystery, maybe even to her.

"Before, I had a kitchen and a room and my own furniture. I had to   9
leave everything and go."

*Editor's title

10   It's two years that she's been on the go, since the rooming houses stopped taking her. "I don't have no place to stay."

11   So she walks. A sturdy coat covers her dress and worn leather boots are on her feet. But her big legs are bare and chapped and she has a ragged cough.

12   Yes, she says, her legs get tired. She has swollen ankles and, with no socks in her boots, she has blisters. She says she has socks — in the suitcase — but they make her feet itch.

13   As for money, "I bum on the street. I don't like it, but I have to. I have to survive. The only pleasure I got is my cigaret." She lights another one. "It's not a life."

14   She recalls the Saturday, a long time ago, when she made $27, and laughs when she tells about how she had to make the money last through Sunday, too. Now she gets "maybe $7 or $8," and eats "very poor."

15   When she is asked how people treat her, the answer is very matter-of-fact: "Some give money. Some are very polite and some are rude."

16   In warm weather, she passes her time at the big square in front of City Hall. When it's cold she takes her suitcase west to the doughnut shop.

17   The waitresses who bring food to the woman look upon her with compassion. They persuaded their boss that her sitting does no harm.

18   Where does she sleep? "Any place I can find a place to sleep. In the park, in stores — like here I stay and sit, on Yonge Street." She shrugs. Sometimes she goes into an underground parking garage.

19   She doesn't look like she knows what sleep is. "This week I sleep three hours in four days. I feel tired but I wash my face with cold water and I feel okay." Some questions make her eyes turn from the window and stare hard. Then they well over with tears. Like the one about loneliness. "I don't talk much to people," she answers. "Just the elderly, sometimes, in the park."

20   Her suitcase is full of dreams.

21   Carefully, she unzips it and pulls out a sheaf of papers — "my concertos."

22   Each page is crammed with neatly written musical notes — the careful writing she does on the doughnut shop table — but the bar lines are missing. Questions about missing bar lines she tosses aside. Each "concerto" has a French name — Tresor, La Tempete, Le Retour — and each one bears the signature of the Vicomtesse. She smiles and points to one. "A very lovely piece of music. I like it."

23   She digs in her suitcase again, almost shyly, and produces a round plastic box. Out of it emerges a tiara. Like a little girl, she smooths back her dirty hair and proudly puts it on. No one in the doughnut shop seems to notice.

24   She cares passionately about the young, the old and the ones who suffer. So who takes care of the suitcase lady?

"God takes care of me, that's for sure," she says, nodding thoughtful-   25
ly. "But I'm not what you call crazy about religion. I believe always try
to do the best to help people — the elderly, and kids, and my country,
and my city of Toronto, Ontario."

STRUCTURE:

1. "Suitcase Lady" appeared as a feature article in the Toronto *Globe and Mail*. Name all the ways that you can think of in which, as a piece of newspaper journalism, it differs from the typical ESSAY in this book.
2. What does McLaren achieve in the opening description?
3. How do the frequent quotations help McLaren to build her description?
4. McLaren's photograph of the "Vicomtesse" originally accompanied McLaren's article in the *Globe and Mail*. Does a descriptive piece of writing like "Suitcase Lady" need an illustration? What does the photograph do that the article cannot do? And what does the article do that the photograph cannot do?
5. What effect does McLaren achieve in the closing?

STYLE:

1. How difficult or easy is the vocabulary used in "Suitcase Lady" compared to that of most essays you have read in this book? Why?
2. "With her words she spins herself a cocoon," states McLaren in paragraph 8. Point out another vivid METAPHOR, a statement that is literally false but poetically true.
3. Of the many concrete details, point out the ones that you think most strongly convey the flavour of this suitcase lady's life and discuss why these particular details are effective.

IDEAS:

1. If you have read "The Firewood Gatherers," by Thierry Mallet, compare the hardships faced by the Eskimo great-grandmother in the arctic with those faced by the suitcase lady in Toronto. In what ways is each of these two persons better off? In what ways is each worse off? If you had to be one of these two women, which would you choose to be and why?
2. "It's not a life," says the "Vicomtesse" in paragraph 13. What is our society doing, either through acts of individuals or acts of institutions such as church and government, to try to make it "a life" for people like the suitcase lady? What more could society do? What prevents society from doing more?

3. How do you react to people who, like the suitcase lady, "bum on the street"? Do you divide them into categories? When do you give and when do you not give? How does the giving or not giving make you feel, and why? Have you ever "bummed on the street" yourself? How much did you make? How did it make you feel, and why?

4. If you have read Ian Adams' "Living with Automation in Winnipeg," compare the ways in which our urban and industrialized society affects the narrator of that description with the ways in which society affects McLaren's suitcase lady.

5. In paragraph 6, the suitcase lady talks of her son in Toronto: "We never got along well because I didn't bring him up. I was too poor. He never call me mama." Discuss the effects of poverty on family life: In the area where you live, how much money does a family need to stay together? To avoid quarrels over money? To feel hopeful about the future?

6. Interview a person who in economic status, age, culture, values or in some other way is radically different from yourself. Then write a vividly descriptive profile of that person, as Christie McLaren has of the suitcase lady.

(NOTE: See also the Topics for Writing at the end of this chapter.)

Emily Carr

D'Sonoqua

Although Emily Carr (1871-1945) is known mainly as a painter, she was also a writer of finely crafted prose. Born in Victoria, B.C., Carr studied art in San Francisco, London and Paris. The forests and Indian villages of the British Columbia mainland and of the Queen Charlotte Islands provided most of the subject matter for her powerful, energetic paintings. (Three of her many expeditions to these sites are described in our selection, "D'Sonoqua.") Carr spent much of her life in poverty, because public recognition of her art was very late in coming. And in her last years, plagued by ill health, she was forced to abandon painting for writing. Our selection comes from her first and most highly regarded book, Klee Wyck *(1941). During her lifetime she published two more books,* The Book of Small *(1942) and* The House of All Sorts *(1944). Others did not appear until after her death:* Growing Pains *(her autobiography, 1946),* The Heart of a Peacock *(1953),* Pause: A Sketch Book *(1953), and finally her journals* Hundreds and Thousands *(1966) and* Fresh Seeing *(1973).*

I was sketching in a remote Indian village when I first saw her. The village was one of those that the Indians use only for a few months in each year; the rest of the year it stands empty and desolate. I went there in one of its empty times, in a drizzling dusk. 1

When the Indian agent dumped me on the beach in front of the village, he said "There is not a soul here. I will come back for you in two days." Then he went away. 2

I had a small Griffon dog with me, and also a little Indian girl, who, when she saw the boat go away, clung to my sleeve and wailed, "I'm 'fraid." 3

We went up to the old deserted Mission House. At the sound of the key in the rusty lock, rats scuttled away. The stove was broken, the wood wet. I had forgotten to bring candles. We spread our blankets on the floor, and spent a poor night. Perhaps my lack of sleep played its part in the shock that I got, when I saw her for the first time. 4

Water was in the air, half mist, half rain. The stinging nettles, higher than my head, left their nervy smart on my ears and forehead, as I beat my way through them, trying all the while to keep my feet on the plank walk which they hid. Big yellow slugs crawled on the walk and slimed it. My feet slipped, and I shot headlong to her very base, for she had no feet. The nettles that were above my head reached only to her knee. 5

It was not the fall alone that jerked the "Oh's" out of me, for the great wooden image towering above me was indeed terrifying. 6

The nettle-bed ended a few yards beyond her, and then a rocky bluff jutted out, with waves battering it below. I scrambled up and went out on 7

95

the bluff, so that I could see the creature above the nettles. The forest was behind her, the sea in front.

8   Her head and trunk were carved out of, or rather into, the bole of a great red cedar. She seemed to be part of the tree itself, as if she had grown there at its heart, and the carver had only chipped away the outer wood so that you could see her. Her arms were spliced and socketed to the trunk, and were flung wide in a circling, compelling movement. Her breasts were two eagle heads, fiercely carved. That much, and the column of her great neck, and her strong chin, I had seen when I slithered to the ground beneath her. Now I saw her face.

9   The eyes were two rounds of black, set in wider rounds of white, and placed in deep sockets under wide, black eyebrows. Their fixed stare bored into me as if the very life of the old cedar looked out, and it seemed that the voice of the tree itself might have burst from that great round cavity, with projecting lips, that was her mouth. Her ears were round, and stuck out to catch all sounds. The salt air had not dimmed the heavy red of her trunk and arms and thighs. Her hands were black, with blunt finger-tips painted a dazzling white. I stood looking at her for a long, long time.

10   The rain stopped, and white mist came up from the sea, gradually paling her back into the forest. It was as if she belonged there, and the mist were carrying her home. Presently the mist took the forest too, and, wrapping them both together, hid them away.

11   "Who is that image?" I asked the little Indian girl, when I got back to the house.

12   She knew which one I meant, but to gain time, she said, "What image?"

13   "The terrible one, out there on the bluff." The girl had been to Mission School, and fear of the old, fear of the new, struggled in her eyes. "I dunno," she lied.

14   I never went to that village again, but the fierce wooden image often came to me, both in my waking and in my sleeping.

15   Several years passed, and I was once more sketching in an Indian village. There were Indians in this village and in a mild backward way it was "going modern." That is, the Indians had pushed the forest back a little to let the sun touch the new buildings that were replacing the old community houses. Small houses, primitive enough to a white man's thinking, pushed here and there between the old. Where some of the big community houses had been torn down, for the sake of the lumber, the great corner posts and massive roof-beams of the old structure were often left, standing naked against the sky, and the new little house was built inside, on the spot where the old one had been.

16   It was in one of these empty skeletons that I found her again. She had once been a supporting post for the great centre beam. Her pole-mate,

representing the Raven, stood opposite her, but the beam that had rested on their heads was gone. The two poles faced in, and one judged the great size of the house by the distance between them. The corner posts were still in place, and the earth floor, once beaten to the hardness of rock by naked feet, was carpeted now with rich lush grass.

I knew her by the stuck-out ears, shouting mouth, and deep eye-sockets. These sockets had no eye-balls, but were empty holes, filled with stare. The stare, though not so fierce as that of the former image, was more intense. The whole figure expressed power, weight, domination, rather than ferocity. Her feet were planted heavily on the head of the squatting bear, carved beneath them. A man could have sat on either huge shoulder. She was unpainted, weather-worn, sun-cracked, and the arms and hands seemed to hang loosely. The fingers were thrust into the carven mouths of two human heads, held crowns down. From behind, the sun made unfathomable shadows in eye, cheek and mouth. Horror tumbled out of them. 17

I saw Indian Tom on the beach, and went to him. 18

"Who is she?" 19

The Indian's eyes, coming slowly from across the sea, followed my pointing finger. Resentment showed in his face, greeny-brown and wrinkled like a baked apple, — resentment that white folks should pry into matters wholly Indian. 20

"Who is that big carved woman?" I repeated. 21

"D'Sonoqua." No white tongue could have fondled the name as he did. 22

"Who is D'Sonoqua?" 23

"She is the wild woman of the woods." 24

"What does she do?" 25

"She steals children." 26

"To eat them?" 27

"No, she carries them to her caves; that," pointing to a purple scar on the mountain across the bay, "is one of her caves. When she cries 'OO-oo-oo-oeo', Indian mothers are too frightened to move. They stand like trees, and the children go with D'Sonoqua." 28

"Then she is bad?" 29

"Sometimes bad . . . sometimes good," Tom replied, glancing furtively at those stuck-out ears. Then he got up and walked away. 30

I went back, and, sitting in front of the image, gave stare for stare. But her stare so over-powered mine, that I could scarcely wrench my eyes away from the clutch of those empty sockets. The power that I felt was not in the thing itself, but in some tremendous force behind it, that the carver had believed in. 31

A shadow passed across her hands and their gruesome holdings. A little bird, with its beak full of nesting material, flew into the cavity of her 32 mouth, right in the pathway of that terrible OO-oo-oo-oeo. Then my eye caught something that I had missed — a tabby cat asleep between her feet.

33 This was D'Sonoqua, and she was a supernatural being, who belonged to these Indians.

34 "Of course," I said to myself, "I do not believe in supernatural beings. Still — who understands the mysteries behind the forest? What would one do if one did meet a supernatural being?" Half of me wished that I could meet her, and half of me hoped I would not.

35 Chug — chug — the little boat had come into the bay to take me to another village, more lonely and deserted than this. Who knew what I should see there? But soon supernatural beings went clean out of my mind, because I was wholly absorbed in being naturally seasick.

36 When you have been tossed and wracked and chilled, any wharf looks good, even a rickety one, with its crooked legs stockinged in barnacles. Our boat nosed under its clammy darkness, and I crawled up the straight slimy ladder, wondering which was worse, natural seasickness, or supernatural "creeps." The trees crowded to the very edge of the water, and the outer ones, hanging over it, shadowed the shoreline into a velvet smudge. D'Sonoqua might walk in places like this. I sat for a long time on the damp, dusky beach, waiting for the stage. One by one dots of light popped from the scattered cabins, and made the dark seem darker. Finally the stage came.

37 We drove through the forest over a long straight road, with black pine trees marching on both sides. When we came to the wharf the little gas mail-boat was waiting for us. Smell and blurred light oozed thickly out of the engine room, and except for one lantern on the wharf everything else was dark. Clutching my little dog, I sat on the mail sacks which had been tossed on to the deck.

38 The ropes were loosed, and we slid out into the oily black water. The moon that had gone with us through the forest was away now. Black pine-covered mountains jagged up on both sides of the inlet like teeth. Every gasp of the engine shook us like a great sob. There was no rail round the deck, and the edge of the boat lay level with the black slithering horror below. It was like being swallowed again and again by some terrible monster, but never going down. As we slid through the water, hour after hour, I found myself listening for the OO-oo-oo-oeo.

39 Midnight brought us to a knob of land, lapped by the water on three sides, with the forest threatening to gobble it up on the fourth. There was a rude landing, a rooming-house, an eating-place, and a store, all for the convenience of fishermen and loggers. I was given a room, but after I had blown out my candle, the stillness and the darkness would not let me sleep.

In the brilliant sparkle of the morning when everything that was not 40 superlatively blue was superlatively green, I dickered with a man who was taking a party up the inlet that he should drop me off at the village I was headed for.

"But," he protested, "there is nobody there." 41

To myself I said, "There is D'Sonoqua." 42

From the shore, as we rowed to it, came a thin feminine cry — the 43 mewing of a cat. The keel of the boat had barely grated in the pebbles, when the cat sprang aboard, passed the man shipping his oars, and crouched for a spring into my lap. Leaning forward, the man seized the creature roughly, and with a cry of "Dirty Indian vermin!" flung her out into the sea.

I jumped ashore, refusing his help, and with a curt "Call for me at 44 sundown," strode up the beach; the cat followed me.

When we had crossed the beach and come to a steep bank, the cat ran 45 ahead. Then I saw that she was no lean, ill-favoured Indian cat, but a sleek aristocratic Persian. My snobbish little Griffon dog, who usually refused to let an Indian cat come near me, surprised me by trudging beside her in comradely fashion.

The village was typical of the villages of these Indians. It had only one 46 street, and that had only one side, because all the houses faced the beach. The two community houses were very old, dilapidated and bleached, and the handful of other shanties seemed never to have been young; they had grown so old before they were finished, that it was then not worth while finishing them.

Rusty padlocks carefully protected the gaping walls. There was the 47 usual broad plank in front of the houses, the general sitting and sunning place for Indians. Little streams ran under it, and weeds poked up through every crack, half hiding the companies of tins, kettles, and rags, which patiently waited for the next gale and their next move.

In front of the Chief's house was a high, carved totem pole, sur- 48 mounted by a large wooden eagle. Storms had robbed him of both wings, and his head had a resentful twist, as if he blamed somebody. The heavy wooden heads of two squatting bears peered over the nettle-tops. The windows were too high for peeping in or out. "But, save D'Sonoqua, who is there to peep?" I said aloud, just to break the silence. A fierce sun burned down as if it wanted to expose every ugliness and forlornness. It drew the noxious smell out of the skunk cabbages, growing in the rich black ooze of the stream, scummed the water-barrels with green slime, and branded the desolation into my very soul.

The cat kept very close, rubbing and bumping itself and purring 49 ecstatically; and although I had not seen them come, two more cats had joined us. When I sat down they curled into my lap, and then the strangeness of the place did not bite into me so deeply. I got up, determined to look behind the houses.

50 Nettles grew in the narrow spaces between the houses. I beat them down, and made my way over the bruised dank-smelling mass into a space of low jungle.

51 Long ago the trees had been felled and left lying. Young forest had burst through the slash, making an impregnable barrier, and sealing up the secrets which lay behind it. An eagle flew out of the forest, circled the village, and flew back again.

52 Once again I broke silence, calling after him, "Tell D'Sonoqua—" and turning, saw her close, towering above me in the jungle.

53 Like the D'Sonoqua of the other villages she was carved into the bole of a red cedar tree. Sun and storm had bleached the wood, moss here and there softened the crudeness of the modelling; sincerity underlay every stroke.

54 She appeared to be neither wooden nor stationary, but a singing spirit, young and fresh, passing through the jungle. No violence coarsened her; no power domineered to wither her. She was graciously feminine. Across her forehead her creator had fashioned the Sistheutl, or mythical two-headed sea-serpent. One of its heads fell to either shoulder, hiding the stuck-out ears, and framing her face from a central parting on her forehead which seemed to increase its womanliness.

55 She caught your breath, this D'Sonoqua, alive in the dead bole of the cedar. She summed up the depth and charm of the whole forest, driving away its menace.

56 I sat down to sketch. What was this noise of purring and rubbing going on about my feet? Cats. I rubbed my eyes to make sure I was seeing right, and counted a dozen of them. They jumped into my lap and sprang to my shoulders. They were real — and very feminine.

57 There we were — D'Sonoqua, the cats and I — the woman who only a few moments ago had forced herself to come behind the houses in trembling fear of the "wild woman of the woods" — wild in the sense that forest-creatures are wild — shy, untouchable.

STRUCTURE:

1. Emily Carr's opening sentence is, "I was sketching in a remote Indian village when I first saw her." Why are we not shown "her" identity until paragraph 6?

2. How many basic parts form this description? Where do they join each other and how do they differ?

3. Are the images of D'Sonoqua merely different from each other or do they form a progression?
4. Since each image is in a different location, the sections of the description are separated by travel. In addition to its organizational function, does the travel have a symbolic function? Consider this passage from paragraph 38:

> There was no rail round the deck, and the edge of the boat lay level with the black slithering horror below. It was like being swallowed again and again by some terrible monster, but never going down. As we slid through the water, hour after hour, I found myself listening for the OO-oo-oo-oeo.

STYLE:

1. Although Emily Carr is respected as a writer, she is known primarily as a painter. What aspects of her prose remind you of the visual arts? Point out passages that illustrate your answers.
2. What effect is achieved by Carr's use of the words "scuttled" (par. 4), "slithered" (par. 8), "grated" (par. 43) and "ooze" (par. 48)?
3. Carr plays with words. Instead of describing the walk as "slimy," she writes that the slugs "slimed" the walk. Where else do you find words used in unusual and fresh ways?
4. When Carr describes the wharf as having "crooked legs stockinged in barnacles" (par. 36), what FIGURE OF SPEECH is she using? Where else does it occur? What effect does it have on the description?
5. Emily Carr is noted for the extreme CONCISENESS of her writing. Identify some of the techniques through which she achieves it, and point out examples of their use.

IDEAS:

1. In paragraph 31, Carr states of the second D'Sonoqua: "The power that I felt was not in the thing itself, but in some tremendous force behind it, that the carver had believed in." And in paragraph 53, she states of the third D'Sonoqua: ". . . sincerity underlay every stroke." Is skill itself insufficient to create art? Must the artist believe in some "tremendous force"?
2. What is art for? As you seek answers to this far-reaching question, think of varous manifestations of art:
   —Monumental architecture, as in cathedrals, banks and large train stations
   —Pretty paintings and photographs on living room walls
   —Heroic sculptures of politicians and generals riding their horses or standing on pedestals in parks
   —"Unrealistic" art in its many forms: impressionism, cubism, surrealism, expressionism, etc.
   —The images of D'Sonoqua described by Emily Carr

3. The narrator, the Indian girl and Indian Tom are all afraid of D'Sonoqua. Do humans create monsters because they need something to fear? Think of Polyphemus, Grendel, Frankenstein's monster, Dracula, Moby Dick, King Kong, witches, ghosts and the bogeyman.
4. Write a vivid and detailed description of any one work of art that you see every day (it could be a well-designed building, a public sculpture, a photograph or painting on your wall, etc.).

(NOTE: See also the Topics for Writing at the end of this chapter.)

Hugh MacLennan
*A Sound Beyond Hearing**

Hugh MacLennan is one of Canada's best-known novelists and essayists, the author of over a dozen books and winner of five Governor General's Awards. He was born in 1907 in Glace Bay, Cape Breton, Nova Scotia, and studied at Dalhousie, Oxford and at Princeton, where he earned a Ph.D. in classics. From 1951 until his retirement in 1982, he taught in the English Department of McGill University. MacLennan has published several books of essays: Cross-Country *(1949),* Thirty and Three *(1954),* Scotchman's Return and Other Essays *(1960) and* The Other Side of Hugh MacLennan *(1978). Among his novels are* Each Man's Son *(1951),* The Watch that Ends the Night *(1959) and* Voices in Time *(1980).* Two Solitudes *(1945), which contrasts the French and English Canadian cultures, is his most widely read novel; but* Barometer Rising *(1941), from which our selection comes, is thought by many to be his best. "A Sound Beyond Hearing," MacLennan's account of an event he witnessed at age 10, is one of the best-known passages in Canadian literature: it describes the explosion that, on December 6, 1917, levelled much of Halifax and killed about 2,000 people.*

T he *Mont Blanc* was now in the Narrows and a detail of men 1 went into her chains to unship the anchor. It would be dropped as soon as she reached her appointed station in the Basin. A hundred yards to port were the Shipyards and another hundred yards off the port bow was the blunt contour of Richmond Bluff; to starboard the shore sloped gently into a barren of spruce scrub. During the two minutes it took the *Mont Blanc* to glide through this strait, most of Bedford Basin and nearly all its flotilla of anchored freighters were hidden from her behind the rise of Richmond Bluff.

Around the projection of this hill, less than fifty fathoms off the port 2 bow of the incoming *Mont Blanc*, another vessel suddenly appeared heading for the open sea. She flew the Norwegian flag, and to the startled pilot of the munitioner the name *Imo* was plainly visible beside the hawse. She was moving at half-speed and listing gently to port as she made the sharp turn out of the Basin to strike the channel of the Narrows. And so listing, with white water surging away from her fore-foot, she swept across the path of the *Mont Blanc*, exposing a gaunt flank labeled in giant letters BELGIAN RELIEF. Then she straightened, and pointed her bow directly at the fore-quarter of the munitioner. Only at that moment did the men on the *Imo's* bridge appear to realize that another vessel stood directly in their path.

Staccato orders broke from the bridge of the *Mont Blanc* as the two 3 ships moved toward a single point. Bells jangled, and megaphoned shouts came from both bridges. The ships sheered in the same direction,

*Editor's title

103

then sheered back again. With a violent shock, the bow of the *Imo* struck the plates of the *Mont Blanc* and went grinding a third of the way through the deck and the forward hold. A shower of sparks splashed out from the screaming metal. The canisters on the deck of the *Mont Blanc* broke loose from their bindings and some of them tumbled and burst open. Then the vessels heeled away with engines reversed and the water boiling out from their screws as the propellers braked them to a standstill. They sprawled sideways across the Narrows, the *Mont Blanc* veering in toward the Halifax shore, the *Imo* spinning about with steerageway lost entirely. Finally she drifted toward the opposite shore.

For a fraction of a second there was intense silence. Then smoke appeared out of the shattered deck of the *Mont Blanc*, followed by a racing film of flame. The men on the bridge looked at each other. Scattered shouts broke from the stern, and the engine-room bells jangled again. Orders were half-drowned by a scream of rusty metal as some sailors amidships followed their own inclination and twisted the davits around to lower a boat. The scurry of feet grew louder as more sailors began to pour out through the hatches onto the deck. An officer ran forward with a hose, but before he could connect it his men were ready to abandon ship.

The film of flame raced and whitened, then it became deeper like an opaque and fulminant liquid, then swept over the canisters of benzol and increased to a roaring tide of heat. Black smoke billowed and rolled and engulfed the ship, which began to drift with the outgoing tide and swing in toward the graving-dock of the Shipyards. The fire trembled and leaped in a body at the bridge, driving the captain and pilot aft, and there they stood helplessly while the tarry smoke surrounded them in greasy folds and the metal of the deck began to glow under their feet. Both men glanced downward. Underneath that metal lay leashed an incalculable energy, and the bonds which checked it were melting with every second the thermometers mounted in the hold. A half-million pounds of trinitrotoluol and twenty-three hundred tons of picric acid lay there in the darkness under the plates, while the fire above and below the deck converted the hollow shell of the vessel into a bake-oven.

If the captain had wished to scuttle the ship at that moment it would have been impossible to do so, for the heat between decks would have roasted alive any man who tried to reach the sea-cocks. By this time the entire crew was in the lifeboat. The officers followed, and the boat was rowed frantically toward the wooded slope opposite Halifax. There, by lying flat among the trees, the sailors hoped they would have a chance when their ship blew up. By the time they had beached the boat, the foredeck of the *Mont Blanc* was a shaking rampart of fire, and black smoke pouring from it screened the Halifax waterfront from their eyes. The sailors broke and ran for the shelter of the woods.

By this time men were running out of dock sheds and warehouses and 7
offices along the entire waterfront to watch the burning ship. None of
them knew she was a gigantic bomb. She had now come so close to the
Shipyards that she menaced the graving-dock. Fire launches cut out from
a pier farther south and headed for the Narrows. Signal flags fluttered
from the Dockyard and the yardarms of ships lying in the Stream, some
of which were already weighing anchor. The captain of the British cruiser
piped all hands and called for volunteers to scuttle the *Mont Blanc;* a few
minutes later the cruiser's launch was on its way to the Narrows with two
officers and a number of ratings. By the time they reached the burning
ship her plates were so hot that the seawater lapping the plimsoll line was
simmering.

The *Mont Blanc* had become the center of a static tableau. Her plates 8
began to glow red and the swollen air inside her hold heated the cargo
rapidly towards the detonation point. Launches from the harbor fire department surrounded her like midges and the water from their hoses
arched up with infinite delicacy as they curved into the rolling smoke.
The *Imo,* futile and forgotten, was still trying to claw her way off the farther shore.

Twenty minutes after the collision there was no one along the entire 9
waterfront who was unaware that a ship was on fire in the harbor. The
jetties and docks near the Narrows were crowded with people watching
the show, and yet no warning of danger was given. At that particular moment there was no adequate centralized authority in Halifax to give a
warning, and the few people who knew the nature of the *Mont Blanc's*
cargo had no means of notifying the town or spreading the alarm, and no
comfort beyond the thought that trinitrotoluol can stand an almost unlimited heat provided there is no fulminate or explosive gas to detonate
it.

Bells in the town struck the hour of nine, and by this time nearly all 10
normal activity along the waterfront had been suspended. A tug had
managed to grapple the *Mont Blanc* and was towing her with impercept-
ible movement away from the Shipyards back into the channel of the
Narrows. Bluejackets from the cruiser had found the bosun's ladder left
by the fleeing crew, and with flesh shrinking from the heat, were going
over the side. Fire launches surrounded her. There was a static concentration, an intense expectancy in the faces of the firemen playing the
hoses, a rhythmic reverberation in the beat of the flames, a gush from the
hose-nozzles and a steady hiss of scalding water. Everything else for
miles around seemed motionless and silent.

Then a needle of flaming gas, thin as the mast and of a brilliance unbe- 11
lievably intense, shot through the deck of the *Mont Blanc* near the funnel
and flashed more than two hundred feet toward the sky. The firemen
were thrown back and their hoses jumped suddenly out of control and

slashed the air with S-shaped designs. There were a few helpless shouts. Then all movement and life about the ship were encompassed in a sound beyond hearing as the *Mont Blanc* opened up. . . .

12   Three forces were simultaneously created by the energy of the exploding ship, an earthquake, an air-concussion, and a tidal wave. These forces rushed away from the Narrows with a velocity varying in accordance with the nature of the medium in which they worked. It took only a few seconds for the earthquake to spend itself and three minutes for the air-expansion to slow down to a gale. The tidal wave traveled for hours before the last traces of it were swallowed in the open Atlantic.

13   When the shock struck the earth, the rigid ironstone and granite base of Halifax peninsula rocked and reverberated, pavements split and houses swayed as the earth trembled. Sixty miles away in the town of Truro windows broke and glass fell to the ground, tinkling in the stillness of the streets. But the ironstone was solid and when the shock had passed, it resumed its immobility.

14   The pressure of the exploding chemicals smashed against the town with the rigidity and force of driving steel. Solid and unbreathable, the forced wall of air struck against Fort Needham and Richmond Bluff and shaved them clean, smashed with one gigantic blow the North End of Halifax and destroyed it, telescoping houses or lifting them from their foundations, snapping trees and lampposts, and twisting iron rails into writhing, metal snakes; breaking buildings and sweeping the fragments of their wreckage for hundreds of yards in its course. It advanced two miles southward, shattering every flimsy house in its path, and within thirty seconds encountered the long, shield-like slope of the Citadel which rose before it.

15   Then, for the first time since it was fortified, the Citadel was able to defend at least a part of the town. The airwall smote it, and was deflected in three directions. Thus some of its violence shot skyward at a twenty-degree angle and spent itself in space. The rest had to pour around the roots of the hill before closing in on the town for another rush forward. A minute after the detonation, the pressure was advancing through the South End. But now its power was diminished, and its velocity was barely twice that of a tornado. Trees tossed and doors broke inward, windows split into driving arrows of glass which buried themselves deep in interior walls. Here the houses, after swaying and cracking, were still on their foundations when the pressure had passed.

16   Underneath the keel of the *Mont Blanc* the water opened and the harbor bottom was deepened twenty feet along the channel of the Narrows. And then the displaced waters began to drive outward, rising against the town and lifting ships and wreckage over the sides of the docks. It boiled over the shores and climbed the hill as far as the third cross-street, carrying with it the wreckage of small boats, fragments of fish, and some-

where, lost in thousands of tons of hissing brine, the bodies of men. The wave moved in a gigantic bore down the Stream to the sea, rolling some ships under and lifting others high on its crest, while anchor-chains cracked like guns as the violent thrust snapped them. Less than ten minutes after the detonation, it boiled over the breakwater off the park and advanced on McNab's Island, whre it burst with a roar greater than a winter storm. And then the central volume of the wave rolled on to sea, high and arching and white at the top, its back glossy like the plumage of a bird. Hours later it lifted under the keel of a steamer far out in the Atlantic and the captain, feeling his vessel heave, thought he had struck a floating mine.

But long before this, the explosion had become manifest in new forms 17 over Halifax. More than two thousand tons of red hot steel, splintered fragments of the *Mont Blanc,* fell like meteors from the sky into which they had been hurled a few seconds before. The ship's anchor soared over the peninsula and descended through a roof on the other side of the Northwest Arm three miles away. For a few seconds the harbor was dotted white with a maze of splashes, and the decks of raddled ships rang with reverberations and clangs as fragments struck them.

Over the North End of Halifax, immediately after the passage of the 18 first pressure, the tormented air was laced with tongues of flame which roared and exploded out of the atmosphere, lashing downwards like a myriad blowtorches as millions of cubic feet of gas took fire and exploded. The atmosphere went white-hot. It grew mottled, then fell to the streets like a crimson curtain. Almost before the last fragments of steel had ceased to fall, the wreckage of the wooden houses in the North End had begun to burn. And if there were any ruins which failed to ignite from falling flames, they began to burn from the fires in their own stoves, onto which they had collapsed.

Over this part of the town, rising in the shape of a typhoon from the 19 Narrows and extending five miles into the sky, was poised a cloud formed by the exhausted gases. It hung still for many minutes, white, glossy as an ermine's back, serenely aloof. It cast its shadow over twenty miles of forest land behind Bedford Basin.

STRUCTURE:

1. To what extent is "A Sound Beyond Hearing" based on chronological order? Could it have been placed in our first chapter, "Narration"? What qualifies it to appear in this chapter instead?
2. To what extent does this selection trace the causes and effects of the great Halifax explosion? Could it have appeared in our later chapter, "Cause and Effect"?

3. Why does MacLennan classify the effects of the explosion into three parts, one each for land, air and sea? Could "A Sound Beyond Hearing" have appeared in our later chapter, "Classification"? Why do you think it appears in this chapter instead?
4. Roughly what percentage of this selection is devoted to description? How close did MacLennan come to making you feel as though you were there? Which passage most strongly gave you the feeling of being a spectator?
5. Does MacLennan's use of narration, cause and effect, classification and description, all in the same selection, give an effect of confusion? Or do these methods of development work smoothly together? Do you think MacLennan consciously planned all these interlocking methods? Would you attempt to combine methods as you plan a piece of writing?

STYLE:

1. This explosion scene, from MacLennan's novel *Barometer Rising,* is recognized as one of the most vivid passages in all of Canadian literature. One reason is the profusion of SENSE IMAGES. Point out one striking example each of appeals to sight, hearing, touch and smell.
2. In paragraph 3, MacLennan uses the image of "screaming metal" and in paragraph 18, the image of "tongues of flame." Point out three other examples of PERSONIFICATION, in which an inanimate object is described in human terms.
3. In paragraph 17, MacLennan writes that fragments of red hot steel "fell like meteors." Point out at least five other SIMILES, figures of speech in which one thing is said to be like another.
4. In paragraph 15, MacLennan writes that "windows split into driving arrows of glass." Point out at least five other METAPHORS, figures of speech in which one thing is said to *be* another.
5. What do "port," "starboard," "hawse," "scuttle" and all the other nautical terms do for this selection? Would a reader's unfamiliarity with some of these specialized words detract from the effect? Why or why not?

IDEAS:

1. Name all the novels and films you can think of that are about disasters. Why is such entertainment popular? Do people like to be scared? If so, why?
2. The blast that killed about 2000 people in Halifax, on December 6, 1917, is said to be the world's most disastrous man-made explosion before the atomic bomb. If you have read about the atomic blast that destroyed Hiroshima in Kildare Dobbs' essay "The Scar," compare

the two events in their magnitude and their effect upon the inhabitants.

3. Do you sense moments of beauty in MacLennan's description of the disaster? If so, where? Is it appropriate or even moral to see beauty in destruction?

4. Write a description of a disaster that you have seen, or of whatever you have seen that comes closest to being a disaster. Your subject could be a fire, an explosion, an automobile accident, a drowning, etc. Use a great many SENSE IMAGES to recreate for the reader what you experienced in person.

(NOTE: See also the Topics for Writing at the end of this chapter.)

Topics for Writing

Chapter 3: Description

(Note also the topics for writing that appear after each selection in this chapter.)

Describe one of the following as vividly as you can:

1. The nursery of a maternity ward
2. The locker room before or after a game
3. A retirement home or nursing home
4. A funeral parlour during visiting hours
5. A swamp, a meadow, the deep woods or the seashore
6. Your favourite park
7. A thunderstorm, blizzard, tornado, hurricane, flood or earthquake
8. The most architecturally interesting building in your town or city
9. A building that seems out of place in your neighbourhood
10. Your town or city as you imagine it in the year 2000
11. The interior of your church, chapel, cathedral, synagogue, mosque or temple during a service
12. The waiting room of a doctor's office or of the emergency ward of a hospital
13. The waiting room of a Canada Manpower office
14. A police station, courtroom or jail
15. A truck stop
16. A laundromat
17. A garage or body shop in operation
18. The appearance of your best friend
19. The appearance of your best-remembered public or high school teacher
20. Your own appearance at age fifty
21. Rush hour on the expressway, subway, streetcar, bus or sidewalk
22. A pool hall, bowling alley or amusement arcade
23. A strike or demonstration
24. A carnival, a circus or the midway of an amusement park
25. The entertainment district of your town or city on a Saturday night

Cartoon by Brian F. Reynolds.

"The problem is simple: information is power, and when you have a vast amount of information, especially about people, as videotex will give to its planners and operators, then you have a vast amount of power."

Andrew Osler, "Warily into a Wired-Up World"

Here's why . . . .

CAUSE AND EFFECT

One of our most human traits is a desire to make sense of things by asking *"why?"*. If something good happens, we naturally want to know *why* so we can repeat it. If something bad happens, we want to know *why* so we can avoid it in the future. And other times we want to know *why* out of plain curiosity. These motives are so strong that cause and effect reasoning is one of our chief ways of thinking, and one of our most effective ways of organizing essays.

When you investigate causes and effects, try to get them right. A few years ago, a church in Florida began a campaign to burn records by Elton John and other rock stars. A survey had reported that 984 out of 1000 girls who had become pregnant out of wedlock had "committed fornication while rock music was played." The assumption was automatic: rock music causes pregnancy. Before it lit the first match, though, the church might have asked what *other* causes contributed to the effect. How many of the music lovers had also taken alcohol or drugs? How many had failed to use means of birth control? Was the music played because "fornication" generally takes place inside a building, where sound systems also happen to be? The church might also have investigated causes further in the past: What kinds of family backgrounds and what influences of society prepared the fornicators to enter the situation in the first place? And, finally, the church might have asked how often people in this age group listened to Elton John and his friends while *not* fornicating. Rock music may still be to blame — but who knows without a more objective and thorough search of causes? When you trace causes and effects, consider these principles:

Just because one event follows another, don't assume the first causes the second. If a black cat crosses the road just before your car blows up, put the blame where it belongs: not on the cat but on the mechanic who forgot to replace your crankcase oil.

Control your prejudices. If the bank manager refuses to give you a loan, is it because bankers are capitalist exploiters who like to keep the rest of us down? Or is it because this one had to call the collection agency to get his last loan back from you?

Explore causes behind causes. Your employer promoted you because you work hard. But why do you work hard: because you are afraid of being fired? Because you need the money to pay off your car? Because your parents set a workaholic example for you? Or because in fact you like the job?

Many events have multiple causes and multiple effects:

In addition, each of these causes may have one or more causes behind it, and each of these effects may produce further effects, leading to an infinite chain of causality receding into both the past and future. Where, then, do you draw the boundaries as you plan an essay of cause and effect? The answer lies in your own common sense: Include enough to make your point clearly and fairly, then stop. If your parents are workaholics, a description of their behaviour may help a reader to understand your own. But do we need to hear about your grandparents as well? If we do, would a quick summary be enough, since we've already heard the details in your parents' case?

Some events or situations have very clear-cut causes, as in Gregory Clark's essay which uncovers the origin in childhood of a "dread" held by Clark in adulthood. Others have very complicated causes, as in Maryon Kantaroff's essay which explores the many reasons why female artists have been suppressed. Like Clark, Kantaroff and all good essayists, tailor your argument to the requirements of the subject.

Gregory Clark

The Cat

Greg Clark (1892-1977) was a story teller. For many years on the inside back page of Weekend Magazine *he told a story each week about the war, or his hunting and fishing pals, or characters he knew or the odd events that came his way in Toronto. And in his last years, living in Toronto's old King Edward Hotel, he would delight staff and friends in the dining room by spinning tales from a long and colourful life. Hardly believing that so many things could happen to one person, his readers or listeners often wondered if the stories were true. "What a question to ask!" Clark would reply. He was born in Toronto, and was a newspaperman — reporter, feature writer and columnist — for over sixty years. He began with the paper his father edited, the Toronto* Star. *When World War I came, he tried several times to enlist but was turned down for being too small. When Clark finally got into the army, though, he rose quickly from private to major and won the Military Cross for courage under fire at Vimy Ridge. Afterwards he returned to the* Star, *where he worked with Ernest Hemingway, Morley Callaghan and Gordon Sinclair. During the next war, he served as a war correspondent until his own son was killed in action. Clark's greatest popularity came with the column he wrote for* Weekend Magazine *from 1952 almost to the end of his life. Many of these pieces — short, funny, warm-hearted and full of homely wisdom — were gathered in books, among them* Hi There! *(1963) from which our selection comes.*

As far, far back as I could remember. I had a dread of cats. Dread, I think, is the word. Not fear. Not hatred. Not revulsion. Just dread.   1

One time, my fishing companion, W.C. Milne asked me   2
to pick up his fishing trackle at his house, and gave me the key. His wife was out of town.

I didn't know the Milnes had acquired a cat. I opened the front door   3
and started through the vestibule for the living room, where the tackle was heaped on a chair. I froze in my tracks.

Somebody was in the house!   4

"Margaret?" I called.   5

No answer.   6

From a golf bag in the vestibule I took an iron.   7

Everything in my nature told me SOMEBODY was in the house. As an   8
old soldier, though only 30, I had an instinct for danger. I could FEEL it.

From wall to wall, I slid to the back door, finding it locked. With the   9
niblick ready to throw or to swing, I sidled up the stairs, knowing any instant I would have to strike. In those days, I was not afraid of men.

Along the hall, into one room, then another, I moved, all tight as a   10
stretched elastic band. In the front bedroom, on the bed was a black-and-

yellow cat, arching aristocratically on being disturbed. I yelled, and chased it from the room and down the stairs and out the back door, which I opened, banging the golf stick.

11   "Ah, yes," said Billy Milne, when I told him. "That's our new cat."

12   But as I remember it, it never came home.

13   As a child, I used to cross the street, on my way to school, if I saw a cat in my path. In my teens, at the age when we look for chosen friends, I lost sundry friends because they had a cat in the house. In World War I, as a young fellow with the lives of thirty-eight men on my mind and soul, I led a night patrol into a ruined farmhouse and made an utter ass of myself because I let fly with a Very light pistol into a black cellar empty save for a poor mangy cat.

14   But I was certain it had been the enemy.

15   It took me weeks to restore the faith of my thirty-eight men.

16   Ah, cats!

17   "It," said my doctor friends, consolingly, "is one of those mysterious, unexplainable phobias . . . "

18   I was in the back half of my fifties when I visited my Aunt Minnie Greig, in Seaforth, Ont. She was my stylish aunt, a beautiful woman.

19   We sat on her veranda, rocking; and she, being my elder by twenty or more years, was regaling me with stories of times past.

20   "You were an awful little shrimp," she said.

21   "Was I?" I regretted.

22   "So timid," said Aunt Min.

23   "Was I?" I muttered.

24   "Do you remember your white Cat?" she asked.

25   MY white cat?" I barely whispered.

26   "Joe, your dad," said Aunt Minnie, rocking idly, "bought you a white cat, since your mother wouldn't have a dog in the house. It was a beauty, that cat. Snow white."

27   I had a strange feeling, as I sat watching Aunt Minnie rocking, that I was in the act of taking off a heavy coat, a coat with pockets full of things.

28   "How old was I?" I said.

29   "Two," said Aunt Minnie. "You still had diapers. Do you remember what the back yard was like?"

30   "Yes," I said. "I was eight when we left there. There was a grape vine on the fence at the far end."

31   "Right," said Aunt Minnie. "A grape arbor."

32   "And over that fence," I said, "was Lilley's greenhouses."

33   "Good for you!" cried Aunt Minnie. "The Lilleys were the florists, and they had those greenhouses . . ."

34   "What," I interrupted cautiously, "about the cat?"

"I'm coming to that," said Aunt Minnie. "Well, the Lilleys had trou- 35
ble with mice and rats in the greenhouses. So they used to put out poison.

"Did I," I asked, "like the cat? The white cat?" 36

"LIKE it!" cried Aunt Minnie. "There you'd go, staggering around
with that cat draped over your skinny little arm."

"I . . . " I said, and stopped. 38

"You took the cat to BED with you," said Aunt Min. "I told your 39
mother, Sarah Louisa, never, never to let a cat in bed with an infant. But
there you were with that blamed cat on the pillow beside your head."

"Well, I . . . " I tried again, my body prickling, my back hair creep- 40
ing as it did in that ruined farmhouse in Flanders.

"The cat," said Aunt Min, "seemed as attached to you as you were to 41
it. It followed you everywhere, around the house, out the door, in the
back yard."

I pressed my back against the back of my chair. 42

"It was white?" I asked. 43

"Snow white, I told you," said Aunt Min. "Well, here's what hap- 44
pened. Your lovely white cat disappeared!"

"Disappeared?" 45

"I was staying with your mother at the time," said Aunt Min. "The 46
cat vanished. It was gone all night. It didn't come home the next day.
You kept toddling around, hunting for it, upstairs, downstairs, out the
door, all around the yard, back in the door, upstairs, downstairs, until
we were sick of the sight of you."

"Did I cry?" 47

"No, you just went wandering around, looking under everything. It 48
was kind of pitiable, really."

"So?" I said, my back no longer twitching. 49

"We were sitting in the kitchen, having a cup of tea," said Aunt Min- 50
nie. "Your mother, Mamie Armour, Mrs. Taylor from next door, and
your Aunt Mart.

"Then," said Aunt Min, "up the back steps from the yard you came, 51
CARRYING your white cat!"

I tightened. 52

"It was DEAD!" cried Aunt Min. "STIFF dead! It had been dead two 53
days. Poisoned from Lilley's greenhouses. Its tail was sticking out stiff.
Its white fur was all matted, damp. And you were HUGGING it to your little chest, your chin over it."

"What happened?" I got the question out. 54

"Why, we all screamed!" said Aunt Min. "Your mother was first to 55
reach you, and she snatched the cat from you so violently, you fell back
on the steps; and she THREW it half way down the yard, and we were all

screaming and yelling, and Aunt Mart had a fainting spell, and you were howling, and your mother was grabbing at you . . . ''

• • •

56   Do you know what I wish you for a Happy New Year?

57   I wish you the luck to find YOUR Aunt Minn, and have her tell you anecdotes about your childhood.

58   For in them, you may find, as I found, absolution from ancient fears, and mysterious dreads, and the strange darknesses that lie beyond the horizon of consciousness.

59   To know is to understand, even yourself.

STRUCTURE:

1 .Point out several effects achieved by the introduction (pars. 1-17).
2. Is Clark's "dread" of cats caused by only one event? Or is there a chain of cause and effect?
3. Most of this essay takes the form of narration. Who does the narrating?
4. Gregory Clark's usual way of exploring a subject was to tell a story. Do you think the cause and effect analysis of this selection is helped or harmed by the narrative form in which it appears?

STYLE:

1. Although this selection is short, it contains 59 paragraphs. Give as many reasons as you can for their short length.
2. How FORMAL or INFORMAL is the STYLE of this selection? Refer to passages that illustrate your answer.
3. Explain the effect of paragraph 27: "I had a strange feeling, as I sat watching Aunt Minnie rocking, that I was in the act of taking off a heavy coat, a coat with pockets full of things."

IDEAS:

1. For many years the inside back page of *Weekend Magazine* featured Clark's "shorties," as he called them. When he was first offered that page to fill, he wondered if he could write anything in so few words. "It's quite simple," his editor said, "write about small things." Is Clark's story of the cat a "small thing"? In what ways is it larger than it may seem at first?
2. Discuss the emotions that the women exhibit to young Clark in paragraph 55. How would you have reacted if you had been one of those women, and why?

3. The process that Clark describes is similar to that of psychoanalysis: learning about oneself in order to find "absolution from ancient fears, and mysterious dreads, and the strange darknesses that lie beyond the horizon of consciousness" (par. 58). Clark found his "absolution." But do you believe that self-knowledge always has a good result? How does self-knowledge help us in life? Can you think of any way in which it could harm us?

4. Do you have any unexplained "dreads," like Clark's dread of cats? Name one or two and invent possible causes for them. Join class members in inventing possible causes of each other's dreads.

5. Write a true narrative or invent a fictitious but plausible one to explain the cause or causes of one of your strongest attitudes (the attitude could be a fear, a hatred, a love, a prejudice, etc.).

(NOTE: See also the Topics for Writing at the end of this chapter.)

Al Pittman

The Day I Became a Canadian

Al Pittman was born in St. Leonard's, a Newfoundland fishing village, in 1940. Although he is known mainly as a poet, he is also a dramatist, a writer of children's books, an anthologist, a teacher at Memorial University's regional college in Corner Brook, and a publisher. In 1973 he co-founded Breakwater Press, which publishes work by Pittman, Ray Guy and other Newfoundlanders. He has written several books of poetry, including The Elusive Resurrection *(1966),* Down by Jim Long's Stage: Rhymes for Children and Young Fish *(1976), and* Once When I Was Drowning: Poems *(1978). With Adrian Fowler he edited* Thirty-One Newfoundland Poets *(1979). Our selection, "The Day I Became a Canadian," appeared in 1979 in* Weekend Magazine.

1　　It is April, finally, and 11 days from now I will be 9. Breakfast is over and I am in an awful hurry to get outdoors. Before I can escape from the kitchen, my father, standing in the doorways, says to me, "From now on you can call yourself a Canadian." It is April Fool's Day, and I have to be careful.

2　"What's a Canadian, Dad?"

3　"A Canadian is someone who lives in Canada."

4　"Do we live in Canada, Dad?"

5　"We do now. Yesterday we didn't. But today we do. And that's why from now on you can call yourself a Canadian."

6　"How come we still live in the same house, if we moved to Canada?"

7　"Well, we didn't move at all. Come here and I'll try to explain to you."

8　And he did. I'm not sure I understood, but I remember walking away from the conversation that morning feeling different. Different like you felt walking out of church on Confirmation Day, or different like you felt later on when you climbed all the way to the top of the Red Scrape without anyone around to watch. That kind of difference.

9　On April 1, 1949, Newfoundland became Canada's 10th province. Whatever it meant inside my nine-year-old mind, there seemed to be little evidence around the neighborhood that anything momentous had happened. Later on I heard about people hanging black flags out the window and wearing black armbands in protest, and other people gathering in halls to celebrate. But where I lived, it seemed to me that my father had shared a solemn secret with me. And what a secret to have hold of, to reveal or conceal according to my will.

10　I went off to find Johnny Moynahan. He beat me in every subject in school, and here he was, a Canadian, and didn't even know it. I've seldom felt such a delightful sense of triumph. Johnny denied it, of course. He was good in geography and he knew all about Canada and he certainly was not a Canadian. Off he went to his father to confirm my stupidity. Poor old Johnny! I don't think he ever lived it down. He was a Canadian, of course, and had been for half a day. And so was Margaret, and Eddie, and Mom, and my brothers, and my sister Alice. And the rocks and the trees and the sky. Even the sky was Canadian now. And this ground I stood upon, this brown slope at the edge of the woods, this was Canada. Yesterday I had stood on this very spot and I was only in Newfoundland. Today I was in Canada.

Other people had other considerations, no doubt, but to me it was a   11 miracle of time and space. I looked up that morning to watch a flock of Canadian snowbirds pitch in the Canadian trees above my head. I suppose only someone just about to be 9 could be so amazed.

Today, 30 years later, I have other recollections, other realizations.   12 Now, because memories are not instant reactions, because they gather and grow and recreate themselves as they like without any reverence for fact, I recall the referendums. The blaring loudspeakers, the fuss on the radio, the arguments in the kitchen, the words "baby bonus" as common as coughs, and the incredible flurry of it all.

"God bless Joey!" Mr. Sparkes would say to every customer who   13 walked into his store.

"Goddamn Joey!" Mr. Shears replied. You could hear them going at   14 it half way down Mountbatten Road.

It was all Joey and the baby bonus. Canada had nothing to do with it   15 until it was all over. There might have been a few intellectuals at Memorial University and the odd Water Street merchant who considered the politics of Confederation before they made up their minds how to vote. But for the vast majority of Newfoundlanders it was simply a matter of the baby bonus versus the return to responsible government, to the sovereignty that was ours for 78 years until the country went bankrupt in 1933.

Newfoundland families were large families. A family of 12 was not   16 considered overly large and the promise of an allowance for each child, no matter how small, added up to a substantial amount of money.

In 1949 Newfoundlanders had little but patriotism to be patriotic   17 about. Conditions for most people were poor by any standard. Tuberculosis was on the rampage. There was a shortage of schools, hospitals, roads and jobs. The fishery was in a desperate state of disrepair, and it was all the Commission of Government could do to dig the country out of the ruins of bankruptcy. And along comes Joseph R. Smallwood, with his promise of the baby bonus.

It is no less amazing that so many Newfoundlanders resisted with such   18 determination. Could it have been anything other than clear recognition that they were being tempted to sell out their country, their nationality, their souls, for the dollars offered? Perhaps. It could have been that they were swayed by the rhetoric of the anticonfederates, gifted orators like Major Peter Cashin, or that they believed the propaganda disseminated by the St. John's merchant class (Confederation would bring economic ruin), or by the Catholic Church hierarchy (Confederation would bring an end to Catholic education). For whatever reason, half the population of Newfoundland resisted Confederation to the bitter end, and many resisted it all their lives after.

19   For most of those who did not resist, the baby bonus made the difference. On the final ballot it came down to "Do we go back to self-government and do without the baby bonus, or do we join Canada and wait for the cheques to arrive?" It was not an easy choice. Say what you like about a people's sense of self-identity and independence, it is not commensurate with economic woe. So after two bitterly fought referendum campaigns, the confederates won by the slimmest possible majority (52.24 percent), and Newfoundland became a province of Canada.

20   "Listen Johnny," I said as soon as I got the chance, "you know what this means, now that we're living in Canada?"

21   "Of course I do," replied Johnny. But he didn't. So I told him.

22   "It means all kinds of things. It means maybe now we'll be able to wear those U.S. Keds sneakers that they wear in the comics, instead of these old gum boots."

23   "How come?"

24   "Because Canada is a big place, my son. Bigger than the States even. My father said so."

25   "So?"

26   "So, if Canada is as big as the States, then it must have all that stuff in it."

27   "What stuff?"

28   "You know. The stuff in the comics. Like where you can join a club and get all kinds of free prizes like spy glasses and roller skates and model airplanes and Double Bubble Gum."

29   "So what? My mother won't let me chew bubblegum. She says it's rude to blow bubbles, and it causes germs."

30   "Still, I bet you'd sneak a chew if it could make you fly."

31   "What do you mean, fly?"

32   "You know, like the kid in the comics. The one who blows big bubbles and flies all over the place. If you could blow a bubble big enough you could go right over your house, over the school even. If it was Double Bubble Gum you could."

33   "Go on! That's just comic book stuff."

"No. It's real. Cross my heart and hope to die. They really have things 34
like that in places like the States and Canada. And now that we live in
Canada, we'll have them too. Just imagine, being able to fly!''

Johnny was a real skeptic and refused to believe a word of it. But back 35
then, when it all began, when I was 9, I, for one, firmly believed in Double Bubble Gum ads. The comic books had convinced me that if we could
get Double Bubble Gum, then I could fly like the fat boy in the adver-
tisements and float, borne up by the biggest bubble imaginable, over
buildings and hills. And I could catch bank robbers if there were ever any
around to catch, and I'd be a hero then to everyone who knew me. As far
as I was concerned, it was all part of becoming Canadian. Since then I've
learned that my childhood notions about Canada were no more unin-
formed than the notions a lot of Newfoundland adults had at the time.

Canada was a most foreign place to us in 1949. Until then, and until 36
we got used to the fact that the border had been lifted between us and the
Canadians, our familiar North American neighbors were the French islands of St. Pierre and Miquelon and the Boston States (which is what we
called the United States of America). Until then Canada had been, for
the most part, an unknown country to us.

We knew Halifax because it was a frequent port of call for ships en- 37
route to Boston, and if you cared to go ashore there you had to put up
with the rigmarole of Canadian customs regulations. We knew of Shelburne because of the Shelburne dory; many of our own dories came from
Shelburne, Nova Scotia, and many that didn't were fashioned by our
own boat builders according to the revered Shelburne design. But of
Canada we knew little else. One older friend of mine recalls he knew
Canada then only "as that place on the Bay of Fundy" because he used
to "run rum up there in prohibition years." Another friend tells me his
concept of Canada was "a place up there that had Montreal in it."
Because of our involvement in the foreign fish trade, many Newfoundlanders were more familiar with the European ports of Cadiz and Oporto
and the islands of the West Indies than they were with most of Canada.
This was not idle ignorance on our part. We simply did not need to
know.

Before the migration of Newfoundlanders to Toronto began in the mid 38
'50s, we had been moving to the Boston States for years in numbers that
would astound the statisticians. On my first trip to Boston in 1960, I
parked my car, bearing Newfoundland licence plates, in the cobblestone
square at the entrance to the Boston Fish Pier. Before I had the motor
turned off I was surrounded by men anxious to talk about things back
home. I spent the day with dozens of them in the bars around the pier.
Most hadn't been back home since they came to Boston during the Depression. They had come to fish on the beam trawlers out of Boston,

New Bedford and Rockland. Their wives had joined them along the way and their children had grown up American. All seven of my father's family went to the States in the '20s and '30s, and only my father came back to live in Newfoundland. I am only one of thousands of Newfoundlanders whose cousins are all citizens in the Boston States.

39   Confederation changed all that. In time we got used to thinking of Toronto as the new mecca, and in time we got used to Canadian money, Canadian stamps, Canadian cigarettes and candy and the rest. But it took many of us a lot longer to get used to being Canadian. To this day, most people of my own and older generations think of themselves as Newfoundlanders. Adrian Fowler of Corner Brook, who was three years old at the time of Confederation, told the Task Force on Canadian Unity in the fall of 1977, "I have feelings of intimacy for Newfoundland that I can never have for Canada, which by comparison is an abstraction and claims my allegiance only by law. I am a Newfoundlander first, Canadian a very distant second."

40   Ray Guy, the province's most popular writer (and the man most often credited with, or blamed for, the political demise of Joseph R. Smallwood because of his insistent attacks upon the Smallwood regime in his daily column in the *St. John's Evening Telegram*), resolutely refers to Newfoundland as his "country." There is no doubt that Fowler and Guy express the sentiments most Newfoundlanders feel following 30 years of Confederation. Back in the '50s, such sentiments were often regarded as the silly notions of the "older crowd," the crowd that resisted change of any kind. For back then, among the young, there was an anxious urge to emulate "the mainland."

41   Our images of the mainland were, of course, mostly American because they were inspired by American movies and magazines, with a little help from Eaton's catalogue. Those were the days when people frantically began ripping down the front room walls to put in "picture windows," when they were inclined to keep up by covering their wooden (and often handmade) tables with arborite, when the latest American fashion or fad was adopted unanimously with a rapid passion unknown to urban Canadians who took on the same facades without the feverish compulsion we had here in Newfoundland. When the world press reported the riots inspired by the movie *Rock Around the Clock* in Philadelphia and Melbourne, they failed to mention that the same thing happened in Grand Falls, Newfoundland.

42   Those were sad years. Sad because so many Newfoundlanders had such negative opinions of themselves. They thought, too often and with too much conviction, that they were an inferior people exiled by history to live inferior lives on an ugly rock in the Atlantic Ocean. They rejected their own music, their dances, their speech, their occupations, their customs, their history and their heritage.

It is only in recent years that the trend has reversed itself. Today you   43
are more likely to encounter a young Newfoundlander proclaiming his
origins with arrogant assurance than you are to encounter any of the
apologetic attitudes so prevalent such a short time ago. The gospel in
Newfoundland now is the gospel of pride and patriotism. This is perhaps
more apparent in the arts than anywhere else. Ray Guy and his contemporaries belong to that generation of Newfoundlanders most inwardly
affected by Confederation and the cultural invasion that followed in its
wake. The poets, playwrights and painters strive in much of their work to
define the tensions inherent in the transition of a people from past to present. It's a compelling theme for these artists because the whole of their
own history was abruptly and irrevocably altered in their own lifetime.
Even if they were born after Confederation they could not escape the effects of it, and they could not help but wonder if we had done the right
thing when we joined up with Canada.

For hundreds of years before Confederation almost nothing had   44
changed in Newfoundland. In 1949 the place was essentially the same as
it had been for hundreds of years past. Then suddenly we became part of
a country we hardly knew, and just as suddenly the government exhorted
the people to abandon their old ways and adopt the new, to come out of
their fishing boats to work in factories, to leave their homes on the islands and in the coves to take up residence in the "growth centres" of the
new industrial Newfoundland. The change was sudden and shocking,
and the shock waves have not yet faded.

There is no doubt the 20th century was going to come our way with or   45
without Smallwood dragging us into it. But dragged we were, and the
kicking and screaming is bound to continue for a while yet. It will continue, at least, until we find a way to defend ourselves against those who
would have us deny what we are. After 30 years of living with the constant threat of being swamped in a culture essentially foreign to our own,
the threat remains. We're a little shy of change, the way we've known it,
but there is a change taking place within us, a change in our attitude
about ourselves, a change that permits us now to hang on to our heritage
without forfeiting our aspirations for the future.

One of my friends told me recently that the only thing he remembers   46
about Confederation is his sorrow that his younger brother was born in
May of '49 because if he had been born a few weeks earlier he would
have been a Newfoundlander instead of a Canadian. I think it safe to say
that his younger brother is probably very much a Newfoundlander. Ray
Guy calls Newfoundland "this dear and fine country" and lovingly
declares, "There is no place else." This Newfoundlander, who's been a
Canadian for 30 years now, couldn't agree more.

STRUCTURE:

1. What does Pittman achieve by introducing this essay with an ANEC-DOTE from his childhood? And why is that anecdote told in the present tense?
2. In Pittman's view, what were the *causes* of Newfoundland's joining Confederation?
3. In Pittman's view, what were the major *effects* of Confederation upon Newfoundland?
4. In his closing (pars. 43-46), Pittman describes a counter-reaction to the effects of Confederation. Does he put it at the end only because it is the ultimate effect of Confederation, or does its location at the end have other purposes as well?

STYLE:

1. How FORMAL or INFORMAL is the language of this essay?
2. Why does paragraph 8 so informally use sentence fragments and refer to the reader as "you"?
3. How appropriate is the image "as common as coughs" in paragraph 12?
4. In paragraph 37, Pittman writes, "One older friend of mine recalls he knew Canada then only 'as that place on the Bay of Fundy' because he used to 'run rum up there in prohibition years.' Another friend tells me his concept of Canada was 'a place up there that had Montreal in it.'" Discuss what these short quotations have achieved, and how they have achieved it.
5. What effect is achieved through the CONCRETE examples in paragraph 41?

IDEAS:

1. The existence of "Newfie jokes" implies that we hold a STEREOTYPE of Newfoundlanders. Describe that stereotype. Describe also the most common stereotype of people from your own province or city. Do you know individuals who do not fit the stereotype? If so, describe them.
2. In paragraphs 40, 43 and 46, Pittman refers to Ray Guy, "the province's most popular writer." If you have read Ray Guy's essay "Outharbor Menu," discuss this question: To what extent should a group resist outside influences in an effort to preserve its traditional culture? You may wish to discuss this question not only in relation to Newfoundlanders, but also to Acadians, Québécois, native peoples, the Old Order Mennonites, other ethnic or religious minorities and — on a national scale — Canadians in general.
3. If you are a naturalized citizen of Canada, write your own essay entitled "The Day I Became a Canadian." If you are a citizen by birth, write an essay entitled "What Being a Canadian Means to Me."

If you are not a Canadian citizen, write an essay entitled "Why I Wish (or Do Not Wish) to Become a Canadian."

4. Regionalism vs. centralization has been perhaps the sharpest ongoing conflict in Canadian life. Do you think of yourself — like Pittman — as a member of your province or region first, and as a Canadian second? Or do you think of yourself as a Canadian first? Analyze the *cause* or *causes* of your attitude in essay form.

(NOTE: See also the Topics for Writing at the end of this chapter.)

Andrew Osler
Warily into a Wired-Up World

Andrew Osler is a native of Toronto. He has been a reporter for the Toronto Star and the Toronto Globe and Mail, a freelance journalist, a teacher of political science at Sir Sandford Fleming College in Peterborough, Ontario, an associate professor of communication studies at the University of Windsor, and is now an associate professor of journalism at the University of Western Ontario. With degrees in both journalism and political economy, Osler has written widely on politics, worked at industrial public relations and done governmental studies of the media. In 1980 he completed a survey of Canadian newspaper ownership patterns for the Royal Commission on Newspapers. Osler's concern for the future of our communications media is evident in our selection, "Warily into a Wired-Up World," which appeared in 1981 in Maclean's.

1 I've been looking at the development of videotex interactive television, with Canada's Telidon system acclaimed internationally as the best of the breed, and what I see scares the hell out of me. It's the social equivalent of an atomic bomb with the potential to blow society, as we know it, wide open, and few people seem to be worrying about what to do with the fallout. This new technology could wipe away whatever scraps of individual privacy remain to us, and that's the least of our worries. It also contains the capacity to fine-tune public mind manipulation in a way that makes George Orwell's *1984* scenario look bush league by comparison. Yet Orwell didn't know about computers, with their capacity to sort and filter vast amounts of detailed information about us, when he first imagined the awful future use of two-way television as a social control mechanism. And computers are what videotex is all about.

2 The problem is simple: information is power, and when you have a vast amount of information, especially about people, as videotex will give to its planners and operators, then you have a vast amount of power. It looks benign at first glance. What we have is the marriage of a computer, perhaps thousands of kilometres away, to the familiar family TV. System details vary, but the only new technical wrinkle visible to the living room Telidon user is a push-button control box. By pushing the right sequence of buttons, you can talk to that computer and do such things as comparative grocery pricing, catalogue shopping, personal banking and looking up Aunt Martha's phone number.

3 Eventually, you'll be able to order library books or personalized news summaries; haul in financial advice from a trust company; have your gimpy heart monitored 24 hours a day; or even find a job in the Canada Manpower listings and apply for it electronically. And that's Telidon

from the bright side, the side the federal department of communications and its many private-sector collaborators at places such as Bell Canada want us to see. A bottomless cornucopia of electronic goodies.

Unfortunately, there's a darker view. If interactive television is to work, it will have to know an awful lot about us. If it is to monitor Great Uncle Charlie's heart, it will need his medical history. If it is to help with our financial planning, it will need to know everything about our income and spending habits, and if it is to help us find jobs, it will need our full employment and educational records. And there will be nothing to stop the system from acquiring such things as lists of our department-store purchases and library books we borrow, or from logging all the phone numbers we look up in its directory.

And here comes the catch. If someone should ever decide to put all that information — and much, much more — into one computer (which with satellite and fibre-optic transmission systems is no big deal), then that person, or agency of government, or political party, or multinational corporation, could learn more about us than we know about ourselves. The scenario develops. Individual privacy in tomorrow's wired-up world just beyond 1984 could become as archaic as medieval bear-baiting. Sophisticated surveillance of individuals (not just of those with medical problems), and the talented massaging of public opinion become terrifying possibilities. Voter manipulation prospects make today's pollster politics look naïve, and heaven knows what an enterprising ad agency could do to our buying habits with access to an interactive data base. Of course, it doesn't have to happen this way. Electronic blocks could be built into that computer labyrinth, and we could have protective legislation. Something could even be said about permissible uses in our new constitution.

We still have some precious time, a very little bit of it, to think and plan and to pressure our political representatives into formulating legislation to prevent such abuse. In its first few years, Telidon will be expensive. One estimate indicates you'll need a $70,000-a-year income to be first on the block with Telidon. But the price will plummet once manufacturers figure out the logistics of cheap mass production, and then there'll be no time left. In the meantime, I wouldn't bet on politicians taking any initiatives on our behalf. Not when you look at the record of public computer systems now in place. Every April, when the taxman takes his annual chunk from my backside and I insert my social insurance number (SIN) at the top of the tax-return form, I remember how Prime Minister Lester Pearson stood in the House of Commons in April, 1964, to promise that our SINs were for social welfare bookkeeping, and never, never, would be used for such things as personal income tax. Not to mention the banks and other private-sector concerns that use our SINs so cheerfully at the expense of our privacy.

7   A 30-member committee of government and private-sector people, the
Canadian Videotex Consultative Committee, serves as an advisory board
to Telidon. But only four members represent groups such as the Con-
sumers' Association of Canada, which might be expected to worry about
our rights in tomorrow's wired world. Overwhelmingly, Telidon is in the
hands of bureaucrats, businessmen and engineers, not the sort inclined to
see beyond profit-and-loss columns and technological nuts and bolts.
Some of us will have to do a bit of worrying for them about this electronic monster, and we'd better start now.

STRUCTURE:

1. In the opening paragraph, what strategy does Osler use, and how effective is this strategy in capturing the reader's interest?
2. In the closing paragraph, what strategy does Osler use? How
appropriate is that strategy to the ending of the essay?
3. Point out all the *causes* that Osler gives for the possible loss of privacy
through "interactive television."
4. What part of Osler's essay is based on a contrast?

STYLE:

1. In paragraph 1, Osler writes, ". . . what I see scares the hell out of
me." Point out other COLLOQUIAL or SLANG expressions in the essay.
What effect do they have? Is that effect appropriate or inappropriate?
2. Three sentence fragments appear in this essay. Identify them. State
why you think Osler used them and whether they are effective.
3. Paragraph 4 contains an obvious example of repetition. Point it out.
Do you think it is an accidental error or a deliberate device of style?
What is its effect?
4. Read this statement aloud: "Voter manipulation prospects make
today's pollster politics look naïve. . ." (par. 5). Describe its style.
Could that style be improved? If so, how?
5. In paragraph 7, Osler refers to Telidon as an "electronic monster."
Point out several other METAPHORS, comparisons that are literally
false but poetically true.

IDEAS:

1. If you have read George Orwell's novel *1984,* which Osler refers to in
paragraph 1, describe the extent to which you think Orwell's nightmare has come true. How much of the problem do you think has been
caused by technology?

2. Write a description of a future society in which computerized information systems "wipe away whatever scraps of individual privacy remain to us" and which "fine-tune public mind manipulation."
3. Write a description of a future society in which computerized information systems greatly improve our lives.
4. In an essay of cause and effect, discuss all the ways you can think of, good or bad, in which computers now affect your life.

(NOTE: See also the Topics for Writing at the end of this chapter.)

Margaret Atwood

Canadians: What Do They Want?

If an American or German or Briton knows only one Canadian writer, that writer is likely to be Margaret Atwood. Both poet and novelist, Atwood is a rare example of the serious writer who has met with popular success. Ironically, it is her poetry that many critics consider her best work, while it is her novels that have brought wide recognition from the public. Atwood was born in Ottawa in 1939, earned a B.A. at the University of Toronto in 1961 and a Master's at Radcliffe in 1962. Since then she has published nearly 20 books. The best-known is her novel Surfacing *(1972), also produced as a film. Her other works include* The Circle Game *(poetry, 1966);* The Journals of Susanna Moody *(poetry, 1970);* Power Politics *(poetry, 1971);* You Are Happy *(poetry, 1974);* Selected Poems *(1976);* The Edible Woman *(novel, 1969);* Lady Oracle *(novel, 1976);* Life Before Man *(novel, 1979);* Bodily Harm *(novel, 1981); and* Survival: a Thematic Guide to Canadian Literature *(1972). Atwood's feminism and Canadian nationalism are evident in her books and also in our selection, "Canadians: What Do They Want?" This essay, written for Americans, appeared in 1982 in* Mother Jones, *an American political magazine. "On a recent visit to Canada," wrote editor Mark Dowie, "I noticed that Canadians were even more anti-American than our media were telling us they were . . . . So we asked Canadian novelist and poet Margaret Atwood to explain why her fellow Canadians feel so strongly about their neighbors to the south."*

1 Last month, during a poetry reading, I tried out a short prose poem called "How to Like Men." It began by suggesting that one start with the feet. Unfortunately, the question of jackboots soon arose, and things went on from there. After the reading I had a conversation with a young man who thought I had been unfair to men. He wanted men to be liked totally, not just from the heels to the knees, and not just as individuals but as a group; and he thought it negative and inegalitarian of me to have alluded to war and rape. I pointed out that as far as any of us knew these were two activities not widely engaged in by women, but he was still upset. "We're both in this together," he protested. I admitted that this was so; but could he, maybe, see that our relative positions might be a little different.

2 This is the conversation one has with Americans, even, uh, *good* Americans, when the dinner-table conversation veers round to Canadian-American relations. "We're in this together," they like to say, especially when it comes to continental energy reserves. How do you *explain* to them, as delicately as possible, why they are not categorically beloved? It gets like the old Lifebuoy ads: even their best friends won't tell them. And Canadians are supposed to be their best friends, right? Members of the family?

Well, sort of. Across the river from Michigan, so near and yet so far,   3
there I was at the age of eight, reading *their* Donald Duck comic books
(originated however by one of *ours*; yes, Walt Disney's parents were
Canadian) and coming at the end to Popsicle Pete, who promised me the
earth if only I would save wrappers, but took it all away from me again
with a single asterisk: Offer Good Only in the United States. Some
cynical members of the world community may be forgiven for thinking
that the same asterisk is there, in invisible ink, on the Constitution and
the Bill of Rights.

But quibbles like that aside, and good will assumed, how does one go   4
about liking Americans? Where does one begin? Or, to put it another
way, why did the Canadian women lock themselves in the john during a
'70s "international" feminist conference being held in Toronto? Because
the American sisters were being "imperialist," that's why.

But then, it's always a little naive of Canadians to expect that   5
Americans, of whatever political stamp, should stop being imperious.
How can they? The fact is that the United States is an empire and
Canada is to it as Gaul was to Rome.

It's hard to explain to Americans what it feels like to be a Canadian.   6
Pessimists among us would say that one has to translate the experience
into their own terms and that this is necessary because Americans are in-
capable of thinking in any other terms — and this in itself is part of the
problem. (Witness all those draft dodgers who went into culture shock
when they discovered to their horror that Toronto was not Syracuse.)

Here is a translation: Picture a Mexico with a population ten times   7
larger than that of the United States. That would put it at about two
billion. Now suppose that the official American language is Spanish, that
75 percent of the books Americans buy and 90 percent of the movies they
see are Mexican, and that the profits flow across the border to Mexico. If
an American does scrape it together to make a movie, the Mexicans
won't let him show it in the States, because they own the distribution
outlets. If anyone tries to change this ratio, not only the Mexicans but
many fellow Americans cry "National chauvinism," or, even more effectively, "National socialism." After all, the American public prefers
the Mexican product. It's what they're used to.

Retranslate and you have the current American-Canadian picture. It's   8
changed a little recently, not only on the cultural front. For instance,
Canada, some think a trifle late, is attempting to regain control of its
own petroleum industry. Americans are predictably angry. They think of
Canadian oil as *theirs*.

"What's mine is yours," they have said for years, meaning exports;   9
"What's yours is mine" means ownership and profits. Canadians are
supposed to do retail buying, not controlling, or what's an empire for?
One could always refer Americans to history, particularly that of their

own revolution. They objected to the colonial situation when they themselves were a colony; but then, revolution is considered one of a very few
home-grown American products that definitely are not for export.

10 Objectively, one cannot become too self-righteous about this state of
affairs. Canadians owned lots of things, including their souls, before
World War II. After that they sold, some say because they had put too
much into financing the war, which created a capital vacuum (a position
they would not have been forced into if the Americans hadn't kept out of
the fighting for so long, say the sore losers). But for whatever reason,
capital flowed across the border in the '50s, and Canadians, traditionally
sock-under-the-mattress hoarders, were reluctant to invest in their own
country. Americans did it for them and ended up with a large part of it,
which they retain to this day. In every sellout there's a seller as well as a
buyer, and the Canadians did a thorough job of trading their birthright
for a mess.

11 That's on the capitalist end, but when you turn to the trade union side
of things you find much the same story, except that the sellout happened
in the '30s under the banner of the United Front. Now Canadian workers
are finding that in any empire the colonial branch plants are the first to
close, and what could be a truly progressive labor movement has been
weakened by compromised bargains made in international union headquarters south of the border.

12 Canadians are sometimes snippy to Americans at cocktail parties.
They don't like to feel owned and they don't like having been sold. But
what really bothers them — and it's at this point that the United States
and Rome part company — is the wide-eyed innocence with which their
snippiness is greeted.

13 Innocence becomes ignorance when seen in the light of international
affairs, and though ignorance is one of the spoils of conquest — the
Gauls always knew more about the Romans than the Romans knew
about them — the world can no longer afford America's ignorance. Its
ignorance of Canada, though it makes Canadians bristle, is a minor and
relatively harmless example. More dangerous is the fact that individual
Americans seem not to know that the United States is an imperial power
and is behaving like one. They don't want to admit that empires dominate, invade and subjugate — and live on the proceeds — or, if they do
admit it, they believe in their divine right to do so. The export of divine
right is much more harmful than the export of Coca-Cola, though they
may turn out to be much the same thing in the end.

14 Other empires have behaved similarly (the British somewhat better,
Genghis Khan decidedly worse); but they have not expected to be *liked*
for it. It's the final Americanism, this passion for being liked. Alas,
many Americans are indeed likable; they are often more generous, more
welcoming, more enthusiastic, less picky and sardonic than Canadians,

and it's not enough to say it's only because they can afford it. Some of that revolutionary spirit still remains: the optimism, the 18th-century belief in the fixability of almost anything, the conviction of the possibility of change. However, at cocktail parties and elsewhere one must be able to tell the difference between an individual and a foreign policy. Canadians can no longer afford to think of Americans as only a spectator sport. If Reagan blows up the world, we will unfortunately be doing more than watching it on television. "No annihilation with representation" sounds good as a slogan, but if we run up the flagpole, who's going to salute?

We *are* all in this together. For Canadians, the question is how to survive it. For Americans there is no question, because there does not have to be. Canada is just that vague, cold place where their uncle used to go fishing, before the lakes went dead from acid rain. 15

How do you like Americans? Individually, it's easier. Your average American is no more responsible for the state of affairs than your average man is for war and rape. Any Canadian who is so narrow-minded as to dislike Americans merely on principle is missing out on one of the good things in life. The same might be said, to women, of men. As a group, as a foreign policy, it's harder. But if you like men, you can like Americans. Cautiously. Selectively. Beginning with the feet. One at a time. 16

STRUCTURE:

1. How does the opening ANECDOTE lead to Margaret Atwood's main topic? Upon what organizational device is it based?

2. What technique underlies the closing of Atwood's essay? How effective is it?

3. Identify Atwood's THESIS STATEMENT, the passage that most clearly tells what the essay will be about.

4. As editor Mark Dowie states in his introduction, ". . . we asked Canadian novelist and poet Margaret Atwood to explain why her fellow Canadians feel so strongly about their neighbors to the south." Point out at least ten *causes* given by Atwood for anti-Americanism in Canada.

5. Atwood's economic "translation" in paragraph 7 is a comparison of American control over Canada with a hypothetical Mexican control over the United States. What purpose does this passage serve for the readers it was meant to instruct?

STYLE:

1. How FORMAL or INFORMAL is Atwood's TONE in this essay? Give examples to illustrate your answer.

2. Like much of Atwood's writing, this selection is charged with IRONY. Point out the strongest examples of it. What effect do they achieve?

IDEAS:

1. How well do you think this essay, written for Americans, communicates to Canadians?
2. In paragraph 13, Atwood writes that "empires dominate, invade and subjugate — and live on the proceeds . . . ." Do you agree with her that the United States is an "empire"? And if so, to what extent has it dominated, invaded and subjugated Canada? Give specific examples to support your point of view.
3. What degree of American influence do you detect in these aspects of Canadian life?

   —transportation   —hockey
   —clothing   —music
   —food   —books
   —housing   —language
   —television   —law
   —films   —foreign policy
   —inflation   —interest rates

4. One concern of the Canadian military is a possible invasion by the Soviets. But in his novel *Exxoneration* (1974), Richard Rohmer describes a future military invasion of Canada by the United States. Tell why you think such an event might or might not happen. If it did, what would you do?
5. Discuss the benefits and dangers of nationalism. How nationalistic do you think most Canadians are? Should they become more or less nationalistic? What might be the results?
6. Point out the similarities and/or differences that you have noticed between Americans and Canadians as individuals. Give specific details.
7. If you have read "The Day I Became a Canadian," compare Al Pittman's description of Newfoundlanders reacting to Canadian culture with Atwood's description of Canadians reacting to American culture.
8. If you oppose Atwood's point of view, write a cause and effect essay entitled "What America Has Done for Me." If you agree with Atwood's point of view, write a cause and effect essay entitled "What America Has Done to Me." In either case, give specific examples.

(NOTE: See also the Topics for Writing at the end of this chapter.)

Robert Thomas Allen

"Who Is Your Skinny Friend, Mary?"

Robert Thomas Allen is one of our most prolific humorists. He was born in 1911 in Toronto, a city he has celebrated in witty and nostalgic books about his early years. Allen's first writing job was in the advertising department of the T. Eaton Company, but he soon found a greater interest in magazine journalism. His numerous articles have appeared in Maclean's, the Star Weekly, the Canadian, Today and other periodicals. Allen has also published more than a dozen books, including two winners of the Stephen Leacock Award for Humour: The Grass is Never Greener (1956) and Children, Wives and Other Wildlife (1970). Our selection typifies Allen's nostalgic yet ironic humour, and his clear and seemingly effortless style. It comes from his book We Gave You the Electric Toothbrush! (1971).

It's no wonder kids today think they can't trust the older generation. They must get suspicious very early. You don't have to be very old to realize that something is wrong when five different companies claim over TV that *their* detergents wash whiter than all the others, or when somebody says casually that all housewives know that only every third coffee bean grown beside a mountain stream is fit to grind. The young must wonder how adults are capable of finding their socks in the morning, let alone making important decisions about running the world, when they listen to statistics like: "Fifty percent of some doctors believe that other leading brands are as little as half as effective," and they must wonder if we've completely lost our marbles when we sing that springtime happens with every Salem.

Yet something that never seems to occur to modern psychoanalysts is that most of us middle-aged patients must be largely products of the advertising of the 1930s. No one could read the kind of ads we read during the Depression without carrying permanent traces at lower brain levels; and it seems to me that if today's brilliant young psychoanalysts want to complete our case histories, they should leave us lying on the couch for a few minutes and take a look at some of the ads we had to look at while we chain-smoked Turrets and Millbanks and tried to get through the Depression.

We were warned of smelling, being ignorant, having dandruff, bad breath, stopped–up bowels, flabby gums, attacks of bile and bad nerves; of having bullies knock us off the sidewalk, of picking up the wrong fork, getting fired, losing our girl friends, and mispronouncing brassiere.

137

4   Listerine told us that although a Hawaiian maid's breath was as sweet as a hibiscus, ours — well, we really didn't know — we only hoped — even our best friends wouldn't tell us — and soon we'd get fired and end up going around telling prospective employers we were "formerly with," a phrase that "wrecked 1,000,000 men."

5   If we didn't have halitosis we were warned by the makers of Lifebuoy that we might be guilty of B.O. and not even know it, because, as the ad said (anticipating our protests that we didn't smell all that bad), we quickly got used to ever-present odors. But the odors were soon noticed by others, especially in hot weather, which explained why we got only one dance out of one girl and were likely to be left sitting alone halfway through movies.

6   But Kruschen Salts told us to keep smiling and said, "There isn't a care in the world that won't seem lighter after a dose or two of Kruschen," and told us to look at Grandpa who, as pictured in the ads, always looked as if he were standing in a high wind. "As happy as the day is long. No poison from congested waste matter seeping through *his* intestinal walls!" When Grandpa took Kruschen with his morning coffee, the aperient elements began to liven up his liver, the diuretic elements began to flush his kidneys, all of which gave him "that Kruschen feeling."

7   Advertising men went at our bodies as if they were tackling an engineering job — unplugging our livers and sealing our joints and assuming that we were chronically corroded. Dr. Oliver Taillandier, consultant at L'Hospice de la Salpêtrière, Paris, took time out from his busy schedule to lean out of an ad for Fleischmann's Yeast and say, "We have on hand a remarkable food — yeast — which has an astonishing effect on constipation. Did *you* know that that tired feeling may mean nothing more or less than an unclean condition of the intestines?"

8   Nobody worried about hurt feelings. "Who is your skinny friend, Mary?" one ad hooted at our girl friends. "Tell him to take cod-liver oil for a couple of months to get enough good healthy flesh on his bones to look like a real man!"

9   If the ads weren't calling us "skinny" they were sneering that we were socially impossible.

10   "Everybody knows but *you* when you mispronounce words," chortled John G. Gilmartin, author of *Everyday Errors in Pronunciation.*

11   "A box of cigars says you don't *dare* dance with her," Arthur Murray taunted, "—Wallflower!"

12   By the time we read the ads, looked at Little Orphan Annie, rubbed our feet with Zambuck, took a couple of Bile Beans at bedtime and ankled upstairs to see if our toothbrush had turned pink, we'd taken more of a clobbering than today's generation will take in their lives.

13   The women of our generation didn't get off any easier than the men. A

girl whose boy friend was out of work and who had just about given up ever getting married was told that even if she did get married she wouldn't look as young as she should because she had dishpan hands.

"I thought you said she was just a bride," a neighbor said, and Lux came back cattily with, "So she is, it's dishpan hands that make her seem much older." 14

She was told that she would become "A flirt with an aching heart," "Often a bridesmaid but never a bride," and would be "branded fickle!" because she was never twice with the same man, when the bitter truth was that *she* didn't use Listerine or Lifebuoy. 15

She was asked by the publishers of *The Book of Etiquette,* "Are you conscious of your crudities?" At a time when she was conserving her $8-a-week salary by eating hot dogs in Woolworth's basement, she was thrown a curve with, "Would you use your fork for a fruit salad or a spoon? Would you take an olive with a fork?" She was told that if she ever did get invited out to dinner, waiters would sneer at her. 16

Fleischmann's Yeast told her the reason no employer wanted her was because she had pimples, and the makers of Kelpamalt put the hex on her love affair by saying, "If *your* romance is spoiled by poor health and skinny, scrawny hollows, this may be due to malnourishment." 17

But all in all, advertisers dreamed up their worst situations for men. They never stopped thinking up things that would happen to us. 18

"If you were walking with your mother, sister, or best girl," we read in an ad for a correspondence course in self-defense, just before getting set to spend an evening at our jigsaw puzzles, "and someone passed a slighting remark or used improper language, wouldn't you be ashamed if you couldn't take her part?" 19

There was a picture of what was presumably us, in the hideous situation of having surprised a 240-pound bully by knocking him off the sidewalk and waiting for him to get up. We spread out our jigsaws, knowing that we not only probably had B.O. but that we had no guts. 20

"Bunk!" said Charles Atlas, sensing our timid conviction that it would take too long to become strong. He leaned forward, muscles straining over his leopardskin loincloth. "Just seven days, that's all I need to prove I can make you a new man. Don't get the idea that it takes a lot of time and hard work for you to get smashing strength and powerful muscles. Don't think you need dumbbells, springs or any other contraption. Both those ideas are all *BUNK!*" 21

But he didn't fool us. Anyway, we were too worried about losing our jobs to worry about having bulging muscles. We were told that we could lose our jobs because of having dandruff, pimples, because we didn't take Ex-Lax or shave close enough. Probably no generation ever got fired so often and for so many reasons as we did in the gloomy imaginations of advertising men. 22

23   We were told that although things were tough, they would soon change — they'd get worse. "What will you be doing one year from today?" asked International Correspondence Schools. "Will you still be struggling along at the same old salary — or even less — worried about the future — standing still while other men go ahead?"

24   The Vita Seald Company implied that we were going to leave our children destitute, but they suggested a way out.

25   "This plan would not only keep you from being dependent on your children, it would give you something to pass on to them. You can appoint distributors during your spare time while your wife handles the potato chips, doughnuts, nutri-nuts, fried pies, and fruit fritters in her extra hours. All these items can be turned out easily with the semi-automatic Vita Seald combination cooker in your home."

26   Even the National Casket Company chuckled lugubriously and mimicked us with "No fuss or feathers for me!" and went on to say that they'd known lots of people like that — "Didn't want any show. Any casket would be good enough" — and hinted that we'd be sorry when we were dead.

27   But we could occasionally leer at the girl in the ads for Body by Fisher, and we enjoyed seeing pictures of the Dionne quintuplets in the Palmolive soap ads. We even felt mildly sophisticated reading about the man who had no sox appeal because he didn't wear Paris garters.

28   It was interesting to learn from Artie McGovern that when a doctor started catching cold, getting fat or feeling sluggish, he followed the simple method of lying on his back with a book on his belly. And it was even faintly exciting to read the ads for the Institute of Applied Science, which suggested a way to spend the evenings when we couldn't afford two bits for a movie. "Become a fingerprint operator in your spare time!" or the ads like those for the National Radio Institute, in which Alfred Parkes of 1203 Wellington Street, Ottawa, wrote: "I was working in a grocery but now make $35 to $50 per week! Three times what I earned before!"

29   A few ads were beginning to sound like today's TV commercials. Hockey stars like Eddie Shore and Charlie Conacher looked up from the ice and said, "I top off my morning shave with a refreshing dash of Aqua Velva!" and there was already a forerunner of the singing commercial, although it appeared in print.

30   "I do believe you've lost your grouch, why Bill what's changed you so?"

31   "I've found that Ingram's shaving cream is just as cool as ever.

32   "It tames my beard, it tones my skin, should I be grouchy? No!

33   " *THEM DAYS IS GONE FOREVER.*"

34   General Motors, explaining why they put "knees" in the McLaughlin-Buick, said with a straight face that thousands of customers had urged

them to "abolish jar and bump and bounce from tomorrow's motor ride!"

And Miriam Hopkins said, without batting an eye, "I enjoy brushing my teeth with Calox." 35

But for the most part, advertisers tried to scare us to death, which was probably one reason why we were soon buying self-help books like Walter B. Pitkin's on how to relax, and Dale Carnegie's *How to Win Friends and Influence People.* 36

They were full of bluff, muscular advice, and a cash-and-carry suburban philosophy on a level with Bruce Barton's contention that the Lord Jesus was an advertising man; but they had the right idea for the times. 37

We needed help. We still do. And I think it's largely because of those ads we read twenty-five, thirty years ago. 38

STRUCTURE:
1. Where does Allen first state his main point?
2. Although the main argument of this essay is based on cause and effect, another method of development takes up much of the space in illustrating that main argument. What method is it and what proportion of the essay would you estimate is given to it?
3. Allen divides his examples into four basic sections: paragraphs 3-12, 13-17, 18-26 and 27-35. How does each of these sections differ from the others?
4. If you had to remove one of these four sections while causing the least damage to the essay, which section would you choose and why?

STYLE:
1. How FORMAL or INFORMAL is the language of the ads that Allen quotes? Give a few examples to illustrate your answer.
2. How FORMAL or INFORMAL is the language of Allen himself in this essay? Give a few examples to illustrate your answer.
3. What percentage of this selection would you estimate consists of quotations? Is it possible to include too many quotations in an essay?
4. Why does Allen not footnote his quotations?
5. When did you first realize that this is a humorous essay?
6. Perhaps the main source of humour is the IRONY we see in Allen's use of quotations. When Kruschen Salts says, "No poison from congested waste matter seeping through *his* intestinal walls!" (par. 6), we are impressed not so much with the efficiency of Grandpa's bowels as with the innocence of the ad writer who *thought* we would be impressed.

Find other examples here of 1930s ads that have an ironic effect upon today's readers.

IDEAS:

1. Have the themes of advertising changed since the 1930s? Do we still hear about "smelling, being ignorant, having dandruff, bad breath, stopped-up bowels, flabby gums, attacks of bile and bad nerves; of having bullies knock us off the sidewalk, of picking up the wrong fork, getting fired, losing our girl friends, and mispronouncing brassiere" (par. 3)?

2. Can you think of new themes in advertising that do not appear in Allen's account of the 1930s?

3. In what ways do you think television has changed advertising?

4. How much sexism do you find in these ads from the 1930s? Is there more or less than in today's ads? Find five or ten sexist ads in a current magazine or newspaper and bring them to class for discussion.

5. Discuss the implications of Allen's opening paragraph, which states that "kids today think they can't trust the older generation."

6. Write a contemporary version of Allen's essay, stating the effects you think advertising has had on your own generation and quoting ads or commercials that illustrate your point of view.

(NOTE: See also the Topics for Writing at the end of this chapter.)

Maryon Kantaroff

Breaking Out of the Female Mould

Maryon Kantaroff, born in Toronto in 1933 to a family from Bulgaria, is a sculptor and feminist. In 1957 she graduated from the University of Toronto in archaeology and art, and for a short time was assistant curator of the Art Gallery of Ontario. In 1959 she began further art studies in London, England, and in the following years exhibited her sculpture widely in Europe. Returning to Toronto in 1969, she established her own studio and foundry, and has made her living from gallery sales and commissions of her sculpture. Kantaroff has also been a leading Canadian feminist, delivering fiery speeches as well as expressing feminism through her art. Our selection "Breaking Out of the Female Mould," which appeared in Gwen Matheson's collection of feminist essays Women in The Canadian Mosaic *(1976), explains how Kantaroff combined the two great interests of her life.*

The usual reaction when people learn I am a sculptor is interesting and predictable: they are surprised, impressed and often awed. These reactions arise from certain misconceptions. 1

The first, I think, is the idea that "art" is a man's domain. If a woman does something men have always done, she is considered extraordinary, somehow more than just a mere woman. And this misconception no doubt originates in the relationship between art and religion. God, the prime creator, is, after all, regarded as male. When Western religion began to disintegrate, art inherited a number of its functions, mainly the power to consecrate. An art object has become something to be worshipped, something pregnant with eternal power and meaning. Such an object made by a woman must be unseemly, if not downright blasphemous. This may explain why women's reactions to me convey a certain sense of alienation. In some way I am regarded as a superior being, somehow akin to a male. The same, I might add, is true of men's reactions, except that their discomfort is experienced as threatening rather than alienating. In a very real sense I am no longer a woman in their eyes. Thus the female sculptor is de-sexed by her activity — a real woman wouldn't be doing a man's job. It is absolutely amazing how many people assume that I am a lesbian because I am a sculptor. This is not so much because they suspect that I may love women, but rather that they suspect I must be like a man. 2

Before I became a feminist all this disturbed and mystified me. I sensed this distance from other women while knowing that I wasn't being accepted by men in my field. Our society goes to great lengths to keep a woman in the female mould; if she steps out of it for whatever reason she is subjected to suspicion, alienation and sometimes total social rejection. 3

143

4   The activity of "making art" is itself generally viewed with suspicion, whether engaged in by a man or a woman. It is seen as a threat to established societal norms and values. The artist's job is to observe — to question, probe, re-evaluate — in some ways, the artist is the conscience of society. In this sense, creative activity is allied to the traditional female role: that of the sensitive guardian or nurturer of society. In order to escape the stigma of "femaleness" attached to creative sensitivity, the male artist has become increasingly virile in his work, assuming the pose of judge or authority — the patriarchal arbiter of taste. The female artist is placed in several binds. She is exiled from society not only in her role as artist, but in her role as woman artist. Further, she is exiled from artistic society which is dominated by male aesthetics and male power. And I haven't yet touched on the woman artist's personal relationships with men, in which she is expected to conform to the requirements of her feminine "obligations" (as housewife, mother, cook, hostess, sex partner). When all of this is taken into account, one can see why women artists in Canada are in a dilemma. Their social role, to which they have been conditioned, is always at odds with their creative activity, both being extremely demanding, and forcing these women into a perpetual state either of exhaustion or guilt, or both.

5   Women in Canada — as in other countries — grow up under the influence of a predominantly male culture. All our values, including those of church, state, school and media, derive from male institutions. This male culture is overlaid on our deepest experiences as women. Without fully realizing it, women artists become involved in male aesthetics — the basis of contemporary art modes — which are at odds with their own female experience. When women default in the art world, they blame their lack of talent or application. They judge themselves, finally, by the standards of what is essentially an alien culture — a culture from which they are profoundly excluded by definition of their sex. There have always been a number of women artists who have been able to achieve some success in this male world, but they have done it by accepting and imitating male aesthetics. Actually, a more accurate word would be politics, rather than aesthetics, for the quality I am referring to in male art is that of power.

6   I am speaking from experience, for I produced male sculpture myself for a number of years. Of course I didn't realize what I was doing until some time after my feminist involvement. My work was generally characterized by strong assertive forms and rigid lines of tension. Some of my female experience did enter into my earlier work, but I fought against it. "Soft" or "warm" shapes seemed weak and flabby to me and I used these terms pejoratively, my tastes well-honed by and respectful of masculine values. Anything that had a symbolic association with the female I automatically experienced as inferior and therefore rejected. I

was using male standards against myself, reflecting and reinforcing them in an attack on female standards. I shudder when I think of it now.

The bizarre aspect of all this mimicry of masculinity was that none of it reflected in my personal life. I was just as intensely "feminine" in my everyday behaviour as I was anti-feminine in my sculpture. Male artists, like female artists, are forced to hustle and compete and generally make their presence known. However, my femininity made this most necessary procedure almost impossible for me. This kind of aggressive self- promotion is second-nature to most male artists, as it is a direct application of learned sex role patterns. The female artist, on the other hand, finds that aggressive and assertive behaviour is in direct contradiction to her conditioning and is next to impossible to assume.

Any individual is to a large extent the product of his or her environment and the social values reflected in it. A woman artist cannot possibly escape the deep-rooted prejudices with which she has been inculcated since birth. What have we been surrounded by during our formative years? Women (the grown-up versions of us) involved in the traditional female world — the kitchen, the nursery, the whole domestic life of the unpaid but willing housewife. Or, we have seen them working in the fields, scrubbing floors for other people, or in boring, dead-end jobs undertaken as alternatives. They have been teachers to male principals, secretaries to male executives, nurses to male doctors — or just generally extensions of some male: wife, hostess or someone's date. Whoever heard of great women doctors or politicians or scientists — least of all artists? Women give birth to great artists, they serve great artists, they slave for great artists — but they seldom *are* great artists! How would a young girl conceive of the idea that she could someday become a great artist? There are just no models to aspire to.

In a very real sense, women are outsiders in society, their existence is viewed as peripheral. They have no direct influence on events. The indoctrination of femininity has been a useful tool in keeping us politically passive.

An obvious analogy can be made with native people in Canada. They, too, have been relegated to the periphery by a kind of "femininity". They can be easily distinguished from white people by their physical characteristics and by their own cultural patterns of behaviour. These differences become the rationale for maintaining power in the hands of the white man. Land was taken away from native people in exchange for the dubious security of being cared for on reserves by big white daddy. Native people were effectively incarcerated in a kind of purdah. When women marry they give up their rights and freedoms for the same kind of "security". Just as the native people have lost their dignity and culture, so we lose ours.

Where are the great native artists and achievers? The answer will be the same as it is for women. What they do achieve, is achieved on their own cultural terms and cannot be compared to the products of an alien culture. Native people have come from a hunting culture and cannot be judged by a technological one which excludes them. Similarly, women have come from a domestic culture and are expected to continue in it and define themselves by it. The artistic achievements of both women and natives are relegated to the inferior status of craft. We each have our "cultural slot" and we will be happily tolerated only as long as we stay in it. The real art world is consecrated ground for the superiors — men — and white men at that.

12   If approached, I suspect that the vast majority of Canadian women artists would deny that they were discriminated against, in fact if married would consider themselves lucky to have the financial support of their husbands. The problems of sex-role playing are so subtle that it is often very difficult to pin-point them for others. The male artist, no matter how suspect he may be in the eyes of society in general, has the full support of his male colleagues, the full backing of the powers that be in the art world and most important personally, perhaps, the full support and backing of his wife and family. Everything in the family is geared to his activity. The woman artist, on the other hand, often has none of these areas of support open to her. Certainly she is excluded from rapport with other artists (unless she is personally attached to a male artist) and she is most definitely seen as an anomaly in the art world generally. But most damaging, perhaps, is the lack of support she is likely to find in her personal life. However much her husband may value her artistic activity, he will still be considered the prime breadwinner, while her primary function will be to support him domestically and emotionally. For this reason, many Canadian women artists are invisible in the art world. They are busy creating, all right, but they are squeezing in their art between thousands of fracturing domestic chores. As they can fall back on the financial support of their husbands they rarely exhibit much incentive in trying to sell their work.

13   I don't see extremely talented women artists promoting and competing in the art marketplace. I do see many mediocre male artists doing just that. Women artists seem to share the same deep sense of inadequacy experienced by most women in our society — a society that views men as primary. The married woman artist's basic reality is one of available time and energy. Our society almost makes marriage mandatory for women and marriage almost makes professional creative production impossible. I don't think it is accidental that the only well-known Canadian women artists were unmarried. The painter Emily Carr lived a life more akin to a gypsy's than to that of a typical Canadian woman. And as for the two sculptors Florence Wylie and Frances Loring, there is no doubt they too

completely rejected the traditional feminine sex role. Our society encourages women to gain their status and sense of identity from the men they live with, not necessarily from their own chances of achievement. To live without a man is to choose to be alienated from society. No male artist is expected to forgo a family because he wants to create; he can in fact expect to be serviced by women whether in or out of marriage. The same is obviously not true of women.

The entire situation regarding women in art is problematic when one considers the close association made between creativity and femininity. Certainly it is part of the female role to encourage sensitivity which is a necessary part of creativity. Our contemporary mystique says that women are creative because they bear children — then goes on to say that for this very reason women have no need to create art. This is a politically useful confusion of biological with intellectual function. There is considerable evidence now emerging to suggest that women in ancient cultures played an extremely active role in the arts, but information about their early contributions has not come down to us in the history books written by men. Consequently, it is widely thought and taught today that women as a group were never of much significance in the cultural activities of past societies. People ask, ''Why were there no great women artists?'' with the happy assumption that there were none.

The fact is that there were many great women artists — but they were never publicized, they were little known in their own day and have remained virtually unknown today. The paleolithic cave paintings until recently were attributed to men and were recognized as great art. Now that modern scholarship can attribute them to women artists, it will be interesting to see if they will still be regarded as ''great''.* One of the acknowledged greatest masterpieces of the Middle Ages, the Bayeux tapestry, was designed and executed by women — but the fact that the artists were nuns was not broadcast. In the thirteenth century Sabina von Steinbach carved the most important sculptures, ''The Church'' and ''The Synagogue'', on Strasbourg Cathedral, thus surpassing work of her father. But no one bothered to mention it. The museums of the world are filled with Marietta Tintoretto's paintings happily attributed to her father Jacopo. Judith Leyster's work in the seventeenth century was attributed to Frans Hals. Constance Marie Charpentier's work in the 1800s was credited to the great neoclassic master, J.L. David. If these women's work was good enough to be attributed to the great male masters, obviously it deserves the term ''great''. But who knew any of this before it was unearthed by feminists? I spent four years at a reputable Canadian university studying art history, and the first woman I came across in my

*See *Art and Sexual Politics*, edited by Thomas B. Hess and Elizabeth C. Baker (Toronto: Macmillan, 1973).

studies lived in the late nineteenth century. I call that male-biased education.

16   In examining our views of women and art, it is most important to look at the two most powerful past influences on Western culture today. The first influence was, of course, the classical culture of ancient Greece. The Greeks were openly homosexual and excluded women in all important areas. They used women for procreation or for erotic satisfaction, but were culturally homosexual in that love was a concept reserved for men. Thus the highest form of love was seen as that between men, whether consummated sexually or not. Aristotle wrote: ''The female is a female by virtue of a certain lack of qualities. We should regard the female as afflicted with a natural defectiveness.'' From what we can see in Greek political structures and in their literature, it would appear that Aristotle was not alone in his contempt for women.

17   The second major influence on Western culture was the Christian church. It viewed woman as the root of all evil, accepted and embellished Greek thought on women, and formed the values that are the basis of most of our social and moral attitudes today. In its medieval period, the church burned as witches the most creative women of that time — women numbering into the millions. Both ancient Greece and the Christian church thus clearly expressed male supremacist attitudes to the point of open inhumanity towards women. Discussing women's lack of achievement during their reigns in history is a meaningless exercise, rather like discussing the reasons why no Jews became popes. The concepts are mutually exclusive.

18   Modern Western culture, therefore, has inherited an extreme anti-female bias. It is basically homosexual in the sense that real value is vested in the male. Hence the occurrence of strong male bonding in our society — clubs, sports, business, politics. If a man in our society is to love a woman, he must first elevate her in his imagination, make her an exception to the inferiority of all other women. This need is the basis of the false and romantic illusions perpetuated in our society with regard to love. Romanticizing the woman makes her worthy of the man's love or respect. This attributed value makes her a suitable subject for the artist; the woman (subject) is romanticized while real value remains vested with the male (artist). It is interesting to note that even women artists in the past have romanticized their female subjects (e.g., Constance-Marie Charpentier's portrait of Charlotte du Val d'Ognes).

19   I remember that during my own postgraduate studies, the majority of our models were women. All my professors of sculpture were men, and they arranged for the models. At the time, this didn't seem odd. Even while I was studying sculpture I suspected darkly that there was something wrong with me or I wouldn't be so involved in an activity in which no other woman I knew of was or had been involved. I was further en-

couraged in this prejudice by my professors. When I complained to one of them that he never talked seriously about art with the women students, he answered that as none of us would ever become professionals there wasn't much point in bothering. Interestingly, every one of my female contemporaries did go on to become professional sculptors — with the exception of one, the only one who was married. As for myself, I was only able to take my work seriously once I had made the political connections in regard to my sex. Society has always allowed women a creative outlet — but only to the degree of dilletante. It is positively unwomanly to be professional, even in our own so-called modern times.

North American culture is predominantly male; all power structures   20 are male and the world of ideas is considered the male prerogative — as opposed to feelings, which are the female prerogative. A female who tunes into the culture at any level must take on male value systems. For example, the university educated woman becomes an intellectual extension of the male. She has studied male writers, male philosophers, male historians, male scientific research, male design, male everything. And if she becomes part of this culture and adds to it, she will be making primarily a male contribution to male culture. A rather frightening example of this is the woman Freudian analyst. These women accept the distortions about their own sexuality and continue to conform to male authority in an area which should rightly be their domain. Their "thinking" on the subject is in direct contradiction to their feeling or experience, which must, in fact, be totally negated. By cutting off experience, the female can become totally male-identified in her "thinking". The same applies to aesthetic values. Male aesthetics have come directly out of the experiences and perceptions of male artists, just as Freud's "thinking" was an extension of his experiences as a man, and not as an asexual observer. When a female artist therefore works out of male aesthetics, she is denying the reality of her perceptions as a woman/person and is cutting herself off from her deepest and most meaningful creative sources.

I would like to trace through my own experiences in this connection.   21 From my earliest days as a postgraduate sculpture student I was preoccupied with two subject areas. The first dealt with integrating male and female symbols into one aesthetic concept — that is, going beyond the two distinct forms into the whole. The other was a preoccupation with flight. Neither of these recurring themes was conscious, even though I have referred to them as preoccupations. These themes persisted in emerging during composition classes, even though I was consciously trying to work in totally abstracted forms. The first subject area reflected my deep sense of alienation from the male, and the sculpture was an emotional and symbolic attempt to make the two come together, to find a solution to the dilemma. The flight theme was, I believe, a straightforward way of expressing both escape from oppression and a search for freedom. Both themes were coming directly out of my experience as a woman in society. I did not value either and I constantly strove against their emergence in my work.

22   Even though I was not successful in completely repressing the subject matter, I was far more successful in my stylistic treatment of it, which helped to camouflage the ideas. From the moment I left art college and began having exhibitions, I made concerted efforts to move closer and closer to a male aesthetic. My style became progressively more strident, sharp, angular — in short, "stronger". I even remember making a decision to get rid of all textured surfaces because I thought they were too seductive and sensual. I wanted hard, glossy, cold surfaces with rigidly defined forms. I wanted what I thought was intellectual clarity, without feeling (which I identified as confusion).

23   The change began with my return to Canada after almost ten years of living and working in Europe. Culture shock probably started the process, for I was suddenly able to see the workings of Canadian society somewhat as a "foreigner" and therefore more objectively. In a few weeks I realized the cultural distortion I was confronted with on my return came from a sexist base. I became deeply involved in the feminist movement and through my experiences was able to come to an understanding and acceptance of my womanhood. Naturally this meant a total re-evaluation of the male culture of which I was a product, and the eventual rejection of it and all its implications in my life.

24   During this time my changing attitudes toward myself were of course directly reflected in my work. Interestingly, though, it was more than a year before I recognized that my work was being affected by my new political awareness. My work was beginning to lose its rigidity and was becoming more fluid. The forms were less forcefully defined. Every shape began to undulate, as if looking for its own natural rhythms. My relief constructions, which at one time had been contained within a picture-like frame, began breaking free of confining edges; they became totally free-flowing. Another vast change was in my use of colour. Just as I had previously used low-keyed, "sophisticated" colour schemes, now the work became bright, optimistic, no longer held back or frightened of feelings. The three-dimensional sculpture often began to relate to my earliest lovers groups, but the male and female forms were no longer read specifically. The hard lines of definition between the male and female were gone. They now ebbed and flowed in and out of each other, reflecting, loving, caressing, interchanging, free of confinement and restriction.

25   Possibly most important was the emergence of the egg. The oval form had always been present, almost as if hanging around the periphery of my consciousness. Now it was fully apparent. It emerged as a symbol of

the beginnings of life, the essence of life, the seat of all potential, awareness, and then would change into the head — the centre of all consciousness. It became a belly, pregnant with life — or with an idea. All allusions to phallic shapes which were so evident in my earlier work (the thrusting forms) have increasingly been replaced by the celebration of the egg. The unconscious is really most marvelous. Waiting there ready to be tapped is all knowledge, all feeling, all understanding. The artist has only to respect it and let it out.

For a woman artist that means respecting herself and her own experiences. As long as she allows the male aesthetic to overpower her own, she effectively chokes off the flow of her own creative wealth. When we consider what is known today about social expectations, subtle indoctrination and role guilts, this is a very tall order for any woman living in this world. I must admit, however, to a deep optimism where women and the arts are concerned. This could be due to desperate wishing, or the number of times I have encountered women who no longer view the women's movement as a terrifying threat. Somewhere, somehow, we're beginning to contact each other — or rather, more women are listening to what other women are saying. Not much is happening yet, I can't pretend to that. But we are *beginning*. 26

STRUCTURE:
Unlike Gregory Clark's essay "'The Cat,'' in which one clear-cut chain of events leads to one main effect, Kantaroff's essay contains a complex web of cause and effect relationships. The questions that follow are an attempt to identify the most important strands of that web.

1. How are modern women affected by the culture of classical Greece?
2. How has Western religion hindered female artists?
3. In Kantaroff's view, how have the art schools suppressed female artists?
4. How does marriage affect female artists?
5. Why do male artists promote themselves more effectively than female artists?
6. Why are there few models of female achievement in the art world?
7. Paragraphs 21-25 contain a remarkable contrast, the changing of Kantaroff's art from "male" to "female." What *caused* that change?

STYLE:
1. How appropriate to this essay is the image in its title, "Breaking Out of the Female Mould"?

2. Discuss the implications of the word "pregnant" in this statement from paragraph 2: "An art object has become something to be worshipped, something pregnant with eternal power and meaning. Such an object made by a woman must be unseemly, if not downright blasphemous."
3. What effect is achieved in the final sentence of the essay?

IDEAS:

1. Kantaroff states in paragraph 18 that modern Western culture "is basically homosexual in the sense that real value is vested in the male." Do you agree? If this is an accurate judgment, then why does our society persecute those who are literally homosexual?
2. Discuss Kantaroff's description of romantic love (par. 18), in which the male idealizes a woman in order to raise her above the inferiority of her sex and make her worthy of his attentions. Have you experienced this process, either as a male or a female? Does the original idea of "inferiority" later reappear in new forms?
3. It is a fact of college and university life that in some courses — such as mechanical engineering — nearly 100% of the students are men, while in others — such as nursing — nearly 100% are women. Discuss the course of study that you have chosen: Does one sex predominate? If so, why? Are there practical reasons why the other sex cannot succeed in your field? Or are there artificial social barriers to success by the other sex?
4. Kantaroff writes, "The activity of 'making art' is itself generally viewed with suspicion, whether engaged in by a man or a woman" (par. 4). What do your family and friends think of artists? Do we as a society STEREOTYPE them? If so, in what ways does that stereotype depict artists as "a threat to established societal norms and values"? In what ways do you think an artist can be dangerous to our society? In what ways do you think an artist can improve our society?
5. Kantaroff has given a number of causes for the imprisonment of women in a "mould." In your own essay, discuss the *causes* and also the *effects* of your own conformity or nonconformity to the norms that society has set for your sex.

(NOTE: See also the Topics for Writing at the end of this chapter.)

Topics for Writing

Chapter 4: Cause and Effect

(Note also the topics for writing that appear after each selection in this chapter.)

Analyze the cause(s) and/or effect(s) of one of the following:

1. The use of credit cards
2. Divorce
3. Alcoholism
4. Gambling
5. Smoking
6. Child abuse
7. Vandalism
8. Terrorism
9. Nuclear war
10. Religious conversion
11. Chemical additives in food
12. Obesity
13. Vegetarianism
14. The energy shortage
15. Unemployment
16. Lotteries
17. The popularity of video games
18. The use of robots
19. The use of nuclear power plants
20. The popularity of bicycles or motorcycles
21. Immigration
22. High-rise development
23. Erosion
24. Arson
25. Acid rain

Ontario Ministry of Industry and Tourism.

"Well, the things you can see just standing for ten minutes at a big-city intersec-tion. Lynda can't get over it. But, of course, she comes from a town where the main recreation is drinking."

Philip Marchand, "Learning to Love the Big City"

It's just the opposite of . . . .

COMPARISON
AND CONTRAST

One of the most dramatic ways to make an argument is to compare and contrast. The term "comparison" is often used to mean the showing of both similarities and differences, but in its narrower sense refers only to the showing of similarities. A "contrast" shows differences. Of the two, contrast is the more dramatic and the more frequently used in essays.

You have experienced contrast to the fullest if you have ever experienced culture shock. As you arrive in a new country, the look of the buildings and streets, the smells in the air, the sounds, the language and customs all seem strange — because you are contrasting them to what you just left. And if you stay a long time, the same thing happens in reverse when you come back: home seems strange because you are contrasting it to the place where you've just been. The cars may seem too big, the food too bland, the pace of life too fast. Travel is one of the great educational experiences: through contrast, the one culture puts the other in perspective.

In writing an essay, you can show similarities only, or show both similarities and differences, or show differences only. Do whatever best fits your subject and your message. But whichever way you do it, choose subjects of the same general type: two countries, two sports, two poems or two solutions to the energy crisis. Like Philip Marchand in "Learning to Love the Big City," you might contrast two centres of population — a town and a city — and in doing so make a logical point. But if you write about a city and an ant hill, no matter how much fun you have or what insights you get across, you will prove nothing — because people are not insects. Your argument will be an *analogy,* a more imaginative but less logical kind of argument which we will study in the next chapter.

Once you have chosen your two subjects of the same general type, you face another choice: how to arrange them. There are two basic ways:

Divide the essay into halves, devoting the first half to the town and the second to the city. This system is natural in a very short essay, because your reader remembers everything from the first half while reading the second half. It is also natural when for some reason the items seem most clearly discussed as a whole rather than in parts.

Divide the subjects into separate points. First contrast employment in both town and city, then recreation in both town and city, then social life in both town and city, and so on. This system is most natural in long essays, for in putting related material together it helps the reader to grasp comparisons or contrasts without the strain of remembering every detail from ten pages back.

Marchand organizes mainly by halves, even though his essay is long. The feeling for life in both town and city develops best in long sections that have time to build their effects; if the contrasting feelings appeared in short alternating sections, they would merely cancel each other out. Like Marchand, do whatever works — that is, whatever fits your subject and your message.

Doris Anderson

The 51-Per-Cent Minority

Doris Anderson is one of Canada's most effective advocates of women's rights. She was born in Calgary in 1925. After earning her B.A. at the University of Alberta in 1945 she wrote radio scripts, worked in advertising, then in 1951 joined the staff of Chatelaine. *As editor-in-chief from 1958 to 1977, Anderson added to the magazine's family emphasis an advocacy of higher social and economic status for women. She served as president of the Canadian Advisory Council on the Status of Women. Her sudden resignation from the Council in 1981, in protest against the government's interference and its reluctance to guarantee equality of men and women in the Constitution, sparked a campaign by women that did achieve a constitutional guarantee of their rights. In 1982 she was named president of the National Action Committee on the Status of Women, an umbrella group that represents over a million women in 190 organizations. Anderson has published novels,* Two Women *in 1978 and* Rough Layout *in 1981, in addition to her many editorials and articles. Our selection, "The 51-Per-Cent Minority," appeared in 1980 in* Maclean's. *Anderson has revised it slightly for this book.*

In any Canadian election the public will probably be hammered numb with talk of the economy, energy and other current issues. But there will always be some far more startling topics that no one will talk about at all.   1

No one is going to say to all new Canadians: "Look, we're going through some tough times. Three out of four of you had better face the fact that you're always going to be poor. At 65 more than likely you'll be living below the poverty level."   2

And no one is going to tell Quebeckers: "You will have to get along on less money than the rest of the country. For every $1 the rest of us earn, you, because you live in Quebec, will earn 61 cents."   3

I doubt very much that any policitical party is going to level with the Atlantic provinces and say: "We don't consider people living there serious prime workers. Forget about any special measures to make jobs for you. In fact in future federal-provincial talks we're not even going to discuss your particular employment problems."   4

And no politician is going to tell all the left-handed people in the country: "Look, we know it looks like discrimination, but we have to save some money somewhere. So, although you will go on paying unemployment insurance at the same rates as everyone else, if you get laid off your job, you'll only collect 50 per cent of your salary, whereas everyone else will collect 66 per cent."   5

And no one is going to say to Canadian doctors: "We know you perform one of the most important jobs any citizen can perform, but from now on you're going to have to get along without any support systems.   6

All hospital equipment and help will be drastically reduced. We believe a good doctor should instinctively know what to do — or you're in the wrong job. If you're really dedicated you'll get along.''

7 As for blacks: "Because of the color of your skin, you're going to be paid less than the white person next to you who is doing exactly the same job. It's tough but that's the way it is.''

8 As for Catholics: "You're just going to have to understand that you will be beaten up by people with other religious beliefs quite regularly. Even if your assailant threatens to kill you, you can't do anything about it. After all, we all need some escape valves, don't we?''

9 Does all of the above sound like some nihilistic nightmare where Orwellian forces have taken over? Well, it's not. It's all happening right now, in Canada.

10 It's not happening to new Canadians, Quebeckers, residents of the Atlantic provinces, left-handed people, doctors, blacks or Indians. If it were, there would be riots in the streets. Civil libertarians would be howling for justice. But all of these discriminatory practices are being inflicted on women today in Canada as a matter of course.

11 Most women work at two jobs — one inside the home and one outside. Yet three out of four women who become widowed or divorced or have never married live out their old age in poverty. And the situation is going to get worse.

12 Women workers earn, on an average, only 61 cents for every $1 a man gets — even though on an average, women are better educated than men.

13 And when governments start talking about basing unemployment insurance on family income or introducing the two-tier system of family income, they mean women will pay the same rates as other Canadians but if they lose their jobs, they will collect less, or may not collect at all.

14 What politician could possibly tell doctors to train each other and get along without all their high technology and trained help? Yet a more important job than saving lives is surely creating lives. But mothers get no training, no help in the way of more than a token family allowance, inadequate day-care centres, and almost nonexistent after-school programs.

15 No politician would dream of telling blacks they must automatically earn less than other people. But women sales clerks, waitresses and hospital orderlies almost always earn less than males doing the same jobs. It would be called discrimination if a member of a religious group was beaten up, and the assailant would be jailed. But hundreds of wives get beaten by their husbands week in and week out, year after year. Some die, yet society acts as though it isn't happening at all.

16 Women make up 51 per cent of the population of this country. Think of the kind of clout they could have if they used it at the polls. But to listen to the political parties, the woman voter just doesn't exist. When pol-

iticians talk to fishing folk they talk about improved processing plants and new docks. When they talk to wheat farmers they talk of better transportation and higher price supports. When they talk to people in the Atlantic provinces they talk about new federal money for buildings and more incentives for secondary industry. When they talk to ethnic groups they talk about better language training courses. But when they think of women — if they do at all — they assume women will vote exactly as their husbands — so why waste time offering them anything? It's mind-boggling to contemplate, though, how all those discriminatory practices would be swept aside if, instead of women, we were Italian, or black, or lived in Quebec or the Atlantic provinces.

STRUCTURE:
1. Is this essay mainly a comparison or a contrast?
2. Is the essay organized point by point or by halves?
3. Point out the passage of transition between Anderson's description of minorities and her description of women.
4. In this essay about women, why does Anderson never mention women until halfway through, at paragraph 10?
5. If you have read *1984 or Animal Farm,* by George Orwell, tell how the reference to Orwell in paragraph 9 helps to explain Anderson's point.
6. Why does the closing bring in a series of new examples? And why are these examples so short?

STYLE:
1. How important is the title of an essay? What should it do? How effective is this one, and why?
2. Anderson's essay appeared in *Maclean's,* a magazine for the general reader. Name all the ways you can think of in which her essay seems designed for that person.

IDEAS:
1. Explain the IRONY of Anderson's claim: in what sense are women, 51 per cent of the population, a "minority" in Canada?
2. Anderson describes numerous groups as not being exploited in the ways that women are. Has she missed other groups that you know to be exploited in Canada? If so, name them.
3. Anderson states in paragraph 11, "Most women work at two jobs — one inside the home and one outside." Suppose that at some time you and your spouse both have full-time jobs. If you are a woman, how much of the housework will you expect your husband to do? If you

are a man, how much of the housework will you expect your wife to do? Whatever your answer, give reasons to support it.

4. Anderson writes in paragraph 12, "Women workers earn, on an average, only 61 cents for every $1 a man gets — even though on an average, women are better educated than men." Whether you are male or female, have you personally experienced this difference in wage levels? If so, give an example. How did you feel about it? How do some employers manage to pay men more than women? If you believe the practice is wrong, how could it be fought?

5. In paragraph 16, Anderson writes, "Women make up 51 per cent of the population of this country. Think of the kind of clout they could have if they used it at the polls." Do you agree that women have not yet used their voting power to best advantage? If so, why haven't they? And how could they begin to?

6. In "Canadians: What Do They Want?" Margaret Atwood points out that war and rape are ". . . two activities not widely engaged in by women . . . ." (par. 1). Do you think our world would be different if it were run by women? If so, why and in what ways? If not, why not?

7. If you have read "Breaking Out of the Female Mould," compare discrimination against women as reported by Maryon Kantaroff and as reported by Anderson.

8. Write an essay in which you contrast the way society trains girls to be women to the way society trains boys to be men.

9. Write an essay that compares either men or women to one of these:

servants	prison guards
masters	children
slaves	employers
prison inmates	employees

(NOTE: See also the Topics for Writing at the end of this chapter.)

Catherine Parr Traill

Remarks of Security of Person and Property in Canada

Catherine Parr Traill (1802-1899) belonged to a family of writers, the best-known of whom were her sisters Agnes Strickland (who wrote Lives of the Queens of England*) and Susanna Moodie (who wrote* Roughing It in the Bush*), and her brother Samuel Strickland (who wrote* Twenty-Seven Years in Canada West*). Traill was born in London, England. In 1832 she came with her husband to Upper Canada, where they settled in Douro Township. Despite the labours of pioneer life, Traill found time to express her optimistic spirit and her enjoyment of nature in the several books she wrote.* The Backwoods of Canada, *a collection of letters written to her mother, appeared in 1836. A book for children,* The Canadian Crusoes, *followed in 1852, and in 1854 appeared the work from which our selection comes,* The Female Emigrant's Guide. *An accomplished botanist, Traill wrote about the natural world she loved:* Rambles in the Canadian Forest *was published in 1859,* Canadian Wild Flowers *(illustrated by her niece, Agnes Fitz-Gibbon) in 1869, and* Studies of Plant Life in Canada *in 1885.*

There is one thing which can hardly fail to strike an emigrant from the Old Country, on his arrival in Canada. It is this, — The feeling of complete security which he enjoys, whether in his own dwelling or in his journeys abroad through the land. He sees no fear — he need see none. He is not in a land spoiled and robbed, where every man's hand is against his fellow — where envy and distrust beset him on every side. At first indeed he is surprised at the apparently stupid neglect of the proper means of security that he notices in the dwellings of all classes of people, especially in the lonely country places, where the want of security would really invite rapine and murder. "How is this," he says, "you use neither bolt, nor lock, nor bar. I see no shutter to your windows; nay, you sleep often with your doors open upon the latch, and in summer with open doors and windows. Surely this is fool-hardy and imprudent." "We need no such precautions," will his friend reply smiling; "here they are uncalled for. Our safety lies neither in bars nor bolts, but in our consciousness that we are among people whose necessities are not such as to urge them to violate the laws; neither are our riches such as to tempt the poor man to rob us, for they consist not in glittering jewels, nor silver, nor gold."

"But even food and clothes thus carelessly guarded are temptations."

"But where others possess these requisites as well as ourselves, they are not likely to steal them from us."

And what is the inference that the new comer draws from this statement?

5   That he is in a country where the inhabitants are essentially honest, because they are enabled, by the exertion of their own hands, to obtain in abundance the necessaries of life. Does it not also prove to him that it is the miseries arising from poverty that induce crime. — Men do not often violate the law of honesty, unless driven to do so by necessity. Place the poor Irish peasant in the way of earning his bread in Canada, where he sees his reward before him, in broad lands that he can win by honest toil, and where he can hold up his head and look beyond that grave of a poor man's hope — the parish work house — and see in the far-off vista a home of comfort which his own hands have reared, and can go down to his grave with the thought, that he has left a name and a blessing for his children after him: — men like this do not steal.

6   Robbery is not a crime of common occurrence in Canada. In large towns such acts will occasionally be committed, for it is there that poverty is to be found, but it is not common in country places. There you may sleep with your door unbarred for years. Your confidence is rarely, if ever, abused; your hospitality never violated.

7   When I lived in the backwoods, out of sight of any other habitation, the door has often been opened at midnight, a stranger has entered and lain down before the kitchen fire, and departed in the morning unquestioned. In the early state of the settlement in Douro, now twenty years ago, it was no uncommon occurrence for a party of Indians to enter the house, (they never knock at any man's door,) leave their hunting weapons outside, spread their blankets on the floor, and pass the night with or without leave, arise by the first dawn of day, gather their garments about them, resume their weapons, and silently and noiselessly depart. Sometimes a leash of wild ducks hung to the door-latch, or a haunch of venison left in the kitchen, would be found as a token of gratitude for the warmth and shelter afforded them.

8   Many strangers, both male and female, have found shelter under our roof, and never were we led to regret that we had not turned the house-less wanderer from our door.

9   It is delightful this consciousness of perfect security: your hand is against no man, and no man's hand is against you. We dwell in peace among our own people. What a contrast to my home, in England, where by sunset every door was secured with locks and heavy bars and bolts; every window carefully barricaded, and every room and corner in and around the dwelling duly searched, before we ventured to lie down to rest, lest our sleep should be broken in upon by the midnight thief. As night drew on, an atmosphere of doubt and dread seemed to encompass one. The approach of a stranger we beheld with suspicion; and however great his need, we dared not afford him the shelter of our roof, lest our so doing should open the door to robber or murderer. At first I could hardly understand why it happened that I never felt the same sensation of

fear in Canada as I had done in England. My mind seemed lightened of a heavy burden; and I, who had been so timid, grew brave and fearless amid the gloomy forests of Canada. Now, I know how to value this great blessing. Let the traveller seek shelter in the poorest shanty, among the lowest Irish settlers, and he need fear no evil, for never have I heard of the rites of hospitality being violated, or the country disgraced by such acts of cold-blooded atrocity as are recorded by the public papers in the Old Country.

Here we have no bush-rangers, no convicts to disturb the peace of the   10
inhabitants of the land, as in Australia. No savage hordes of Caffres to invade and carry off our cattle and stores of grain as at the Cape; but peace and industry are on every side. "The land is at rest and breaks forth into singing." Surely we ought to be a happy and a contented people, full of gratitude to that Almighty God who has given us this fair and fruitful land to dwell in.

STRUCTURE:
1. The long first paragraph states all the main ideas of this essay. What, then, does the rest of the essay do?
2. In this contrast between the dangers of life in England and the security of life in Canada, why is so much more of the essay devoted to Canada than to England?
3. The main contrast, between Canada and England, occurs in paragraphs 7-9. Why is this detailed contrast followed, in the last paragraph, by very brief contrasts to Australia and the Cape?

STYLE:
1. Catherine Parr Traill published *The Female Emigrant's Guide* in 1854. Does her style in this selection seem much different from the style of modern writers? Discuss the following:
   A. Word choice
   B. Sentences
   C. Paragraphs
   D. TONE
2. Discuss the meaning of "want" in the phrase "want of security" (middle of par. 1). Do you see other words in this essay that have changed in meaning since 1854?
3. In paragraph 7, Traill writes that Indians ". . . never knock at any man's door . . . ." In paragraph 9, she states that ". . . your hand is against no man, and no man's hand is against you." In fact, she mentions men so often that only once in the essay does she specifically re-

fer to women — yet she entitled her book *The Female Emigrant's Guide.* Discuss your feelings about our traditional male-centred grammar. Should the generic "he" be changed? If so, how?

4. Do you think our language has deteriorated or improved since the time of Catherine Parr Traill?

IDEAS:

1. Does modern Canada more closely resemble the new land which Traill describes in this essay, or the old land she left behind?

2. If you have moved to Canada from another country, as Traill did, have you experienced any of the benefits she describes?

3. Traill states that "... it is the miseries arising from poverty that induce crime" (par. 5). Do you agree? Or does crime have other causes as well?

4. Traill states, "... I, who had been so timid, grew brave and fearless amid the gloomy forests of Canada" (par. 9). The frontier has always been regarded as a place to make a new start, leaving one's problems in the past. In our increasingly crowded and industrialized world, do frontiers remain? If so, name some. What sacrifices would we have to make in order to live there?

5. Can a "frontier" exist in the city? Are there new ways of living in old places, by which people can free themselves from problems of the past?

6. Write an essay in which you compare and/or contrast life in two towns, cities, provinces or countries.

(NOTE: See also the Topics for Writing at the end of this chapter.)

Philip Marchand

Learning to Love the Big City

Born in Massachusetts in 1946, Philip Marchand studied English language and literature at the University of Toronto. After earning his M.A. in 1970, he worked as a manuscript editor and freight car loader, then became a freelance writer. Since 1971, his articles about social trends have appeared regularly in Saturday Night, Chatelaine *and other Canadian magazines. He says, "I like to write about individual personalities reacting to a larger social scene, reacting to expectations they feel this scene imposes on them." Until recently Marchand was heavily influenced by the "New Journalism" of the American writer Tom Wolfe. In this approach to writing, the subject is thoroughly researched but is presented in a subjective, personal style meant to heighten its appeal to the reader. One of these "non-fiction short stories," as they have been called, is our selection "Learning to Love the Big City." It appeared first in* The Canadian, *then in Marchand's book* Just Looking, Thank you *(1976).*

Man does not live by bread alone, but by fantasy and   1
daydream as well. Young men and women are sitting
behind desks in downtown Toronto, Montreal, and Vancouver and thinking, when I get my grubstake I'm going to
leave this scene for good. I'm heading for the country. Get a place ten
miles from the nearest town and only come in on weekends for supplies,
like lentils and Crunchy Granola. Yes. A little homestead far from the
Great Urban Maw . . . and at the same time as these visions are being
entertained, other young men and women are flocking to Toronto and
Montreal and Vancouver, from places like Marathon, Ont., and Gyp-
sumville, Man., and Vanderhoof, B.C., for jobs in life-insurance offices
and a comfortable nook in some monstrous high-rise. It's not the popular dream, to settle down in the big city, but there you have it — real
alternatives are simply too scarce. Small-town life practically doesn't *exist* in Canada anymore. Or rather it exists, but it's fading all the time.
We're in a stage roughly analogous to the Late Roman Republic, when
poets and politicians were praising the virtues of the simple old Roman
country life, sturdy farmers worshipping the household gods and taking
cold-water baths, while everybody who had the chance was heading for
the city for some fast money and funky entertainment.

For people like Lynda, eighteen years old and fresh into Toronto from   2
a town of 5,000 in the wilds of northern Ontario, all this talk about getting out of the city is definitely puzzling. For a weekend, sure — who
doesn't like the peace and quiet? But the city is fascinating. The first few
weeks she was here she would spend ten minutes at a time standing on a
street corner like the Bloor–Yonge intersection, just watching. She would

see, for instance, this young man with a shaved head and a saffron robe dogging passersby on the sidewalk, talking it up for the Lord Krishna. Disgusting! Nobody she had ever known in her whole life would act like such an idiot, but she had to watch. This guy would attack some poor timorous girl going back to work at a reception desk and stick to her like a horsefly, threatening her with his humbleness, his shamelessness, asking for money, asking for her name, her address, silently hinting that if she yielded a little bit he would never let up until she was there in the temple babbling insane praise to Lord Krishna for the rest of her natural life. He did this until he tried it on one guy in a business suit, who just grabbed him by his saffron robes and threw him off the sidewalk, into the traffic.

3   Well, the things you can see just standing for ten minutes at a big-city intersection. Lynda can't get over it. But, of course, she comes from a town where the main recreation is drinking. It overshadows such country sports as ice-fishing, snowmobiling, backpacking, even hockey. At school dances the Ontario Provincial Police officer is standing by the door watching fourteen- and fifteen-year-old kids reel in, and the only time he interferes is if they start attacking each other. Of course, the booze is cheap up there in the north country — you go to one of the three hotels in the town and get a bottle of beer for 50 cents, or a shot of vodka for 70 cents. It always surprised Lynda when people in Toronto would say they were going out drinking, and then they'd end up having only three shots of rye the whole evening. That was not Lynda's idea of serious drinking. She would be having her sixth or seventh vodka, and calmly watching her boyfriend knocking over chairs as he stumbled back to their table from the men's room — she would be just getting warmed up, you see, and here he was losing control of his basic motor functions after consuming the same quantity of booze.

4   But after a while Lynda began to grasp the point, which is that you don't really have to get drunk in the big city. Lynda gets drunk in Toronto, and all she wants to do is go home and sleep. That means, really, that she misses all the weird and wonderful action around her, the satin freaks in star-spangled boots, the criminal types with tattoos on their arms, premed students wearing sleeveless sweaters and Bulova watches, the whole urban monkey house drinking draught beer out of jugs and having their ear membranes warped from the rock music.

5   Back home there was a point to getting drunk. You could not conceive, in fact, of having a party or a dance without getting ripped before 10 p.m. You'd end up rolling around on the floor, and the guys would be shouting at each other — "George, get your arms off me, you queer!" — like a class of ten-year-olds who had just been forced to sit a whole half-hour with their feet still and their hands on top of their desks, and the girls would be giggling at the sight of their boyfriends making such utter

fools of themselves. And, of course, a few party games. In this one game a person would doodle a few lines on a piece of paper and then another person who didn't know what the game was about would take a strand of hair and try to bend and twist the hair so it covered the lines on the paper, and meanwhile some girl who knew Pitman shorthand would be recording his remarks on the sly. These remarks would then — surprise! — be read back to the guy later as the things he would say on his "wedding night". With half a pint of rye, rum, vodka, gin, or Zing under their belts, the kids would kill themselves laughing at remarks like "Geez, I can't keep hold of this thing." Party night for the young folks in ——, Ont.

But at least it was something to talk about in school on Monday, the number of bottles consumed, and what happened to so and so who was found with his head resting on the toilet, and this other couple who disappeared a little after midnight, under a bed, or some place. A few of the guys, and the girls even, would have arguments about just how much each person drank, it being a point of honour, of course, to hold your liquor and not act too foolish unless the kidneys and the lobes of the brain were actually getting soggy from alcohol. These are all, indeed, lively topics of conversation . . . but after a while it does get tiresome, Monday after Monday, the endless gossip about drinking, and sometimes about sex. Kids couldn't possibly have a little sexual adventure without everybody they met on the street knowing about it within a few days. Sometimes the people on the street even knew about things that never happened. A girl might enter the hospital to have her appendix removed and come out to discover her friends and neighbours all firmly believed she'd had an abortion.

But what else is there to talk about? Lynda is not an intellectual, but sometimes during conversations she tried to discuss topics of wider interest than, say, last night's alcoholic blowout — like what is the future of life in this town, for instance — and her friends started examining their fingernails and clearing their throats and after 30 seconds the conversation slid back into the old, hairy trough of local gossip. Or she used words like "progressive" or "confrontation" in conversation, and they asked, "What's with the vocabulary?" These people are all carrying on like Leo Gorcey and his Bowery Boys. Great for nostalgia, watching Gorcey movies from the forties, but it's not so funny in real life.

The guys, for instance, have two alternatives facing them when they leave high school. They can work in the mines or they can work in a garage somewhere. Either way, they will get married and have a family and try to get on the graveyard shift, so they can goof off and sleep for a few hours and brag about it afterwards to their buddies in the beverage room of the hotel. They will actually do things like trade war comics with their co-workers, the kind that feature granite-jawed Marines with five-o'clock shadows, blasting away at Japs on Gizo Island. They will get their greatest excitement from picking fights with guys who come in for the hockey tournament with their team, from some town a hundred miles away, and they will continue to do this until their bellies turn soft from drinking and they can't take the punishment anymore. That will be a sad day for them, incidentally, because they do like picking fights with strangers. The adrenalin wash helps clear up the brainstem and, besides, it's one of the few things they can do that girls can't, with their blue jeans and T-shirts and ability, some of them, to out-gross and out-drink even the hairiest males.

9   But this is their future, ladies and gentlemen. And their girlfriends do not exactly have it better. They will work in the bank or an insurance office after they leave school, and then they will get married and tend to the kids. Some of them will skip the high school graduation and employment part of it and get married out of Grade 11 or 12. Indeed, it is not uncommon for fourteen-year-old girls to get married in this town. These blossoming children who would prefer scar tissue to wearing something other than their blue-jean-and-T-shirt ensemble — except maybe a short skirt with lime- or raspberry-coloured nylons, for the glamorous occasions.

10   Lynda recalls that the girl she admired most in this town was a secretary who had her own apartment, her own money, her own definite views on life — she knew definitely where she was going in this world. This was a girl Lynda actually thought stood out from the crowd. This was a girl Lynda thought really had an interesting point of view, some unique statements on life to make, as opposed to the general numbness of intellect around town. If you want to know what a boy you're thinking of marrying is going to be like 20 or 30 years from now, she would say to Lynda, take a look at his father. That's what he's going to be like. Truly a sobering thought . . . and she had more, much more, to say in this vein. Well, when Lynda came back from Toronto for her first homecoming, her first Christmas visit, and met this girl again, somehow she appeared in an entirely different light. Instead of being a person of strongly held views and unique personal vision, she just seemed . . . well, opinionated, and as set in her ways as any middle-aged lady with tortoise-shell glasses and menthol cigarettes whose greatest challenge in life is deciding on what cheese dip to serve for the weekly meeting of her canasta club. Now her discussion of young men centred on whether or not they were "self-starters". That, apparently, is more important than what their fathers are like, because she has just gotten herself engaged to a young engineer at the mines, whose father spends most of his time down in his basement with some ice water and Saltines, going over his stamp collection.

11   Had this girl changed — or had Lynda changed, in the four months she had spent away from home for the first time in her life, back there in the big city? Lynda suspects that she herself has changed. She suspects

that if she had lived in Toronto before, she would never have been taken in by this secretary. One thing she has learned in Toronto is not to take people for granted. They just aren't moulded in those cast-iron, unbreakable reputations that are given to people past the age of five in small towns. In Toronto you have to find out for yourself what they're like; you have to pick up all the subtle little indicators — practically in the first few minutes you meet them.

With guys, for instance, Lynda now can tell how promising they look   12
after two or three minutes. It's all based on the degree of shyness they present to you when they talk to you in your favourite bar, the Nickelodeon, say, or the Generator, or Zodiac I. At one end of this spectrum you find guys who are not shy at all. A guy like this sits down at your table and turns around and leans forward so his face is squarely in front of yours and there's an upbeat, lively tone in his voice as he starts talking about how boring this whole scene is, and what a drag so many of these girls are, they look like they're out on horse tranquillizers, and you know that before the evening's over he'll be suggesting that someone like you is obviously cut out for finer things, like going over to his apartment above an Army-Navy store on Yonge Street and shooting up. Most aren't this extreme, but if there's no *hint* of shyness in the character it often means there is a definite tilt to psychopathic lunacy here.

And at the other end of the spectrum is the guy who is tormented by   13
shyness, but obviously driven, forced, impelled to seek out contact, so he talks to you with his eyes fluttering back and forth between your own two eyes and the little pools of beer on the tabletop, talking with such effort that it is obvious he must have worked himself up to come here tonight by performing unspeakable acts in front of some *Penthouse* nudes.

But Lynda has discovered that it isn't all that difficult to meet reason-   14
able people somewhere in the middle of the shyness spectrum, even in bars. Curiously enough, the fact she was from a small town made it much easier, in a way, because she thought nothing of starting up a conversation with the people sitting next to her in the Nickelodeon or the Generator. Hard-bitten Torontonians do not as a rule do things like this, because they're already sure the person sitting next to them is somebody who will respond to their friendliness by putting a hand on their thigh, or quoting whole passages from the Book of Revelations at them, or shutting them up with their Penetrating Death Stare.

But Lynda, as I say, came from a small town where you speak to peo-   15
ple who sit next to you in public places, as a matter of course. And not only does she meet a lot of *nice* guys this way, but she can tell how much other girls sitting around get absolutely burned up at her for it. I mean, she knows they're carrying on as if she were Little Orphan Annie befriending the poor and the outcast, and they're just sitting by doing a pictorial spread for *Vogue,* but — well, that's not her problem. Let them

wobble by on their platform shoes, with their slithery satin gowns coming down low under the shoulder blades, let them entice these young men with such obvious displays of themselves; Lynda knows that guys also appreciate a girl who can talk to them, a girl they can approach without feeeling they've strayed into a walk-in refrigerator. Good conversations can be sexy, too, as Lynda knows, who comes from a place where they are nonexistent. It kills her, for instance, that Lennox there, who she met at the Nickelodeon two or three months ago and with whom she has been more or less going steadily ever since, was actually interested, in one conversation they had, in the details of how people go about ice-fishing back home in ——. Lennox, who was born in Morocco and has lived in about three different countries in Europe, interested in how Lynda's friends and neighbours ice fish! I mean! Well, Lennox, how you do it is you start cutting a hole in the ice with a pick, and . . . and this is what Lynda came to Toronto for, to meet people and *talk,* to share experiences, to learn, to — oh, Lynda doesn't know, but to — to widen her horizons a bit beyond the world of the mines and incipient alcoholism.

16   This is what makes it worthwhile for Lynda — her boyfriend Lennox, who is interested in how you go about ice-fishing, and things like the whole variety of clothing stores in the city where you can buy practically anything outrageous or elegant, and you can dress like a lady and put on the nail polish and the green eyeliner without people staring at you in the pub and your friends calling you "green eyes", and you can get your hair cut'n'curled any way you want, and you can get a decent Chinese meal and you can take long walks in the city and admire everything from the skyscrapers to odd little filigreed Victorian houses, and you can even stand at the corner of Yonge and Bloor and watch altercations between secretaries and Hare Krishna mendicants.

17   Yes, this is what makes it all worthwhile, and at times Lynda actually has to remind herself that for the first two or three months she was here she was often on the verge of packing it in and going home. For those first few months, the fascination of life in Toronto was balanced by certain of its more frightening aspects. It was just all so *unknown.* Before she met Lennox, for instance, she really was dependent on some of the bars in town, the ones with the ear-warping rock music, for meeting people. But it was more than that. It was going into the subway at rush hour, and having people rush by you on the steps in panic, like a scene out of the fall of Berlin. It was the feeling of being a stranger, a foreigner almost, in your own country, riding the elevator in your apartment building every morning and hearing all these different languages, seeing black people for the first time, Sikhs, Chinese . . . I mean, Lynda is no bigot, but she was not quite ready for a lot of the cosmopolitan mix here in the city, the Detroit dudes in the peach-coloured suits, say, with matching fedoras, introducing some of that U.S.-patented pimp-flash to Toronto,

looking as if any minute they would approach you on the sidewalk and say something like "Hey, honey, you so *fine*."

It was the feeling of having to be on your guard all the time, of riding   18
the subway and finding yourself sitting next to some drunk talking to you at the top of his voice, asking you all these questions, like did you know about this here Bermuda Triangle, and everybody else in the car looking at you to see how you're going to handle the situation. It was the feeling of wanting to go for a walk by yourself, late in the evening perhaps, and being afraid to, because guys on the street would be eyeing you, staring hard as if you were swinging a purse and wearing a leopard skin coat and white vinyl boots. One night Lynda was eating by herself in a restaurant and a table full of men in business suits kept *looking* at her the whole time. When Lynda walked by their table on her way out she couldn't take it anymore, she was so annoyed — she said something sarcastic to them like, "Have you fellas had a good look?" and one of them stood up and started yelling at her, calling her names, telling her to get out — it was a thoroughly bad scene. But why can't she eat by herself in a restaurant without being gawked at? And why can't she go out by herself late at night, if that is her wish? It's her right, isn't it? It was certainly her right back home. But then, of course, this is the big city, and we have different rules here, lady.

Most disturbing of all, perhaps, was something more subtle,   19
something Lynda found hard to put her finger on. In its more extreme forms, it was, she guessed, simple big-city rudeness. All those waitresses who never seemed to crack a smile, for instance, and rolled their eyes in exasperation when you pointed out that you ordered your fried eggs done on both sides, not sunny-side up. But even when people in the city were not rude, when they had no intention of being anything other than decent and friendly and sociable, they still seemed curiously indifferent to other people's feelings. At work, for instance, Lynda will be doing these letters, not a rush job but she can't take forever on them. Her boss will ask another typist to do something, and that typist will say, right in front of Lynda, "Oh why can't you give it to Lynda? She never has that much to do." Or at lunch one of the girls will say to another, who is eating a full slice of rich, creamy cheesecake in spite of some obvious weight problems, "Are you sure you should be eating all that?" They don't seem to *care* about what other people think or feel, and they say these things that just cut you, things that people back home would never say.

But at Christmas, when Lynda went back home for the first time, she   20
acquired a little perspective on the whole thing. She found that, yes, people in her town were friendly. Folks had a big smile for her when they met her on the street, and asked her questions— "Have you met anybody in Toronto?" — and seemed just full of concern. But after a while Lynda noticed how they kept giving her these surreptitious stares in the hotel

bar when she walked in wearing a pantsuit and all this makeup. She noticed that when she talked about Toronto, especially in an enthusiastic tone of voice, the look on their faces began to get more and more quizzical, as if they couldn't figure her out, as if they were thinking — is this girl turning *strange* on us? And then she remembered all the times she felt she *had* to smile at people on the streets, greet them nicely, be careful of what she said, because, after all, this was a small town and you were going to have to live with these people whether you liked it or not. It was certainly true that she did have a definite place in this town, that her absence from it had been noted, that the merchants here never hesitated to cash one of her cheques. All this was a comfort when you thought about that big-city anonymity . . . but it hardly seemed worth it when you considered how hollow much of this recognition, this position in the community, actually was. I mean, Lynda's family happened to live in —— Heights, the most prosperous area of town and her address alone guaranteed that a cheque of hers would be cashed anywhere in town, even if the merchant or clerk didn't know her personally. But there are, of course, other areas in town that aren't so nice, areas closer to the mines where families with eight or ten kids live and the old man works as a gas station attendant. Lynda recalls that a lot of this small-town friendliness begins to evaporate when it comes to dealing with people like this, and you will never find them hanging out with the —— Heights United Church Women, for instance.

21   So all in all, Lynda finds herself voting for the big city. People who have lived in the city for a long time will no doubt continue to complain about it, and dream of the day they can settle down in the country on a farm perhaps, but for the vast majority of these people it will always be a dream. Economic pressure alone will continue to coerce people into living in the great cities. But there is something else involved. In 1806 John Loudon, in *A Treatise on Forming, Improving and Managing Country Residences,* wrote, "Such is the superiority of rural occupations and pleasures, that commerce, large societies, or crowded cities, may be justly reckoned unnatural. Indeed, the very purpose for which we engage in commerce is, that we may one day be enabled to retire to the country, where alone we picture to ourselves days of solid satisfaction and undisturbed happiness. It is evident that such sentiments are natural to the human mind." Such sentiments may indeed be natural to the human mind, but as long as there are cities there will always be a counter-appeal, expressed in the medieval proverb that city air breeds freedom. For the foreseeable future, the city will continue to draw people like Lynda with this lure — the freedom of lifestyle, the freedom of movement, the freedom of anonymity itself.

STRUCTURE:
1. What basic organizational technique underlies both the introduction, in paragragh 1, and the closing, in paragraph 21?
2. Most of the essay is divided into two sections, one describing the small town and the other describing the big city. Point out where each begins and ends.
3. What is the function of paragraph 11?
4. To what extent is "Learning to Love the Big City" based on narration? Where does the narrative begin?
5. To what extent is this essay based on examples? Point out a few of the more vivid ones.

STYLE:
1. On a scale of 1 to 10, with INFORMAL style as 1 and FORMAL style as 10, where would you place this essay?
2. Read paragraph 15 aloud, then describe its style, especially toward the end. How appropriate to the essay form is this style? When would you avoid it? Name other essays that you have read in this book whose style is in sharp contrast to that of "Learning to Love the Big City."
3. In paragraph 3, Marchand uses the word "booze" and in paragraph 5, the word "ripped." Point out other COLLOQUIAL and SLANG terms in the essay. Can any of these words be used in a more FORMAL sense?
4. A.   What device does Marchand use in the phrase "stick to her like a horsefly" (par. 2)?
   B.   What device does he use in "the whole urban monkey house" (par. 4)?
5. Read paragraph 16 aloud. How many sentences does it contain? Is this passage a grammatical error? Is it effective?

IDEAS:
1. In closing, Marchand quotes the medieval proverb "city air breeds freedom." Name as many ways as you can in which this proverb holds true for modern city life. Name as many ways as you can in which it does not hold true.
2. If you, like Lynda, have come from the small town to the big city, describe as vividly as you can several of your first impressions. If you have been in the city for some time now, tell which of these first impressions were true and which were false.
3. If you live on a farm or in a small town, describe several ways in which your friends and neighbours amuse themselves.
4. If you live in the big city, describe rush hour as you experience it.
5. Do city dwellers really think that a stranger, when spoken to, "will respond to their friendliness by putting a hand on their thigh, or quoting whole passages from the Book of Revelations at them, or shutting them up with their Penetrating Death Stare" (par. 14)? Tell your tech-

niques for meeting people in the city, or tell your techniques for avoiding people in the city.

6. If you have read "Suitcase Lady," by Christie McLaren, compare and contrast the experiences of the "Vicomtesse" with those of Lynda.

7. In essay form, contrast Saturday night in two different neighbourhoods, towns or cities.

(NOTE: See also the Topics for Writing at the end of this chapter.)

Cindy Titus

The Debate

Cindy Titus was a first-year social work student at Ryerson Polytechnical Institute in 1981 when she wrote her short composition in class (it has been revised slightly for this book). She says that writing is normally hard work for her, but that this time her involvement with the topic — her struggle between wanting to enjoy life in the present and wanting to succeed at school and career — made the writing easy. As she describes it, "What came out just went down." Titus was born in 1958 in Toronto but grew up in Cobourg, a town whose natural surroundings contrast sharply to the Toronto she describes in her composition. She has worked in group homes in both Stratford and Toronto, is sure that her future is in social work, and now thinks that the choice she describes in "The Debate" was the right one.

The debate's on. Two recalcitrant foes cannot find a happy medium. God tells me that in the past two months of school I haven't stored a single good memory. "You may have knowledge but the days pass and you have no beautiful moments to remember. Why live a day if the day's not worth a memory? You have parted with your beloved moon. The intricate paintings on the leaves I did for you, you have no time for. You begrudge the snowflakes. Look at them: they are fascinating, like a universe of stars close enough for you to touch. You curse them. You suffocate your soul, hiding yourself from the sun. Do you prefer being on the corner of Yonge and Dundas in a concrete building swarming with people? Escape, get out and live, let your soul breathe."

The Devil defends me: "God, be easy on the girl. She must make a living for herself soon. Perhaps she will have time for this wonderland you created when she finishes school. She will resuscitate her soul. Perhaps the job she finds will give her more spare time than school has provided for her and she will choose to spend that time with your lakes, trees and moonlit nights. She will walk in the spring and fall more often than she is given the chance to now. First let her make money. She needs security, a place to live, food and clothing."

The debate continues. And while they struggle, each with unshifting views, I continue with the Devil.

STRUCTURE:

1. Is "The Debate" long enough to be an essay? How short can an essay be? What must it do to be considered an essay?

175

2. Is "The Debate" a comparison, a contrast, or a comparison and contrast?
3. Describe the basic organization of "The Debate."

STYLE:

1. A. God mentions ". . . the intricate paintings on the leaves I did for you . . ." (par. 1). What FIGURE OF SPEECH is used here?
   B. God describes the snowflakes as ". . . fascinating, like a universe of stars close enough for you to touch" (par. 1). What FIGURE OF SPEECH is this comparison?
   C. God describes ". . . a concrete building swarming with people" (par. 1). What FIGURE OF SPEECH is represented by the word "swarming"?
2. Is the final sentence effective? If so, why?

IDEAS:

1. The biblical account of Creation states:

   So God created man in his own image, in the image of God created he him; male and female created he them.

   And God blessed them, and God said unto them, Be fruitful, and multiply, and replenish the earth, and subdue it: and have dominion over the fish of the sea, and over the fowl of the air, and over every living thing that moveth upon the earth" (Genesis 1: 27-28, King James Version).

   Contrast God's values as they appear in this well-known scriptural passage to God's values as they appear in "The Debate."
2. In "The Debate," God asks, "Why live a day if the day's not worth a memory?" What is your answer to that question? To what degree should the present be sacrificed for future gain?
3. "The Debate" is a personal essay, an expression of the author's own feelings about her life at the time the essay was written. Think about your own life right now, then write your own version of "The Debate," choosing as foes one of these pairs or another pair that you think is more appropriate to your purpose:

   God and the Devil
   Reason and Passion
   Good and Evil
   Pleasure and Duty
   Nature and Civilization
   Freedom and Responsibility
   Present and Future

(NOTE: See also the Topics for Writing at the end of this chapter.)

Austin Clarke

*Old Year's Night**

Austin Chesterfield Clarke is Canada's best-known black writer. He was born in Barbados in 1932, went to school there, then in 1955 moved to Canada and studied at the University of Toronto. Not all of Clarke's professional life has been spent in Canada. He has served as advisor to the prime minister of Barbados, as cultural attaché of the Embassy of Barbados in Washington, D.C., and as general manager of the Caribbean Broadcasting Corporation. He has also been a visiting professor at numerous universities in the United States as well as in Canada. Now he lives in Toronto. Since 1964 Clarke has written or edited some twenty books, among them a widely read trilogy of novels about West Indians living in Toronto: The Meeting Point *(1967),* Storm of Fortune *(1973) and* The Bigger Light *(1975). Although our selection comes from* Growing Up Stupid Under the Union Jack *(1980), Clarke's account of his own boyhood, it shares the vivid dialogue and rich style of his fiction.*

Everyone in the village — our mothers, big sisters, aunts, uncles and fathers — worked at some time at the Marine Hotel. It was a huge building washed in pink, with tall casuarina trees for miles and miles up in the blue sky; and at night it almost touched the stars which we counted beyond five hundred, although the sages of little boys among us said, "If you ever count past five hundred stars, yuh going *drop-down* dead, yuh!"

After midnight only ghosts and fowl-cock thieves walked the streets from the Marine, past the church which had a graveyard of dead Englishmen and English vicars and an English sailor which a tombstone called an "ensign."

And when we ventured too close to the walls of the Marine Hotel on Old Year's Night — the highest moment in our lives — the watchman, dressed in an old black jacket to suit the night, and khaki trousers rolled up above the ankles, and who knew the lay and geography of each rock and glass-bottle in the roads and lanes surrounding the grounds, this night watchman would challenge us. "Where the arse wunnuh think wunnuh going?"

If we stood our ground, which we never did, and stated our mission, which he never accepted, we would end up running from him, with the fear of his bull-pistle* in our back. We soon learned that we could take liberties only when he had a woman in the flower bed of blooming begonias.

*Editor's title
*bull-pistle: a whip made from the penis of a bull

5   On Old Year's Night there would be balloons with faces painted on them, bigger and prettier than we had ever seen before. And music by the best dance bands in the country. Coe Alleyne's Orchestra, Percy Greene's Orchestra and others. The music would slip over the wall which was too high and treacherous for us to climb.

6   Outside the free wall hundreds of boys and unemployed men, and some girls who were old enough to have boyfriends and be out at night, would stand in the dew dressed in men's jackets, always black, to keep the dew from seeping into our bones, so the old people said, and to give us consumption, which was our term for tuberculosis. We would dance to the music in our native rhythmic steps, moving over the pebbles in the road, and watch the white people inside because the Marine was "blasted serrigated."*

7   The men inside wore formal black suits that turned them into undertakers. And the women were white in long dresses skating over the huge dance floor, slippery and dangerous to unpractised steps from the waxing which the watchman had given it the day before. "Woe betide the man who don't know a waltz from a trot when he step 'pon that floor!" he would boast to us.

8   We watched them from below the wall. And we dreamed of becoming powerful and rich, to join them, to be like them. The waiters, our "relatives," our family, were mingling among them now: our fathers, uncles and older brothers. And if we were looking at the right moment, we would see a wink cast in our direction, and in the wink the promise of a turkey leg, or a rum for the older boys. Perhaps a funny hat or a balloon that was not trampled at the stroke of midnight.

9   Once one of them, braver than the watchman, and smarter, sneaked a leg of turkey out to us before the ball was over. And we chomped on the cold strange-tasting meat all the way through "The Blue Danube," all the while making mincemeat with prettier steps than those trudging ladies and drunken gentlemen on the grand ballroom floor.

10   Five minutes before midnight it would become very quiet. Quiet like my old school down the gap fifty yards away, silent and asleep at this time of grave-digging darkness. The watchman would stand at attention. And when he knew that we had all seen him, he would walk through the midst of us like a general, like a plantation overseer; come right up to each one of us, twirling his stick right in our faces, like the drum major in the Volunteer Force, and say, "Don't mek no noise in front of the white people, you hear me?"

11   Four minutes before midnight. And we can see the *musicianers* with their instruments at the ready, and the ladies and gentlemen in the grand ballroom skipping here and there, looking for husbands or partners. And

*serrigated: segregated

the lights would go off one by one, and suddenly the place would be like
a fairy garden with only coloured bulbs, and the balloons like beads of
sea water on the skin. And then the counting in a collection of voices,
ours and theirs inside. "Twelve . . . eleven . . . ten . . . nine . . ."

All of us outside counting in a year that would bring us more war, and 12
nothing like what it would bring the ladies and gentlemen on the other
side of the wall.

The counting growing louder now. ". . . five . . . four . . ." And we 13
continue to ignore the watchman, whom we had long ago nicknamed
"Hitler." And suddenly he too joins in the counting.

And then, on the stroke of midnight, the eruption of motorcar horns 14
blowing, balloons popping; the waiting taxicabs honking, with a hint of
deliberate impatience; and the ringing of bells, dinner bells and church
bells; and the bursting of balloons, and the scuffling and fighting for the
balloons thrown over the wall and floating in our direction; and the good
fortune of a funny hat which has landed in our midst, barely destroyed,
which we patched and for days afterwards wore as a statement: "Man,
you went to the Marine Old Year's Ball? I went, man. I got this hat.
Look!" Or a noise-maker sneaked out from behind the wall by a maid or
a mother; and the boiled unsalted rice carried in paperbags; "them
tourisses is people who suffer from sugar in the blood!"

We would walk back, happy, to our district, memorizing the night of 15
magic and revelry and choruses and words of the most popular tune
played by the Percy Greene Orchestra. *Goodnight, Irene* . . .

"Percy blow that tenor sax like po'try, boy! You hear how he take 16
them riffs in the first chorus? Pure po'try, boy!"

STRUCTURE:

1. How fully does Clarke develop a *contrast* between the tourists and the
   islanders? What are the main differences that he describes?
2. To what extent does Clarke *compare* the tourists and the islanders?
   Point out the main similarities that he describes.
3. How does Clarke organize his comparison and contrast: by halves, or
   by switching from one side to the other with each new topic?
4. To what extent is "Old Year's Night" a narrative? Point out at least
   ten words or phrases that signal the flow of time.
5. To what extent is "Old Year's Night" supported by description?
   Point out the most vivid passages.

STYLE:

1. Point out all the passages of local dialect quoted in this selection and

discuss what they contribute to Clarke's description of life in Barbados. Why didn't Clarke write the whole selection in dialect, since he is narrating in first person?

2. In what ways do the visual images of the opening paragraph appeal to our attention?

3. Point out all the appeals that paragraph 14 makes to our sense of sound.

4. When Clarke says the tourists are "skating over the huge dance floor" (par. 7), he uses a METAPHOR — a figure of speech that is literally false but poetically true. And when he says the watchman is "like a general" (par. 10), he uses a SIMILE — a figure of speech saying that one thing is like another. Which of the following are metaphors and which are similes? And what is the effect of these FIGURES OF SPEECH?

   A. "It was a huge building washed in pink" (par. 1)
   B. "The men inside wore formal black suits that turned them into undertakers" (par. 7)
   C. "All the while making mincemeat with prettier steps" (par. 9)
   D. "Five minutes before midnight it would become very quiet. Quiet like my old school down the gap fifty yards away, silent and asleep at this time of grave-digging darkness" (par. 10)
   E. "And the lights would go off one by one, and suddenly the place would be like a fairy garden with only coloured bulbs, and the balloons like beads of sea water on the skin" (par. 11)
   F. "The eruption of motorcar horns blowing" (par. 14)
   G. " 'Percy blow that tenor sax like po'try, boy!' " (par. 16)

5. In what ways is the wall a SYMBOL?

IDEAS:

1. The islanders described by Clarke envy the tourists ("we dreamed of becoming powerful and rich, to join them, to be like them" — par. 8), yet the same islanders "would walk back happy" to their "district" (par. 15). How do you explain this apparent discrepancy?

2. In what ways do the islanders feel superior to the tourists?

3. What benefits does tourism bring to a small country like Barbados? What economic and cultural problems can extensive tourism bring?

4. Is it possible for a tourist from a relatively wealthy country like Canada to be responsible in visiting a poor country? If so, name some characteristics of the responsible tourist.

5. Write an essay contrasting either of these two pairs:
   The good tourist and the bad tourist
   My best holiday and my worst holiday

(NOTE: See also the Topics for Writing at the end of this chapter.)

Pierre Berton

The Dirtiest Job in the World

Few people are better known to Canadians than Pierre Berton — journalist, humorist, social critic, popular historian and television personality. He was born in 1920 in Whitehorse, the Yukon, and studied at the University of British Columbia. In 1942 he began his career in journalism at the Vancouver News-Herald. *After wartime service in the Canadian Information Corps, Berton returned to journalism as a feature writer for the* Vancouver Sun, *moved in 1947 to an editorial position at* Maclean's, *then in 1958 became a daily columnist for the* Toronto Star. *For over two decades Berton has appeared regularly on television series such as* Front Page Challenge *and* The Great Debate, *and since 1954 has written over twenty books, several of them best sellers. His most widely read have been* The National Dream *(1970) and* The Last Spike *(1971), the massively researched and highly readable two-volume history of the CPR which in 1974 was serialized on CBC-TV with Berton as narrator.* The Invasion of Canada, 1812-13 *appeared in 1980 and* Flames Across the Border *in 1981. Whatever Berton's subject, his writing is full of human interest and concern for social justice. Nowhere are these traits more evident than in our selection, "The Dirtiest Job in the World," which appeared in Berton's 1968 book* The Smug Minority.*

On my seventeenth birthday, which fell on July 12, 1937, one of the worst years of the Depression, I went to work for pay and there was jubilation among my friends and relatives. In an era when jobs were scarce I had a job; and having a job was the goal of everyone in those days. Having a job in the Thirties was a bit like having a swimming pool in the Sixties; it conferred status. It didn't really matter what the job was. It could be unrewarding, mindless, foolish, unproductive, even degrading — no matter: it set you apart as a paying member of a society whose creed was that everyone must work at something, and the harder the better, too.

My job was in a mining camp in the Yukon some 1,500 miles from my home in Victoria, B.C. I worked ten hours a day, seven days a week, and I was paid $4.50 a day plus my board. Almost everybody who learned about my job had the same thing to say about it: "It will make a man out of you!" And when the job came to an end at the start of my university term, almost every adult I knew examined my hands to note with satisfaction the heavy callouses. Back-breaking work was considered to be a high form of human endeavour. A man who worked hard couldn't be all bad, whether he was a convict breaking rocks in a prison yard or an executive neglecting his family by toiling weekends at the office.

I worked for three summer seasons at that same job and it was commonly held that I was "working my way through college," another laudable endeavour in a society which believed, and still believes, that every individual must pay his own way regardless of position, health, mental ability, or physical condition.

4 The first year I worked on a construction gang; the following years I worked on the thawing crew, engaged in preparing the ground for the actual gold mining that was to follow. Thawing permafrost with cold water is a fascinating process to almost everyone except those actually employed in it. As far as I know, it is the world's muddiest job, involving as it does the pumping of millions of gallons of cold water into the bowels of the earth.

5 In earlier days steam had been used to thaw the permanently frozen ground so that the dredges could reach the gold; but the lovely, verdant valleys had long since been denuded of their timber and no fuel was left to operate the old-time boilers. So now a new process had been devised to tear the valley apart and convert it into a heaving sea of mud.

6 On Dominion Creek in the Klondike watershed, where I toiled those three Depression summers, the gold lay hidden in crevices of bedrock some twenty or thirty feet beneath the surface. The valley was perhaps a mile wide at this point and it was being ripped to pieces so that man might reach this gold. First, every shred of plant life was sheared off by a bush-cutting crew. Then all the black topsoil, most of it frozen hard as granite, was sluiced away by giant nozzles flinging water against the banks at a pressure so high it could cut a man in half. By the time the thawing crew arrived, the sinuous valley, misty green each spring, flaming orange each fall, had been reduced to a black, glistening scar.

7 It was our task to dam the creek anew to build up water pressure and then introduce a spider web of pipes across the newly ravaged valley floor. From these pipes at sixteen-foot intervals there protruded an octopus-like tangle of hoses. On to each hose was fastened a ten-foot length of pipe, known as a "point," because of the chisel-bit at the end. This point was driven into the frozen soil by means of a slide hammer. When it was down the full ten feet, an extension pipe was screwed onto the end and this was driven down, too, inch by painful inch. If necessary, further extensions were added. And all the time, without cessation, ice cold water was being pumped through every pipe at high pressure. In this way an underground lake was created beneath the valley floor and, though its waters were only a few degrees above freezing, that small change in temperature was enough to thaw the permafrost.

8 And so we toiled away, up to our ankles, our knees, and sometimes even our hips in a pulsating gruel of mud and ice-water. The men who drove those points into the rock-like soil were soaking wet most of the time, for it was difficult to add extensions or withdraw a point without water spurting in all directions. All day long they laboured, with their fingers curled around the handles of their slide hammers, their torsos rising and falling as they drove each pipe inch by inch into the earth. When

a point became plugged it had to be hauled up and unplugged while the ice-water squirted in their faces. Each man was logged on the amount of footage he had driven in a day, and if that footage was seen to be too low he could expect to draw his time slip that evening. There was a story current in my day that the general manager had come out from Dawson on a tour of inspection and seen a man standing immobile in the distance. "Fire that man!" he cried. "I've been watching him and he hasn't moved for half an hour." Later it was discovered that he *couldn't* move; he was up to his hips in mud.

As the water continued to flow into the ground, the floor of the valley began to go to pieces. Immense craters ten or twenty feet deep began to appear. Whole sections fell away, sometimes taking men with them. The mud grew thicker. The pipeline supports toppled as the soil crumbled, and the pipes themselves — mainlines and feeder lines — began to buckle and break and to shoot icy fountains in every direction. When this occurred it was the job of the pipeline crew, of which I was a member, to replace the pilings, drive new pipes and repair leaks. Sometimes the sun was out and we stripped to our shorts; sometimes a bone-chilling wind swept down the valley accompanied by a sleety rain. It did not matter. We worked our ten hours (later it was reduced to a merciful nine) day in and day out, without a holiday of any kind.

When you work for ten hours at hard labour, whether you are seventeen or fifty-seven, there is precious little time or energy left for anything else. We rose at six, performed our swift ablutions, wolfed an enormous breakfast, and headed for the job which had to begin at seven. At noon we started back up the valley slopes through the mud to the messhall, wolfed another vast meal, and finished it just in time to head back once more. At six we were finished, in more ways than one. I have seen men so tired they could not eat the final meal of the day which was always consumed in silence and at top speed. (It was said that any man who stumbled on the messhall steps on the way in found himself trampled by the rush coming out.) When this was over, large numbers of men of varying ages simply lay down on their bunks, utterly fagged out, and slept. There was nothing else to do anyway: no library, no recreation hall, no lounge, no radio or films — nothing but a roadhouse five miles distant where you could buy bootleg rum. Civilization was represented by Dawson, forty miles away; we never visited it. We were like men in a prison camp, except that we worked much harder.

Under such conditions any kind of creative act or thought is difficult. I remember one man, a German immigrant, who was trying to learn to draw by correspondence. He had some talent but in the end he had to give it up. He was too tired to draw. I had brought along a pile of books required in my university course for summer reading, but most of the time I found I was too tired to read. Those who did not immediately go to sleep after supper spent their spare time washing their work clothes or lying in their bunks indulging in verbal sexual fantasies. I often wondered if this was what the adults meant when they said that mining camp life would make a man of me. Certainly I learned a great deal more from these sexual bull sessions than I had at my mother's knee. It was not until many years later that I discovered most of it was wrong.

12   It is difficult to describe the absolute dreariness and hopelessness of this kind of job. The worst thing about it was that there was no respite, since — in a seven-day-a-week job — there were no breaks of any kind to look forward to until the coming of winter rendered further toil impossible. There was one wit among us who used to leap from his bunk once a week, when the bull cook banged the triangle at 6:00 A.M., crying jubilantly: "Thank God, it's Sunday!" This always provoked a bitter laugh. Without any change of pace, time moves sluggishly; without any break in the routine, a kind of lethargy steals over the mind. The blessed winter seemed eons away to all of us.

13   Yet for me, in my late teens, life in this mining camp was immeasurably easier than it was for the others. There were men here in their sixties who had lived this way all their lives. There were men in their prime with wives and children to support — families they did not see for half of every year. There were all kinds of men here and few who were really stupid. I worked with immigrants from Austria, Germany, Switzerland, Italy, Sweden, Norway, and Denmark, as well as with Canadians. Most were intelligent and a great many were extremely sharp and able. All were industrious. Each had displayed enough courage and independence to somehow make his way several thousand miles to the one corner of North America where a job of sorts was comparatively easy to get. But all had one thing in common: according to my observation, none had been educated up to his ability.

14   There were many men in that mining camp easily capable of obtaining a university degree; and there were many more who might have completed highschool and then gone on to technical school. I saw them each evening, lying on their bunks and trying to force their hands open — hands that had been curled into almost permanent positions around cold pipes; I saw them each morning, shambling down to that grotesque mud-pie of a valley; during the day I saw them — scores of ant-like figures, bent double over their slide hammers, struggling in the gumbo, striving and groaning; and the thought that came to my mind was ever the same: "What a waste of human resources!"

15   For this "job," which everybody had congratulated me upon getting, which was supposed to be so ennobling, which was to make a man of me, was actually degrading, destructive, and above all useless. It was degrading because it reduced men to the status of beasts. There was one wag who went around with his zipper purposely undone and his genitals

exposed. "If I'm working like a horse, I might as well look like one," he'd say. It was destructive because it reduced a glorious setting to a black obscenity. And it was useless because the gold, which was mined at such expense and human cost, was melted into bars and shipped to Fort Knox in the United States where it was once again confined below ground. Every manjack of us knew this; it was the subject of much bitter banter and wisecracking; each of us, I think, was disturbed by the fact that we were engaged in an operation which was essentially unproductive. If we'd been growing wheat, we would at least have had the satisfaction of knowing our labours were useful. The whole, vast, complicated operation seemed to me to be pointless: even the stockholders failed to profit by it greatly; for years the company was forced to pass its dividends. Would we or the nation have been worse off if we had stayed drunk all summer?

For myself, as a teenager, there were certain minor advantages that did   16
not apply to those older men who worked out of necessity and desperation. Certainly it was healthy enough. Certainly I got to know a bit more about my fellow men. It occurs to me now, however, that both these goals could have been achieved in a pleasanter and more productive fashion. As for the financial gain, much of that was illusory. After I paid for my equipment and my return fare home, there was precious little left. The first year I scarcely broke even. In succeeding seasons I was able to pay my university tuition but not much more. Like my fellow students, I could say that I was working my way through college, but like most of them I could not have continued a university career had I not been able to board at home and take money for clothing and extras from my parents. During four years at university, I met only a handful of students who were able to support themselves wholly through summer employment.

The one valuable asset that I recovered from my mining camp experi-   17
ence was status. It allows me to use a line in my official biography which I notice is seized upon joyfully by those who have to introduce me when I make after-dinner speeches: "During the Thirties, he worked in Yukon mining camps to help put himself through university." When that line is uttered the audience is prepared to forgive me almost anything: outlandishly radical opinions, dangerous views on matters sexual, alarming attitudes toward religion. I am pronounced worthy because, in that one sentence, is summed up the great Canadian myth: that work — *any* work — is the most important thing in life, and that anybody who is willing to work hard enough can by his own initiative get as far as he wants.

STRUCTURE:

1. In this contrast between society's high opinion of work and Pierre Berton's low opinion of his job, why is so much more of the argument devoted to the job than to society's opinions?
2. How is the essay organized? Does Berton finish with one view before presenting the other?
3. Berton's argument against the idea of hard labour as "a high form of human endeavour" basically takes the form of one extended example. Has this example enabled Berton to *disprove* society's view of work?
4. Paragraph 15 is filled with short comparisons and contrasts. Point out each one.

STYLE:

1. Is the TONE of Berton's essay OBJECTIVE or SUBJECTIVE? Point out passages that illustrate your answer.
2. In paragraph 5, Berton describes the valley as "a heaving sea of mud." Find other METAPHORS or SIMILES which poetically describe one thing as another.
3. In paragraph 10, the crew "wolfed an enormous breakfast" and later "wolfed another vast meal." Have you heard this figure of speech before? How effective is it?

IDEAS:

1. Do we still believe, or did we ever believe, in what Berton calls "the great Canadian myth: that work — *any* work — is the most important thing in life, and that anybody who is willing to work hard enough can by his own initiative get as far as he wants"?
2. Is work necessary for human happiness? How are prisoners, pensioners, the unemployed and the rich affected by large amounts of leisure time? Give examples from the experience of people you know.
3. To what extent does our society still believe that "every individual must pay his own way regardless of position, health, mental ability, or physical condition" (par. 3)?
4. Berton seems to view education as the means of escape from "back-breaking work" (see par. 14). Was that view correct during the Depression in which the essay is set? Was it correct in 1968 when the essay was first published? Is it correct now?
5. How much did Berton learn from his experience in the gold fields? How large a part of your own education has come from summer or part-time work?
6. If you have read "Living with Automation in Winnipeg," compare and contrast work as Ian Adams describes it to work as Berton describes it.
7. Write an essay contrasting the most socially useless job and the most socially useful job that you can think of.

(NOTE: See also the Topics for Writing at the end of this chapter.)

Topics for Writing

Chapter 5:   Comparison and Contrast

(Note also the topics for writing that appear after each selection in this chapter.)

Compare and/or contrast one of the following pairs:

1. The pessimist and the optimist
2. The conformist and the nonconformist
3. The introvert and the extrovert
4. The idealist and the realist
5. The liberated woman and the liberated man
6. Morning people and night people
7. City people and country people
8. Americans and Canadians
9. The metric system and the Imperial system
10. AM and FM radio programming
11. Diesel and gasoline engines
12. Reptiles and mammals
13. Incandescent and fluorescent lighting
14. Active and passive solar heating
15. A large university and a small college
16. Life in a high-rise apartment and in a house
17. Marriage and living common law
18. Cross-country and downhill skiing
19. Two ways to get a job
20. Two ways to get rich
21. Two ways to celebrate Christmas
22. Two ways to lose weight
23. Two neighbourhoods that you know
24. Two current fads in clothing
25. Two current fads in music

"We were all, brothers and sisters alike, born in a long three-storey wooden house, a house as humped and crusty as a loaf of homemade bread, as warm and clean inside as the white of the loaf."

Félix Leclerc, "The Family House"

In a way, it's like . . .

ANALOGY and Related Devices

One student wrote this memory of his childhood in Toronto:

> I heard and felt a rumbling from the ground, looked up and saw a huge red metallic monster with a tail on the end approach us. "Run, run" I said, "before it eats us." My mother reassured me that no fear was necessary. The monster slowly rolled up beside us, opened its mouth, and we went in.

As adults, we know that monsters have not roamed the shores of Lake Ontario for many millions of years, and that they were not red but green! We also know that monsters and streetcars have little in common. Yet who would say that this *analogy* does not clearly explain the child's first encounter with a streetcar? It may even help us, as adults, to view with new eyes something that we have taken for granted.

In the last chapter, we discussed how two items from the same category — say, two centres of population — can be explained logically through comparison and contrast. By seeing how the town and the city

189

are alike or unlike, we gain a clearer understanding of both. An *analogy,* though, brings together two apparently unlike items from different categories. And instead of using both items to explain each other, it more often uses one as a device to explain the other. It is not the monster we care about but the monstrous aspects of the streetcar.

In the last chapter, we speculated whether, instead of comparing a city and a town, we could compare a city and an ant hill. To those of us who live in chambers along the corridors of apartment buildings or who each day crowd into holes in the ground to take the subway, the similarities may be all too clear. We see right away that such an argument is hardly logical, for the very good reason that people are not ants. Yet the analogy may be a fresh, thought-provoking way to describe some aspects of life in a city.

As the selections in this chapter demonstrate, an entire essay can be built on one analogy developed with details. The more similarities between the two items, the stronger and more satisfying the analogy. Our account of the city as an ant hill should no doubt include more items than the apartment buildings and subway, and those items should be described and explained in some detail. Yet even a brief statement, "The city is like an ant hill," has value. As a *simile,* it is not much of an argument in itself, but is a vivid statement that can be used in support of another argument.

While a *simile* states that one thing is *like* another, a *metaphor* states that one thing *is* another ("The city is an ant hill"). Both devices occur often in poetry and in fiction, and both are effective in essays. The last selection in this chapter, Félix Leclerc's description of his boyhood home, contains a steady stream of similes and metaphors that convey a vividly poetic sense not only of the place but also of the author's feelings toward the place. Perhaps nothing objective has been proven, but a message has certainly been given.

Robertson Davies
The Decorums of Stupidity

If any Canadian can be called a Renaissance Man, it is Robertson Davies. The breadth of his knowledge, the variety of his interests, and the polish and wit and dramatic flair with which he writes make him one of Canada's most versatile and popular authors. He was born in 1913 in Thamesville, Ontario. After attending Upper Canada College, he studied at Queen's University and in 1938 earned his B. Litt. at Balliol College, Oxford. For a time he was an actor in the English provinces, then joined the Old Vic Company to act and teach in its Drama School. He returned to Canada in 1940, and in 1942 began a distinguished career in journalism as editor of the Peterborough Examiner. *He returned to academia in 1963 as Master of Massey College, University of Toronto, a post which he held until retirement. Despite his busy schedule, Davies has written numerous plays, books of literary criticism, and the works for which he is best known, his novels.* Tempest Tost *appeared in 1951,* Leaven of Malice *in 1954,* A Mixture of Frailties *in 1958 and* The Rebel Angels *in 1981. But Davies' reputation, both at home and abroad, rests chiefly on his Deptford Trilogy of novels:* Fifth Business *(1970),* The Manticore *(1972) and* World of Wonders *(1975). Our selection comes from a collection of Davies' essays,* A Voice from the Attic, *1960.*

Not all rapid reading is to be condemned. Much that is badly written and grossly padded must be read rapidly and nothing is lost thereby. Much of the reading that has to be done in the way of business should be done as fast as it can be understood. The ideal business document is an auditor's report; a good one is finely edited. But the memoranda, the public-relations pieces, the business magazines, need not detain us. Every kind of prose has its own speed, and the experienced reader knows it as a musician knows Adagio from Allegro. All of us have to read a great deal of stuff which gives us no pleasure and little information, but which we cannot wholly neglect; such reading belongs in that department of life which Goldsmith called "the decorums of stupidity." Books as works of art are no part of this duty-reading. 1

Books as works of art? Certainly; it is thus that their writers intend them. But how are these works of art used? 2

Suppose you hear of a piece of recorded music which you think you might like. Let us say it is an opera of Benjamin Britten's — *The Turn of the Screw.* You buy it, and after dinner you put it on your record player. The scene is one of bustling domesticity: your wife is writing to her mother, on the typewriter, and from time to time she appeals to you for the spelling of a word; the older children are chattering happily over a game, and the baby is building, and toppling, towers of blocks. The records are long-playing ones, designed for 33 revolutions of the turn- 3 table per minute; ah, but you have taken a course in rapid listening, and you pride yourself on the speed with which you can hear, so you adjust your machine to play at 78 revolutions a minute. And when you find your attention wandering from the music, you skip the sound arm rapidly from groove to groove until you come to a bit that appeals to you. But look — it is eight o'clock, and if you are to get to your meeting on time, Britten must be choked off. So you speed him up until a musical pause arrives, and then you stop the machine, marking the place so that you can continue your appreciation of *The Turn of the Screw* when next you can spare a few minutes for it.

4   Ridiculous? Of course, but can you say that you have never read a book in that fashion?

5   One of the advantages of reading is that it can be done in short spurts and under imperfect conditions. But how often do we read in conditions which are merely decent, not to speak of perfection? How often do we give a book a fair chance to make its effect with us?

STRUCTURE:
1. In discussing "duty-reading" that is best done at high speed, how does paragraph 1 prepare us for the main point?
2. Where is the main point first stated?
3. Paragraph 3 develops the analogy upon which this essay is based: listening to music as reading a book. Books have been discussed in the introduction but why are they not mentioned in the analogy itself?
4. Davies uses a standard technique in closing his essay: the asking of questions. Are these true questions that are open to debate, or are they rhetorical questions designed to make us agree with the author?

STYLE:
1. Why is this essay so much shorter than others you have read in this book? Has Davies failed to develop his point fully?
2. Why are paragraphs 1 and 3 so long while paragraphs 2 and 4 are so short?
3. What FIGURE OF SPEECH does Davies use in this sentence from paragraph 1: "Every kind of prose has its own speed, and the experienced reader knows it as a musician knows Adagio from Allegro"?
4. Is Davies entirely serious, as his elevated and dignified style would suggest? Or is humour important to his argument? Give examples.

IDEAS:
1. Is a desire to read fast like a desire to eat fast? To drive fast? To work fast? To live fast? Why is speed so highly regarded in our culture? Are

you familiar with another culture that encourages a slower pace? If so, which do you prefer and why?

2. Before writing was invented, all stories and poems were of course spoken aloud. What advantages do you think a listener has over a reader? What advantages do you think a reader has over a listener?

3. If you have read "D'Sonoqua," compare Emily Carr's approach to experiencing sculpture with Davies' approach to experiencing books.

4. Francis Bacon said, "Some books are to be tasted, others to be swallowed, and some few to be chewed and digested . . . ." Make a list of the five or ten books you have most recently read. Which did you "taste," which did you "swallow" and which did you "chew and digest"? What factors influenced your method in each case?

5. In an essay based on analogy, tell how you "taste," "swallow" or "chew and digest" different kinds of music.

(NOTE: See also the Topics for Writing at the end of this chapter.)

Barry Dickie

The Only Lesson I Still Remember

Barry Dickie was born in 1949 in Halifax and now lives in Toronto. He has led a varied life: earning a bachelor's degree at the University of Toronto, travelling in South America, working at the many jobs described in his essay, and experiencing what he calls "frequent intervals of happy unemployment." Dickie maintains that "the finest ambition a writer can have is to entertain his reader. . . . In fact, the word enter-tainment means 'to hold between' or 'to communicate,' which is the purpose of words. The subject matter is never more important than this communication between reader and writer; it is only an 'excuse' to write." He seems to follow his own advice in our selection "The Only Lesson I Still Remember," which appeared in 1980 in the Toronto Globe and Mail.

1   Everything I learned at university I owe to a janitor. Indeed, this Man of the Broom taught me the only lesson I still remember.

2   I met him during a mathematics lecture at the University of Toronto. He was a skinny man with a black mustache and a grey uniform. He entered our class, checked his watch and started pushing his broom.

3   We hardly noticed. Our eyes were glued to the blackboard where the professor was proving a theorem called Russell's Paradox. This is no ordinary theorem; it is more like a poem — a passionate burst of logic which proves that there is no universe. You can imagine the suspense on that fateful morning in 1970.

4   After the janitor had finished sweeping, he took a brush from the blackboard ledge and was beginning to erase the theorem. Using broad, lazy strokes he was demolishing Bertrand Russell's masterpiece faster than the professor could write it down. It was a race between brush and chalk, Time and Truth. The professor once stopped to glare at the janitor, but he didn't say anything. Maybe he was afraid of Big Labor, or maybe he had personal reasons. Soon the janitor caught up to the professor and settled into a yet slower pace, killing the logic one line at a time. After writing the last line and watching it vanish, the professor walked to the window and looked out. The janitor checked his watch again and left the room.

5   The incident changed my life. I sensed that the janitor knew something we didn't. I wondered if all people with simple jobs knew something I didn't know. For 10 years now, I have been trying to find out.

6   It hasn't been easy. The first problem was finding a simple, menial job. I went to CN and asked to be hired on as a Lantern-Swinger: some-

one who walks beside the train swinging a lantern and smoking a pipe. CN didn't want me. They gave me an aptitude test and told me I wasn't mentally fit to be a Lantern-Swinger. It hurt. As consolation, they offered to train me as a computer programmer, but the damage had already been done.

So I lowered my sights and got a clerical job with the federal Government. I was a CR-2 working in the Old Age Security Department. It was fun: all I had to do was carry papers back and forth between the filing cabinets and the desk where the CR-3 sat. The fun lasted until they promoted me to a CR-3. As a CR-3, I had to do complex arithmetic; I also had to tell pensioners their Guaranteed Income Supplement had been cut off. I lacked the social finesse for this, so I quit and shovelled snow for the Toronto Transit Commission.

This was my big break. The moment I touched the shovel something clicked inside me. A new vitality surged through my body. I felt alive. It is hard to describe the joy of pushing slush off a bus stop. For once, I knew who I was: I was a laborer.

Since then I have had dozens and dozens of laboring jobs. I have laid sod, picked worms, mixed cement, crushed rock, dug holes, sawed trees, loaded trucks and slung garbage *ad euphoria*. Each job has been special in its own way. Each job has brought me a step closer to the wisdom of that skinny janitor.

Of course, the Path has crossed some rough terrain. I dodged rats while loading sacks of flour into a Russian ship moored in Halifax Harbor. I watched a man lose his arm under a bending machine in a steel factory. I forfeited my dream of being a concert pianist, for my hands are numb with callouses. I have known boredom and I have known pain.

There has been beauty, too. I watched rainbows dance as I swept the morning dew from a golf-green with a bamboo pole. I heard the earth sigh as I scratched her back with a pickaxe. I heard hailstones playing drums on my hardhat.

There has been heroism. I remember one September afternoon in 1972 when I was picking tomatoes on a farm near Chatham, Ont. The farmer ran from his house, shouting across the field to us: "We won! We won!" I learned later, after many cruel hours in the field, why the farmer was so excited: it was because Paul Henderson had scored the winning goal for Team Canada. Yes, it was a glorious day: it was the day I picked 120 hampers of back-breaking, homegrown Canadian tomatoes. It was a day of tears, a day of joy.

Most laborers have a specialty. I do not. I am a general, all-round, unskilled laborer. You might call me freelance. Leaving a job is half the fun. The very notion of a permanent job disturbs me: it is a total contradiction of what the janitor was trying to teach me about Time and the passing of all things.

14   Now I am working for Metro Parks, laying sod and putting up snow fences. It's getting chilly. I am looking forward to winter layoff. There's something romantic about a Separation Certificate: it is like a ticket into the Unknown.

15   I still think about the janitor. Last week I was at the university, looking everywhere for the janitor. I couldn't find him. I asked a few students if they had seen him but, no, students don't take much notice of janitors. Oh, well, maybe he retired.

16   Hmmm . . . maybe the university is looking for a good man to fill his shoes.

STRUCTURE:

1. Explain the analogy upon which this essay is based: how is the janitor's action of erasing the blackboard related to what the author has experienced and learned about life?
2. To what extent is this essay a narrative?
3. Which section of this essay is a process analysis, showing how something was done?
4. To what extent is this essay based on examples?
5. What effect do the last two paragraphs achieve? Is that effect appropriate to the ending?

STYLE:

1. How serious or light is the TONE of this essay? Give examples to illustrate your answer.
2. "Our eyes were glued to the blackboard," writes Dickey in paragraph 3. Is this image effective or ineffective? Why?
3. Why does Dickie use capitals where he does not need to — in "Man of the Broom" (par. 1), "Time and Truth" (par. 4), "Big Labor" (par. 4), "Lantern-Swinger" (par. 6), "the Path" (par. 10), "Time" (par. 13), "Separation Certificate" (par. 14) and "the Unknown" (par. 14)?
4. Describe the language of paragraph 11: how are the descriptive effects achieved?

IDEAS:

1. Barry Dickie has admitted, in conversation with this author, that his story is made up. Although Dickie has held all the jobs he describes, he never saw a "Man of the Broom" erasing Russell's Paradox. Did you suspect that he made the story up? If not, do you feel cheated now that you know? Can Dickie's essay be dismissed as a fraud, or has

Dickie told a truth that rises above specific facts? And in what form of writing does an author habitually make up the "facts" while pursuing the truth?

2. Describe the most important lesson that you have learned so far about life. Did you learn it through abstract logic or through concrete experience? And how have you applied it?

3. In paragraph 14, Dickie states that "There's something romantic about a Separation Certificate: it is like a ticket into the Unknown." Compare the merits of a steady long-term career at one job with the merits of periodic job changes. In your field, which approach is better professionally? Financially? Personally?

4. If you have read "The Dirtiest Job in the World," contrast the attitudes of Pierre Berton and of Barry Dickie toward manual labour. Which writer's view do you come closer to sharing, and why?

5. A job has often been described as a kind of marriage. Develop this analogy in an essay, noting as many similarities between the two relationships as you can.

(NOTE: See also the Topics for Writing at the end of this chapter.)

Alan Stewart

Cars Make the Man a Boy

Alan Stewart was born in 1943 in Glasgow, Scotland. He immigrated to Canada, earned a B.A. and M.A., then taught for a time. Now he writes regularly for the Toronto Globe and Mail. *"Cars Make the Man a Boy" appeared in 1981 in the* Globe and Mail *column "Between the Sexes." Like his other contributions to this column, our selection examines an aspect of sex in modern society.*

1   One of the signs of the creeping androgyny that is skulking around everywhere these days, coming on little cat feet to fog up our precious and time-honored sexual distinctions, is the growing lack of masculine absorption in cars. I have met very few women who really cared at all about cars, cared in the same sense that they care about ecology or world peace or bringing home the constitution; traditionally, it was always men who clustered in corners at otherwise boring parties to discuss transmissions or the evolution of the Plymouth tail-light during the 50s. It was men who wrote car magazines and men who read them. It was men who, with the instinctive regularity of swallows homing in on Capistrano, visited the automobile showrooms every fall, not because they needed a car but just to have a look.

2   It seemed the younger the man, the greater the interest and nowhere was the interest more ardent than among boys approaching 16, the magical age at which you could get your driver's licence and hence be able, in theory at least, to drive a Ferrari. I was lucky to be that age during a time when cars were taken very seriously by all right-thinking people, and no one took cars more seriously than I did.

3   It was not odd that I wanted to stop being a pedestrian at about the same stage that I wanted to stop being a virgin; the connection between automobiles and sex, in the masculine mind, has been extensively documented. I remember that someone came up with a theory that when a man was buying a car, he went at it in the same way he chose a woman. What he really wanted, according to the theory, was a convertible, because a convertible represented the glamor and excitement of having a mistress.

4   However, there being a crust of solid citizenship over the seething ooze of his libido, he usually settled for a sedan, which represented the more sensible and socially acceptable wife. Egged on by this research, the manufacturers came up with the hardtop convertible, a sexy compromise which enabled a man to have a car that he could park in the bedroom as well as in the kitchen.

Almost everything is a sedan these days, which certainly does not say   5
much for the sexual aspirations of modern men. The writer Trevanian, in
his novel Shibumi, argues that Italian men drive as if the car were an extension of their penis, while Frenchmen drive as if it were a substitute for
one. How does this jibe with the current trend of each year's cars seeming smaller than those of the year before? Even the Cadillac, perhaps the
Burt Reynolds of the automotive world, proudly offers a smaller edition
than it once did.

Some wet blankets claim that sex should be sex and cars should be   6
cars. But if everything from gardening to politics can be appreciated for
its sexual overtones, why must sexual equality and the price of gasoline
stamp all the raunchiness out of driving a car? Why must a man's attach-
ment to his automobile be considered puerile and silly? If I can manage
to hold down a halfway respectable job, pay the rent on time, and refrain
from littering our parks, I should be allowed to enjoy a little fantasy as I
crawl up the Parkway during rush hour.

As a teenager, I fantasized of one day owning my own car. It would be   7
a brassy convertible with a very loud radio and I would zoom around
town in it with my sleeves rolled up, smoking cigarets, wearing sunglasses, and looking out at the world like Steve McQueen. From my current vantage point of incipient middle age, I can see that all this was
mindless and juvenile. Nevertheless, a few years ago I did get such a car.
It was a sprawling, eight-cylinder Mustang, and I had it painted what the
Ford people called Deep Orchid. On summer evenings I would put on my
sunglasses, roll up my sleeves, and wheel along Yonge Street with the top
down and the radio way up.

Was it possible to go back and experience an adolescent thrill I had   8
missed the first time around? Could a grown man enjoy making an
empty-headed spectacle of himself? Can you go home again?

You bet your life.   9

STRUCTURE:
1. Where does the THESIS STATEMENT of this essay appear?
2. What is the analogy upon which this selection is built, and which
   sentence introduces it?
3. How do paragraphs 7-9 develop the main point?
4. Why does the last paragraph contain only four words?

STYLE:
1. Alan Stewart uses words normally found in serious writing — "androgyny" (par. 1), "libido" (par. 4), "puerile" (par. 6) and "inci-

pient" (par. 7) — in the same essay with expressions more likely to be heard in casual conversation: "egged on" (par. 4), "jibe" (par. 5), "wet blankets" (par. 6), "raunchiness" (par. 6), "zoom" (par. 7) and "You bet your life" (par. 9). For what sort of reader do you think this mixture of FORMAL and INFORMAL language is intended? How effective do you think it is?

2. Point out at least one passage that deliberately uses repetition to achieve an effect.

3. The emotionally loaded words "creeping" and "skulking," in Stewart's opening sentence, convey bias. Point out other words or phrases like them in the rest of the essay.

4. Use a desk-size dictionary to find the origins of the word "androgynous." Discuss how "androgynous" and "androgyny" are related to the words "androgen," "android," "gynecology," "gynecocracy" and "misogyny."

IDEAS:

1. How serious is Stewart in his argument against "creeping androgyny" (par. 1) when he makes an "empty-headed spectacle of himself" (par. 8) in his own male-centred enjoyment of cars? Point out passages that support your interpretation.

2. Point out all the ways in which Stewart's analogy links cars and sex.

3. Does this essay have anything to say to women? If men symbolize their sexuality through driving cars, how do women symbolize theirs?

4. Do we STEREOTYPE people by the vehicles they drive? What kind of person do we think of as driving a "muscle car"? A van? A station wagon? A semitrailer truck? A pickup truck? A Buick? A Volvo? A Volkswagen? A motorcycle? Or no vehicle at all? If you recognize such stereotypes, do you know individuals who are exceptions to the rule? If so, describe them and their vehicles.

5. Many critics see the automobile as a threat to our society. It has killed more North Americans than have all of our wars combined; it consumes large amounts of fossil fuel, making us dependent upon oil imports; it pollutes our cities; and it causes our farmland to disappear under pavement. Yet neither these problems nor the rapidly rising costs of cars, fuel and insurance have stopped North Americans from driving. Why do we love cars so much? Are there reasons other than the one Stewart has given?

6. Are you familiar with a culture in which most people do not have a car? What advantages and disadvantages do they experience? What are their methods for getting along without a car?

7. Write an essay based on an analogy between cars and one of the following:

—horses
—elephants
—dinosaurs
—one's clothes
—one's own body
—loaded guns
—houses

(NOTE: See also the Topics for Writing at the end of this chapter.)

David Macfarlane

Skin Trade

David Macfarlane is a freelance writer who lives in Toronto. He has published articles in Saturday Night, Maclean's, Weekend Magazine, Today *and other periodicals, writing on topics as diverse as women's rights among the Mormons, extrasensory perception, Ken Thomson, cable television, Canadian sculptors living in Italy, book publishing and Maple Leaf Gardens. Our selection, "Skin Trade," was published in* Weekend Magazine *in 1979. Although it takes the form of a news feature, it has quite another purpose.*

1   Higsley, Ontario, a tiny community about 20 miles from the Manitoba border, has since January 1 been the site of an unorthodox experiment, conducted under the auspices of the provincial government. As the result of a rare amendment to the Liquor Licensing Act of 1876, retail grocers in the town have been granted the right to sell "liquors, wines, ales and other kindred spirits," while the former outlets of the Liquor Control Board — there are two in Higsley — now specialize in "the procurement and general sale of high quality pornography."

2   According to Earl Hooper, general manager for stock purchasing and quality control, the new Pornography Control Board of Ontario (PCBO) is a result of intense market research and the weakening social fibre of the western world. "Our government has always believed that substandard service and outrageous prices are highly profitable sales techniques, especially in situations where the customer is buying something he knows he shouldn't be buying. But times are changing. The boom years of liquor sales are numbered."

3   Government analysts agree. A highly controversial report compiled by a team of leading sociologists reveals that at some point in the future, probably within the next 10 years, Ontario citizens will learn that nowhere else is drinking regarded as a sin punishable by a 600 percent markup per bottle. Already there have been ominous rumblings of liberalization; recent changes in provincial liquor laws permit consenting adults to consume alcoholic beverages in their gardens, and tavern patrons may now transport drinks from table to table without fear of arrest. If this trend continues, liquor sales, now worth $365 million a year to the government, will be transferred from the public to the private sector. "We're preparing for the inevitable," says Hooper. "Pornography is the money-making, government-controlled commodity of the future."

4   The PCBO remains an explosive issue. The Ontario Censor Board is continuing its efforts to ban "all films, books and magazines that por-

tray or otherwise allude to where babies come from,'' which makes government distribution of pornography seem paradoxical. But the government has always been adept at ''controlling'' what it considers a socially undesirable product and, at the same time, making a killing on it. Addressing an irate gathering of surviving members of the Women's Christian Temperance Union, a spokesman for the Department of Consumer and Commercial Relations said, ''We believe that if we can't beat it, our duty is to sell it.''

What sells one vice apparently sells another. Although advertising executives have long been puzzled by the antidrinking posters displayed on liquor store walls, no change is foreseen in government marketing policy now that alcohol is being replaced by pornography. Posters in the Higsley retail outlets graphically portray the ravages of advanced syphilis and warn that self-abuse can lead to blindness, baldness and loss of teeth. Walls, floors and counters are painted battleship grey, and employees, chosen for their surly indifference, are not allowed to show any interest in, or knowledge of, their product. Each magazine and book is number coded (*Penthouse* is 4496-B; *Girls in Leather,* 1168-S; *The Diviners,* 536-H) and listed according to category (American Unnatural, French Decadent, Canadian Wildlife). Items are rated from 0 to 10 according to their degree of eroticism, and young clients are required to carry government-issued identification cards that read: ''Remove all doubt, fill it out!''

On a recent Friday night, business was brisk at the Main Street outlet in Higsley. The sidewalk in front of the wide glass doors was lined with old men in crumpled raincoats. Holding out their gnarled hands, they asked passersby for ''a quarter for a copy of *Maclean's.*'' Inside the PCBO, customers eagerly filled out the complicated order forms and passed them, along with their money, to the expressionless female cashier. After it was rung up, the order was passed across a long service counter where a second clerk pulled a pencil from behind his ear, scribbled mysteriously on the form, then disappeared to the shelves behind. When he returned, the purchased article was abruptly rolled in brown paper and shoved into a bag. Although PCBO policy forbids employees to speak to customers, one clerk proved willing to explain why only one magazine is wrapped if two are purchased: ''That's the way we always do it, eh?''

Despite almost weekly price hikes, the PCBO reports that sales of skin magazines and dirty paperbacks are healthy. Officials blame the exponential price increases on international inflation and the rising popularity of sexual activity. But as prices continue to rise the clientele seems ever more eager to buy. Having purchased a recent issue of *Hustler,* a magazine that retails for $37.40, one customer commented, ''It's imported. Frankly, the Canadian stuff is not very interesting. You have to pay for quality.''

8   While the PCBO admits that the pricing system favors inferior Canadian products, officials insist that such protection is essential to the establishment of a robust national pornography industry. Earl Hooper believes there have already been signs of improvement. "Look at the first issue of *Baby Bear*," he recently told reporters. "It's a naive domestic without any breeding, but we think the public will be amused by its presumption."

STRUCTURE:

1. In what ways does "Skin Trade" follow the form of a news feature? How much research do you believe David Macfarlane did in writing the "article"?
2. How fully developed is this analogy between the sale of alcohol and of pornography? List the basic similarities included in the analogy.
3. In the closing, Earl Hooper says, " 'Look at the first issue of *Baby Bear* . . . . It's a naive domestic without any breeding, but we think the public will be amused by its presumption.' " To what do you think *Baby Bear* alludes? And what qualifies this passage to act as the closing of the article?

STYLE:

1. In a SATIRE such as "Skin Trade," careful word choice is important. Discuss the effects achieved by these phrases:

   A. "the procurement and general sale of high quality pornography" (par. 1)
   B. "consenting adults" (par. 3)
   C. "without fear of arrest" (par. 3)
   D. "where babies come from" (par. 4)
   E. "making a killing" (par. 4)
   F. "self-abuse" (par. 5)
   G. "battleship grey" (par. 5)
   H. "Canadian Wildlife" (par. 5)
   I. "business was brisk" (par. 6)
   J. "price hikes" (par. 7)
   K. "sales of skin magazines and dirty paperbacks are healthy" (par. 7)
   L. "a robust national pornography industry" (par. 8)

2. Look up the origins of the word "pornography" in a desk-size dictionary. How is "pornography" related to the words "autograph," "graphite," "orthography" and "seismograph"?

IDEAS:

1. Give your definition of pornography and name specific examples of it.
2. Paragraph 5 lists as pornography *Penthouse, Girls in Leather* and *The Diviners*. Certain school boards have, in fact, removed Margaret Laurence's novel *The Diviners* from reading lists. If you have read it, do you consider it pornography? Or is Macfarlane satirically implying that its censors are prudes?
3. To what extent, if any, should society control the sale of pornography? To what extent, if any, should society control the sale of alcohol? Are you familiar with another province or country whose government has a different attitude toward these "vices" than does the Province of Ontario as portrayed by Macfarlane? If so, describe the difference.
4. Canadian wineries used to specialize in sweet and heavy wines that they labelled as "ports" and "sherries." Then they responded to a change in public demand by producing more dry red table wine. Now they are struggling to meet the demand for light white table wine. Give as many reasons as you can why the market is changing.
5. Name all the dubious or even destructive industries you can think of that are condoned by your provincial or national government.
6. The legalization of marijuana and its regulated sale in government outlets are prospects often discussed. Write a report on the new marijuana outlet that has just opened in your home town, as Macfarlane has written about the PCBO in Higsley, Ontario.

(NOTE: See also the Topics for Writing at the end of this chapter.)

Farley Mowat

The One Perfect House[*]

Farley Mowat is one of Canada's more flamboyant public figures. Soldier, traveller, writer, anthologist, story teller, conservationist and public gadfly, Mowat has always been more warmly received by the reading public than by the critics, who are only now recognizing him as a serious writer. He was born in 1921 in Belleville, Ontario. From 1940 to 1946 he served in the Canadian army in Europe, then after the war spent two years in the arctic, and in 1949 earned a B.A. at the University of Toronto. Since then Mowat has written or edited more than 25 books, and his work has been translated into more than 20 foreign languages. Among his works are children's books (Lost in the Barrens, 1956; Owls in the Family, 1961), light humour (The Boat Who Wouldn't Float, 1969), accounts of his experiences in the arctic (People of the Deer, 1952; The Desperate People, 1959; Never Cry Wolf, 1963; Sibir, 1970), numerous anthologies, and a highly acclaimed account of his experiences at war (And No Birds Sang, 1979). Our selection, "The One Perfect House," comes from People of the Deer, *Mowat's study of the Ihalmiut among whom he stayed in the arctic barrens. These original Canadians, who called themselves "The People," have since vanished.*

1   As I grew to know the People, so my respect for their intelligence and ingenuity increased. Yet it was a long time before I could reconcile my feelings of respect with the poor, shoddy dwelling places that they constructed. As with most Eskimos, the winter homes of the Ihalmiut are the snow-built domes we call igloos. (Igloo in Eskimo means simply "house" and thus an igloo can be built of wood or stone, as well as of snow.) But unlike most other Innuit, the Ihalmiut make snow houses which are cramped, miserable shelters. I think the People acquired the art of igloo construction quite recently in their history and from the coast Eskimos. Certainly they have no love for their igloos, and prefer the skin tents. This preference is related to the problem of fuel.

2   Any home in the arctic, in winter, requires some fuel if only for cooking. The coast peoples make use of fat lamps, for they have an abundance of fat from the sea mammals they kill, and so they are able to cook in the igloo, and to heat it as well. But the Ihalmiut can ill afford to squander the precious fat of the deer, and they dare to burn only one tiny lamp for light. Willow must serve as fuel, and while willow burns well enough in a tent open at the peak to allow the smoke to escape, when it is burned in a snow igloo, the choking smoke leaves no place for human occupants.

3   So snow houses replace the skin tents of the Ihalmiut only when winter has already grown old and the cold has reached the seemingly unbearable

*Editor's title

extremes of sixty or even seventy degrees below zero. Then the tents are grudgingly abandoned and snow huts built. From that time until spring no fires may burn inside the homes of the People, and such cooking as is attempted must be done outside, in the face of the blizzards and gales.

Yet though tents are preferred to igloos, it is still rather hard to understand why . . . Great, gaping slits outline each hide on the frame of a tent. Such a home offers hardly more shelter than a thicket of trees, for on the unbroken sweep of the plains the winds blow with such violence that they drive the hard snow through the tents as if the skin walls did not really exist. But the People spend many days and dark nights in these feeble excuses for houses, while the wind rises like a demon of hatred and the cold comes as if it meant to destroy all life in the land.

In these tents there may be a fire; but consider this fire, this smoldering handful of green twigs, dug with infinite labor from under the drifts. It gives heat only for a few inches out from its sullen coals so that it barely suffices to boil a pot of water in an hour or two. The eternal winds pour into the tent and dissipate what little heat the fire can spare from the cook-pots. The fire gives comfort to the Ihalmiut only through its appeal to the eyes.

However, the tent with its wan little fire is a more desirable place than the snow house with no fire at all. At least the man in the tent can have a hot bowl of soup once in a while, but after life in the igloos begins, almost all food must be eaten while it is frozen to the hardness of rocks. Men sometimes take skin bags full of ice into the beds so that they can have water to drink, melted by the heat of their bodies. It is true that some of the People build cook shelters outside the igloos but these snow hearths burn very badly, and then only when it is calm. For the most part the winds prevent any outside cooking at all, and anyway by late winter the willow supply is so deeply buried under the drifts, it is almost impossible for men to procure it.

So you see that the homes of the Ihalmiut in winter are hardly models of comfort. Even when spring comes to the land the improvement in housing conditions is not great. After the tents go up in the spring, the rains begin. During daylight it rains with gray fury and the tents soak up the chill water until the hides hang slackly on their poles while rivulets pour through the tent to drench everything inside. At night, very likely, there will be frost and by dawn everything not under the robes with the sleepers will be frozen stiff.

With the end of spring rains, the hot sun dries and shrinks the hides until they are drum-taut, but the ordeal is not yet over. Out of the steaming muskegs come the hordes of bloodsucking and flesh-eating flies and these find that the Ihalmiut tents offer no barrier to their invasion. The tents belong equally to the People and to the flies, until midsummer brings an end to the plague, and the hordes vanish.

9   My high opinion of the People was often clouded when I looked at their homes. I sometimes wondered if the Ihalmiut were as clever and as resourceful as I thought them to be. I had been too long conditioned to think of home as four walls and a roof, and so the obvious solution of the Ihalmiut housing problem escaped me for nearly a year. It took me that long to realize that the People not only have good homes, but that they have devised the one perfect house.

10   The tent and the igloo are really only auxiliary shelters. The real home of the Ihalmio is much like that of the turtle, for it is what he carries about on his back. In truth it is the only house that can enable men to survive on the merciless plains of the Barrens. It has central heating from the fat furnace of the body, its walls are insulated to a degree of perfection that we white men have not been able to surpass, or even emulate. It is complete, light in weight, easy to make and easy to keep in repair. It costs nothing, for it is a gift of the land, through the deer. When I consider that house, my opinion of the astuteness of the Ihalmiut is no longer clouded.

11   Primarily the house consists of two suits of fur, worn one over the other, and each carefully tailored to the owner's dimensions. The inner suit is worn with the hair of the hides facing inward and touching the skin while the outer suit has its hair turned out to the weather. Each suit consists of a pullover parka with a hood, a pair of fur trousers, fur gloves and fur boots. The double motif is extended to the tips of the fingers, to the top of the head, and to the soles of the feet where soft slippers of harehide are worn next to the skin.

12   The high winter boots may be tied just above the knee so that they leave no entry for the cold blasts of the wind. But full ventilation is provided by the design of the parka. Both inner and outer parkas hang slackly to at least the knees of the wearer, and they are not belted in winter. Cold air does not rise, so that no drafts can move up under the parkas to reach the bare flesh, but the heavy, moisture-laden air from close to the body sinks through the gap between parka and trousers and is carried away. Even in times of great physical exertion, when the Ihalmio sweats freely, he is never in any danger of soaking his clothing and so inviting quick death from frost afterwards. The hides are not in contact with the body at all but are held away from the flesh by the soft resiliency of the deer hairs that line them, and in the space between the tips of the hair and the hide of the parka there is a constantly moving layer of warm air which absorbs all the sweat and carries it off.

13   Dressed for a day in the winter, the Ihalmio has this protection over all parts of his body, except for a narrow oval in front of his face — and even this is well protected by a long silken fringe of wolverine fur, the one fur to which the moisture of breathing will not adhere and freeze.

In the summer rain, the hide may grow wet, but the layer of air between deerhide and skin does not conduct the water, and so it runs off and is lost while the body stays dry. Then there is the question of weight. Most white men trying to live in the winter arctic load their bodies with at least twenty-five pounds of clothing, while the complete deerskin home of the Innuit weighs about seven pounds. This, of course, makes a great difference in the mobility of the wearers. A man wearing tight-fitting and too bulky clothes is almost as helpless as a man in a diver's suit. But besides their light weight, the Ihalmiut clothes are tailored so that they are slack wherever muscles must work freely beneath them. There is ample space in this house for the occupant to move and to breathe, for there are no partitions and walls to limit his motions, and the man is almost as free in his movements as if he were naked. If he must sleep out, without shelter, and it is fifty below, he has but to draw his arms into his parka, and he sleeps nearly as well as he would in a double-weight eiderdown bag.

This is in winter, but what about summer? I have explained how the porous hide nevertheless acts as a raincoat. Well, it does much more than that. In summer the outer suit is discarded and all clothing pared down to one layer. The house then offers effective insulation against heat entry. It remains surprisingly cool, for it is efficiently ventilated. Also, and not least of its many advantages, it offers the nearest thing to perfect protection against the flies. The hood is pulled up so that it covers the neck and the ears, and the flies find it nearly impossible to get at the skin underneath. But of course the Ihalmiut have long since learned to live with the flies, and they feel none of the hysterical and frustrating rage against them so common with us.

In the case of women's clothing, home has two rooms. The back of the parka has an enlargement, as if it were made to fit a hunchback, and in this space, called the *amaut,* lives the unweaned child of the family. A bundle of remarkably absorbent sphagnum moss goes under his backside and the child sits stark naked, in unrestricted delight, where he can look out on the world and very early in life become familiar with the sights and the moods of his land. He needs no clothing of his own, and as for the moss — in that land there is an unlimited supply of soft sphagnum and it can be replaced in an instant.

When the child is at length forced to vacate this pleasant apartment, probably by the arrival of competition, he is equipped with a one-piece suit of hides which looks not unlike the snow suits our children wear in the winter. Only it is much lighter, more efficient, and much less restricting. This first home of his own is a fine home for the Ihalmio child, and one that his white relatives would envy if they could appreciate its real worth.

18   This then is the home of the People. It is the gift of the land, but mainly it is the gift of Tuktu*.

STRUCTURE:

1. In this selection, where does the analogy begin?
2. To what extent is the analogy developed? Point out all the ways in which the clothes of the Ihalmiut are described in terms of a house.
3. Why is this discussion of Eskimo clothing in terms of a house considered an analogy rather than a comparison and contrast?
4. Paragraphs 1-9 describe the qualities of the igloo and the tent. Is this passage an analogy or a comparison and contrast? Why?
5. In what way does Farley Mowat's discussion of the igloo and tent prepare us for his discussion of Eskimo clothing?

STYLE:

1. A SIMILE states that one thing is like another, while a METAPHOR states poetically that one thing is another. Which of the following are similes and which are metaphors?

   A. " . . . the wind rises like a demon of hatred . . . . " (par. 4)
   B. " . . . almost all food must be eaten while it is frozen to the hardness of rocks." (par. 6)
   C. " . . . the hot sun dries and shrinks the hides until they are drum-taut . . . ." (par. 8)
   D. "The real home of the Ihalmio is much like that of the turtle, for it is what he carries about on his back." (par. 10)
   E. " . . . a long silken fringe of wolverine fur. . . . " (par. 13)
   F. "A man wearing tight-fitting and too bulky clothes is almost as helpless as a man in a diver's suit." (par. 14)
   G. " . . . the porous hide nevertheless acts as a raincoat." (par. 15)

2. To what extent has Mowat used SENSE IMAGES to make this selection vivid? Give one example each of appeals to sight, hearing, touch, taste and smell.
3. Hold your book at arm's length so that you have an overall view of the selection's appearance. Does Mowat's writing seem to consist mostly of long words or short words? What effect do you think his preference for long or for short words has upon his style?

IDEAS:

1. Dying cultures such as those of the Inuit are being recorded by anthropologists, and dead cultures are being reconstructed by archae-

---

*Tuktu: the caribou.

ologists. Why do we study ways of life that are passing or past? Can such study in any way improve our present lives?

2. Over the last decades, the federal government has provided the Inuit of Canada with houses so that, except on hunting trips, they no longer need the igloos or tents described by Farley Mowat. Do you agree with the government's actions? Did it make more sense to reduce physical hardships among the Inuit, or would it have made more sense to preserve at least some of their stone-age culture? And would such preservation have been possible?

3. A North American Indian once observed that the White Man works in an office fifty weeks of the year so he can live like an Indian the other two weeks. How much truth do you find in this statement? In what ways does a temporary outdoor experience differ from a permanent one?

4. If you have read "D'Sonoqua," discuss the ways in which both Emily Carr and Mowat portray native peoples as a part of nature.

5. Write an essay based on an extended analogy between a house and one of the following:

—a nest
—the burrow or den of an animal
—a car or van
—the earth's atmosphere
—our government's system of social benefits
—a complicated theoretical argument
—a person's system of psychological defences

(NOTE: See also the Topics for Writing at the end of this chapter.)

Félix Leclerc

The Family House*

translated from the French by Philip Stratford

Félix Leclerc, born in 1914 at La Tuque, Quebec, is a singer and writer. From 1934 to 1942 he was an announcer, actor and writer with Radio-Canada, occasionally singing his own songs as well. For a few years he acted with a theatre company, then from 1951 to 1953 lived in Paris, where his music hall appearances as "le Canadien" won him immense popularity. In Quebec he is now considered the original chansonnier — as singer Gilles Vigneault puts it, "the father of us all." Yet Leclerc thinks of himself as primarily a writer. He has published more than a dozen books, including poetry, plays, fables, stories and novels. Among his most widely read have been Adagio (1943) and Allegro (1944), two collections of his fables and stories written for radio; Pieds nus dans l'aube (1946), the autobiographical novel from which our selection comes; and his novel Le fou de l'île (1958), translated by Philip Stratford in 1976 as The Madman, the Kite and the Island.

1   We were all, brothers and sisters alike, born in a long three-storey wooden house, a house as humped and crusty as a loaf of homemade bread, as warm and clean inside as the white of the loaf.

2   Roofed over with shingles, harbouring robins in its gables, it looked itself like an old nest perched up there in the silence. Taking the north wind over the left shoulder, beautifully adjusted to nature, from the roadside one might also have mistaken it for an enormous boulder stranded on the beach.

3   In truth it was a stubborn old thing, soaking up storms and twilight, determined not to die of anything less than old age, like the two elms beside it.

4   The house turned its back squarely on the rest of town so as not to see the new subdivision with its shiny little boxes as fragile as mushrooms. Looking out over the valley, highroad for the wild St. Maurice river, it focused as if in ecstasy on the long caravan of blue mountains over there, the ones that flocks of clouds and the oldest seagulls don't seem able to get over.

5   With its rusty sides, its black roof and its white-trimmed windows, our common cradle crouched over a heavy cement foundation sunk solidly in the ground like a ship's anchor to hold us firm, for we were eleven children aboard, a turbulent, strident lot, but as timid as baby chicks.

*Translator's title

A big, robust, rough fieldstone chimney, held together by trowel-   6
smoothed mortar, began in the cellar near the round-bellied furnace just
above that drafty little iron door that sticking a mirror into you could see
the stars. Like the hub of a wheel it rose through the floors distributing
spokes of heat, then broke through to the outside as stiff as a sentinel
with a plumed helmet and smoked there with windswept hair, close to a
grey ladder lying along the roof. The grey ladder and the sooty little
door, we were told, were not for human use, but for an old man in red
who in winter jumped from roof to roof behind reindeer harnessed in
white.

From top to bottom our home was inhabited: by us in the centre like   7
the core of a fruit; at the edges by parents; in the cellars and attics by
superb and silent men, lumberjacks by trade. In the walls, under the
floors, between the joists, near the carpets, and in the folds of the lamp-
shades lived goblins, gnomes, fairies, snatches of song, silly jokes and
the echoes of games; in the veins of our house ran pure poetry.

We had a chair for rocking in, a bench for saying prayers, a sofa to cry   8
on, a two-step staircase for playing trains. Also other fine toys that we
didn't dare touch, like the two-wired bird with its long beak and the bell
in its forehead that talked to the grown-ups. A flower-patterned linoleum
was our garden; a hook in the wall, a bollard to tie up our imaginary
boats; the staircases were slides; the pipes running up the walls our
masts; and armchairs miniature stages where we learnt with the hats,
gloves and overcoats of our elders how to make the same faces that we
wear today but without finding them funny.

A vast corridor divided the ground floor lengthwise. A few rung-   9
backed chairs made a circle in one corner; above them a row of hooks
like question marks disappeared beneath the coats of visitors who came
to consult Papa, the biggest timber merchant in the valley. The living
room and a bedroom for visitors stood side by side. The living room,
with its black piano, its net curtains, its big blue armchair, its gold- fram-
ed pictures, a few old-style chairs upholstered in satin (particularly a
spring-rocker dressed up like an old lady out of the past with tassels on
the hem of her dress) gave our lives a quality of Sunday celebration. Our
parents' bedroom closed its doors on impenetrable secrets. In its obscuri-
ty slumbered an old dresser full of camphor-scented sheets between
which my mother hid mysterious notebooks, repositories of the exact
hour of our birth, the names of godfathers and godmothers, and very
private family events.

To the left of the hall a smoking room served as my father's study and   10
as library for all of us. A door opened to the dining room — classroom
would be more exact, for we only ate there once or twice a year. In the
sewing room between the sewing machine and an enormous cupboard

stood the sofa, ready to be cried on. At the back of the house, spreading the full width, was our gay and singing kitchen: the cast-iron stove with its built-in mirror, the red kitchen cupboards, the white muslin curtains hanging like fog in the narrow windows, and the patches of sunlight playing on the left of the long family table. There shone the ever-burning lamp, known to all people throughout all time as the soul of the home. There we were told of good news and bad. There Papa signed our school report cards. There in the high rocking chair we would often sit in silence to think of facts of creation discovered that day and ponder on the strange and marvellous world we had fallen into.

11   The first floor was lined with children's bedrooms. There were eight, I think, divided between girls and boys. In the girls' rooms it was cleaner, rosier, airier, more airy than the boys'. On the walls they pinned up tiny frames, graceful silhouettes and sprigs of flowers. On ours we stuck huge vulgar calendars, of hunters waiting for game and old gents smoking rubbed tobacco.

12   Our room, the most spacious on the floor, looked out on the garden, its black earth full as a cornucopia, and cut through with straight little paths that we walked down every evening, watering under the watching eyes of the cottontails.

13   We each had our own bed, a little white bed with a real straw mattress and iron bedposts ending in brass knobs where we hung our clothes, our slingshots, and our hands clasped in prayer.

14   On the second floor a screened veranda jutted out in a bow like a pilot-house. It was a veritable observation post dominating the waves of the valley like those of the sea: waves of snowstorms, waves of loggers in springtime, waves of poor families gathering wild fruit, waves of falling leaves, of showers of sunshine, of the beating of birds' wings, of paths traced by children, hunters and fishermen. On hot nights we slept there above the waves on that wooden porch which was also the children's playroom. Soldiers, teddy bears, drums, little wooden shoes, dolls seated at table before empty china plates, all keeping good company together. A tin bridge built long ago by my eldest brother served as access to this cardboard world.

15   On the floor above, behind a bull's-eye window, stretched the attic, a long deserted dusty cage, dormitory in winter for several lumberjacks. Between the three-legged chairs and the family portraits, these men on their mattresses, devoured by fatigue, tumbled headlong each night into sleep.

16   And like the crew of a happy ship, thinking neither of arrivals nor of departures, but only of the sea that carries them, we sped through childhood all sails set, thrilled with each morning and every night, envying neither distant ports nor far cities, convinced that our ship was flying the

best colours and that we carried on board all necessary potions to ward off pirates and bad luck.

The house we lived in was number 168, rue Claire-Fontaine.   17

STRUCTURE:

1. This selection is filled with figures of speech — SIMILES, METAPHORS and PERSONIFICATION — but only one is developed extensively enought to be considered an analogy. What is it and which paragraphs develop it?
2. What is the main purpose of this selection, and where does Leclerc most openly state it?

STYLE:

1. Roughly how many METAPHORS and SIMILES appear in this selection as compared to the other selections in this book? Twice as many? Four times as many? Ten times as many? And what effect does Leclerc achieve through such a concentration of FIGURES OF SPEECH?
2. Among his other achievements, Félix Leclerc is a poet and is one of Quebec's best-loved singers. What relationship, if any, do you find between his experience as poet and singer and the approach he took to writing "The Family House"?
3. Point out at least ten SIMILES in this selection. Point out at least ten METAPHORS. Point out at least five examples of PERSONIFICATION. Do these figures of speech work together to build a dominant impression or do they seem to be used separately for their own sake?
4. Do you suppose "The Family House" was easy or difficult to translate from French to English? Is a perfect translation possible? If you know two languages, how easy or difficult is it to translate words and expressions from one to the other?

IDEAS:

1. In paragraph 8, Leclerc describes how he and his brothers and sisters imitated their elders, learning "how to make the same faces that we wear today but without finding them funny." Do you sense in this passage (and perhaps in the whole selection) a regret for lost childhood? Do you ever regret your own lost childhood? Do most people? If so, what might be the reasons?
2. "Coming of Age in Putnok" is the opening of George Gabori's autobiography, while "The Family House" is the opening of Félix Leclerc's autobiographical novel. If you have read both, compare

them. Which gives more facts? Which gives more feeling? Which seems to give a greater insight into the author's background and personality? Do the two openings differ in TONE? And which would more strongly motivate a reader to finish the book?

3. If you have read "The One Perfect House," compare the ways in which Farley Mowat describes that "house" with the ways in which Leclerc describes the house of his childhood.

4. Using a great many METAPHORS and SIMILES, describe your own childhood home in such a way as to strongly convey the feelings you have toward it and toward the life you led there.

(NOTE: See also the Topics for Writing at the end of this chapter.)

Topics for Writing

Chapter 6:   ANALOGY and related devices

(Note also the topics for writing that appear after each selection in this chapter.)

Develop one of the following topics into an extended analogy:

1. Manners as a mask
2. A person you know as the pet he or she keeps
3. A large corporation as an octopus
4. A town, city, province or country as the animal it reminds you of
5. A sports team as an army
6. Chess as war
7. Capitalism or communism as a religion
8. Knowledge as light
9. A computer as a brain
10. A camera as an eye
11. Football as life
12. Or hockey as life
13. Or soccer as life
14. A motorcycle as a horse
15. A newborn child as an astronaut in space
16. Home as a nest
17. Home as a fortress
18. Crime as war
19. Crime as disease
20. An industrial worker as a robot
21. Television as a drug
22. Television as a desert
23. School as a factory
24. The atom as a solar system
25. The earth as a spaceship

Ontario Ministry of Industry and Tourism.

"There isn't a reason in the world to suppose that twenty million people really enjoy going fishing . . . ."

Roderick Haig-Brown, "Articles of Faith for Good Anglers"

There are three kinds of them. . . .

CLASSIFICATION

Our world is so complex that without classification we would be lost. To call a friend we use an alphabetized phone book. To buy a steak we go to the meat section of the supermarket. To buy a used car we open our newspaper to the *classified* section. Putting things into categories is one of our most common methods of thought, both for good and for bad. Who would look through the whole dictionary when the word in question begins with "T"? What school child would enter a grade one *class*room when he has been *class*ified into grade five?

Yet as Hitler and other bigots have demonstrated, classifying people by skin colour, race or religion can lead to stereotypes and from stereotypes to violence. Ethnic jokes may seem innocent (*Why does it take two WASPs to change a light bulb? One makes the gin and tonics while the other calls the repairman*). But such a characterization of a group makes it harder for others to view a member of that group as an individual. If all WASPs (or all Newfoundlanders or Torontonians or Jews or Indians or bankers or postal workers) are classified as the same, we have dehumanized them. Dislike and even persecution are now possible. Be careful, then, not to let a classification become a stereotype. For example, you may have a practical reason to group people by age, but do leave room for individuals: not all teenagers are delinquents, not all forty-year-olds are getting a divorce and not all retired people are ready for the rocking chair.

Whatever its subject, your essay of classification should have at least three categories, because only two would form a comparison and contrast. And it should have no more than you can adequately develop — perhaps six or seven at the most. To be logical your essay will follow these principles:

Classify all items by the same principle. An essay on sources of energy for home heating might include oil, natural gas, hydro, coal, wood and solar heat. But it would not include insulation as a category, for insulation is not a *source* of energy but a means of *retaining* energy.

Do not leave out an obvious category. Would you discuss six artists in an essay about the Group of Seven?

Do not let categories overlap. An essay on the major types of housing might include the detached single-family house, the semi-detached house, the row house and the high-rise apartment. The bungalow has no place in this list, though, because it *is* a detached single-family house. And rental units have no place in the list, because any of the above forms of housing can be rented.

Classifying is not easy; it is a real exercise in logic. But it will become easier when you observe the most important principle of all: *Know your purpose.* Is one form of housing cheaper, more pleasant, more appropriate to the city, more energy efficient, better suited to singles or to families or to retired people? Let that idea, whatever it is, underly your classification so that your essay will emerge as a clear and unified message.

Roderick Haig-Brown
Articles of Faith for Good Anglers

Since the time of Izaak Walton, enthusiasts of fishing have written eloquently about their sport. The best of these writers in North America, and the man often called Canada's finest essayist, was Roderick Haig-Brown (1908-1976). Born in England to an aristocratic family, he moved at age 17 to the State of Washington and worked as a logger and semi-pro boxer. After a short return to England he settled in British Columbia, where he worked as a guide, logger, trapper, bounty hunter for cougars, and fisherman. Then in 1941 he was appointed magistrate and judge at Campbell River, B.C. Sometimes late to court sessions because of his fishing, Haig-Brown retained a passion for the sport to the end of his life, and in flawless prose imparted his experiences, his close observations of nature, his code of sportsmanship and his devotion to conservation. The best-loved of his many books are A River Never Sleeps *(1946),* Fisherman's Spring *(1951) and* Fisherman's Summer *(1959). A shortened version of our selection, "Articles of Faith for Good Anglers," appeared in* Life Magazine *in 1960; the complete version was collected in* The Master and His Fish *(1981).*

Some twenty million angling licences a year are sold on the North American continent and considerably more than twenty million people go fishing each year. There isn't a reason in the world to suppose that twenty million people really enjoy going fishing; a remarkably high proportion of them contribute vastly to the discomfort of others while finding little joy in the sport for themselves. This is sad but inevitable; it grows directly out of the misconception that anyone with two hands, a hook, and a pole, is equipped to go fishing. After all, the beloved fable has it that the boy with the worm on a bent pin always does far better than the master angler with his flies and intricate gear, so it follows logically that a state of blissful ignorance, combined with youthful clumsiness, is the perfect formula for success. If the formula doesn't prove itself, the trouble is probably the weather. 1

Fishing is not really a simpleton's sport. It is a sport with a long history, an intricate tradition, and a great literature. These things have not grown by accident. They have developed by the devotion of sensitive and intelligent men and they make not only a foundation for rich and satisfying experience but the charter of a brotherhood that reaches around the world and through both hemispheres. 2

It is a brotherhood well worth joining. There are no papers to sign, no fees to pay, no formal initiation rites. All that is required is some little understanding of the sport itself and a decent respect for the several essentials that make it. 3

4   The first purpose of going fishing is to catch fish. But right there the angler separates himself from the meat fisherman and begins to set conditions. He fishes with a rod and line and hook — not with nets or traps or dynamite. From this point on, man being man, further refinements grow naturally and the sport develops. The fisherman is seeking to catch fish on his own terms, terms that will yield him the greatest sense of achievement and the closest identification with his quarry.

5   This establishes the first unwritten article of the brotherhood. Fishing is a sport, a matter of intimate concern only to fish and fisherman; it is not a competition between man and man. The man's aim is to solve by his own wits and skill the unreasoning reaction of the fish, always within the limits of his self-imposed conditions. Besides this, any sort of outshining one's fellow man becomes completely trivial. The fisherman is his own referee, umpire, steward, and sole judge of his performance. Completely alone, by remote lake or virgin stream, he remains bound by his private conditions and the vagaries of fish and weather. Within those conditions, he may bring all his ingenuity to bear, but if he departs from them or betrays them, though only God and the fish are his witnesses, he inevitably reduces his reward.

6   This total freedom from competitive pressure leads the fisherman directly to the three articles of faith that really govern the brotherhood: respect for the fish, respect for the fish's living space, and respect for other fishermen. All three are interrelated and, under the crowded conditions of today's fishing waters, all three are equally important.

7   Respect for other fishermen is simply a matter of common courtesy and reasonably good manners. The more crowded the waters the more necessary manners become and the more thoroughly they are forgotten. The rule can be expressed in a single golden-rule phrase: "Give the other guy the kind of break you would like to get for yourself." Don't crowd him, don't block him, don't push him. If he is working upstream, don't cut in above him; if he is working downstream, don't pile in directly below him. If you see he is hooking fish along some favourite weed bed, don't force your boat in beside him and spoil it for both. Don't park all day in what you think is a favourite spot so that no one else can get near it — give it a fair try and move on.

8   On uncrowded waters a self-respecting fisherman always gives the other fellow first chance through the pool or the drift; as often as not the second time through is just as good. On crowded waters give whatever room and show whatever consideration you can and still wet a line; better still, try somewhere else. The crowds are usually in the wrong places anyway.

9   If you would be part of the brotherhood, be generous. Don't hide the successful fly or lure or bait; explain every last detail of it and give or lend a sample if you can. Show the next man along where you moved and

missed the big one, make him aware of whatever little secret you may have of the river's pools or the lake's shoals or the sea's tides — but only if the other guy wants it. If he doesn't, be generous still and keep quiet. If he wants to tell you his secret instead of listening to yours, reach for your ultimate generosity and hear him out as long as you can stand it. Good things sometimes come from unlikely sources.

Respect for the fish is the real base of the whole business. He is not an enemy, merely an adversary, and without him and his progeny there can be no sport. Whatever his type and species, he has certain qualities that make for sport and he must be given a chance to show them to best advantage. He is entitled to the consideration of the lightest gear and the subtlest method the angler can use with a reasonable chance of success. Trout deserve to be caught on the fly; other methods may be necessary at times, but it is difficult to believe they give much joy to the fisherman. A northern pike or a muskie taken by casting is worth half a dozen taken by trolling. A black bass tempted to the surface is a far greater thrill than one hooked in the depths; an Atlantic salmon or summer steelhead risen to a floating fly is a memory that will live forever. If it takes a little time to learn such skills, there is no doubt the fish is worthy of them. And if the angler is any kind of a man he is unlikely to be satisfied with less. 10

Even in the moment of success and triumph, when the hooked fish is safely brought to beach or net, he is still entitled to respect and consideration: to quick and merciful death if he is wanted, to swift and gentle release if he is not. Killing fish is not difficult — a sharp rap on the back of the head settles most species. Releasing fish is a little, but only a little, more complicated. Fly-caught trout of moderate size are easy. Slide the hand down the leader with the fish still in the water, grip the shank of the hook, and twist sharply. Where it is necessary to handle the fish, a thumb and finger grip on the lower jaw does the least harm and is usually effective. If not, use dry hands and a light but firm grip on the body just forward of the dorsal fin. Wet hands force a heavier grip which is extremely likely to injure vital organs. For heavily toothed fish like northern pike and muskies many fishermen use a grip on the eye sockets or the gill-covers. The first may be all right, but seems dangerous and unnecessarily cruel. The second is destructive. Fish up to ten pounds or so can be gripped securely on the body just behind the gill-covers and should not be harmed. 11

Larger fish that have fought hard are often in distress when released and need to be nursed in the water until they can swim away on their own. Generally little more is needed than to hold them on an even keel, facing upstream, while they take a few gulps of water through their gills. If they lack the strength for this, draw them gently back and forth through the water so that the gills will be forced to work; all but the most exhausted fish will recover under this treatment and swim smoothly 12 away. Fish that have bled heavily or fish that have just swum in from salt water are less likely to recover and should be kept.

13   Respect for the fish's living space should be comprehensive. It includes the water, the bed of the stream or lake, the land on both sides of the water, and all the life that grows there, bird or mammal, plant or fish or insect. There isn't an excuse in the world for litter-leavers, tree-carvers, brush-cutters, flower-pickers, nest-robbers, or any other self-centred vandals on fishing waters. The fisherman comes at best to do some damage — to the fish — and the best he can do is keep it to that. He doesn't need to junk-heap the place with cartons and bottles and tin cans; he need not drop even so much as a leader case or cigarette pack; he can afford to remember that no one else wants to be reminded of him by his leavings.

14   These are elementary and negative points and if parents raised their children properly there would be no need to mention them in this context. A fisherman, any kind of a fisherman, should know better than to spoil the place that makes his sport. But a true share in the brotherhood calls for a little more. The fisherman is under obligation to learn and understand something about the life of his fish and the conditions it needs, if only so that he can take his little part in helping to protect them.

15   All fish need clean waters and all nations, if they know what is good for them, can afford to keep their waters clean. Pollution, whether from sewage or industrial wastes, starts as a little thing scarcely noticed and goes on to destroy all the life of the waters. Its damage can be repaired, slowly, painfully, expensively, but there is no excuse for it in the first place, though many are forthcoming.

16   Besides clean water for their own lives and the many living things they depend on, fish need special conditions for spawning and hatching and rearing. Migratory fish need free passage upstream and down. These things and many others like them are worth understanding not merely because they suggest protections and improvements, but because knowledge of them brings the fisherman closer to the identification he seeks, makes him more truly a part of the world he is trying to share.

17   The old days and the old ways, when every stream was full of fish and empty of people, are long gone. They weren't as good as they sounded anyway. It took time and the efforts of good fishermen to learn what could be done and should be done to produce the best possible sport. North American angling has now come close to full development. No one is going to get what he should from the sport by simply buying some gear and going out on the water, nor can he achieve very much by sneering at better men than himself who do take the trouble to learn the delicate skills of the subtler methods. The real world of fishing is open to anyone, through the literature and the generosity of the brotherhood. Once entered upon, the possibilities are limitless. But even the casual, oc-

casional fisherman owes the sport some measure of understanding — enough, shall we say, to protect himself and others from the waste and aggravations of discourtesy and bad manners that are so often based on ignorance.

In Winchester Cathedral, not far from a famous trout stream in Hampshire, England, is the tomb of William of Wykeham, a great fourteenth-century bishop and statesman who left a motto to a school he founded: "Manners makyth man." Within the same cathedral lie the bones of our father, Izaak Walton, who remarked three hundred years ago: "Angling is somewhat like poetry, men are to be born so." Perhaps Izaak's precept is for the inner circle of the brotherhood, but William's is certainly universal. It is just possible that nice guys don't catch the most fish. But they find far more pleasure in those they do get.

18

STRUCTURE:

1. Haig-Brown states four "articles of faith" for anglers, the first one serving as a general introduction to the three that "really govern the brotherhood" (par. 6). Point out all four articles of faith, specifying where each occurs.
2. Point out all the contrasts that you find in the first four paragraphs of the essay.
3. Which paragraphs make fullest use of examples as a means of development?
4. In the last paragraph, what does Haig-Brown achieve by quoting William of Wykeham's motto, "Manners makyth man"?
5. Can you think of a relevant "article of faith for good anglers" that Haig-Brown has omitted from his classification?

STYLE:

1. How FORMAL or INFORMAL would you judge the style of Haig-Brown's essay to be?
2. Largely because of his prose style, Haig-Brown is sometimes described as Canada's finest essayist. Analyze two especially good examples, paragraphs 5 and 9: In what ways is their STYLE effective?
3. Careful word choice is a central trait of Haig-Brown's style. In paragraph 10, why does Haig-Brown point out that the fish "is not an enemy, merely an adversary. . . ."?
4. In this 1960 essay, Haig-Brown continually uses expressions such as "brotherhood," "fisherman," "competition between man and man," "if the angler is any kind of man" and so on, as if no woman has ever fished. If Haig-Brown were writing today, do you think he would use this traditionally male-centred language? Would you?

IDEAS:

1. In our modern society, which produces food industrially and scientifically, why do people still hunt and fish?

2. According to a Chinese proverb, the time a person spends fishing is not subtracted from that person's life. Discuss the ways in which this philosophy may be true.

3. Many people consider overtly competitive and even violent sports, such as hockey and football, to be the best ones. Yet according to Haig-Brown, it is an absence of competition between anglers that contributes to the best qualities of fishing as a sport (par. 5). In your opinion, what makes a sport good? Is competition necessary? Is body contact or even violence desirable? Illustrate your answers by referring to sports you have experienced.

4. Haig-Brown writes, "Pollution, whether from sewage or industrial wastes, starts as a little thing scarcely noticed and goes on to destroy all the life of the waters" (par. 15). By 1980, twenty years after those words were published, acid rain had killed 140 lakes in Ontario. An Ohio state government survey quoted by *Maclean's* (June 30, 1980) warned that "if something is not done quickly, 2,500 lakes a year to the end of the century will die in Ontario, Quebec and New England." Are there ways in which we as individuals might reduce this damage, caused mainly by the fumes of oil refineries, chemical plants, smelters, coal-fired power plants, paper mills, factories and the private automobile?

5. Write an essay classifying the different types of hunters, hikers, boaters, skiers, snowmobilers or campers.

(NOTE: See also the Topics for Writing at the end of this chapter.)

Edgar Roussel

*Letter from Prison**

Translated from the French by Mary Conrad and Jean-Paul Chavy

Edgar Roussel is considered one of Canada's most dangerous convicts. In 1974 he was among the gunmen who entered the Gargantua Bar in Montreal, locked thirteen patrons in a closet and burned the place down. Roussel was found guilty of two of those murders, and in 1978 was sentenced to life imprisonment. That same year he led hostage-taking uprisings at both Dorchester Penitentiary and the St. Jerome provincial jail, and as a result was sent to a super-maximum security unit within Laval Institute, the Correctional Development Centre. It is this place that he describes in his long and impassioned letter of April 12, 1980 which was sent to External Affairs Minister Mark MacGuigan and a few months later appeared in the Montreal newspaper Le Devoir. *Three months after he sent the letter, Roussel was transferred from the CDC to Laval Institute. A few weeks after that he tried to escape.*

Since March 29, 1978, I have been detained in the Correctional Development Centre (the CDC) where I am serving a life sentence with eligibility for parole in twenty years.

Everything has been said about federal penitentiaries. All I can do is retell it — except when it comes to special detention units such as the CDC, the subject of this letter. The purpose of such centres, according to Directive 174 of the national commissioner, is to prepare "dangerous" prisoners for reintegration into the penitentiary.

To do this, the administration has set up a program that I'd like to examine carefully, to discover in what original way the system works to bring about the desired metamorphosis, so that the caterpillar might become a butterfly — how, in cutting us off from life, they claim to reacquaint us with it. They carry out this program within four boundaries placed like watch towers: a cell, a common room, an outside courtyard, and on top of all that, a Socialization Division.

At the CDC the amount of time spent in the cell is even greater than at most Canadian federal penitentiaries. To keep the prisoner from sinking into boredom or even madness, the administration grants what other institutions categorically forbid: a television set. This gift to the prisoner is important in view of his mental state caused by being alone. But it is even more a confession of failure and, worse yet, a flagrant lack of imagination.

During the first days it is used all the time, then gradually less, and finally more again but this time to drown out the noises that the prisoners never noticed before.

*Editor's title

227

6   Sometimes the television is an aspirin that relieves suffering and at other times it is a window to the outside world. After months of this routine come nausea and disgust; you turn off the machine only to learn a new phenomenon: noise! Searches, guards' rounds, everything takes second place to noise, which in the cells is louder than anywhere else, with never a lull. Very late at night, when sleep finally comes and re-establishes the equalibrium so dangerously broken during the day, the night rounds begin. Each hour, without fail, the loud steps of the guard making his rounds ring on the ceiling of the cell. At the CDC they've found a new way to count the prisoners — from above. The guard can get a full view of the captive through an opening in the ceiling. It's always possible to make up lost sleep by sacrificing the daily walk. But this is just the time the guards choose to search the cells of prisoners who are outside. They arrive in the cell-block corridors in a mob, their noses in the air, and bang! on the walls to see if there are any holes, bang! on the ceiling to see if the opening has been tampered with and bang! on the air vent. Once their work is done they leave, deliberately slamming all the cell doors shut at once in an infernal din. Good-bye sleep and calm.

7   It would be hard to speak of ventilation because there isn't any; there are no windows, and the doors are solid. The air is so heavy that it hangs over you like a thick fog.

8   In summer it's a furnace and our inactivity makes the heat unbearable; we sweat from doing nothing. In the morning, there is a symphony of throat clearing, of nose blowing, and of hoarse coughing to clear respiratory passages.

9   I've been sleeping right on the floor of my cell for nearly two years, my head at the bottom of the door to catch the smallest breeze, an incomparable luxury.

10   For time spent outside the cell, a common room is available every night from 6:30 to 10:30 but never for more than ten inmates at a time. This is part of the socialization; they want to teach us to get along in small groups, in order to plunge us into a population of three or four hundred other prisoners, with the problems of adjustment which that implies.

11   Several group games, another television set, and above all, surveillance. Apart from its larger size, this common room is just another cell like the ones we spend most of our time in.

12   Outside we use a 75-foot-square courtyard where again never more than ten prisoners are let in; no more, no less — it's an administrative fixation. In summer, the high walls keep out any breeze, and from the asphalt pavement rises a stifling heat. No greenery, no benches, nothing but asphalt, cement and iron.

For exercise we practice boxing on a punching bag that cost $172 of our own money. The administration lost a good chance to demonstrate justice, for in all the other prisons punching bags are paid for out of the recreation budgets. All physical activity is risky because of the asphalt surface. Almost all of us suffer from some muscle problem; it would be interesting to see the medical requests and to count the inmates who have asked for special shoes. [13]

Our visits are our greatest comfort and only contact with the outside world; these are timed by the administration for the day and hour that suit them. The privilege of a visit is stingily granted on Wednesdays and Thursdays. At the CDC, visits are considered favours and are scrutinized carefully. [14]

There's no contact with parents, wives and children; it's in this way that the administration promotes individual development. [15]

Several years ago some officials of a zoo travelled across the world to find a female elephant so the captive male wouldn't get bored. The animals' space is constantly being relandscaped so it will be as much as possible like their natural habitat. In their parks, the animals actually have more space than we do. [16]

A Socialization Division, staffed by an evaluation officer and a psychologist, completes the program and is without a doubt the worst problem of all. We get to meet these social science experts when we're at our wits' end; it's when things are ready to blow up that we get to benefit from their bright ideas. [17]

Their main concern is determining whether we're so disturbed that we might attack a staff member, or, much less importantly, whether we might attack fellow prisoners. Once they find this out, these servants of the administration report their conclusions, and it's on the basis of their testimony that the National Special Handling Unit Review Committee will transfer a prisoner. So more often than not, the decision of the committee, though well intentioned, will be based on erroneous reports that were warped from the beginning because they were based on an abnormal situation in which the prisoner was totally confused. [18]

Experts all agree that a prison term longer than five years creates irreversible problems, not to mention the special problems created by units like ours. What we undergo only turns us into animals, bringing out our killer instincts. There are several cases of criminals who were kept in isolation, some longer than others, and who are good examples of what I'm saying. [19]

I'll name just four I knew personally and whose fate I was able to learn: Jacques Mesrine, Richard Blass, Jean-Paul Mercier and Jean Lachapelle. [20]

21   All have certain things in common: they spent several years in isolation and they are all dead today because they refused to relive, even for one day, what they had known in the past.

22   It might be useful to know just what they did after experiencing this isolation.

23   Jean Lachapelle was imprisoned about six years in one cell. Upon his return behind bars, he pleaded guilty to nine charges of murder, not to mention the fact that during his escape — the last, it goes without saying — he was himself shot full of holes.

24   As for Richard Blass, only his death kept him from being charged with fifteen murders. And as for Jean-Paul Mercier (like Blass, isolated for three years), he confessed to murdering two guards after his escape, to avoid being recognized and getting several more years in solitary. As for Jacques Mesrine, a close reading of his two books clearly reveals the mental state produced by his years of isolation in a cell.

25   None of these four individuals had been found guilty of murder before their time in isolation. Was this a coincidence? You can draw your own conclusions. The system aims to make the criminal feel small, to repress the least initiative, and in a word to assassinate his personality so it will conform to the closed prison world in which they force it to develop. When the inmate has become enough of a cheat, hypocrite and liar that he can fake gratitude to his torturers, then he's eligible for a transfer.

26   The individuals considered "dangerous" cases are the product of a myth perpetuated by rituals meant to remind us of our past crimes.

27   Nothing can erase a criminal act, and to think that punishment causes redemption is a trap. When they intend to change the individual, arbitrarily deciding to make him the same as everyone else — then I claim the right to be different.

28   All the inmates brought here when I was have since been transferred. Only an unchanging thirst for vengeance can explain my presence at the CDC. The last inmate of the group left April 10, 1980 and his honours list speaks for itself; recently this guy was hit with a one-year sentence for assaulting two officers of the CDC with a knife. At first he had been charged with attempted murder, but his jurors accepted the reduced charge; according to them, the inmate could not judge the nature of his act, because the conditions during his imprisonment had altered his reason.

29   Some time ago they released a prisoner from the CDC directly into society, although only a few months before he had been considered too dangerous for transfer to a maximum security penitentiary.

30   In this long and detailed letter I have tried to give you an inside view of the situation that I have endured for too long. These days I talk to myself, laugh without reason or shake from nervous spasms. I sense that

something in me is breaking down, and if no-one intervenes on my behalf the worst will happen. I've reached a point of saturation where the slightest incident could trigger a desperate act.

For two long, endless years I have not hugged my wife, my mother or my daughter, and for two long years I have not seen the moon or stars. Even the lowest of animals is not denied this right. Konrad Lorenz maintains that it is dangerous to corner an animal with no chance of escape. Friedrich Nietzche states in his book *Thus Spake Zarathustra* that man has made the wolf into a dog and has made himself into man's best domestic animal. In the introduction to the same book, he also denounces cruelty clothed in justice, saying that it is in tragedies, bullfights and crucifixions that man has felt best on earth; when he invented hell, that was his paradise on earth.

31

It is in the name of these great men and in the veneration of their thought that I ask you now to intercede on my behalf. Already in 1976 as president of a subcommittee investigating violence in the penitentiaries, you denounced the ineptitude of administrators. Now your new position gives you the influence and power to improve my condition. This is the purpose of my request.

32

If this document one day serves as a defence before the courts, it will be because the change from caterpillar to butterfly has not taken place.

33

I dare hope, Honourable Minister, that despite all the responsibility and work that your new position brings, my appeal will not be in vain.

34

STRUCTURE:

1. This selection was written as a letter to an individual, External Affairs Minister Mark MacGuigan. Why, then, has it been made public in *Le Devoir* and in this book? In what ways might this specific case be of general interest?

2. Where does Edgar Roussel first name the four categories of his classification?

3. In this classification of the CDC environment, paragraphs 4-9 are devoted to the cell, 10 and 11 to the common room, 12 and 13 to the outside courtyard, and 17 and 18 to the Socialization Division. Why does Roussel devote as many paragraphs to the cell as he does to all the other categories combined?

4. Do the four "boundaries" of the CDC program overlap at all, or are they mutually exclusive, as befits the parts of a logical classification?

5. The classification of Roussel's prison environment ends with paragraph 18. In what ways do the classification and the rest of Roussel's letter support each other?

6. Identify and discuss the cause and effect argument upon which "Letter from Prison" is to a large extent based: what are the causes? What are the effects?

STYLE:

1. Analyze the sources of power in this passage from paragraph 31: "For two long, endless years I have not hugged my wife, my mother or my daughter, and for two long years I have not seen the moon or stars. Even the lowest of animals is not denied this right."

2. Point out two FIGURES OF SPEECH in paragraph 3 and discuss their relevance to the subject.

3. What technique gives life to paragraph 12?

IDEAS:

1. Edgar Roussel's letter to Mark MacGuigan apparently made its point: three months after it was sent, Roussel was released from the CDC and returned to the general prison population of Laval Institute. But a few weeks after that, Roussel attempted to escape from the prison altogether. Discuss this act: does it demonstrate that Roussel was insincere in writing his so carefully reasoned letter? Or does it merely prove his own point that the program of the CDC is a failure?

2. Roussel writes, ". . . to think that punishment causes redemption is a trap" (par. 27). Do you agree or disagree? What, if anything, does redeem a criminal? Does the Correctional Development Centre, as described by Roussel, seem designed for punishment? For redemption? For some other purpose?

3. If you have read "Living with Automation in Winnipeg," what similarities do you find between the lives of industrial workers, as described by Ian Adams, and the lives of CDC inmates, as described by Roussel?

4. If you have read "Warily into a Wired-Up World," what similarities do you find between the collecting of information by computers, as described by Andrew Osler, and the surveillance of inmates by guards and psychologists, as described by Roussel?

5. If you have read "Breaking Out of the Female Mould," what similarities do you find between Maryon Kantaroff's description of the female artist in society and Roussel's description of the inmate in the CDC?

6. Write a letter requesting something that is very important to you, addressed to the person or organization that could grant your request. Include many supporting details, as Roussel does.

7. Write an essay that classifies the "boundaries" of your present life (these could include home, school, employment, etc., but should be mutually exclusive as are the "boundaries" that Roussel names in paragraph 3).

(NOTE: See also the Topics for Writing at the end of this chapter.)

Susan G. Cole

Jesse James & the New Frontier

Susan G. Cole is a media specialist and feminist. She was born in 1952 and raised in Toronto. In 1974 she received a Bachelor's degree in Greek and Latin from Harvard University, then lived for a year in Greece before returning to Toronto. She began her career in communications as researcher and editor for TV Ontario's Education of Mike McManus, *then became Peter C. Newman's personal researcher, conducting interviews and business research for Newman's book* The Bronfman Dynasty *(1978). Since then Cole has written for the Toronto* Globe and Mail *(our selection appeared in the Fanfare section in 1982) and for Canadian Business, has co-published a monthly feminist review called* Broadside, *has lectured extensively on pornography and is planning a book on that subject. Cole now works in the programming department of the pay television network* First Choice Canadian.

1   The Computer Age is here, and we love it: video games fill up our leisure hours and keep the kids quiet. We fear it, too — especially when the bank teller is peering at her terminal screen to see if we're solvent. And we respect it, so much so that Harvard University requires that liberal arts students show they can program a computer before granting their degrees. In future, every child will be expected to have the vocabulary of the computer at his fingertips.

2   Now, the office is a whirr, a symphony of percussive chugs as the cheques, pre-signed, of course, come churning out of the machines. EDP personnel tap away at the terminals. The accounting manager sighs with satisfaction as the computers spit up printouts of the payroll — right on time. It's a push-button operation, a manager's dream.

3   EDP stands for Electronic Data Processing. Information that used to be stored by manual file in six different offices now spews forth from one terminal; accounting that demanded scores of man-days can be handled in a matter of seconds. Electronic Word Processing (EWP) allows secretaries to do volumes of correspondence and have it filed away in a memory bank that never forgets.

4   Computers are the brainchildren of the omnipotent scientist, his gift to the rest of us who marvel at what he knows and at what, we assume, we can never understand. But not everyone is standing by, overcome with awe. There's always someone out to beat the system, and programmers and police are getting ready for the crime wave of the future, the Jesse James of the scientific era.

5   "There's no evidence *yet* that computer crime is a problem," says Detective-Inspector Peter Campbell of the Ontario Provincial Police

anti-rackets branch. "What we're talking about is the enormous potential for abuse of computer systems."

The word efficiency was wasted until EDP came along, and managers   6
were so excited about it that they forgot that the information inside the machines can be very valuable. "The emphasis," Campbell explains, "is on getting the system working and worrying about security later. Sometimes, later never comes."

John Carroll, a professor of computer science at the University of   7
Western Ontario, is working on his third book on computer security. "People are lazy," he says, "and lack responsibility. It's a disease and it starts at the top. They close their eyes to the losses, if the losses are cost-effective. And the middle manager will close his eyes, too, if it's a question of being a nice guy."

Of course, it's possible that middle manager never opened his eyes to   8
begin with. He may even have clasped hands with the programmer who put the wrench in the works. In fact, employees with access to business computers often aren't even given a security check.

"There's a desperate need for computer-trained personnel," Carroll   9
explains. "They'll take any warm body that can program. Besides, how do you clear staff without having the Human Rights Commission and the unions crying discrimination? Screening means interviewing school teachers, checking criminal records, dredging up old files. A lot of people find it repulsive."

The systems may be perfect, but human error makes them perfectly   10
vulnerable. According to Carroll, the new Jesse James can fashion any number of computer capers, like the one aptly named The Trojan Horse. The middle manager beaming away at sight of his payroll printout may have been the victim of a simple sabotage for anyone with basic programming skills.

The programmer is asked to design Program SORT which puts   11
employees' names in alphabetical order. He does that and, indeed, every time a new employee comes onto the roster, an operator presses SORT and the new employee is sorted.

But the programmer does something else while he's at it. He develops   12
program AORT, which not only puts the payroll in order but makes sure his own remittance is considerably higher than it should be. He assumes (and rightly so) that an operator will make the common typographical error of pushing A instead of S. Every time the error is made, the computer caper works. Naturally, the programmer arranges it so that his extra program will erase itself.

The Logic Bomb has much more dire consequences. The vice-president   13
fires his programmer for seeking an exorbitant raise. The programmer takes his revenge. He inserts into the existing sequence of instructions a message to erase all files if his name doesn't appear on the payroll. Of

course, he doesn't bother to make his program disappear because he's caused the entire system to self-destruct. The Logic Bomb goes by another name: extortion.

14 The Salami Technique sounds more like a how-to guide for delicatessen owners but it refers to another computer crime. Not all of us calculate how benefit premiums are deducted from our paycheques, and most of us would never miss a few cents. The programmer slices off a fraction of a dollar say, 87 cents from 2,000 employees' paycheques, places it in another account he's programmed, and it adds up to $1,740 a week. It comes spewing out of the computer, a cheque made out to the felonious fiddler himself. Who's to know? The cheques are all pre- signed.

15 "All you have to do," says Flora Macquarrie, a computer programmer working for one of Canada's fastest-growing software specialists, "is find out what the system doesn't care about and then exploit it."

16 It's amazing what loopholes can be unearthed. With a little help from friendly computers, interest payments are calculated to the smallest fraction of a cent. If interest works out to $25.324, the figure is dutifully rounded off by the computer to $25.32, and that extra .4 of a cent goes floating back into the black void, lost forever. But not if an enterprising programmer gets to it first. He'll set up an account of his own with a variation of the Salami technique and funnel those fractions of cents into his own pocket.

17 EDP systems may be efficient but sometimes the sheer expense of operating them makes room for another caper. If a customer overpays his mortgage by less than a dollar, it's often not worth it for the computer to spew out yet another cheque and for the system to provide an envelope and postage for the client's minuscule rebate. So the computer ignores the overpayment, balances the account, and more money goes into the black void waiting for a programmer to snap it up.

18 Programmers couldn't weave this magic without access to the computer facility, but limiting access would be like forbidding a doctor to visit his patient. EDP systems are not designed like Fort Knox and when something goes wrong — and anything can — it's a programmer who has to fix it. Some systems, for example, went crazy when interest rates hit double-digit figures.

19 Macquarrie explains, "If systems were designed to deal with single-digit interest rates, they crashed as soon as interest went up to 10 per cent. The same kind of problem can occur if mortgages have to be paid over a 25-year period. As soon as the billing date goes over the year 2,000 and my system is programmed to function only with the years beginning with 19, the systems will go crazy."

20 Corporate dependence on computers almost guarantees that the word

"crash" will never again refer to a depression, and will always conjure up the image of a computer failing to compute. A crash can be disastrous. Every second lost means the loss of precious revenue. It's estimated that if an EDP system goes down for anywhere from five to 10 days, a business will go under.

Imagine the operator who beeps his SOS to the programmer on call. 21 Enter the fixer, usually on his own, sometimes in the middle of the night, often unsupervised by a manager who would rather stay in bed. There is not much to stop him from some dangerous diddling. "One of the biggest exposures," Carroll warns, "is during the debugging stage or during the recovery from a crash."

"You don't have to be a genius to commit these crimes," Macquarrie 22 says with a smile. In fact, you don't even have to be a programmer to hop onto the criminal bandwagon. Just one week's training can make you an operator and gives you knowledge of whatever security measures are in place — passwords, for example. A password is the special combination of digits that clears the terminal for use. A password gives automatic access to vital data, some of which can be used for blackmail, some of which you may just want to get at without having to pay for it. Passwords, of course, are for sale.

If you can't buy it you can always guess at it, particularly if, as is often 23 the case, computer terminals are not kept under lock and key. "If a password has eight digits," says Colin Rous, "and you have a computer handy, then very quickly you can feed into the computer every combination of digits until you get the right password. But if I program the computer so that anyone who tries more than three times and fails to get entry gets cut off, then it's not worth the thief's while to keep at it."

Providing such deterrents is precisely Colin Rous's business. He runs 24 Cerberus Computer Security Inc., a consulting firm that specializes in beefing up computer security. "I'm trying to increase the cost of penetrating the system so that the costs are greater to a potential thief than the value of getting access."

Since passwords come and go on the black market and employees 25 come on and off an office payroll, changing passwords makes a great deal of sense. Not everybody makes the sensible move, though. Rous tells the story of meeting a systems operator employed three years ago in a municipal office. "We wanted to see if he could dial by his phone into his old terminal from a computer he operated on his own desk. He did, and everything was still the same. He could have changed his utility and natural gas bills with ease."

John Swinden, a specialist in computer security, is a partner of 26 Clarkson Gordon, one of the country's largest accounting institutions. "I like to use the analogy of your own home," Swinden says. "If you change all the locks all the time, add bolts, bar your windows, make it really secure, it makes it harder for you to get in and harder for you to live in it. Executives are asking what the practical possibilities are.''

27   "It's still difficult to convince the EDP departments to take action because anything we recommend hampers the system," Rous confesses. "We're a pain."

28   The difference between the computer caper and any other inter-office espionage has to do with the nature of the beastly computer itself: programs vanish. "If I'm smart enough to manipulate a computer, then I'm smart enough to make sure that the programs disappear," says Detective-Inspector Campbell, who has been on the computer-crime case for more than 10 years. "At least if I've stolen a manual file, I've left some evidence. But if I hook into a terminal from a thousand miles away, I don't leave any fingerprints." It's the kind of thing that gives crime detectors fits.

29   Catching up with the culprit sometimes doesn't help matters much. Two years ago, two former University of British Columbia professors hooked into a terminal owned by the University of New Brunswick, and helped themselves to some information. They were convicted of theft, but only the theft of $26, the value of the paper on which the information was printed.

30   "Let's say information is the basis on which you function, your source of revenue," Campbell explains. "I steal it. I sell it. Unless the information is a trade secret, I can't be charged with anything else but theft of paper." Why such a minor offence? Because technically nothing has been stolen. The information, after all, is still where it was. Had the thieves in New Brunswick copied the information off the terminal screen, they couldn't have been charged with theft of anything.

31   Film director Stanley Kubrick tried to sound the alarm in 2001: A Space Odyssey. He predicted that HAL, the master computer, would confound his operators and program them. But Kubrick sounded the wrong alarm. Computers don't lie, cheat or steal. The people around them can and do. Even if the potential for computer crime remains devastatingly high, it's obvious that computers are still senseless assemblages of basic hardware. They're still, after all, susceptible to the human touch.

STRUCTURE:
1. In what way does the opening paragraph prepare us for the topic?
2. What is Susan G. Cole's THESIS STATEMENT?

3. The classification of computer crime occupies paragraphs 10-17. How many categories are there within this space, how are they labelled and which paragraphs does each take up?
4. Once the classification of computer crimes is made, what does the large remainder of the essay do?
5. Discuss the analogy upon which paragraph 26 is based. Is it clear? Does it seem appropriate?
6. In what ways are paragraphs 28-30 based on contrast?
7. Is the final paragraph effective as a closing? Why or why not? Is it ominous or is it reassuring?

STYLE:

1. Point out all the FIGURES OF SPEECH in paragraph 18 and judge how effective each is.
2. Discuss the term "crash" as applied to computers (par. 20 and elsewhere). Is "crash" a good word for this meaning? State all the other computer JARGON that you know. Are these terms newly invented or have they been borrowed from our standard vocabulary?

IDEAS:

1. Some people who would never consider shoplifting or burglary would not hesitate to steal thousands of dollars through such white-collar devices as computer crime. Do white-collar criminals view their acts as less serious than other crimes? How much of a criminal is the new "Jesse James" compared to someone like Edgar Roussel, who wrote our previous selection "Letter from Prison"?
2. Write an episode for the autobiography of the new Jesse James, narrating in first person how a computer crime was committed.
3. Many people love computers while many others hate them. Why do computers tend to provoke extreme reactions?
4. Do you agree with film director Stanley Kubrick (par. 31) that computers such as "HAL" in *2001: A Space Odyssey* may someday control us? Or do you agree with Cole that people, whether honestly or dishonestly, will control the computers?
5. It is often said that as technology grows more complicated, our society grows more vulnerable. Discuss this concept as it applies to these areas and to any others that come to mind:
   computers
   agriculture
   energy
   transportation
   warfare

6. In an essay, classify one of the following:
    computer games
    computer languages
    computer malfunctions
    benefits of computers
    dangers of computers
    views of the role that computers will play in our future society

(NOTE: See also the Topics for Writing at the end of this chapter.)

David Godfrey

No More Teacher's Dirty Looks

For years David Godfrey has been on the leading edge of things, moving regularly from one avant-garde to the next. He has served with CUSO in Ghana, written experimental fiction, been an outspoken socialist and Canadian nationalist, begun three anti-establishment publishing houses, and now that the Information Age is upon us has become a proponent of computers in education. Godfrey was born in Winnipeg in 1938 and was educated at the Universities of Toronto and Iowa. He has worked mainly as a teacher (now chairman of the Creative Writing Department of the University of Victoria, B.C.), and as a publisher and writer. Godfrey co-founded the House of Anansi Press in 1967, New Press in 1969 and Press Porcépic (which he still heads) in 1972, and in 1970 co-founded the Independent Publishers' Association. His own first book was a highly experimental collection of short stories, Death Goes Better with Coca-Cola (1968). He drew upon his CUSO experience to produce a novel about Africa, The New Ancestors, which won the 1970 Governor General's Award. Godfrey has co-authored books about subjects such as CUSO, economic nationalism and Canadian books, and in 1978 published a second collection of short stories, Dark Must Yield. Our selection, drawn from his recent work with computers, comes from the book he co-authored in 1979, Gutenberg Two.

> *No more pencils, no more books*
> *No more teacher's dirty looks.*

I t is generally agreed that perhaps the most startling of changes envisaged in education over the next 10-15 years will be the extent to which technological systems will be employed. For instance, Information Retrieval Television systems (IRTV) would probably be employed in most schools to provide audio-visual television rather than decentralized type systems. There is also considerable discussion in informed circles of the possible diminution of the role of the school itself. Evolving concurrently with the implementation of the technological systems for education, audio-visual communications could transform the home into part-time school. According to a study by Bell Canada, within a decade a significant number of homes could be equipped with home terminals capable of utilizing IRTV and computerized library systems. Consequently, it is quite likely that significant numbers of post secondary students will spend more time working at home or in small groups by 1990. Secondary students could follow by 1993 and primary students by the year 2010 (1).

Before you put too much trust in that prediction you might note that its source was a 1971 document and all that I have done is add ten years to every date mentioned in the original.

3   Although the media . . . see growth as well as vulnerability in the new technologies, on the whole the teaching establishment sees, quite rightly, nothing but danger. Why did this revolution predicted by Bell not come about? Partly because of the teaching establishment's relatively firm control of both Content and Carrier aspects of education (can a student bring his own textbook to class?), and partly because those who became involved in the technology early were quickly absorbed by the fascinating techniques available and failed to pose the deeper philosophic questions that will probably have to be answered before the revolution is actually implemented.

4   Anyone who has taught for a number of years comes to recognize a set of problems which exist beneath the set of problems that occupy one's teaching efforts and hours.

5   Because these deeper problems seem insoluble, they tend to disappear from view. The evolution of the Electronic Highway and NABU's forces one to consider them, however, and once they are considered as solvable, then major structural changes within the educational system become almost inevitable. In many instances, the unhappiness that attends all such structural changes will attach itself to the mechanisms of solution rather than to the deeper set of problems, and it would be unwise to underestimate either the changes or the unhappiness likely to be involved, but in the beginning at least one can concentrate upon the problems themselves.

6   My personal terms for these problems are a little unusual, but perhaps useful.

LOCKSTEPS	TRANSCRAPS
MR. GRUNDY	BULL CURVES
STUDENT X	PRE-SOLUTIONS

7   By LOCKSTEPS, I attempt to summarize those problems generated by the requirement to process a large number of students through the same teaching sequence at the same moment. The result, of course, if the teacher is reasonably honest, is that 90% of the students are bored, lost, or out of phase at least 90% of the time and most actual learning takes place outside of the sequence or on its peripheries while the main talents of the teachers are best described in entertainment terms. The result for students is twofold: a general mistrust of education and the development of individual adaptative techniques to bypass the structure they find themselves enmeshed within.

8   MR GRUNDY refers to those inevitable disasters that occur as LOCKSTEPS ensures that certain teachers will be notched with certain students for fixed periods. All students have had the experience of a year or course of excitement and stimulation followed by one of extreme boredom, non-comprehension, or personality clashes. Teachers some-

times find themselves turned into MR GRUNDY simply by the particular chemistry of a group of students.

The system and the students still make some attempts to grade teachers, but the MR GRUNDY factor makes such comparisons more or less useless. It is possible to grade teachers on their effectiveness within a general population, but their effectiveness range with specific groups of students will likely vary far more than the comparative range of their effectiveness measured against that of other teachers. 9

The question of defining effectiveness of teaching is thus shuffled to one side and only random attempts can be made to match teachers and students according to such factors as personality type, cultural backgrounds, teaching modes, degree of authoritarianism, libertarianism, intelligence quotients. 10

STUDENT X represents the other side of the equation. Except at the graduate level, the process of education remains largely exterior to the students. They are processed through a system that must seem almost totally artificial to them and are graded on accomplishment only. Rare indeed are the skylights of a sympathetic and knowledgeable teacher, a well-trained educational counsellor, or a co-op or intern program that demonstrates how the real world goes about its learning. 11

At the extremes, something is known of STUDENT X as he or she passes through the kinks of the system: honour students and trouble makers impose their presence on the system; but in general, each new teacher takes on STUDENT X as a fully unknown quantity. 12

After a lecture on *The Heart of Darkness,* I once had a first year student wax enthusiastic over my presentation. I woke up when she said, "That's the first time I ever understood that book." In high school, it turned out, she had studied the text three times. No one had kept track of this fact, nor of her failure to ever understand the book. 13

The list of factors that can affect learning accomplishment is large: social background, personality factors, motivation, right brain/left brain development, aural/visual/conceptual modes of learning, skill mastery, reading habits, etc., but the system cannot afford to record and report on these factors let alone restructure itself to take account of their impact upon actual learning. 14

We all know the student who can recite every Vezina Trophy winner from 1904 on, but can't remember the dates of the War of 1812; none of us really have time to understand why that is so. 15

STUDENT X enters our range of vision, absorbs a vaguely measured quantity of what we push out into his or her domain by methods almost totally unknown to us, and then passes on to the next strange MR GRUNDY with a duly rewarded B- or 63 or Pass or one line comment. 16

Cumulatively, these strange little marks make up a very formal and 17 imposing document which may allow or prevent STUDENT X from entering Law School or graduating from Veterinarian College. TRAN-SCRAPS represent just that, scraps of information of very dubious value carried from step to step of the system and acting as cryptic symbols of STUDENT X's contacts with MR GRUNDY. In the aggregate, like tribal scars, they do identify the failures and the superstars.

18   The fact that TRANSCRAPS can be produced is a major self-ratification of the system, but as anyone knows who has looked at two or three hundred of them, looking for the one best employee or for the thirty most innovative students, the usefulness of the record is not very high; at the best, it records about 10% of what you really want to know.

19   Looking at the changing ability of certain high schools in Ontario to produce Ontario Scholarship students before and after the elimination of provincial examinations, one can understand the notion of a BULL CURVE as a representation of the system's ability to manipulate its relative grading in order to justify its existence. In B.C., teachers who mark firmly find that their students move to other classes where high grades are easier to obtain and the "offending" teacher discovers that his or her effectiveness is graded downward. In another variation of the BULL CURVE, B.C. secondary schools whose failure rate exceeds a certain percentage may find themselves in trouble with the certification bodies.

20   The fundamental problem here is that the system finds it difficult to define mastery and degrees of mastery within its disciplines. How much French does STUDENT X know? Not enough. The causes may be diverse, ranging from mere hesitancy, through conflicting approaches and varied environments, to the real problems of advanced disciplines that are in constant flux.

21   I recently gave some assistance to a student finishing her MA at the Sorbonne on a West Indian writer. There were gaps in her knowledge of literature that absolutely astounded me. She felt, for example, that the writer was racist because many of his characters made racist remarks about Jews in Toronto. Nonetheless, she passed her MA from the Sorbonne. MR GRUNDY'S law of the BULL CURVE might be expressed as follows:

> The knowledge received by any given teacher of any given new student from a TRANSCRAP is always less than 5% of the ideal and the knowledge passed on varies directly with the peculiarities of the institution's grading system but is never greater than the original knowledge.

22   The cumulative result of many of these factors is one I term PRE-SOLUTIONS. A metaphor that seems applicable is that of the meat-

grinder; in goes pork, veal, beef and perhaps a little venison, pony and turtle; out comes hamburger. A few students escape almost completely and most learn to learn despite the system, but all are damaged to some extent and the process itself remains unchanged. The amount of adaptation to the variables of time, innovation and personality is minuscule and the awareness of those involved is but a fraction of what it might be.

All the teacher can do is carry into the classroom a set of pre-solutions,   23
ideas, concepts and methods of presentation which have been used in the past, and hope that they will work as well as they did last time; however well that might be. The dedicated teachers manage to change a small percentage of those PRE-SOLUTIONS every year; the less dedicated don't.

The fascination of computers, databanks and cheap long-distance   24
communications for the innovative teacher is obvious and quite enormous. One can now begin to deal with all of these deeper problems. Let me start with a small example. During the seventies, the teaching of English in the secondary schools began at last to stress the creative and personal rather than strict rules of composition. This was quite a breakthrough, provided that the teachers were excellent and had the necessary time to devote to this quite difficult task. Many teachers were excellent and made the time to encourage students to write out of their own experience and desires.

But the "basics" did suffer, punctuation, grammar, and structure. In   25
fact, of course, these "basics" are much easier to teach than a sense of creativity and provide ideal material for experimental computer-aided courses. I no longer "teach" punctuation in any of my classes. Students who haven't mastered that particular aspect of the discipline receive an 80 page manual covering over 180 rules of punctuation and an introduction to the computer. Then, at their own speed, they master the rules and demonstrate that mastery to the computer/program which is endlessly patient, keeps track of exactly which rules have been mastered and which not, never asks them anything they already know and politely refers them back to the manual if they miss a test question too many times. In addition, it allows the students to decide if they want me to be able to see the computer's evaluation of their current session.

Obviously not all educational material is suitable for this type of CAL   26
(Computed Assisted Learning) presentation, but far more is than is not. There are a number of centres of excellence in the country involved with computer systems and satellites, especially the University of Quebec (2) which has thirteen campuses deliberately linked together by computerized communications to encourage all the segments to function as an Omnibus Network, and the Ontario Institute for Studies in Education (3) which will be one of the primary foci for experiments involving education.

27   The National Research Council has sponsored the development of a new language, designed for educational purposes, which makes the writing of courses far easier. Unlike the PLATO and TICCIT systems, NATAL is not restricted to a single terminal type nor to a single manufacturer's equipment with all the limitations and often unnecessary expense implicit in such a restriction. NATAL currently supports a variety of terminals ranging from basic alphanumeric units to graphics units incorporating local processing and is capable of accommodating new hardware developments such as the Telidon terminal.

28   NATAL now functions on the Digital Equipment Corporation's PDP10 and implementation is underway on other large, general purpose, time-sharing systems and on a dedicated mini-computer. These efforts will result in a standard specification for NATAL, implementations of which are expected to be available from a wide variety of sources.

29   One of its many features is that it is bilingual. For every command in the language there is a French and English version, so that programmers can work in the language of their own choice with the same system being capable of running both English and French programs (4).

30   Let us look at my "class" in terms of the six problems:

31   LOCKSTEPS. Bob does not have to listen as I explain comma splices to Peter for the 27th time. In fact, Bob isn't even present while Peter spends the ten minutes (or fifty minutes) necessary to master this particular unit. If a new student enters the "class" and has problems with only five of the 180 units, then graduation may take place within twenty minutes. All the time-oriented functions of education (periods, days, Grades, Years, Majors and Degrees) are unnecessary for those portions of knowledge available in similar CAL courses. On Monday, the student might improve his mastery of punctuation by three percent, of trigonometry by one percent and of French Vocabulary Level Five by six percent. Every student would thus have a completely distinct learning track in all segments of all disciplines.

32   MR GRUNDY does not completely disappear, but little is left beyond the memory. As students become more aware of the process of learning and more of the routine aspects of teaching are taken over by programs, teachers will be able to be matched with those students with whom they function well rather than those whom the timetable demands. Neither a student nor teacher will have to face a year with a "fink," or a "complete idiot." Most courses will contain a shadow of their originator, of course, but teachers or students will be able to select different courses covering the same material. From the teacher's point of view, dealing with students who have self-selected themselves, with the more theoretical and complex aspects of the subject, all with a minimum of grading, must surely reduce frustration.

The STUDENT X problem will be reduced in a number of ways. Primarily, the student will be able, and ought to be encouraged, to examine the process by which a given body of material is being taught. That is, the program itself will be available to the student and the student's suggestions will be part of the continual amendment of the program. Questions that are ambiguous, elements that are unclear, options that should be added, can all be dealt with in discussions, either group or individual.

Properly constructed programs will also provide a great deal of information to the student about the process of learning so that each student will be able to develop an individual profile of learning skills and difficulties. If some students wish to keep most of this fairly private, they should be allowed to.

In other instances, acceptance into certain learning situations might require some documentation of learning skills rather than merely learning accomplishments, but in these instances the student would at least be able to improve the skills before application.

In the majority of cases, a student moving to a new learning situation would carry with them a great deal of information which would greatly improve their chances of success.

The TRANSCRAP as such would lose most of its functions. Employers would have their own ways of examining in detail for the skills and accomplishments they required and so would graduate schools. Since education would be far less time-bound and place-bound than it is now, one could expect a far greater degree of transfer between the private sector and the formal educational system. The actuality of failure would not disappear, of course, but the recording of it on TRANSCRAPS would. A case can be made that most educational failures represent either inadequate teaching or inadequate self-analysis that draws the student into a particular LOCKSTEPS situation from which the only exit door is marked Failure. Individualized learning should consist of individually established goals as well as individual learning speed, routing and approach.

BULL CURVES are not entirely the educational system's responsibility. The society's general fear of the twenty-hour work week has created a hidden demand on the system, which might be expressed in the vernacular as "teach the buggers anything, movies, bowling, science fiction even sex, but keep them out of the labour market as long as possible."

The universities have listened to this message (suitably translated of course) with more care than most of the community colleges who, out of fear or intelligence, have felt that students might like to be employed once they do graduate. As one result, unlike the universities, many of the community colleges have two applicants for every position.

But much of the responsibility remains within the system. Faced with declining enrolments and uncertain about its functions because of society's own uncertainty about the future, the system becomes terrified at the thought of a fifty percent "failure" rate and the moment of truth is put off, either until university or until the student enters the real work world.

41   Let us assume, however, that a university develops a computer-based course in Physics with a reasonable effectiveness ratio. What is to prevent secondary school teachers from taking the course, from letting their best students take the course in their senior year, from revising the course for their other students? Only a few technical considerations which will soon become quite minor.

42   As such transfers become more common, fraudulent grades will become obviously fraudulent. At the moment, most university departments have learned to recognize the schools which prepare students well and those which don't, but no action can be taken of any real effectiveness. Being able to send back some detailed comparative statistics drawn out automatically by the program and demonstrating that an A in Physics from School Bloat is comparative to a C- from School Honest, will be a start at least.

43   But it is in the elimination of PRE-SOLUTIONS that the most excitement lies. The creative teacher will be delighted to see 80% of the rote aspects of any discipline adapted for presentation by this methodology for many reasons. First of all, it forces one to examine the content of what is being taught. Since the information presented is public in ways that a lecture or discussion are not, even this initial step can be salutary. Secondly, one must seriously examine one's assumptions about how the material might best be presented. LOCKSTEPS simplifies presentation in many ways. But suppose one needn't worry about holding up the entire class for a half hour while Paul grasps the second law of thermodynamics; suppose it doesn't matter if he needs fifteen examples instead of two. Do you have fifteen? Why didn't the first fourteen work? Perhaps what is needed is more drama, or humour, or a game context?

44   The program can store data about hundreds of reactions to specific questions and summarize them in patterns that help indicate why some elements didn't work for certain students; the students themselves will discuss their reactions and suggest improvements. Most amendments can be made fairly quickly. In addition, other teachers can utilize the program and report on it to the originator. One thus begins to seriously analyse the educational process itself in addition to participating in it.

45   Programs should act as a neutral buffer between teacher and student. Both can amend it; both can draw information from it that is not normally available. Rather than guessing as to whether or not a particular segment works, one can compare its effectiveness with other segments of the same course and even with other experiences of that particular class.

46   The time saved by this method of presentation of rote portions of the material can be spent not only upon specific difficulties and the complex-

ities of a particular discipline, but upon the larger questions of how we acquire and retain knowledge.

This is not to say that adaptation of a large proportion of the curriculum to this teaching method will come about overnight. For every program that is complete and functioning, there seem to be a dozen horror stories of disasters, fantasies, meanderings or brave beginnings best forgotten. There are at least three major categories of error: inadequate equipment, over-ambitious plans, and lack of comprehension of what it is that is to be taught.

Nonetheless, successful programs do exist and if the educational establishment fails to recognize the innovation it will simply have to watch as the new methodology establishes itself outside of the existing institutions.

The establishment of schools as we know them was influenced greatly by Gutenberg's inventions. J.L. Vives was describing a revolution when he wrote in 1531:

> The man desirous of wisdom must make use of books, or of those men who take the place of books . . . Let a school be established in every township, and let there be received into it as teachers men who are of ascertained learning, uprightness and prudence. Let their salary be paid to them from the public treasury . . . Let the teacher know the mother-tongue of the boys exactly, so that by means of their vernacular he may make his instruction easier and more pleasant . . .; the teacher should keep in his mind the earlier history of his mother-tongue (5).

The innovations we term Gutenberg Two do not have a "schoolroom" as their natural environment: an appendage of a library, a room in which books can be distributed, collected and stored. There is no technical reason why a student in my punctuation "class" couldn't "pass" the course without leaving home. It is inevitable that some . . . entrepreneurs . . . will recognize the possibilities of educational content within the new electronic environment and promote the advantages of home learning via the friendly NABU.

Education has existed for a long time without serious competition, partly because of its social function and partly because of its high labour content; competition is about to arrive. As in all instances where a social group faces a threat from mechanical innovation, we can expect a good deal of protest, intensified in this instance by the prior lack of competition and the articulateness of the threatened group. The educational system at the present is a Carrier whose Content is the accepted and valued knowledge of the society. It is place-bound, time-bound and unused to competition or innovation. No other sector of society is more vulnerable to the new technologies. I will predict, however, that within the system (after an initial period of protest), terror will become the mother of adaptation, and although the formal structures will continue to shrink as the work week shortens, creative teachers will have tasks and opportunities that they had previously never even considered possible.

52   Vulnerability Coefficient: .75
Prognosis: Small craft warnings in the straits at last. High winds. Danger of capsizing for the ill-prepared. Light in distant harbours for the adventurous.

REFERENCES . . . .

1. *The Film Industry in Canada: Report,* prepared by The Bureau of Management Consulting for the Department of the Secretary of State, Arts and Culture Branch, Ottawa, 1977, p. 107.
2. The address of the Universite du Quebec is 2875, boulevard Laurier, Sainte-Foy, Quebec, G1V 2M3, Management of Omnibus Network project.
3. The address of the Ontario Institute for Studies in Education is 252 Bloor St. W., Toronto, Ontario, M5S 1V6.
4. For more information on NATAL write J.W. Brahan, Senior Research Officer, Information Science Section, National Research Council, Montreal Road, Ottawa, K1A 0R8.
5. From Hirsch, Rudolf, *Printing, Selling and Reading: 1450-1550,* Otto Harrassowitz, Wiesbaden, 1967, p. 152.

_____

STRUCTURE:

1. In what way does the schoolyard rhyme "No more pencils, no more books /No more teacher's dirty looks" help to introduce the topic?
2. The six problems of traditional schooling are discussed once in paragraphs 6-25 and again in paragraphs 30-48. In what major way does the purpose of the second section differ from that of the first?
3. Are the six categories of David Godfrey's classification mutually exclusive?
4. Why does Godfrey save "PRE-SOLUTIONS" for last?
5. Point out the ways in which examples help to develop paragraph 31.
6. Discuss the comparison that Godfrey makes (in pars. 49 and 50) between Gutenberg's invention of printing and modern technology's invention of computers.

STYLE:

1. Do you find the METAPHOR of the meat grinder (par. 22) to be appropriate?

2. In paragraph 36, Godfrey writes, "In the majority of cases, a student moving to a new learning situation would carry with them a great deal of information which would greatly improve their chances of success." In making the plural pronouns "them" and "their" refer to the singular noun "student," has Godfrey committed a grammatical error? Or has Godfrey, in the past known as a highly politicized writer, tried to avoid the sexism of making "he" and "his" refer to "student"? If you think the latter is true, is there a way to make this passage avoid bad grammar and sexism at once?

3. What FIGURE OF SPEECH does Godfrey use in paragraph 51 when he states that ". . . terror will become the mother of adaptation. . . ."?

IDEAS:

1. To what extent does your own experience confirm or deny the problems that David Godfrey labels as "LOCKSTEPS," "MR. GRUNDY," "STUDENT X," "TRANSCRAPS," "BULL CURVES" and "PRE-SOLUTIONS"?

2. Godfrey states in paragraph 25, "I no longer 'teach' punctuation in any of my classes." Would you prefer to study punctuation in class or by computer? Why? Is there a way to bypass both of these alternatives and still master punctuation?

3. If you have read "Warily into a Wired-Up World," contrast Andrew Osler's warnings of public manipulation and invasion of privacy to Godfrey's predictions of efficiency in education. Do you think computers and telecommunications are a threat or an opportunity? Could they be both at once?

4. If you have read the previous essay, "Jesse James & the New Frontier," compare and contrast the view of computers given by Susan G. Cole and by Godfrey.

5. Do you agree or disagree with Godfrey when he describes universities as trying to keep students out of the labour market while community colleges are trying to get students into it (pars. 38 and 39)? What can universities do for students that community colleges cannot do? And what can community colleges do for students that universities cannot do?

6. Can you imagine your schooling taking place at home, as Godfrey suggests in paragraph 50? What might be the advantages? What might be the disadvantages?

7. Either verbally or in writing, describe a day at college or university as you imagine it in the year 2000.

8. Write an essay based on a classification of one of the following:
      Uses of computers
      Types of computers
      Types of computer enthusiasts
      Types of computer haters
      Types of English classes
      Types of English teachers

(NOTE: See also the Topics for Writing at the end of this chapter.)

Topics for Writing

Chapter 7: Classification

(Note also the topics for writing that appear after each selection in this chapter.)

Develop one of the following topics into an essay of classification:

1. Gamblers
2. Drinkers
3. Writers
4. Sports fans
5. Dancers
6. Drivers
7. Garage mechanics
8. Farmers
9. Weightlifters
10. Unidentified flying objects
11. Hair styles
12. Cameras
13. Musical instruments
14. Book bindings
15. Film theatres
16. Restaurants
17. Snow (from the skier's point of view)
18. Home heating systems
19. House insulation
20. Parents
21. Wives
22. Husbands
23. Friends
24. Neighbours
25. Districts of your town or city

© Miller Services Limited, Photograph by Denes Baracs, Camera Press, London, England.

"The Peking we came to love was not the city we first arrived in."

John Fraser, "Strangers"

Here's how it's done. . . .

PROCESS ANALYSIS

In the last quarter century, how-to-do-it books and magazines have flourished. Perhaps we have lost the skills we need to build a garage, grow cabbages or bake bread, and need to look them up. Perhaps the increasing cost of labour has driven us to do our own work. Or perhaps increased leisure has led us to new hobbies. Whatever the reason, we are very familiar with the practical writing known as *process analysis.*

It is a sort of narrative, taking us from the beginning to the end of a task, usually in the strict time order required to build the garage, grow the cabbages or make the bread. It includes every step, for each is necessary to the success of the whole project. And if it is written for the amateur, it includes *all* the details right down to the size of the nails, or the spacing and depth of seeds in the ground, or the amount of yeast or salt in the dough. A highly experienced cook might just say "add some yeast" or "put in a little salt," but the writer of a recipe tries to save us from failure by giving measurements. The main thing to remember in giving directions is to *keep the reader in mind.* If you are writing in your area of expertise, you'll be tempted to take short cuts, leaving out details the reader will be lost without. And you'll be tempted to load your writing with technical terms. But if you accurately estimate your reader's level of knowledge and write accordingly, your directions will stand a greater chance of working.

Another kind of process analysis satisfies not our practical needs but our curiosity. You may enjoy learning how a space satellite is launched, how stockholders are swindled, how liquor is distilled, how World War II was won or how a heart is transplanted — without ever doing these things yourself. Of course not every detail must be given in armchair reading such as this: only as many as it takes to clearly convey the information and to interest the reader.

Sometimes a writer will use process analysis not to instruct or inform, but for a totally different reason. When W.P. Kinsella tells how he became a "Junk Mail Junkie," his real subject is not mail but alcohol and drugs, and his purpose is not to confess but to amuse. And when Stephen Leacock tells us "How to Live to Be 200," he advises us to eat cement — a strange way to reach the goal — until we see that his goal is not longevity but laughs.

Whether you aim to help the reader accomplish a task, or to satisfy the reader's curiosity, or just to entertain, your process analysis will work only if you observe the most basic principle of writing any essay: know your purpose at the beginning and keep it firmly in mind as you write.

Stephen Leacock

How to Live to Be 200

During his lifetime, Stephen Leacock became the best-known humorist writing in English, and he remains Canada's favourite writer of all time. Even today, no Canadian author has more books in print. Leacock was born in England in 1869, but at age 6 came with his family to Ontario. He studied at Upper Canada College, the University of Toronto and the University of Chicago where, in 1903, he was awarded a Ph.D. In the same year, McGill hired him to teach political science, and from 1908 until his retirement in 1936, he served as head of his department. He died in 1944. Leacock wrote over forty books, many on academic subjects, but of course it is for his books of humour that he is treasured. The best-loved have been Literary Lapses *(1910),* Nonsense Novels *(1911),* Sunshine Sketches of a Little Town *(1912),* Arcadian Adventures with the Idle Rich *(1914) and* My Remarkable Uncle and Other Sketches *(1942). Our selection, which comes from a later edition of* Literary Lapses, *is vintage Leacock: through exaggeration and incongruities, it reduces to absurdity a topic that many people, today as in Leacock's time, take seriously.*

Twenty years ago I knew a man called Jiggins, who had the Health Habit. 1

He used to take a cold plunge every morning. He said it opened his pores. After it he took a hot sponge. He said it closed the pores. He got so that he could open and shut his pores at will. 2

Jiggins used to stand and breathe at an open window for half an hour before dressing. He said it expanded his lungs. He might, of course, have had it done in a shoe-store with a boot stretcher, but after all it cost him nothing this way, and what is half an hour? 3

After he had got his undershirt on, Jiggins used to hitch himself up like a dog in harness and do Sandow exercises. He did them forwards, backwards, and hind-side up. 4

He could have got a job as a dog anywhere. He spent all his time at this kind of thing. In his spare time at the office, he used to lie on his stomach on the floor and see if he could lift himself up with his knuckles. If he could, then he tried some other way until he found one that he couldn't do. Then he would spend the rest of his lunch hour on his stomach, perfectly happy. 5

In the evenings in his room he used to lift iron bars, cannon-balls, heave dumb-bells, and haul himself up to the ceiling with his teeth. You could hear the thumps half a mile. 6

He liked it. 7

He spent half the night slinging himself around the room. He said it made his brain clear. When he got his brain perfectly clear, he went to 8 bed and slept. As soon as he woke, he began clearing it again.

9   Jiggins is dead. He was, of course, a pioneer, but the fact that he dumb-belled himself to death at an early age does not prevent a whole generation of young men from following in his path.

10   They are ridden by the Health Mania.

11   They make themselves a nuisance.

12   They get up at impossible hours. They go out in silly little suits and run Marathon heats before breakfast. They chase around barefoot to get the dew on their feet. They hunt for ozone. They bother about pepsin. They won't eat meat because it has too much nitrogen. They won't eat fruit because it hasn't any. They prefer albumen and starch and nitrogen to huckleberry pie and doughnuts. They won't drink water out of a tap. They won't eat sardines out of a can. They won't use oysters out of a pail. They won't drink milk out of a glass. They are afraid of alcohol in any shape. Yes, sir, afraid. "Cowards."

13   And after all their fuss they presently incur some simple old-fashioned illness and die like anybody else.

14   Now people of this sort have no chance to attain any great age. They are on the wrong track.

15   Listen. Do you want to live to be really old, to enjoy a grand, green, exuberant, boastful old age and to make yourself a nuisance to your whole neighbourhood with your reminiscences?

16   Then cut out all this nonsense. Cut it out. Get up in the morning at a sensible hour. The time to get up is when you have to, not before. If your office opens at eleven, get up at ten-thirty. Take your chance on ozone. There isn't any such thing anyway. Or, if there is, you can buy a Thermos bottle full for five cents, and put it on a shelf in your cupboard. If your work begins at seven in the morning, get up at ten minutes to, but don't be liar enough to say that you like it. It isn't exhilarating, and you know it.

17   Also, drop all that cold-bath business. You never did it when you were a boy. Don't be a fool now. If you must take a bath (you don't really need to), take it warm. The pleasure of getting out of a cold bed and creeping into a hot bath beats a cold plunge to death. In any case, stop gassing about your tub and your "shower," as if you were the only man who ever washed.

18   So much for that point.

19   Next, take the question of germs and bacilli. Don't be scared of them. That's all. That's the whole thing, and if you once get on to that you never need to worry again.

20   If you see a bacilli, walk right up to it, and look it in the eye. If one flies into your room, strike at it with your hat or with a towel. Hit it as hard as you can between the neck and the thorax. It will soon get sick of that.

But as a matter of fact, a bacilli is perfectly quiet and harmless if you   21
are not afraid of it. Speak to it. Call out to it to "lie down." It will
understand. I had a bacilli once, called Fido, that would come and lie at
my feet while I was working. I never knew a more affectionate companion, and when it was run over by an automobile, I buried it in the
garden with genuine sorrow.

(I admit this is an exaggeration. I don't really remember its name; it   22
may have been Robert.)

Understand that it is only a fad of modern medicine to say that cholera   23
and typhoid and diphtheria are caused by bacilli and germs; nonsense.
Cholera is caused by a frightful pain in the stomach, and diphtheria is
caused by trying to cure a sore throat.

Now take the question of food.   24

Eat what you want. Eat lots of it. Yes, eat too much of it. Eat till you   25
can just stagger across the room with it and prop it up against a sofa
cushion. Eat everything that you like until you can't eat any more. The
only test is, can you pay for it? If you can't pay for it, don't eat it. And
listen — don't worry as to whether your food contains starch, or
albumen, or gluten, or nitrogen. If you are a damn fool enough to want
these things, go and buy them and eat all you want of them. Go to a laun-
dry and get a bag of starch, and eat your fill of it. Eat it, and take a good
long drink of glue after it, and a spoonful of Portland cement. That will
gluten you, good and solid.

If you like nitrogen, go and get a druggist to give you a canful of it at   26
the soda counter, and let you sip it with a straw. Only don't think that
you can mix all these things up with your food. There isn't any nitrogen
or phosphorus or albumen in ordinary things to eat. In any decent
household all that sort of stuff is washed out in the kitchen sink before
the food is put on the table.

And just one word about fresh air and exercise. Don't bother with   27
either of them. Get your room full of good air, then shut up the windows
and keep it. It will keep for years. Anyway, don't keep using your lungs
all the time. Let them rest. As for exercise, if you have to take it, take it
and put up with it. But as long as you have the price of a hack and can
hire other people to play baseball for you and run races and do gym-
nastics when you sit in the shade and smoke and watch them — great
heavens, what more do you want?

STRUCTURE:

1. This essay is divided into two main parts. How do they differ from
   one another and where do we pass from one to the other?

2. Is the story of Jiggins explained in any particular order? And what effect is achieved at the end of his case (par. 9)?
3. Are Stephen Leacock's health instructions organized according to the order in which they should be applied?
4. What is our first clue that Leacock's process analysis is meant not to instruct but to entertain?

STYLE:

1. Leacock uses the word "eat" seven times in this passage from paragraph 25:

> Eat what you want. Eat lots of it. Yes, eat too much of it. Eat till you can just stagger across the room with it and prop it up against a sofa cushion. Eat everything that you like until you can't eat any more. The only test is, can you pay for it? If you can't pay for it, don't eat it.

Is this repetition accidental or deliberate? What effect does it achieve? Where else in the essay does Leacock use repetition?
2. In paragraph 25, Leacock writes: "That will gluten you, good and solid." What is the effect of the word "gluten" as used in this sentence?
3. In paragraph 21, Leacock writes: "I had a bacilli once, called Fido, that would come and lie at my feet while I was working." Analyze the sources of humour in this sentence.
4. Reduction to absurdity is a comic device often used by Leacock. One good example is the analogy of "bacilli" as insects being swatted or as a favourite dog being run over by a car. Where else in this essay is an idea reduced to absurdity?

IDEAS:

1. Do you have the "Health Habit," like Jiggins, or do you prefer comfort and luxury, like our narrator? Give reasons to justify your preference.
2. How would you revise Leacock's essay for our times? Which aspects of the "Health Mania" would you drop from the argument, which would you keep, and which might you add?
3. If you are following a serious program of physical fitness, describe in a process analysis exactly how you do it. At the end, describe the effects of the program.
4. Write a serious or humorous process analysis on the topic of how to attain old age in good health. Be as specific as possible.

(NOTE: See also the Topics for Writing at the end of this chapter.)

Judy Stoffman

The Way of All Flesh

Judy Stoffman has been a senior editor of Today *magazine, and author of articles that have appeared in* Today *and other periodicals. She grew up in Vancouver, studied English literature at the University of British Columbia and at Sussex University, England, where she earned an M.A., and studied also in France. Her future seemed decided as early as grade two: when a teacher read out to the class her composition on recess, Stoffman knew she wanted to be a writer. At UBC she wrote for the student newspaper. And now, living in Toronto, she writes on a broad variety of subjects. "I love the research and dread the writing," she says. "Before I start writing I have a kind of stage fright and from talking to other writers I know they have it too, but they persist because when the words finally start to flow there is an exhilaration nothing else can give." Our selection, "The Way of All Flesh," appeared in* Weekend Magazine *in 1979. Before writing it Stoffman did extensive research: she read ten books on aging and interviewed three gerontologists, a family doctor and a sex therapist. "Then," she says, "I tried to synthesize what I had learned, while exploring my own deepest fears. But you'll notice that I never used the word 'I'."*

When a man of 25 is told that aging is inexorable, inevitable, universal, he will nod somewhat impatiently at being told something so obvious. In fact, he has little idea of the meaning of the words. It has nothing to do with him. Why should it? He has had no tangible evidence yet that his body, as the poet Rilke said, enfolds old age and death as the fruit enfolds a stone.

The earliest deposits of fat in the aorta, the trunk artery carrying blood away from the heart, occur in the eighth year of life, but who can peer into his own aorta at this first sign of approaching debility? The young man has seen old people but he secretly believes himself to be the exception on whom the curse will never fall. "Never will the skin of my neck hang loose. My grip will never weaken. I will stand tall and walk with long strides as long as I live." The young girl scarcely pays attention to her clothes, she scorns makeup. Her confidence in her body is boundless; smooth skin and a flat stomach will compensate, she knows, for any lapses in fashion or grooming. She stays up all night, as careless of her energy as of her looks, believing both will last forever.

In our early 20s, the lung capacity, the rapidity of motor responses and physical endurance are at their peak. This is the athlete's finest hour. Cindy Nicholas of Toronto was 19 when she first swam the English Channel in both directions. The tennis star Bjorn Borg was 23 when he triumphed this year at Wimbledon for the fourth time.

It is not only *athletic* prowess that is at its height between 20 and 30. James Boswell, writing in his journal in 1763 after he had finally won the favors of the actress Louisa, has left us this happy description of the sexual prowess of a 23-year-old: "I was in full glow of health and my bounding blood beat quick in high alarms. Five times was I fairly lost in supreme rapture. Louisa was madly fond of me; she declared I was a prodigy, and asked me if this was extraordinary in human nature. I said twice as much might be, but this was not, although in my own mind I was somewhat proud of my performance."

5   In our early 30s we are dumbfounded to discover the first grey hair at the temples. We pull out the strange filament and look at it closely, trying to grasp its meaning. It means simply that the pigment has disappeared from the hair shaft, never to return. It means also — but this thought we push away — that in 20 years or so we'll relinquish our identity as a blonde or a redhead. By 57, one out of four people is completely grey. Of all the changes wrought by time this is the most harmless, except to our vanity.

6   In this decade one also begins to notice the loss of upper register hearing, that is, the responsiveness to high frequency tones, but not all the changes are for the worse, not yet. Women don't reach their sexual prime until about 38, because their sexual response is learned rather than innate. The hand grip of both sexes increases in strength until 35, and intellectual powers are never stronger than at that age. There is a sense in the 30s of hitting your stride, of coming into your own. When Sigmund Freud was 38 an older colleague, Josef Breuer, wrote: "Freud's intellect is soaring at its highest. I gaze after him as a hen at a hawk."

7   Gail Sheehy in her book *Passages* calls the interval between 35 and 45 the Deadline Decade. It is the time we begin to sense danger. The body continually flashes us signals that time is running out. We must perform our quaint deeds, keep our promises, get on with our allotted tasks.

8   Signal: The woman attempts to become pregnant at 40 and finds she cannot. Though she menstruates each month, menstruation being merely the shedding of the inner lining of the womb, she may not be ovulating regularly.

9   Signal: Both men and women discover that, although they have not changed their eating habits over the years, they are much heavier than formerly. The man is paunchy around the waist; the woman no longer has those slim thighs and slender arms. A 120-pound woman needs 2,000 calories daily to maintain her weight when she is 25, 1,700 to maintain the same weight at 45, and only 1,500 calories at 65. A 170-pound man needs 3,100 calories daily at 25, 300 fewer a day at 45 and 450 calories fewer still at 65. This decreasing calorie need signals that the body consumes its fuel ever more slowly; the cellular fires are damped and our sense of energy diminishes.

10   In his mid-40s the man notices he can no longer run up the stairs three at a time. He is more easily winded and his joints are not as flexible as

they once were. The strength of his hands has declined somewhat. The man feels humiliated: "I will not let this happen to me. I will turn back the tide and master my body." He starts going to the gym, playing squash, lifting weights. He takes up jogging. Though he may find it neither easy nor pleasant, terror drives him past pain. A regular exercise program can retard some of the symptoms of aging by improving the circulation and increasing the lung capacity, thereby raising our stamina and energy level, but no amount of exercise will make a 48-year-old 26 again. Take John Keeley of Mystic, Connecticut. In 1957, when he was 26, he won the Boston marathon with a time of 2:20. This year he is fit and 48 and says he is as fiercely competitive as ever, yet it took him almost 30 minutes longer to run the same marathon.

In the middle of the fourth decade, the man whose eyesight has always   11
been good will pick up a book and notice that he is holding it farther from his face than usual. The condition is presbyopia, a loss of the flexibility of the lens which makes adjustment from distant to near vision increasingly difficult. It's harder now to zoom in for a closeup. It also takes longer for the eyes to recover from glare; between 16 and 90, recovery time from exposure to glare is doubled every 13 years.

In our 50s, we notice that food is less and less tasty; our taste buds are   12
starting to lose their acuity. The aged Queen Victoria was wont to complain that strawberries were not as sweet as when she was a girl.

Little is known about the causes of aging. We do not know if we are   13
born with a biochemical messenger programed to keep the cells and tissues alive, a messenger that eventually gets lost, or if there is a 'death hormone,' absent from birth but later secreted by the thymus or by the mysterious pineal gland, or if, perhaps, aging results from a fatal flaw in the body's immunity system. The belief that the body is a machine whose parts wear out is erroneous, for the machine does not have the body's capacity for self-repair.

"A man is as old as his arteries," observed Sir William Osler. From   14
the 50s on, there's a progressive hardening and narrowing of the arteries due to the gradual lifelong accumulation of calcium and fats along the arterial walls. Arteriosclerosis eventually affects the majority of the population in the affluent countries of the West. Lucky the man or women who, through a combination of good genes and good nutrition, can escape it, for it is the most evil change of all. As the flow of blood carrying oxygen and nutrients to the muscles, the brain, the kidneys and other organs diminishes, these organs begin to starve. Although all aging organs lose weight, there is less shrinkage of organs such as the liver and kidneys, the cells of which regenerate, than there is shrinkage of the brain and the muscles, the cells of which, once lost, are lost forever.

For the woman it is now an ordeal to be asked her age. There is a fine   15
tracery of lines around her eyes, a furrow in her brow even when she

smiles. The bloom is off her cheeks. Around the age of 50 she will buy her last box of sanitary pads. The body's production of estrogen and progesterone which govern menstruation (and also help to protect her from heart attack and the effects of stress) will have ceased almost completely. She may suffer palpitations, suddenly break into a sweat; her moods may shift abruptly. She looks in the mirror and asks, "Am I still a woman?" Eventually she becomes reconciled to her new self and even acknowledges its advantages: no more fears about pregnancy. "In any case," she laughs, "I still have not bad legs."

16   The man, too, will undergo a change. One night in his early 50s he has some trouble achieving a complete erection, and his powers of recovery are not what they once were. Whereas at 20 he was ready to make love again less than half an hour after doing so, it may now take two hours or more; he was not previously aware that his level of testosterone, the male hormone, has been gradually declining since the age of 20. He may develop headaches, be unable to sleep, become anxious about his performance, anticipate failure and so bring on what is called secondary impotence — impotence of psychological rather than physical origin. According to Masters and Johnson, 25 percent of all men are impotent by 65 and 50 percent by 75, yet this cannot be called an inevitable feature of aging. A loving, undemanding partner and a sense of confidence can do wonders. "The susceptibility of the human male to the power of suggestion with regard to his sexual prowess," observe Masters and Johnson, "is almost unbelievable."

17   After the menopause, the woman ages more rapidly. Her bones start to lose calcium, becoming brittle and porous. The walls of the vagina become thinner and drier; sexual intercourse now may be painful unless her partner is slow and gentle. The sweat glands begin to atrophy and the sebaceous glands that lubricate the skin decline; the complexion becomes thinner and drier and wrinkles appear around the mouth. The skin, which in youth varies from about one-fiftieth of an inch on the eyelids to about a third of an inch on the palms and the soles of the feet, loses 50 percent of its thickness between the ages of 20 and 80. The woman no longer buys sleeveless dresses and avoids shorts. The girl who once disdained cosmetics is now a woman whose dressing table is covered with lotions, night creams and makeup.

18   Perhaps no one has written about the sensation of nearing 60 with more brutal honesty than the French novelist Simone de Beauvoir: "While I was able to look at my face without displeasure, I gave it no thought. I loathe my appearance now: the eyebrows slipping down toward the eyes, the bags underneath, the excessive fullness of the cheeks and the air of sadness around the mouth that wrinkles always bring. . . . Death is no longer a brutal event in the far distance; it haunts my sleep."

In his early 60s the man's calves are shrunken, his muscles stringy looking. The legs of the woman, too, are no longer shapely. Both start to lose their sense of smell and both lose most of the hair in the pubic area and the underarms. Hair, however, may make its appearance in new places, such as the woman's chin. Liver spots appear on the hands, the arms, the face; they are made of coagulated melanin, the coloring matter of the skin. The acid secretions of the stomach decrease, making digestion slow and more difficult.

Halfway through the 60s comes compulsory retirement for most men and working women, forcing upon the superannuated worker the realization that society now views him as useless and unproductive. The man who formerly gave orders to a staff of 20 now finds himself underfoot as his wife attempts to clean the house or get the shopping done. The woman fares a little better since there is a continuity in her pattern of performing a myriad of essential household tasks. Now they must both set new goals or see themselves wither mentally. The unsinkable American journalist I.F. Stone, when he retired in 1971 from editing *I.F. Stone's Weekly*, began to teach himself Greek and is now reading Plato in the original. When Somerset Maugham read that the Roman senator Cato the Elder learned Greek when he was 80, he remarked: "Old age is ready to undertake tasks that youth shirked because they would take too long."

However active we are, the fact of old age can no longer be evaded from about 65 onward. Not everyone is as strong minded about this as de Beauvoir. When she made public in her memoirs her horror at her own deterioration, her readers were scandalized. She received hundreds of letters telling her that there is no such thing as old age, that some are just younger than others. Repeatedly she heard the hollow reassurance, "You're as young as you feel." But she considers this a lie. Our subjective reality, our inner sense of self, is not the only reality. There is also an objective reality, how we are seen by society. We receive our revelation of old age from others. The woman whose figure is still trim may sense that a man is following her in the street; drawing abreast, the man catches sight of her face — and hurries on. The man of 68 may be told by a younger woman to whom he is attracted: "You remind me of my father."

Madame de Sévigné, the 17th-century French writer, struggled to rid herself of the illusion of perpetual youth. At 63 she wrote: "I have been dragged to this inevitable point where old age must be undergone: I see it there before me; I have reached it; and I should at least like so to arrange matters that I do not move on, that I do not travel further along this path of the infirmities, pains, losses of memory and the disfigurement. But I hear a voice saying: 'You must go along, whatever you may say; or indeed if you will not then you must die, which is an extremity from which nature recoils.'''

23   Now the man and the woman have their 70th birthday party. It is a sad affair because so many of their friends are missing, felled by strokes, heart attacks or cancers. Now the hands of the clock begin to race. The skeleton continues to degenerate from loss of calcium. The spine becomes compressed and there is a slight stoop nothing can prevent. Inches are lost from one's height. The joints may become thickened and creaking; in the morning the woman can't seem to get moving until she's had a hot bath. She has osteoarthritis. This, like the other age-related diseases, arteriosclerosis and diabetes, can and should be treated but it can never be cured. The nails, particularly the toenails, become thick and lifeless because the circulation in the lower limbs is now poor. The man has difficulty learning new things because of the progressive loss of neurons from the brain. The woman goes to the store and forgets what she has come to buy. The two old people are often constipated because the involuntary muscles are weaker now. To make it worse, their children are always saying, "Sit down, rest, take it easy." Their digestive tract would be toned up if they went for a long walk or even a swim, although they feel a little foolish in bathing suits.

24   In his late 70s, the man develops glaucoma, pressure in the eyeball caused by the failure of the aqueous humour to drain away; this can now be treated with a steroid related to cortisone. The lenses in the eyes of the woman may thicken and become fibrous, blurring her vision. She has cataracts, but artificial lenses can now be implanted using cryosurgery. There is no reason to lose one's sight just as there's no reason to lose one's teeth; regular, lifelong dental care can prevent tooth loss. What can't be prevented is the yellowing of teeth, brought about by the shrinking of the living chamber within the tooth which supplies the outer enamel with moisture.

25   Between 75 and 85 the body loses most of its subcutaneous fat. On her 80th birthday the woman's granddaughter embraces her and marvels: "How thin and frail and shrunken she is! Could this narrow, bony chest be the same warm, firm bosom to which she clasped me as a child?" Her children urge her to eat but she has no enjoyment of food now. Her mouth secretes little saliva, so she has difficulty tasting and swallowing. The loss of fat and shrinking muscles in the 80s diminish the body's capacity for homeostasis, that is, righting any physiological imbalance. The old man, if he is cold, can barely shiver (shivering serves to restore body heat). If he lives long enough, the man will have an enlarged prostate which causes the urinary stream to slow to a trickle. The man and the woman probably both wear hearing aids now; without a hearing aid, they hear vowels clearly but not consonants; if someone says "fat," they think they've heard the word "that."

At 80, the speed of nerve impulses is 10 percent less than it was at 25,   26
the kidney filtration rate is down by 30 percent, the pumping efficiency
of the heart is only 60 percent of what it was, and the maximum
breathing capacity, 40 percent.

The old couple is fortunate in still being able to express physically the   27
love they've built up over a lifetime. The old man may be capable of an
erection once or twice a week (Charlie Chaplin fathered the last of his
many children when he was 81), but he rarely has the urge to climax.
When he does, he sometimes has the sensation of seepage rather than a
triumphant explosion. Old people who say they are relieved that they are
now free of the torments of sexual desire are usually the ones who found
sex a troublesome function all their lives; those who found joy and
renewal in the act will cling to their libido. Many older writers and artists
have expressed the conviction that continued sexuality is linked to continued creativity: "There was a time when I was cruelly tormented, indeed obsessed by desire," wrote the novelist André Gide at the age of 73,
"and I prayed, 'Oh let the moment come when my subjugated flesh will
allow me to give myself entirely to. . .' But to what? To art? To pure
thought? To God? How ignorant I was! How mad! It was the same as
believing that the flame would burn brighter in a lamp with no oil left.
Even today it is my carnal self that feeds the flame, and now I pray that I
may retain carnal desire until I die."

Aging, says an American gerontologist, "is not a simple slope which   28
everyone slides down at the same speed; it is a flight of irregular stairs
down which some journey more quickly than others." Now we arrive at
the bottom of the stairs. The old man and the old woman whose progress
we have been tracing will die either of a cancer (usually of the lungs,
bowel or intestines) or of a stroke, a heart attack or in consequence of a
fall. The man slips in the bathroom and breaks his thigh bone. But worse
than the fracture is the enforced bed rest in the hospital which will probably bring on bed sores, infections, further weakening of the muscles and
finally, what Osler called "an old man's best friend": pneumonia. At 25
we have so much vitality that if a little is sapped by illness, there is still
plenty left over. At 85 a little is all we have.

And then the light goes out.   29

The sheet is pulled over the face.   30

In the last book of Marcel Proust's remarkable work *Remembrance of*   31
Things Past, the narrator, returning after a long absence from Paris,
attends a party of his friends throughout which he has the impression of
being at a masked ball: "I did not understand why I could not immediately recognize the master of the house, and the guests, who seemed
to have made themselves up, in a way that completely changed their appearance. The Prince had rigged himself up with a white beard and what

looked like leaden soles which made his feet drag heavily. A name was mentioned to me and I was dumbfounded at the thought that it applied to the blonde waltzing girl I had once known and to the stout, white haired lady now walking just in front of me. We did not see our own appearance, but each like a facing mirror, saw the other's." The narrator is overcome by a simple but powerful truth: the old are not a different species. "It is out of young men who last long enough," wrote Proust, "that life makes its old men."

32   The wrinkled old man who lies with the sheet over his face was once the young man who vowed, "My grip will never weaken. I will walk with long strides and stand tall as long as I live." The young man who believed himself to be the exception.

STRUCTURE:

1. "The Way of All Flesh" is a striking example of chronological order used to organize a mass of information. Point out at least ten words, phrases or sentences that signal the flow of time.
2. Does Judy Stoffman's process analysis tell the reader how to do something, how something is done by others, or how something happens?
3. How long would this essay be if all its examples were removed? How interesting would it be? How convincing would it be?
4. What device of organization underlies both paragraphs 14 and 16?
5. What effect does Stoffman achieve when, in the last paragraph, she refers to the first paragraph?

STYLE:

1. Why are paragraphs 29 and 30 so short?
2. To what extent does Stoffman rely on statistics? What do they do for her argument?
3. To what extent does Stoffman rely on quotations? Would you call this selection a research essay? Why or why not?
4. In a desk-size dictionary, look up the origins of the word "gerontologist" (par. 28). How is it related to the words "geriatrics," "Geritol," "gerontocracy," "astrology" and "zoology"?

IDEAS:

1. Did this essay frighten or depress you? If so, was this effect a failure or a success on the part of the author?
2. Do you share the attitude of Stoffman's young man who "has seen old people" but who "secretly believes himself to be the exception on

whom the curse will never fall'' (par. 2)? What are the benefits of such an attitude? What are the dangers?

3. Jonathan Swift said, ''Every man desires to live long, but no man would be old.'' How do you explain the apparent contradiction in this PARADOX?

4. In paragraph 21, Stoffman contrasts our ''subjective'' and ''objective'' realities. Which do you think is more important in forming our self-image? Which do you think *should* be more important, and why?

5. Is compulsory retirement at 65 good for the individual? For the company? For society? When would you retire if you had the choice, and why? Would you apply a standard other than age?

6 .If you have read ''The Firewood Gatherers,'' compare the description of old age given by Thierry Mallet with that given by Stoffman.

7. Using examples to illustrate your points, write a process analysis on one of these topics:

How to stay physically fit past thirty

How to retain a feeling of self-worth in old age

How to help parents and grandparents to be happy in their old age

(NOTE: See also the Topics for Writing at the end of this chapter.)

Kenneth Mews

You Dirty Rat!

Kenneth Mews, born in Toronto in 1946, spent years training to be a scholar before he became a journalist. He holds a B.A. and M.A., and, after studying for his Ph.D. in English, completed what he calls the A.B.T. (All But the Thesis). For a time he worked as sub-editor of The Victorian Periodicals Newsletter *(now* Journal*). In 1977 he moved to the world of electronics and of popular journalism, joining the staff of* AudioScene Canada *(now* Audio Canada*), of which he is now managing editor. Mews thinks that writing is all too often mechanical and dull. For magazine writers in particular, he recommends "taking your reader by the hand, getting his attention, taking him on a brisk walk through the subject, pointing out the most interesting things to see along the route you've chosen, and leading him home at the end — if only with a bit of a chuckle. . . ." In "You Dirty Rat!" — from a 1981 issue of* AudioScene Canada *— Mews has certainly followed his own advice.*

1   A writer has only words; a stage, film, or TV director has visual images, music, and sound. A radio producer falls somewhere in the middle. He isn't as restricted as a writer, yet he doesn't have the rich variety of the visual to draw on. His job is to create the illusion of reality — or a believable fantasy — by using a script, appropriate music, and sound effects. More than just the equivalent of spectacular visual effects like the battle scenes from *Star Wars*, sound effects create a mood, advance the action, in fact, provide aural treats that can be more fun than the movies.

2   The building is dark. A great mass of sombre Victorian brick. Big oak doors creak open and close with a heavy thud. Narrow, dingy, linoleum-covered corridors lead off in all directions. Distant, hollow footsteps and creaking floorboards. At the end of one long corridor stands an open door. Excited voices become clearer as we approach. Then a man screams, the scream fading off into a groan. What is going on here?

3   "In the dream you are falling, plummeting through a dark, seemingly bottomless chasm. You scream in terror with the wind. Suddenly you come awake, bathed in a cold sweat, chills down your spine, heart pounding . . . it's *Nightfall*." Luther Kranst, your mysterious host with the gravelly, insinuating voice, is introducing another segment in the CBC radio drama series *Nightfall*, tales of the weird, the uncanny, and the good old-fashioned horrible.

4   When the scream heard from outside the studio is mixed with a composite effect of several close-miked fires, it will form the climax of a half-hour radio drama by Mavor Moore, called "The Book of Hell," a

guided tour by a full-time resident. The book is so hot, the manuscript literally burns up the man who is trying to get it published.

Bill Robinson, a veteran sound effects technician, is the man who pro- 5 vides the fire that makes the scene and any number of other bizarre effects called for by producer Bill Howell. Robinson admits that he is sometimes hard-pressed to come up with some of the things he's asked to make sound convincing. But the challenge is what makes it fun. Howell aims to include at least one effect in every show that will make listeners wonder: "How the hell did they do that?"

Sometimes it's the simple sound that poses unexpected difficulties. 6 The script of "The Telltale Heart" called for the close-miked sound of a human heart picking up speed. If Robinson had been content to record his own heart and change the speed on playback, the frequency of the sound would have changed so much as to make it unrecognizable. He tried the old trick of slapping the two halves of an open telephone book together rhythmically; but wasn't convinced. He ended up on the floor of the studio, in a suitably hollow spot, pounding the floor rhythmically to imitate the changing heart rate of the victim in the story.

"Anybody coming into the studio, seeing me lying on the floor, 7 pounding it with my fist, would have been sure I'd really flipped. But it sounded just fine when we got it on tape," says Robinson, with a grin.

An attack by an undersea monster in "The Devil's Backbone" re- 8 quired some unorthodox props and a risky miking technique. Robinson got some condoms from the corner drugstore, fitted them around his expensive Neumann mike, and plunged it into three feet of water. Blowing gently through a hose, he duplicated the sound of the diver's scuba breathing gear; plunging the mike into the water became the monster's first attack; sounds made through the hose sounded like convincing underwater screams and the ripping off of the diver's face-mask; even rocks moving around on the bottom of the ocean could be imitated by rubbing and tapping the outside of the pail.

Although Robinson has access to a library of stereo effects of over 9 1,000 cartridges, he finds that he has to record fresh ones to fit the demands of this show, or at least combine and modify what he has on hand. A cartridge of seagull noises, when speeded up, turned into the high-pitched squealing of a horde of rats on the rampage. Robinson then added the sound of the anguished hero beating them off by squashing oranges with the broad side of an axe.

In fact, he uses a whole cartful of groceries to achieve some of his 10 more gruesome effects. Chopping a chunk off a pineapple substitutes nicely for chopping off someone's hand, since it's hard and the tough outer layer sounds like bone. It also bounces nicely.

Watermelons are very versatile. When dropped from a height, they can 11 sound like a body crashing to earth. Blows to the head of all kinds can be imitated from the stunning thud of a nightstick, to a splitting hammer stroke, to the grisly squelch of an axe buried in the skull by Lizzie Borden.

12   It is the immediacy of such an effect, gruesome as it may sound, that Bill Howell is striving for in *Nightfall.* By using closer miking techniques and focus, combined with spectacular effects and the emotional colouring of music, he wants to bring the listener right into the action. What Howell calls "television for the mind" succeeds if it gets you caught up in the action, emotion, and imaginary reality of the story, using sound alone.

13   If sound effects paint vivid pictures with sound, the background mood and colouring come from ambience effects and music. Obviously a scene in a park must sound different from one in a small room. A continuous loop on the cartridge machine will provide background noise, careful adjustment of large baffles in the studio will give a realistic lack of echo suggesting an outdoor setting, and more extreme acoustic environments — an eerie, echoing cavern, for example — can be synthesized on a signal processor.

14   Robinson records his background noise effects live, with a portable cassette machine, transferring them later to broadcast cartridges. He will go to almost any lengths to get the right effect. He toured a number of small towns before he found one with just the right combination of vintage cars and old pick-ups to get the effect of Main Street, Anywhere, circa 1940.

15   Obviously his effects must be tailored to fit the ambience of the scene they illustrate, and that sometimes causes problems. Background noise for a scene taking place inside a car was too obtrusive when he used the real thing. So he hunted through his collection, deciding finally on a recording of a waterfall. When equalized and slowed down, it provided just the right quality of background roar, deadened by the car interior acoustic, to suggest the right setting.

16   Background effects may be required only for short periods of time, or they may have to support a whole scene. The format used is a small cartridge, an endless loop 20 or 40 seconds long, with a cue track. The broadcast cartridge is a predecessor of the nasty old consumer eight-track, and it looks like one. It uses quarter-inch tape, but in the full or half-track format to improve signal-to-noise ratio. The playback unit has a cue defeat feature that allows it to play over and over again, endlessly if need be.

17   When it comes time to make the mix, the process whereby the edited voice tracks, music, and sound effects are combined to produce the master tape at 38 cm/s. Robinson has a small mixing board with six

stereo outputs through which he can mix, equalize, pan, and enhance the effects recorded on up to nine cartridges simultaneously.

John Jessop, the recording engineer, mans a larger board that deter- 18 mines the final mix, controls input from the voice tracks, adds music from studio production discs on two turntables, more broadcast cart- ridges, or two open-reel tape recorders. Meanwhile he is spraying the board with anti-static spray to keep down the pops and crackles in the tinder-dry control booth.

Robinson is building up the convincing background of a chaotic fire 19 scene with four cartridges — one each of fire engines, a separate siren, fire, and crowd ambience — while Howell is choosing music — two syn- thesizer tracks, one on cartridge and the other to be played doused with record-cleaning fluid on one of the turntables — and Jessop is putting it all together with the dialogue at his board.

The scene is short, less than two minutes long, but somehow it all fits 20 neatly, despite the pandemonium in the studio that echoes the chaos of the scene. This frantic multi-machine technique is the way these "mad scientists" prefer to work, since it gives them the flexibility and im- mediacy they're trying to capture for broadcast.

Multi-tracking, the obvious alternative, is more costly, time- 21 consuming, and frustrating, since it ties you down to real time much sooner than their method. Because they're not overdubbing, but mixing all the elements at once — music at 76 cm/s, effects at 38 cm/s, and voice at 19 cm/s — they can get a master on the second generation, rather than on the first as with multi-tracking. It all has to be transferred to a 19 cm/s broadcast master anyway, and a further generation is lost in the automatic delay system which distributes programs across the country's different time zones.

Despite the limitations, though, these wildmen are producing a show 22 that, if it doesn't exactly plant an axe in the middle of your head, does grab you firmly by the throat. And that's in no small part due to the vividness of Bill Robinson's sound effects, creating a mood, setting a scene, and then going for the jugular.

Though it may sound like the real thing, the next time you hear a heart 23 being ripped out of a man's chest, it may be only the slowed-down tear- ing and crunching of chicken breasts, followed by the squeezing of a ball of wet paper towels. A falling body may be a bucket of wet rags on a slab of cement. Breaking bones may be old-fashioned berry boxes instead, equalized and slowed down to sound right (Robinson has a secret lifetime supply of these).

Indeed, sounds are rarely what they seem when they come out of Bill 24 Robinson's shop. The recording of smashing a lightbulbs may sound like a lightbulb being smashed; but what does a wheelchair sound like? Practically silent. If Robinson is supplying the effect, though, it sounds more like a wheelchair than a wheelchair — or the rear wheel of a ten-speed bike spinning. And that's the illusion, folks.

STRUCTURE:

1. What is a title for? Is "You Dirty Rat!" a good title? In answering these questions, look not only at the title of this essay but also at the titles of other essays in the book.
2. How does the closing (par. 24) reflect the opening (par. 1)?
3. What is the purpose of paragraphs 2 and 3?
4. Where does the process analysis of sound effect production begin?
5. Does this essay describe one ongoing process or a number of processes?
6. How are paragraphs 17-21 organized?
7. Discuss the role of examples in this essay.

STYLE:

1. Two sentence fragments appear in paragraph 2. Where are they and why do you think the author uses them?
2. Read this sentence aloud, with expression, then discuss the effect created by its style: "Big oak doors creak open and close with a heavy thud" (par. 2).
3. In this essay about radio, a number of specialized terms are used. If you or another class member can define them for the other students, do so:

    close-miked (par. 4), miking (par. 8), mike (par. 8)
    playback (par. 6)
    signal processor (par. 13)
    endless loop (par. 16)
    cue track (par. 16)
    signal-to-noise ratio (par. 16)
    cue defeat feature (par. 16)
    mix, equalize, pan and enhance (par. 17)

4. If you do not understand some of the terms in question 3 above, to what extent did the presence of the terms reduce your enjoyment and understanding of the essay as a whole? What difficulties do you think the author might have in trying to explain the "mix" by using only terms known to the general reader? In summary, when should technical JARGON be used or avoided in essays?
5. Mews uses the technical terms "input" (par. 18) and "output" (par. 17). What is the effect of these terms in the non-technical uses to

which they are so often put? Can you think of other electrical JARGON that has passed into general use?

6. Why do you think Mews uses the non-technical terms "mad scientists" (par. 20) and "wildmen" (par. 22) alongside the very technical language of paragraphs 16-21?

7. List ten or twenty technical terms from your own field of study, which you suspect the average person would not know. Read them to the class (or to someone outside the class if your classmates are all studying the same subject) to see whether you were right.

IDEAS:

1. Mews states in paragraph 1, "A writer has only words; a stage, film, or TV director has visual images, music, and sound. A radio producer falls somewhere in the middle." Contrast in more detail the technical advantages and disadvantages of literature, drama, film, TV and radio.

2. Interview an older person who grew up without television. What were his or her favourite radio programs? How exciting did they seem? Was radio a kind of "television for the mind" (par. 12)? Was radio used mainly as a background to other activities or was it actively listened to? How interesting does television now seem in comparison with the way radio seemed before television? Which seems more interesting now and why?

3. What are your favourite kinds of radio programs and why? What degree of attention do you give to them when they are on, and why?

4. What attracts people to horror programs like those described in paragraphs 2-4? Do people enjoy being scared?

5. According to Mews, ". . . sounds are rarely what they seem when they come out of Bill Robinson's shop" (par. 24). Discuss the place of illusion in radio, TV, film and the stage. To what extent can and should each of these media simulate reality?

6. Write a process analysis in which you instruct your reader as to how to do one of the following:

—select a sound system
—select a television set
—select a videotape system
—select radio or TV programs wisely
—stop the TV habit
—help children to use radio or TV wisely
—reduce the effect of commercials on one's life

(NOTE: See also the Topics for Writing at the end of this chapter.)

W.P. Kinsella

Junk Mail Junkie

W.P. Kinsella was born in 1935 and raised in a remote area of Alberta. He never attended school until grade five. Before he earned an M.F.A. at the Iowa Writers' Workshop and began teaching fiction writing at the University of Calgary, he held a number of jobs in the business world: selling advertising, running a credit bureau and a pizza restaurant, and selling life insurance. He has published over 50 short stories in literary magazines as well as books of his stories: Dance Me Outside *(1977),* Scars *(1978),* Shoeless Joe Jackson Comes to Iowa *(1980) and* Born Indian *(1981). Upon the invitation of an American book editor, Kinsella expanded his short story about baseball, "Shoeless Joe Jackson Comes to Iowa," into a novel.* Shoeless Joe *was published in 1982 and was awarded the Houghton Mifflin Literary Fellowship. Our selection, "Junk Mail Junkie," appeared in 1979 on the* Funny Page *of* Weekend Magazine.

1 It started when I was 6. A small ad in a children's magazine set me going: it offered a free stamp. It seemed like such a simple thing. How could one stamp hurt me? I printed out the address with a stubby pencil in my stubby fingers. While my letter was in the mail I suddenly realized I had something to live for. I began skipping my grade one classes in order to hide in the caragana and wait for the mailman. I cannot describe the excitement of finding a letter in the mailbox with my own name on it. Once I had taken that first letter it was too late. My parents warned me that some people are not meant to use the mails: it took me years of suffering and hard mail use to discover that I was one of them.

2 During the rest of my childhood, instead of spending my allowance on bubble gum and cigarettes, I was paying the weekly instalments on my Charles Atlas Bodybuilding Course, which I ordered from a coupon on the back of a comic book. I was always one jump ahead of the credit agencies. In high school I never had money for dating. I was too busy selling Regal Christmas cards and Cloverdale salve in order to pay for my selections from all the book and record clubs I had joined. I am one of those people who wrote to the Canadian Wildlife Service for more information on the moose, the coyote and the ptarmigan. You have to understand! I couldn't help myself!

3 The week I landed my first full-time job I celebrated by sending away for a reprint of an article from *Reader's Digest*. I managed to keep my job for many years. At first I was a spree mailer. I'd mail only from Friday night until Monday morning. I'd go to work red-eyed and exhausted, chewing mints and claiming I was just hung over, but I never missed a

day of work because of my mailing. I kept telling myself everything was all right, I could take junk mail or leave it alone.

I married a woman who worked at the general delivery window of the post office. By then I was filling out coupons indiscriminately, sometimes 200 a week. I'd do anything for a 10-cent stamp. I knew what the Rosicrucians knew. The One True Church of God's Redemption and Reaffirmation of Biloxi, Mississippi, sent me their complete sermons of 1954. I became a mail-order minister. I got a PhD from Rochdale College. I collected recipes from a famous cheese company. I received a free tape recording from an evangelical organization in Miami.   4

To an addict, a day without junk mail is hell. By the end of every weekend I was a retching, pitiful excuse for a man. Long weekends were too awful to describe in a family magazine. I compensated by mailing more and more on weekdays. My family became virtual strangers. I think they suspected but tried to pretend that nothing unusual was happening, even though I regularly came late to birthday dinners and anniversaries, disheveled, incoherent, a telltale bulge in my inside suit pocket.   5

As my craving grew, so did my capacity. It got to the point where I'd start the day by reading a piece of junk mail. Soon junk mail replaced breakfast. I owned the 12-record series of someone reading what sounds like a novel in Serbo-Croatian, and I'd listen to that until the post office opened and I could return the 10-day card from the Canadian Patriot Record Club. I kept caches of unmailed letters all about my house, hiding them away in ingenious places and then forgetting where they were.   6

My marriage broke up after I acquired a copy of the *National Hog Farmer* and ordered a Scanopreg, an electronic device that tells if sows are pregnant, and predicted that our son would be a girl. My wife gave me an ultimatum: either her or junk mail. I loved her dearly, and I wish her well. The divorce petition reached me by registered mail — a red-letter day.   7

The next step in my degradation was unavoidable: in order to support my habit I became a pusher. I started a direct mail business. God help me, I sold to women, children, anyone with the strength to fill out a coupon. I soon began having blackouts. My doctor told me that if I didn't give up junk mail my tongue would quit functioning. It wasn't long before I was on the street. Broke, unemployed, uncaring, I began loitering around magazine stands where I would surreptitiously rip advertising inserts from magazines.   8

Then one Sunday morning I woke up in the gutter. My clothes were threadbare and I needed a bath and a haircut. Well dressed people stepped around me on their way to church. In the hospital I went through   9 the horrors of withdrawal. I lay for week in the fetal position. Japanese bonsai tree offers oozed from my pores. Every inch of my body felt as if it were being tattooed with postmarks. I finally had to admit that junk mail was stronger than I was.

10   I still am a junk mail junkie, though I'm learning to taper off. I still take the occasional magazine containing ads with box numbers and coupons, but I only read them socially. I'm on the mail wagon. Like most reformed junkies, however, I am most concerned with the rehabilitation of fellow junkies.

11   A few of us have organized Junk Mail Anonymous. Doctors are reluctant to treat junk mail junkies. Addicts are brought into emergency rooms unshaven, mucilage on their breath, ink stains on their fingers. Nurses wrinkle their noses, orderlies mutter under their breath, doctors are suddenly needed in surgery. Junk mail junkies often lie for hours unattended: hospital waiting rooms are known as "dead letter offices."

12   Concerned parents ask me how they can tell if their child is using junk mail. I have compiled the following five-point guide:

13   1. Smell his clothes. The cheap ink used in junk·mail has a harsh, acrid aroma that clings to clothes for hours.

14   2. Smell his breath. If it has glue on it, prepare yourself for the worst.

15   3. Check his eyes. Reading the small print in junk mail ads leaves the eyes red and the pupils enlarged.

16   4. Study his fingers for ink stains. Junk mail addicts spend a lot of time writing.

17   5. Does he always try to be at the mailbox first? Does he appear anxious and withdrawn if the postman is late or on strike?

18   For more information on the junk mail junkie, write to the Canadian Wildlife Service.

STRUCTURE:

1. Is the opening sentence effective? If so, why?
2. Both kinds of process analysis occur in this selection: the kind that gives directions to follow and the kind that merely describes a process that occurs. Where does each appear?
3. "Junk Mail Junkie" is more than a process analysis. Several other basic means of development, examined in other chapters, contribute as well. Name them and tell briefly what they do for this selection.
4. Point out several of the examples that most vividly describe the narrator's "addiction."
5. What effect is achieved by the final sentence?

STYLE:

1. Our narrator says, "My parents warned me that some people are not meant to use the mails" (par. 1), "I managed to keep my job for many years" (par. 3), "Then one Sunday morning I woke up in the gutter" (par. 9) and "I finally had to admit that junk mail was stronger than I was" (par. 9). Where have you heard expressions like these before? What effect do they have in this selection?

2. What device of humour is Kinsella using in paragraph 7 when he writes, "The divorce petition reached me by registered mail — a red-letter day"? And where else is this device used?

3. Name the device Kinsella uses in paragraph 9 when he writes: "Then one Sunday morning I woke up in the gutter. My clothes were threadbare and I needed a bath and a haircut. Well dressed people stepped around me on their way to church."

IDEAS:

1. Is this piece of writing a SATIRE on drug addiction or on alcoholism?

2. Is addiction to drugs or alcohol a suitable topic for humour? Does Kinsella make fun of the victims? Or is he making fun of something else?

3. Name all the purposes that you think Kinsella may have had in writing "Junk Mail Junkie."

4. Compare junk mail to other commercial invasions of your home such as telephone solicitation, door-to-door peddling and television advertising. Are any or all of these beneficial? How do you respond to each?

5. Write an essay of process analysis, either humorous or serious, telling how to combat junk mail.

(NOTE: See also the Topics for Writing at the end of this chapter.)

Martin Allerdale Grainger

In Vancouver

Born in London, England, and educated at Cambridge, Martin Allerdale Grainger (1874-1941) might have led a conventional life. But a love of action led him to British Columbia where he worked as a backpacker, miner, hunter, logger and writer. He also fought in South Africa and for a time taught jujitsu in London, but it was logging that became the main interest of his life and the subject of his book. Woodsmen of the West, *the semi-autobiographical novel from which our selection "In Vancouver" comes, appeared in 1908 and was dedicated by Grainger "TO MY CREDITORS AFFECTIONATELY." Grainger went on to become an influential conservationist, governmental official and businessman in the forest industry of British Columbia.*

1   As you walk down Cordova Street in the city of Vancouver you notice a gradual change in the appearance of the shop windows. The shoe stores, drug stores, clothing stores, phonograph stores cease to bother you with their blinding light. You see fewer goods fit for a bank clerk or man in business; you leave "high tone" behind you.

2   You come to shops that show faller's axes, swamper's axes — single-bitted, double-bitted; screw jacks and pump jacks, wedges, sledge-hammers, and great seven-foot saws with enormous shark teeth, and huge augers for boring boomsticks, looking like properties from a pantomime workshop.

3   Leckie calls attention to his logging boot, whose bristling spikes are guaranteed to stay in. Clarke exhibits his Wet Proof Peccary Hogskin gloves, that will save your hands when you work with wire ropes. Dungaree trousers are shown to be copper-riveted at the places where a man strains them in working. Then there are oilskins and blankets and rough suits of frieze for winter wear, and woollen mitts.

4   Outside the shop windows, on the pavement in the street, there is a change in the people too. You see few women. Men look into the windows; men drift up and down the street; men lounge in groups upon the curb. Your eye is struck at once by the unusual proportion of big men in the crowd, men that look powerful even in their town clothes.

5   Many of these fellows are faultlessly dressed: very new boots, new black clothes of quality, superfine black shirt, black felt hat. A few wear collars.

6   Others are in rumpled clothes that have been slept in; others, again, in old suits and sweaters; here and there one in dungarees and working boots. You are among loggers.

They are passing time, passing the hours of the days of their trip to   7
town. They chew tobacco, and chew and chew and expectorate, and look
across the street and watch any moving thing. At intervals they will exchange remarks impassively; or stand grouped, hands in pockets, two or
three men together in gentle, long-drawn-out conversations. They seem
to feel the day is passing slowly; they have the air of ocean passengers
who watch the lagging clock from meal-time to meal-time with weary effort. For comfort it seems they have divided the long day into reasonable
short periods; at the end of each 'tis "time to comeanavadrink." You
overhear the invitations as you pass.

Now, as you walk down the street, you see how shops are giving place   8
to saloons and restaurants, and the price of beer decorates each
building's front. And you pass the blackboards of employment offices
and read chalked thereon:—

"50 axemen wanted at Alberni
5 rigging slingers $4
buckers $3½, swampers $3."

And you look into the public room of hotels that are flush with the street
as they were shop windows; and men sit there watching the passing
crowd, chairs tipped back, feet on window-frame, spittoons handy.

You hear a shout or two and noisy laughter, and walk awhile outside   9
the kerb, giving wide berth to a group of men scuffling with one another
in alcohol-inspired play. They show activity.

Then your eye catches the name-board of a saloon, and you remember   10
a paragraph in the morning's paper —
"In a row last night at the Terminus Saloon several men . . ."
and it occurs to you that the chucker-out of a loggers' saloon must be a
man "highly qualified."

•   •   •   •   •   •

The *Cassiar* sails from the wharf across the railway yard Mondays and   11
Thursdays 8 P.M. It's only a short step from the Gold House and the Terminus and the other hotels, and a big bunch of the boys generally comes
down to see the boat off.

You attend a sort of social function. You make a pleasing break in the   12
monotony of drifting up the street to the Terminus and down the street
to the Eureka, and having a drink with the crowd in the Columbia bar,
and standing drinks to the girls at number so-and-so Dupont Street —
the monotony that makes up your holiday in Vancouver. Besides, if you
are a *woodsman* you will see fellow aristocrats who are going north to
jobs: you maintain your elaborate knowledge of what is going on in the
woods and where every one is; and, further, you know that in many a
hotel and logging-camp up the coast new arrivals from town will shortly

be mentioning, casual-like: "Jimmy Jones was down to the wharf night before last. Been blowing-her-in in great shape has Jimmy, round them saloons. Guess he'll be broke and hunting a job in about another week, the pace he's goin' now."

13   You have informed the *Morning Post!*

14   If logging is but the chief among your twenty trades and professions — if you are just the ordinary western *logger* — still the north-going *Cassiar* has great interest for you. Even your friend Tennessee, who would hesitate whether to say telegraph operator or carpenter if you asked him his business suddenly — even he may want to keep watch over the way things are going in the logging world.

15   So you all hang around on the wharf and see who goes on board, and where they're going to, and what wages they hired on at. And perhaps you'll help a perfect stranger to get himself and two bottles of whisky (by way of baggage) up the gang-plank; and help throw Mike M'Curdy into the cargo-room, and his blankets after him.

16   Then the *Cassiar* pulls out amid cheers and shouted messages, and you return up town to make a round of the bars, and you laugh once in a while to find some paralysed passenger whom friends had forgotten to put aboard. . . . And so to bed.

•   •   •   •   •   •

17   The first thing a fellow needs when he hits Vancouver is a clean-up: hair cut, shave, and perhaps a bath. Then he'll want a new hat for sure. The suit of town clothes that, stuffed into the bottom of a canvas bag, has travelled around with him for weeks or months — sometimes wetted in rowboats, sometimes crumpled in a seat or pillow — the suit may be too shabby. So a fellow will feel the wad of bills in his pocket and decide whether it's worth getting a new suit or not.

18   The next thing is to fix on a stopping-place. Some men take a fifty-cent room in a rooming house and feed in the restaurants. The great objection to that is the uncertainty of getting home at night. In boom times I have known men of a romantic disposition who took lodgings in those houses where champagne is kept on the premises and where there is a certain society. But that means frenzied finance, and this time you and I are not going to play the fool and blow in our little stake same as we did last visit to Vancouver.

19   So a fellow can't do better than go to a good, respectable hotel where he knows the proprietor and the bartenders, and where there are some decent men stopping. Then he knows he will be looked after when he is drunk; and getting drunk, he will not be distressed by spasms of anxiety lest some one should go through his pockets and leave him broke. There are some shady characters in a town like Vancouver, and persons of the under-world.

Of course, the first two days in town a man will get good-and-drunk. 20
That is all right, as any doctor will tell you; that is good for a fellow after
hard days and weeks of work in the woods.

But you and I are no drinking men, and we stop there and sober up. 21
We sit round the stove in the hotel and read the newspapers, and discuss
Roosevelt, and the Trusts, and Socialism, and Japanese immigration;
and we tell yarns and talk logs. We sit at the window and watch the
street. The hotel bar is in the next room, and we rise once in a while and
take a party in to "haveadrink." The bar-tender is a good fellow, one of
the boys: he puts up the drinks himself, and we feel the hospitality of it.
We make a genial group. Conversation will be about loggers and logs, of
course, but in light anecdotal vein, with loud bursts of laughter. . . .

Now one or two of the friends you meet are on the bust; ceaselessly 22
setting-up the drinks, insisting that everybody drink with them. I am not
"drinking" myself: I take a cigar and fade away. But you stay; politeness
and good fellowship demand that you should join each wave that goes up
to the bar, and when good men are spending money you would be mean
not to spend yours too. . . .

Pretty soon you feel the sweet reasonableness of it all. A hard-working 23
man should indemnify himself for past hardships. He owes it to himself
to have a hobby of some kind. You indulge a hobby for whisky.

About this time it is as well to hand over your roll of bills to Jimmy 24
Ross, the proprietor. Then you don't have to bother with money any
more: you just wave your hand each time to the bar-tender. *He* will keep
track of what you spend. . . .

Now you are fairly on the bust: friends all round you, good boys all. 25
Some are hard up, and you tell Jimmy to give them five or ten dollars;
and "Gimme ten or twenty," you'll say, "I want to take a look round
the saloons" — which you do with a retinue.

The great point now is never to let yourself get sober. You'll feel awful 26
sick if you do. By keeping good-and-drunk you keep joyous. "Look bad
but feel good" is sound sentiment. Even suppose you were so drunk last
night that Bob Doherty knocked the stuffing out of you in the Eureka
bar, and you have a rankling feeling that your reputation as a fighting
man has suffered somewhat — still, never mind, line up, boys; whisky
for mine: let her whoop, and to hell with care! Yah-hurrup and smash
the glass!!

•   •   •   •   •   •

If you are "acquainted" with Jimmy Ross — that is to say, if you have 27
blown in one or two cheques before at his place, and if he knows you as a
competent woodsman — Jimmy will just reach down in his pocket and
lend you fives and tens after your own money is all gone. In this way you
can keep on the bust a little longer, and ease off gradually — keeping

pace with Jimmy's growing disinclination to lend. But sooner or later you've got to face the fact that the time has come to hunt another job.

28   There will be some boss loggers in town; you may have been drinking with them. Some of them perhaps will be sobering up and beginning to remember the business that brought them to Vancouver, and to think of their neglected camps up-coast.

29   Boss loggers generally want men; here are chances for you. Again, Jimmy Ross may be acting as a sort of agent for some of the northern logging-camps: if you're any good Jimmy may send you up to a camp. Employment offices, of course, are below contempt — they are for men strange to the country, incompetents, labourers, farm hands, and the like.

30   You make inquiries round the saloons. In the Eureka some one introduces you to Wallace Campbell. He wants a riggin' slinger: you are a riggin' slinger. Wallace eyes the bleary wreck you look. Long practice tells him what sort of a man you probably are when you're in health. He stands the drinks, hires you at four and a half, and that night you find yourself, singing drunk, in the *Cassiar's* saloon — on your way north to work.

STRUCTURE:

1. Why do you think Grainger begins this selection with a walk down the street?
2. Where does the process analysis begin? What process does it explain? What are its main events?
3. To what extent is "In Vancouver" a narrative? What purpose does this narration serve?
4. What proportion of "In Vancouver" is given to description?
5. Notice the last word of this selection, "work." What qualifies it to occupy that place?

STYLE:

1. Since saws have metal teeth, Grainger is using a METAPHOR when he writes of "great seven-foot saws with enormous shark teeth" (par. 2). Do other metaphors appear in the selection? If so, point them out.
2. In paragraph 18, Grainger mentions "men of a romantic disposition who took lodgings in those houses where champagne is kept on the premises and where there is a certain society." What is he saying? These polite EUPHEMISMS were published in 1908; restate the passage as it might appear if written today.

3. Look up the word "expectorate" (par. 7) in a desk-size dictionary. Why does Grainger prefer it to the word "spit"? What are its origins in Latin? How is it related to the words "expand," "expatriate" and "pectoral"?
4. What has Grainger achieved by combining words, as in "come-anavadrink" (par. 7), "blowing-her-in" (par. 12), "good-and- drunk" (par. 20) and "haveadrink" (par. 21)?
5. Grainger frequently refers to "you," as in ". . . this time you and I are not going to play the fool and blow in our little stake same as we did last visit to Vancouver" (par. 18). What has he achieved in doing so?

IDEAS:
1. What is a holiday for? What benefits do Grainger's loggers derive from their Vancouver holiday?
2. If you have read Pierre Berton's essay "The Dirtiest Job in the World," point out the ways in which the gold miners he describes suffer from lack of time off.
3. Does Grainger glorify the drinking, fighting and whoring that he describes? To what extent does an attitude of machismo underly the philosophy of "In Vancouver"?
4. Choose one section of "In Vancouver" to rewrite from the point of view of a feminist, retaining all the facts but changing the presentation of them.
5. "There are some shady characters in a town like Vancouver, and persons of the under-world" (par. 19), wrote Grainger in this 1908 description. If you know Vancouver, discuss the extent to which his statement is true today. Give specific examples. If you live elsewhere, give examples of "shady characters" and "persons of the under-world" in your town or city.
6. Write a process analysis of any one of these activities:

   Enjoying a party
   Enjoying a concert
   Enjoying a holiday (specify where)
   Enjoying a night out on the town

(NOTE: See also the Topics for Writing at the end of this chapter.)

John Fraser

Strangers

People were understandably surprised when the Toronto Globe and Mail sent John Fraser, former ballet critic, to head the Globe's news bureau in Peking. It was 1977 and Fraser was only 33. First he studied the language intensively. Then when he and his wife Elizabeth MacCallum arrived, they did all they could to skirt the bureaucracies and — as Fraser relates in "Strangers" — meet the people. The result was one of the most spectacular success stories of modern journalism: Fraser was at the centre of things when Chinese citizens, in reaction against the Cultural Revolution and the Gang of Four, openly argued for democracy in posters on the now-famous "Xidan Wall." Fraser's accounts of this remarkable change were already being carried in newspapers across the world, when one day he agreed to talk about democracy to a gathering. Fu Ruizhe (as the Chinese pronounced his name) found himself addressing a crowd of many thousands and being carried on their shoulders as a hero. When The Chinese: Portrait of a People appeared in 1980, it became a runaway best seller, was a main Book of the Month Club selection in both the United States and Canada, and was translated into several other languages. "Strangers" is Chapter 2 of that book.

1   The Peking we came to love was not the city we first arrived in. For anyone who has even the vaguest conception of the unique cultural legacy of China, modern Peking, transformed by thirty years of Communist rule, is devastated territory, a dead place seemingly animated only by the circumspect blobs that move about on foot or by bike. Had we arrived in summer, or especially during the triumphant Peking autumn, this view would have been ameliorated by the abundance of trees whose foliage softens the stark outlines of conformist, Soviet-inspired architecture. But we arrived in the dead of winter, when the city is at its bleakest and the air is often so weighed down by pollution and muck that you can scarcely see a half block ahead.

2   Even in summer, much of the vitality of Peking is hidden behind walls or down narrow lanes, so that if you keep to the main streets, cocooned in a car, the place will seem forever alien. Chang An Avenue, the main thoroughfare, and Tienanmen Square itself are dismal disappointments. The vast acres of pavement bordered by huge, ugly Stalinist buildings seem designed to reduce human beings to minuscule proportions. The architecture, planning and subsequent development of all capital cities define a nation's vision. It's no good arguing that the Communists were handed a bankrupt nation and had to do the best they could. The amount of toil they demanded of their people to tear down the unique and ir-

replaceable city walls and build such monsters as the Great Hall of the People belies a government merely coping with necessity. There was an iconoclastic vehemence behind the act. The Communists wanted a symbol of the kind of changes they planned to bring about in this ancient land, and the vast desert of Tienanmen Square is the result.

I found all this depressing but, fortunately, not dispiriting. It was a challenge, and I didn't intend to be defeated. A few years earlier a Canadian diplomat freshly posted to Peking had been taken on his first tour of the city. He and his wife were driven past all the high points, and with a sense of increasing despair, they realized that this was a city like no other. There was no downtown that the diplomat could recognize as such — no sense of the vitality and mystique that marks an exciting city. As his tour came to its harsh conclusion in Tienanmen Square, he hunched lower and lower in the seat of the car. Finally, he looked around him and surveyed the interminable panorama. "This city sucks," he said. Others like him have asked for immediate transfers within a week of arrival.

Grimy and depressing as it seemed to be, Peking was our new home, and we set about discovering it methodically. We were aided, I suppose, by our own natures, as well as by the daily presence of four remarkable Chinese who worked for the *Globe and Mail* bureau. Lazy unless goaded into action, I would have been content to hibernate in the bureau apartment, waiting for official trips to materialize so I could fill out the cable forms I sent back to Toronto. Elizabeth, however, detests being housebound, and she had us out on bicycles before I even had a chance to devise stratagems to stay inside. My wife was born with a fierce determination, which was often at odds with her shyness and easily aroused fear of being rebuffed or defeated. My own forte is people, all shapes, sizes and colors. I am fascinated by the complexities of human beings and the reasons they do things the way they do. Like Mutt and Jeff, we took our foibles and fancies to an unsuspecting audience, which often responded with affection and curiosity. My gregariousness and indiscriminate snooping were balanced by Elizabeth's prudence and immaculate eye for detail.

I discovered the back lanes of Peking in this manner day after day. It was mostly a view of walls, punctuated by brief glimpses through courtyard doors. When we got off the bikes and walked around, we were invariably surrounded by hordes of giggling kids and curious adults; there would be occasional conversations of an exceedingly superficial sort, which nevertheless left us elated and excited. Sometimes there would be sullen glares too, and these I tried to ignore. It is not possible to walk anonymously through a street in China; you are forced to react in some way. Some foreigners resent being stared at and can get quite snarky and irritable after they have settled down in Peking and are no longer frightened by the setting. For ourselves, we always smiled and often said

"Ni hao?" ("How are you?") to nearly every passing face, because to ignore the effect you are having on people or to be annoyed at it is to admit that there is no possibility of contact, no common ground, no shared humanity.

6   Right from the beginning, albeit unconsciously, that was something I would never admit. Usually when Elizabeth and I were depressed with life in the foreign ghetto, we would go out on our bikes and come back renewed and refreshed. Nothing extraordinary ever happened, but we had forced ourselves, however insignificantly, on the city and its people, and that act alone made me feel that we actually existed in Peking. Even when these outings were disasters, either because we got no response or because our own moods made us indifferent to the passing scenes, we never gave up our manic compulsion to push out beyond the ghetto. To admit defeat also meant that I had to accept life in China exclusively on terms dictated by the Chinese Government, and those terms struck me as being perilously close to the ones I had lived under at private boarding schools in Canada. The Grade Nines rarely mixed with the Grade Tens and never had anything to do with the privileged crowd in the most senior grade. Prefects and teachers, however intelligent or kind, ordered our lives from dawn to dusk. Above all, there was the final authority of the Headmaster. In respecting the various restraints all societies are forced to impose upon themselves, whether it is the governing of a nation or a school, those prohibitions which are arbitrary or fundamentally unfair naturally arouse opposition. I was not an international spy, whatever the Chinese Government thought of all foreign journalists; I was a former dance and theater critic who was now living and working in China, and I was damned if the Headmaster and all his staff were going to prevent me from trying to meet the Grade Nines or the Grade Twelves — or the staff members, for that matter.

7   With such chips on our shoulders, Elizabeth and I gradually expanded our daily excursions. Unlike the diplomats or even the foreign students attending classes at several Peking institutions, I had no fixed schedule that defined the hours I could go out. This gave us flexibility and freedom. One day shortly after arriving, we were cycling through the back lanes in the Drum Tower neighborhood of northwest Peking when we saw some Chinese youths walking ahead of us carrying ice skates. Rounding the next corner, we came to a beautiful little lake completely frozen over, where hundreds of people were whizzing around on the ice. Skating! We were not Canadians for nothing, and the possibility of ice skating dazzled us. For some reason, it was among a number of things I had not thought about before coming, but this was soon rectified with the purchase of Chinese racing skates, which cost only about $9 (absurdly cheap to us, but a sizable dent in a Chinese wallet).

8   Within two days we were out on the ice, and it was a glorious, giddy

experience. We were bundled up in Chinese duffel coats, which toned down our strangeness, and I discovered for the first time that when the Chinese are at play, they are at their most relaxed with foreigners. We bumped and crashed into each other, laughed all the time, shook hands, waved in the distance; none of the encounters, save one, led to anything but brief pleasantries, but the whole business was a considerable step up from bike rides down the lanes.

The other great diversion in those days was hunting for old, broken-down Chinese furniture in Peking's "commission," or secondhand, stores. In our naiveté back in Canada, we had supposed that China would give us a chance to shuck our relentless materialism. Our folly was to have imagined that the Chinese people were not like other mortals, that if they had a bit more purchasing power — as some are beginning to have now — they would not waste it on things which had only ephemeral value, that they cared not a whit about the cut or color of the cloth on their backs.

We also didn't know that the degree to which Chinese society was cut off from foreigners would force us to spend an inordinate amount of time hunting through shops because there was little else to do during leisure time, particularly in the winter. It was also fun. Thus it was that the five or six commission shops around Peking became favorite haunts for hundreds of foreigners, especially the ruthless wives of French diplomats, who learned the game sooner and fought harder than anyone else.

The furniture to be found in these places — scroll tables, money chests, ornate chairs, leather trunks, small side tables — was usually in a completely dilapidated state, and anyone who didn't know how well it could be redone at the local furniture-repair shop would have avoided most of it. Some was very ugly, but it was all Chinese, and the very act of discovery enhanced the appeal. You could easily spend a happy morning scooting about the various shops to see what was in. Inevitably you learned a bit about Chinese crafts, and following the business through to the repair shop was a small but undeniably diverting pleasure. Most of all, it was another one of the exercises that got us out of the foreigners' ghetto.

The best time to go was first thing in the morning, especially in the weeks preceding a major Chinese holiday or festival, when ordinary Chinese sold their few remaining old pieces of furniture to get a bit of extra money for a festive meal or to buy a special gift. No group of foreigners surpassed the French at nabbing the most unusual finds. They reigned as supreme in this area as the Japanese wives did in the Chinese antique stores, although for different reasons — the Japanese came with such large wads of Chinese currency that no one could beat them to anything they really wanted, particularly porcelains.

Right from the beginning, we were helped in our desire to meet and treat Chinese people as equals and friends by the four staff members employed by the *Globe*. The linchpin was the interpreter, Mr. Hao, who guided us through the intricacies of Chinese bureaucracy and was practically our nursemaid during the first confusing days. Then there were the driver, Mr. Wang; the cook, Mr. Chen; and the housekeeper, Mrs. Liu. It was surely an anomaly of remarkable proportions that only in Communist China could two hopelessly Western bourgeois live in a style more suitable to nineteenth-century capitalist compradors. I remember vividly having a conversation with a very rich woman several years before in which she bemoaned the fact that no one seemed to understand the problems of "keeping a good household staff busy and satisfied." I roared my disdain to Elizabeth later. Imagine someone in this day and age talking like that. I vaguely remembered my grandfather's large house in Toronto, which had a household staff, and throughout my youth my parents had always employed a live-in housekeeper and cook. But those days were gone for most of my generation, and had I ever paused to analyze the situation, I would have concluded that they were happily gone, for reasons of romantic egalitarianism as well as the nature of to-day's mobility and leisure time in the affluent world. Even if you had the money, who would want to be tied down to the kind of daily ritual and ordered existence that a household staff would inevitably bring?

14   Not I, anyway, and initially the prospect of ordering the lives of four total strangers — three of whom spoke no English — filled us with trepidation. I shouldn't have worried. It was *they* who set about ordering our lives, once they had learned our particular interests and idiosyncrasies. Mercifully, they didn't live in — no Chinese staff live with foreigners, although they do with important Chinese officials' families — so we had the evenings and weekends to ourselves. We got along famously right from the beginning, and it was from these four that our affection for the Chinese people first grew.

15   Instinctively, we never regarded them as "our staff." Their lives and our lives had come together through a fluke, and since they were already established in the bureau, we turned to them as colleagues for help and understanding. In addition, the system whereby their services were made available to the *Globe* reinforced the idea that they were not beholden to us for their livelihood.

16   The staff worked for an organization called the Diplomatic Service Bureau, and it was to this outfit that all foreigners posted to Peking had to apply if they wanted Chinese workers. I never paid their salaries; instead I sent a sum of money for their services to the bureau, which in turn gave them a salary predetermined by the state. With the interpreter, for example, I sent off 350 yuan (about $275) a month to the bureau, but I'm sure he never received more than 70 or 80 yuan, if not less. At the time this struck me as inherently unfair — not the price I paid the bureau,

which was a very small sum for the services of an educated, perceptive person, but the discrepancy between what he got and what the *Globe* had to put out. If it annoyed any of the Chinese staff working for diplomats or journalists in Peking, I never heard about it. One time I broached the subject to an exceedingly bright interpreter at a European embassy who, after I had got to know him well, never hesitated to make a criticism of his government or "feudal" Chinese habits if he felt so inclined. But he wouldn't hear of my arguments: "I accept this," he said very matter-of-factly, without the least trace of rhetorical grandstanding. "Most people are so poor in this country, I wouldn't feel right taking any more money than I do already. I'm lucky. I live in the city and have an interesting job. It would be wrong to demand more when so many others have so much less." I believed and respected him, even though I knew there were other Chinese who resented the arbitrary way wages were kept so low.

In fact, I remained predisposed to believe the Chinese who talked this way, not because I wanted to believe that people could see beyond self-interest (I knew I could myself, so I didn't need Maoism to persuade me that Chinese people were also capable of it), but because I had the daily example of our own, benevolent Gang of Four — as opposed to the real Gang of Four, the name ascribed to a quartet of state leaders who were purged shortly after Mao Tsetung died — back in the bureau. We discussed most things openly with the *Globe's* Chinese staff and worked out understandings that were models of diplomacy, tact and compromise. When Mr. Wang, the driver, first realized that I wouldn't be able to drive, he volunteered to work after hours. In two years, Elizabeth and I never heard a serious gripe or complaint from them and they never heard one from us. There were misunderstandings and cultural mix-ups, but they were always resolved with laughter and a mutual concern for the other person's feelings.

With the exception of the interpreter, who called us by our given names, the staff used our Chinese names, which had been given to us by language teachers in Toronto — mine was Fu Ruizhe, which means "lucky philosopher," and Elizabeth's was Mai Kailan, which means "generous orchid" (the pronunciation was a Chinese approximation of our family names). By this time we had been accorded one of those signal honors which used to make me swell with pride. We were encouraged by the staff to use the familiar and affectionate prefixes of *lao* or *xiao* (pronounced "shao") with their family names. Thus Mr. Chen, the cook, became Lao Chen, or Old Chen — except that the English doesn't give you the spirit of the term, which is rough and warm at the same time. Mr. Hao, the interpreter, was younger than anyone else, so he became Xiao Hao, or Little Hao; while the housekeeper, Mrs. Liu, let us call her Liu Ayi, or Auntie Liu. If this all sounds a trifle cute and cloying, I don't care: we had a relationship based on respect and fondness, which grew steadily, and I began thinking of us all as a Unit, the basic work and social grouping of all Chinese people under Communism. It was a nice feeling.

19   No one engaged my admiration more than Lao Chen, the cook, who was a Shandong peasant and a man of quiet, unassuming but inestimable wisdom. As time went by, I was to blow hot and cold about the vagaries of Communism in China, but even when I was feeling angriest at the mindless, stupid dogmatism that could dispatch people to prison or even death for their thoughts, I was also forced to remember Lao Chen and what he represented. Shandong people are supposed to produce the best cooks in China. This is a myth, as it turns out: Sichuan or Guangdong people make just as admirable — or bad — cooks. But the myth may well have given Lao Chen his only lucky break in prerevolutionary China: he got a job as a kitchen scullery that eventually led him from his native province to Peking.

20   Until he learned to read in his forties during one of the Communist literacy campaigns, he had had no formal education. He was initially a product of his native wit and his own determination, but the revolution gave him his pride. He had had a miserable job in the old Soviet Embassy in Peking, which as far as I could figure out didn't improve appreciably during the alliance between China and the Soviet Union throughout the 1950s. A visit to Vietnam much later confirmed my view that Soviet comrades with a bit of power and position can be the most pompous, arrogant and abusive masters the world has ever seen, and that their style lacks even the formal etiquette ascribed to the British Raj in colonial India.

21   In any event, Lao Chen had been sacked along with all the other Chinese staff at the Soviet Embassy in 1966 and had come straight to the *Globe and Mail,* where he impressed six correspondents with his hard work, his uncomplicated devotion to Chinese socialism and his uproarious love of life. During the worst madness of the Cultural Revolution, Lao Chen showed through his actions and demeanor that there was at least one Chinese who had integrity and decency, and because he existed, one knew there were more. He did not consider the Communist Party an oppressive menace; for him the Party represented a better life for both him and his children.

22   I could not exclude him from my understanding of China because he was "not typical" in that he was sufficiently trusted to work with foreigners. If I had excluded him, then I couldn't include the host of young people who had so many grievances against the same Party. They too are not supposed to be typical. For me, Lao Chen represented something that was fine and good in China, and because he ascribed his lot to the Communist Party I had to accept that there was something fine and good in it too. He was a product of that prerevolutionary faith and

determination for a better life which helped bring Mao Tsetung to power and defined the new integrity and courage of modern China. He was also a participant in the first few years of postrevolutionary reconstruction, when the government had broad popular support and the future, for the first time in over a century, seemed bright.

As I was not to see the truly dark side of Chinese Communism for nearly a year, at least as it affected us directly, I succumbed to Sinophilia quite quickly. I confused love of the people with love of the system, accepting all the frustrations imposed to divide foreigners and Chinese people with equilibrium, while studiously ignoring certain troubling little details that emerged every now and then. The country was clearly changing radically for the better from its immediate past, and the pace of events was so fast it was almost impossible to stop and reflect on what everything meant. 23

My earliest encounter with a Chinese citizen, free of official circumspection, however, is something I look back on with feelings of personal bitterness and deep regret — although the incident served to remind me to keep my eyes and ears open at all times and push beyond the directly observable routine of Chinese life that foreigners could see. Less than a week after we had arrived, Elizabeth and I joined two Canadian acquaintances at a carpet exhibition assembled for the benefit of "foreign friends." It was a pleasant Sunday-afternoon diversion, and the carpets were of good quality at a fair price. The display room was at the back of a large exhibition hall. There were several rooms you had to pass through first, one of which contained a selection of Chinese-made musical instruments, including an upright piano. As an amateur pianist I was curious about the quality of the local product, and after a half hour of fighting three hundred other foreigners knee-deep in silk carpets, I excused myself for a few minutes and went to look over the instruments. 24

I believe I was playing one of Bach's two-part inventions, or something equally pretentious considering the setting, when a young man of about twenty-five came up to me with a broad, encouraging grin stretched across his handsome face. 25

"Ni hao?" I said. 26

To my surprise, he began speaking in slow but carefully correct English. "You play the piano very well," he said. 27

All Chinese conversations with foreigners seem to begin with a compliment of some sort, and I learned very quickly how to play the game I called "Opening a Conversation." 28

"No. I play very badly," I said. "But you speak English very well." 29

"No, not at all. I speak it only a little and very poorly. I must study much harder. But I think you really do play very well." 30

It was the first time I had played the game, and despite the beginner's luck of the first gambit, I was raw and ignorant. For one thing, I didn't 31 even know that it was supposed to be impossible to have conversations like the one I was about to have.

32   "Are you a diplomat?" he asked me.

33   "No. I'm a journalist."

34   His eyes lit up. "A journalist! I think that must be the most wonderful job in the world. You have the opportunity to travel and make the acquaintance of many people. I think you have to be very intelligent to be a journalist."

35   "It's a good job, all right," I agreed, "but you don't always have to be intelligent."

36   "Oh, I think so. Very intelligent. What country are you from?"

37   "Canada."

38   He stopped for a moment. I was so naive at the time, I was actually being paternalistic to him and hadn't even asked him where he was from and what he did. The remembrance of this ignorance is painful for me to recall now — ignorance of what to ask him, of course, but most of all ignorance of his own courage in even speaking to me in this forthright manner.

39   "Canada? Didn't I hear something about a Canadian journalist who got into trouble with our government?"

40   I was surprised he knew about Munro and his troubles. It was my initial understanding that Chinese people were unaware of the affairs of foreigners. "That was the last correspondent," I said. "He wrote some articles about life in China that the government didn't like, so he had to leave fast and I had to get here faster."

41   "I think that is very wrong, don't you? I think people should be allowed to think and write what they see and feel. I believe our government was wrong to make trouble for him."

42   So help me God, I then indirectly *defended* the Chinese Government by telling him — nay, lecturing — about injustices in Canada and the United States as well as the good things in his country, all based on six days' experience.

43   "But still," he said (and kindly, too, for he must have known I was a fool at that moment), "I think my country is very backward in many ways."

44   I asked him whether he could come and visit me in my apartment, and he smiled. "No. I don't think so. You would get into serious trouble."

45   Dimly, I perceived I was talking to a remarkable person who knew that my trouble would be minuscule compared with the trouble to which he would be subjected. I asked him how long it would be before Chinese people and foreigners could meet naturally in Peking, without either side's feeling any fear.

46   "Maybe fifteen years. Maybe longer. I think my country is very backward in this matter."

That was it. We shook hands, and I went to join Elizabeth and the others. I told them I had had an interesting conversation, and the Canadian couple, who had already been in Peking for several months, was flabbergasted — although nothing had struck me as strange.

"Are you sure he said those things?" asked one of our friends. "I've never heard of anything like that."

The incredulity made me ask several experienced foreigners in Peking about the business, and they all expressed surprise. One United States diplomat was convinced it was a setup and told me I had better watch myself before I fell into a trap. Instinct forced me to write a veiled account of the conversation for my newspaper, being careful to omit any references that might have identified the person. I was grateful for the opportunity because, while I wanted to distance myself from my predecessor's approach to China reporting, I also wanted to show the Chinese authorities that I was not frightened to write what I saw and heard. In this way I established a link between Ross Munro's years and my own, and it is the only thing I look back on without regret in the whole incident.

Within a few months I had forgotten all about it. It seemed a strange thing, almost unreal, and since I never ran across anyone else who spoke like that, I dismissed it. He wouldn't come back to my mind again until the following November, when I would meet thousands of his brothers- and sisters-in-arms at the Xidan (pronounced "she-dan") Democracy Wall and I was able to shed the conceit that I had ever understood Chinese people properly. It was not that I lived unobservant in China until that time. With eyes and ears and a willingness to witness, a professional journalist can pick up a lot, and I set about the business of being just such a professional journalist with enthusiasm.

This was objective journalism with a vengeance, the kind that had regularly poured out of Peking for years. It wasn't false, as such, and my work certainly reflected accurately what I could see. I learned a great deal about how official China operates and the games the senior leadership in the Party's Politburo plays. For the first time in ages, journalists were being allowed to travel all over the country, even to the once-forbidden province of Sichuan, where one hundred million people had gone through a tumultuous two decades which outsiders scarcely knew the first thing about. Increasingly frequent visits by foreign businessmen and government leaders brought far greater access to the thinking and actions of official China, while foreigners and Chinese alike were invited to try their hand at the intricate and complex game of figuring out which faction was winning the day within the power structure of the country. Never in my life had I witnessed the degree to which people picked over and speculated on the significance of government statements and official editorials, trying to winnow the chaff of propaganda from the hard kernels of political action; this wretched metaphor is apt because it was grueling, tedious work.

52 In between the traveling and the winnowing, there was the foreigner's life in Peking to be enjoyed or hated. Elizabeth hated it terribly at first, causing some morose scenes, but she is not a quitter, and by the end of spring we had become regulars. I had also started falling in love with Peking. Images haunted me with their beauty and poignancy. Driving to the cable office late at night, I would pass solitary workers heading off for late-shift work on their bikes. As often as not, they would be singing some complicated Peking Opera aria, or perhaps a lusty peasant song, which filled the still night air with as vibrant and human a sound as I have ever heard. By day, Chinese children were an endless source of hilarity and affection, especially when they played by their grandparents' side. On the face of it, there was a cohesion to everyday life and society that I had never seen in the West, although this was primarily because I was a participant in my own society, while in China I was only an observer.

53 After the late-night drives to the cable office, I would come back to the apartment and tiptoe into the bedroom, trying not to wake my sleeping wife. In the few minutes it took me to doze off, the sweet sounds of a Peking night continued and came into the room through the balcony window. Another singer, perhaps, cycling by. If he was in full voice, one of the guards from the People's Liberation Army outside might shout a sarcastic comment, and there would be a chorus of giggles all along the road. At other times, the wagonloads of produce from the nearby communes would pass through our quarter, and the clip-clop of the mules and horses that pulled them was wildly nostalgic, reminding me of the horse-drawn milk and ice wagons that I heard in my boyhood, during the fifties in Toronto. I had learned that the drovers who brought these wagons into Peking were among the most independent souls in China, thanks to their late-night work and the fact that they were on the road most of the time. How I loved their raucous bark as they urged the animals on. I had survived the initial period of stark terror as a foreign correspondent. Life was becoming more pleasant with every passing day, and I was running my own show halfway around the world. Sleep came very easily.

STRUCTURE:

1. Why does John Fraser paint such a dismal picture of Peking in the introduction, especially in describing the newly arrived Canadian

diplomat who, in paragraph 3, ends his first look at Peking by saying "This city sucks"?

2. Contrast the closing to the beginning: what effect does Fraser achieve in the poetical language of his last two paragraphs?

3. The process through which John Fraser and his wife cease to be "strangers" in Peking can be broken into several phases. Point out each and explain its role in the process.

4. Through which device of organization does Fraser explain his attitude toward the Chinese Government in paragraph 6?

5. Which devices of organization are introduced in paragraph 28 where Fraser writes, "All Chinese conversations with foreigners seem to begin with a compliment of some sort, and I learned very quickly how to play the game I called 'Opening a Conversation'"?

STYLE:

1. John Fraser's book *The Chinese: Portrait of a People,* from which this selection comes, was a publishing sensation: a best seller in Canada, it also appeared in the United States and several other countries. Judging by the style of this selection, what sort of reader do you think Fraser had in mind as he wrote the book?

2. What is the effect of Fraser's referring to "you" in paragraphs 11 and 24?

3. What device is represented by the word "hibernate" in paragraph 4?

4. If you do not already know the origins of the word "Sinophilia" (par. 23), look them up in a desk-size dictionary (you may also have to look under "-phil"). How is this word related to "sinology," "philanthropy" and "philosophy"?

IDEAS:

1. Fraser learned Chinese before he arrived. In what ways would the experiences he relates in "Strangers" be different if he had not learned the language? If you have travelled in an area where English is not spoken, how did your knowing or not knowing the local language affect the experiences you had?

2. Why do some people who move to a new country never learn the language?

3. Most journalists write in an objective way, preferring facts to feelings. But in "Strangers," as well as in much of his newspaper writing, John Fraser takes the personal approach. Which approach do you enjoy more? Which approach teaches you more? Which approach tends to be more accurate?

4. In one way or another, paragraphs 6, 7, 13, 42 and 53 *compare* life in China with life in Canada. Discuss those comparisons, then point out and discuss other passages that *contrast* life in the two countries. Which seem more numerous, the similarities or the differences?

5. Fraser writes of his cook, "During the worst madness of the Cultural Revolution, Lao Chen showed through his actions and demeanor that there was at least one Chinese who had integrity and decency, and because he existed, one knew there were more" (par. 21). Discuss the implications of this observation. To what extent can one learn a culture by learning to know individuals from it?
6. Write an essay of process analysis, telling how you came to know a new country, province, city, town or neighbourhood.

(Note: See also the Topics for Writing at the end of this chapter.)

Topics for Writing

Chapter 8: Process Analysis

(Note also the topics for writing that appear after each selection in this chapter.)

Tell your reader how to perform one of these processes:

1. Select a wife, husband or lover
2. Break off a romance
3. Transplant a tree
4. Paint a house
5. Produce a block print, silk screen, lithograph or photographic print
6. Make wine or beer
7. Win at the race track
8. Order a meal at an expensive restaurant
9. Get a loan at the bank
10. Select a career
11. Have a successful job interview
12. Select a bicycle or motorcycle or car
13. Stop smoking, drinking or overeating
14. Become physically fit
15. Cure insomnia

Explain how one of these processes is performed or occurs:

1. The making of paper
2. The making of gunpowder
3. The making of paint
4. The making of glass
5. The making of cement
6. The sending of messages by the human nervous system
7. The evolution of a species
8. The extinction of a species
9. The formation of soil
10. Desertification
11. The formation of rain
12. The eruption of a volcano
13. Continental drift
14. Nuclear fission
15. Nuclear fusion

© Miller Services. H. Armstrong Roberts.

"As you read this there are 1,800 electrical storms raging throughout the world, and by the time you finish this sentence, lightning will have struck earth 100 times."

Janice McEwen *and the* Harrowsmith *staff,* "Thunderstrokes and Firebolts"

EXTENDED DEFINITION

We are all familiar with the kind of essay introduction that goes something like this:

> Lightning, according to the *Acme Collegiate Dictionary,* is "a flash of light created by a discharge of atmospheric electricity between one cloud and another or between a cloud and the earth."

We recognize the stern language of the dictionary, which in an authoritative and exact way tells us what something is. But after a few words, the definition is over. We have made only a beginning, an introduction to a term but not an exploration of a subject.

In the hands of the essay writer, though, a definition can expand into more and more detail until the whole essay functions to define the topic. In "Thunderstrokes and Firebolts," Janice McEwen has told us probably all we ever wanted to know about lightning: its causes, its various forms, its power and its dangers. By the time we finish her many examples, statistics, reports of research findings and techniques for staying alive in a storm, we have amassed a much clearer and more detailed picture of lightning than the dictionary could ever give us.

The purpose of such an *extended definition* is usually to educate. Although it can also persuade or entertain, as in Harry Bruce's "Johnny Canuck Is a Yuk," a definition exists mainly to give us information. Thus you may find yourself doing research, like McEwen, who found that a lightning bolt "attains a core temperature of about 50,000 degrees Fahrenheit — five times the temperature at the surface of the sun." A specific fact like this is much more interesting and convincing than a vague statement that lightning bolts are very hot. And a large number of such facts will add authority, as well as interest, to your essay. One way to define is to tell what the subject is *not*. Myrna Kostash develops her "Profile of the Rapist as an Ordinary Man" in part by showing that a typical rapist is not an easily recognizable "weirdo," is not insane and does not even consider himself a rapist.

An extended definition can be organized in almost any way or combination of ways. To explain lightning, McEwen brings in nearly all the major techniques we have discussed in other chapters: *narration, example, description, cause and effect, comparison and contrast, metaphor* and *process analysis*. While essays in other chapters of this book have done the same thing, drawing upon a variety of methods, their basic structure usually depends on one organizational form — such as comparison and contrast. But definition is not a *form;* it is a *function.* In constructing your extended definition, you may want to think consciously of forms we have studied — or you may allow these forms to occur naturally as you write. The process is completely open.

Marvin Zuker and June Callwood

You Are a Child

Marvin Zuker is an Ontario Provincial Court Judge. He was born in 1941 in Toronto, studied at the University of Toronto, and in 1966 was awarded the LL.B. from Osgoode Hall Law School. Zuker taught business administration at Centennial College, Toronto, from 1969 to 1972, and at Ryerson Polytechnical Institute, Toronto, from 1972 until his appointment as judge in 1978. He has expressed a strong concern for the average citizen in numerous magazine and newspaper articles that demystify the law by explaining it in everyday language. Zuker has done the same in his books, A Guide to Law for Canadians (1967, 1969, 1975), Canadian Women and the Law (with June Callwood, 1971), and The Law Is Not for Women (with Callwood, 1976). It is from this last book that our selection, "You Are a Child," is taken.

June Callwood, born in 1924 in Chatham, Ontario, has been called "the most successful ghost writer in Canada." Working from taped interviews, she has written the words to "autobiographies" of Dr. Charles Mayo, Barbara Walters, Otto Preminger and several other public figures, American and Canadian. She has also been the real author of magazine columns "written" by others. In her own right Callwood has been a television script writer and broadcaster, a successful journalist, a book writer, and an outspoken social critic, especially on behalf of women and children. It is this last concern, on the part of both Callwood and her collaborator Marvin Zuker, that is most apparent in our selection "You Are a Child."

I f you are under the age of nineteen, you're a child in some 1 of the provinces some of the time, and by a magic trick an adult the rest of the time. It will make life interesting for you, particularly if you leave home legally in one province and get picked up by the police in another for being under-age, or if you forget about provincial borders when ordering beer.

The Canadian Council on Children and Youth received a grant from 2 the Secretary of State in 1974 to discover, among other matters, what *is* a child in Canada. It took a group of industrious researchers an entire summer to discover that we don't know.

You are too young to drink at eighteen in some provinces, and ready 3 for a double in others. You commit a crime at the age of fifteen and you may be tried as a juvenile offender but, on the other hand, you may find yourself in an adult court. If your grandmother left you some bonds, you can have them when you are eighteen if you live in Manitoba, but inches away in Saskatchewan you'll have to wait another year.

If your parents are divorcing, the judge may ask you to make the ugly 4 decision about which one you'll live with, providing you are twelve or more. If you're younger, the judge might talk it over with you but most of them don't. In either case, your wishes don't prevail, anyway.

5   Until you are eighteen or nineteen (depending on where you live in this disunified country), you are legally an "infant." You are not considered by the law to be capable of responsibility for yourself. The law therefore may not recognize any contract you have signed as binding; you cannot sue anyone or be sued directly; you may not be able to own land or write a will.

6   You can, however, drive a car, an expensive, complicated and potentially lethal piece of machinery. You can also become a parent at whatever age nature throws the switch, which can be as young as twelve. If you are female, you may keep the baby if you want to: the unlikelihood that you are knowledgeable or mature enough to care for the baby adequately will not be a factor.

7   Your name can be changed whether you like it or not. Your last name is your father's last name, unless your mother was never married to him. If a foster father turns up on the scene and the adults agree that he can adopt you, your last name becomes his. You can be taken from your parents and placed in a foster home in a strange city if that's what the court decides to do. Your parents or legal guardians have jurisdiction over your body: they can have your healthy kidney removed and donated to an ailing brother or sister without your approval.

8   It's obvious that children require protection. They don't have the experience or sufficient information to make life-changing decisions on their own. In fact, children deserve far more protection than they are now receiving in Canada against neglect, emotional deprivation, malnutrition and the caprice of parents, teachers, and social workers.

9   But the dilemma has been to decide at what age protection becomes stifling and an affliction. When, and in what areas, should autonomy begin? And until the child achieves the agreed-upon age of independence, is it good enough to leave her fate entirely in the hands of one or two parents who may or may not be competent, or even sane?

10   There has been considerable discussion in recent years about what is usually described as "the rights of children." Some feel that children should have an advocate whenever adults plan to do something drastic to them, such as deprive them of their freedom in the name of rehabilitation, or award custody of them to an agency or a divorced parent.

11   The advocate most commonly recommended is a lawyer, which seems reasonable since these crises occur in a courtroom setting. But it might be argued that there is nothing in legal training to equip lawyers to understand the emotional needs of children or to interpret their often confused and confusing behaviour.

12   In the meantime, Canadian children remain the most vulnerable of all citizens.

STRUCTURE:

1. Zuker and Callwood write, "The Canadian Council on Children and Youth received a grant from the Secretary of State in 1974 to discover, among other matters, what *is* a child in Canada. It took a group of industrious researchers an entire summer to discover that we don't know" (par. 2). In the paragraphs that follow, have Zuker and Callwood achieved what the researchers could not?
2. "You Are a Child" has two main parts. Where does the second part begin and how does it differ from the first part?
3. In paragraph 3, the authors write that "If your grandmother left you some bonds, you can have them when you are eighteen if you live in Manitoba, but inches away in Saskatchewan you'll have to wait another year." Point out other short contrasts in this selection.
4. What does the last sentence accomplish?

STYLE:

1. As befits a chapter from a handbook, "You Are a Child" is very concise. How have the authors managed to say so much in so few words?
2. This sentence from paragraph 9 uses "she" instead of "he" as a pronoun representing children in general: "And until the child achieves the agreed-upon age of independence, is it good enough to leave her fate entirely in the hands of one or two parents who may or may not be competent, or even sane?" What is the effect of this reversal of our traditionally male-centred grammar? How do you feel about it?

IDEAS:

1. In many traditional cultures, the male and female assume their adult roles as soon as they are biologically capable of doing so. What are the reasons why, in our culture, adult status is postponed for several years?
2. What do you think should be the legal age for doing each of the following activities, and why?
   - driving   having a full-time job
   - drinking   entering legal contracts
   - voting   serving in the armed forces
   - marrying   serving as an MPP, MP, premier or prime minister
3. When an unmarried high–school student finds that she is pregnant, what are the main arguments for and against marriage with her partner? If marriage is decided against, what are the main arguments for and against abortion? For and against putting the child up for adoption? For and against the single mother or single father raising the child?

4. Do you agree that "Canadian children remain the most vulnerable of all citizens" (par. 12)? How vulnerable are they compared to women? The elderly? The retarded, the physically handicapped and the disabled? The native peoples?

5. If you have read "The Iron Road," by Al Purdy, in what ways would you consider the author, at the time of his narrative, to be a child? In what ways would you consider him to be an adult?

6. Write your own extended definition of an adult in our society.

(Note: See also the Topics for Writing at the end of this chapter.)

Harry Bruce

Johnny Canuck Is a Yuk

If any one quality distinguishes the writings of Harry Bruce, it is a sense of place. Born in 1934 in Toronto, he celebrated his city in the 1960s by writing a series of columns for the Toronto Star *which reported the walks he took through the streets and alleys and neighbourhoods and ravines and waterfront that he had known since childhood. In 1968 these were published in a book as* The Short Happy Walks of Max MacPherson. *In 1971 Bruce moved to Nova Scotia, drawn by old family roots and the prospect of salt-water sailing. Since then he has written lovingly of his adopted province in many articles, in the text for a book of colour photographs,* Nova Scotia *(1975) and in* Lifeline: The Story of the Atlantic Ferries and Coastal Boats *(1977). Bruce has worked for* The Ottawa Journal, *the Toronto* Globe and Mail, Maclean's, Saturday Night, The Canadian Magazine, The Star Weekly *and* Atlantic Insight, *although in recent years he has written mostly on a freelance basis. "Johnny Canuck Is a Yuk" appeared in 1976 in* Saturday Night.

The temperature in Ontario and Québec hung around 100°F, almost enough to boil the blood of your most icy-veined Upper Canadian, and the front page of the Halifax *Mail-Star* happily announced, "Canucks Swelter in Heat." Perhaps I only imagined ill will. Perhaps the deskman who wrote that strange head did not whisper to himself, "and it serves the bastards right."

But something else about the head bothered me, and it wasn't just the redundancy of "swelter in heat." I wondered, why "Canucks"? Surely Canadians don't call one another Canucks. Surely it's only British and American veterans who still use that funny old word. (*Soldier and Sailor Words and Phrases,* 1925, a British dictionary, lists "Canuck: A Canadian" just after "Canteen Eggs: A gas attack.")

But why was a Nova Scotian calling central Canadians "Canucks" unless, deep down somewhere, he regarded all Canucks, Canadians, or whatever you called "them" up there, as foreigners? The headline suggested that, in the mind of one bluenose newspaperman at least, the ancient chasm of Confederation was still too wide for bridges. Not only that, "Canucks" was musty, like a hand-cranked gramophone machine, a photograph of George V, or coy references to Dan Cupid on Valentine's Day. Reading that head was like picking up a newspaper in Memphis or Mobile and finding denunciations of "Yankee carpetbaggers."

But perhaps "Canuck" is not so dated as I want it to be. There's a comic book published for nationalists in short pants and it's called *Captain Canuck.* He's a masked muscle man with a maple leaf on his forehead and colourful long johns; and, although I hate to say this, he bears a suspicious resemblance to American comic-book heroes. Maybe his long johns are Stanfields. He doesn't look at all like Johnny Canuck, who wore a boy-scout hat and a vaguely military tunic. Sartorially, Johnny Canuck was a cross between a retired forest ranger and a sloppy Mountie in brown. He was supposed to be to Canada what John Bull was to England and Uncle Sam to the States and indeed, in political cartoons, he stood around chatting with John and Sam for decades. He was a nice chap, a follower rather than a leader. "I like to walk with a man who can set the pace for me," he told Sir Wilfrid Laurier as they strolled through a cartoon in the Toronto *Globe* in 1908. About all Johnny Canuck and Captain Canuck have in common is their surname and the fact they're both a trifle goody-goody. And, oh yes, a country!

5   U.S. presidential politics gave "Canucks" a deplorable shot of importance in 1972. I want the word to disappear in the quicksand of stale slang but now, dammit, it's a footnote to American history. It helped defeat Senator Edmund Muskie of Maine in his effort to win the Democratic nomination for the presidency of the United States. Muskie's enemies published a letter in which he apparently described New Englanders of French-Canadian descent as "Canucks"; and this evidence of his bigotry, which later turned out to have been a forgery by a Republican dirty-trick artist, was a factor in the sudden collapse of his campaign.

6   The baffling thing, for Canadians, was why anyone would mind being called a Canuck. "In spite of the definition given in many dictionaries still," says *A Dictionary of Canadianisms on Historical Principles* (1967), "the term Canuck, as applied by Canadians to themselves, is not at all derogatory, quite the contrary." Canucks think Canucks are good guys. What they don't know is that many Americans use "Canucks" the way bigots use hunky, bohunk, wop, etc. "Polacks and Canucks," the New York *Evening Post* reported in 1907, "have taken the places of most of the old-time American woodsmen in the Adirondacks."

7   The bias is more ancient than that. As far back as 1840, the Boston *Transcript* reported, "The French Canadian — or Conuck, as Her Majesty's provincial subjects of English and American extraction sometimes call him — can never by any means be induced to lay aside the abominable practice [of smoking and chewing in church]." A character in *Field and Forest* allowed in 1870 that, "I hadn't no 'fection for them pesky half-breeds, nor them French Kanucks nuther. They are thick enough all along the [Arkansas] River."

8   In 1899 a book called *Trooper and Redskin* gave a prime example of U.S. snottiness with regard to Canucks: "But for pure and unadulterated brag I will back the lower-class Canuck against the world." When the insults were not direct, they lurked in descriptions. In *Whispering Hills* (1912) there was "weary contempt" on the face of "the swarthy Canuck

guide." In *Second Base Sloan* (1917), "La Croix was a thickset, hook-nosed Canuck" and, as astute readers of popular fiction have always known, people with hooked noses and thicksets are seldom up to any good.

Sometimes the American opinion that Canucks were an inferior breed revealed itself in contempt and defiance. "Thar ain't no Johnny Canuck kin arrest me," said a rider of the plains in *Riders of the Plains* (1910). More often, the attitude was one of condescension. In 1846, for instance, a W.G. Stewart wrote, "The Cannakers, as they were commonly called, set themselves quietly about reviving their fire." Sturdy primitives they were, with bovine patience. In 1855, another outdoors writer said, "Giving our donkey into the keeping of a lively Canuck . . . we commenced the slow ascent [of Mount Holyoke]." And in 1888, in *Century Magazine:* "One was a short, square-built, good-humoured Kanuck . . . who interlarded his conversation with a mixture of French and English profanity." The *Dictionary of American Slang* (1965 reprint) advises, "Since 1855 the reference is often to a strong, rough woodsman or logger." 9

Strong, yes, but also kind of dumb and smelly. Look what progress had done to the proud *voyageur!* Turned him into a Canuck, by gar. The guy left holding the donkey while better men climb mountains. He's handy enough in a canoe, all right, but hardly the sort you'd invite to opening night at the opera. Good man to have around when you want wood hewed or water drawn but he talks funny and he's got spruce needles growing out of his ears. "What's that?" someone asked in *Landlord at Lion's Head* (1908), and the reply came: "It's that Canuck, chopping in Whitwell's clearing." 10

In *Modern Instances* (1882) a character confides to another, "Fridays I make up a sort of chowder for the Kanucks; they're Catholics, you know." (A "sort of chowder"? One imagines the speaker dumping fishgut stew into a huge trough, and letting the Kanucks go at it in the manner to which they were accustomed.) Anyway, this raises the strange matter of Canucks as all Canadians, and Canucks as French Canadians. The origin of the word may have been a corruption of "Connaughts." That's what French Canadians used to call the Irish in Canada. Somehow, it came out sounding like "Canucks" and English-speaking North Americans then nicknamed the French with the French nickname for the Irish. That's the story anyway. 11

The odd thing is, however, that American authorities are virtually unanimous that, as *A Dictionary of American English* (1936) explains the word, it is "In Canada the nickname of French Canadians; in the U.S. a nickname for all Canadians." Moreover, the 1970 reprint of Eric Partridge's *A Dictionary of Slang and Unconventional English* states under "Canuck": "Originally (1855) a Canadian and American term for 12 a French Canadian which, inside Canada, it still means. Etymology obscure."

13   Time has made lies out of these definitions. It is chiefly in the United States, especially in New England, that "Canuck" still means someone of French-Canadian descent; and there, as we've seen, it's often about as friendly a word as "wetback" is in California. Moreover, though English-speaking Canadians have plenty of nasty words for the French, "Canucks" is certainly not one of them. And Johnny Canuck, who began to appear in English-Canadian political cartoons long before 1900, was about as Gallic as Lord Baden-Powell.

14   I am pleased to report that among all the dictionaries I consulted in this matter, so vital to our national identity, the only one that made any contemporary sense was Canadian. It was *A Dictionary of Canadianisms on Historical Principles* (University of Victoria, 1967) and it specifically denied that, in modern Canadian use, "Canuck" had any French- Canadian association. It conceded the term probably *first* designated a French Canadian but only because, in the early nineteenth century, "the term 'Canadian' itself most often referred to a French Canadian." Whatever other Canadians existed in those days, they were so inconspicuous a bunch they didn't deserve even an insulting nickname.

15   Not only did the Americans perpetuate "Canucks" as an insulting label for people of French-Canadian descent, they also went so far as to suggest Canucks were not even human. They were animals. Horses to be exact. From a piece in the *Congressional Globe* of 1867: "They went from St. Louis to Canada to buy the little Canuck ponies at $130 apiece." And C.D. Ferguson, a U.S. adventure novelist, was talking about horses, not some hombres from Québec City, when he declared in 1888 that "No frontier town ever saw a grander sight than those four Canucks."

16   In American slang, Canuck is also a language. The *American Thesaurus of Slang* (1945) lists it right up there with "Blemish: a mixture of Belgian and Flemish . . . Bohunk: the language of any Slavonic race" . . . "Hunky" for Hungarian . . . and "spick, spic, spig, spigoty" for "the language of any foreigner of dark complexion." The thesaurus also lists, as expressions for Canada, Canuckland, Kanuckland, and Jack Canuck's Country. The best that can be said for them is that they're preferable to "Godamland" for England.

17   We are fortunate that, although a U.S. magazine called *Outing* once carried "Snowshoeing in Canuckia" as a heading, "Canuckia" never really caught on. (Possibly because, "Oh Canuckia, We stand on guard for thee" was hard to sing.) In 1888, *Dominion Illustrated* used "Canuckiana" as a heading and, though I can't swear there isn't a "Canuckiana" sign in at least one of the bookstores that stretch *a mari usque ad mare,* our escape from an epidemic of that word strikes me as both miraculous and kind.

Canuck has popped up as Canack, Canuk, Conuck, Kanuk, K'Nuck, and Cannaker. In *Leaves of Grass,* Walt Whitman preferred Kanuck. I prefer none of them. They're all repulsive. As French Canadians, "Canucks" were backwoods slobs. As an English Canadian, Johnny Canuck had less character than Mr. Clean without the muscles. Worst of all, "Canuck" is an essentially silly word. 18

Say it slowly. Listen to it. Can-uck. It has not one but two K sounds, and K sounds have a mysterious quality of the ludicrous. That's why people get it right in the kisser and fall right on their keisters. That's why it is that, when supposedly hilarious violence occurs in comic books, people and animals and things all go kerbam, kerchunk, kerflooey, kerflop, kerflunk, kerslosh, kersmack, and kerspang. The huge metal spring that shoots a comic-book baddie headfirst into a brick wall (kersplat!) should not merely go boi-i-i-i-n-g-g; it must go *ker*boi-i-i-i-n-g-g. 19

Stand-up comedians have always known the secret of the K. Desperate for a laugh, a cheer, any sign of life from groggy, hostile audiences, they'd mention Saskatoon, Kalamazoo, Hoboken, Albuquerque, Brooklyn. The result? Instant guffaws, titters, whistles. Har, har. Hoo, boy, they're warming up now. Time to hit them with something about Kokomo, the Kootenays, Kirkland Lake, Kelowna: 20

"Hey, listen folks, the other night I met this meathead, said he was from Kamsack, Saskatchewan, Canader. Or maybe it was Kenogami, Kweebec, Canader. Nope, now I remember, it was Keewatin. Key *what* in? Look fella', you think maybe I should know about the sex life of the Keewatians? You think maybe I'm the Margaret Mead of the aurora borealis or something? Anyway, this fruitcake, he was from Lake Couchiching actually, he sez his name's Canuck. That's right, Johnny Canuck. Johnny, as in the little boys' room; and Canuck, as in shmuck, shnook, and jerk. Anyway, so this Canucklehead from Kitchener, he sez to me. . ." 21

Johnny Canuck is a yuk. That's why I wish Canadians would just leave him where he lay: back there in the time before inflatable tires. He's one symbol of our past we can afford to let stay there. Who wants a dink like that as the personification of nationhood? 22

STRUCTURE:

1. This extended definition has a purpose in addition to informing or entertaining the reader. What is that other purpose and where is it most clearly stated?

2. In what ways do the first three paragraphs provide a background for this essay?

3. This investigation into the word "Canuck" appears in sections. How is the word explained in paragraph 4? In paragraph 5? In paragraphs 6-10? In paragraphs 11-14? In paragraphs 15-17? And in paragraphs 18-21?

STYLE:

1. Can an essay with a light TONE have a serious purpose? Is the purpose of this essay serious?
2. In paragraph 4, what is the effect of the phrase "colourful long johns" and the statement "Maybe his long johns are Stanfields"?
3. In paragraph 9, where and how is repetition used deliberately as a device of humour?
4. Point out all the sources of humour in paragraph 10.
5. Contrast the style of paragraph 21 to that of the rest of the essay. Why is it different?

IDEAS:

1. What does the word "Canuck" mean to you? Where in the essay does Harry Bruce come closest to defining the word as you know it?
2. If the "k" sounds funny, as Bruce says, do other sounds also have particular effects? As an example, look at all the words in your dictionary that begin with "sl" (as in "slippery"). Do a large number of these words create the same feeling? Give examples.
3. In paragraph 18, Bruce sums up the STEREOTYPES he has exposed: "As French Canadians, 'Canucks' were backwoods slobs. As an English Canadian, Johnny Canuck had less character than Mr. Clean without the muscles." How often do we think in stereotypes? Do you and the other class members agree on a common stereotype of the French Canadians? The English Canadians? The Germans? The Russians? The Americans? The Chinese? The Italians? Males? Females? Artists? Hockey players? Bankers? Teachers? Do you know of individuals in these groups who do not conform to the common stereotype? If so, give examples.
4. Discuss the dangers of stereotyping.
5. In an essay, develop an extended definition of the word "Yankee" and show the similarities, if any, between this word and "Canuck."

(Note: See also the Topics for Writing at the end of this chapter.)

Myrna Kostash

Profile of the Rapist as an Ordinary Man

Myrna Kostash is a freelance writer whose subjects range from feminism to ethnicity, regionalism, radical politics and Canadian literature. Born in Edmonton in 1944 to a family of Ukrainian background, she has lived in Europe, Toronto, Montreal and now Edmonton again. In 1968 Kostash earned an M.A. in Russian literature at the University of Toronto, and in 1970 published her first magazine article. Since then she has written a great many articles for Saturday Night, Maclean's, Chatelaine, The Canadian Forum *and other magazines, has published short stories, and has written scripts for film and television. Her book about Ukrainians in Canada,* All of Baba's Children, *appeared in 1977, and* Long Way from Home: The Story of the Sixties Generation in Canada *in 1980. Our selection, "Profile of the Rapist as an Ordinary Man," illustrates her feminism. It appeared in 1975 in* Maclean's.

I was hitchhiking from my parents' place to the city and got 1 a ride with a man. When I first got into his car, he looked like a nice, gentle, innocuous guy who wouldn't bother me. He said he was 25 years old and had been out of school for a couple of years. We got to talking and he seemed okay but after about an hour he said he wanted to pull over to the side of the road and rest. I told him I was kind of in a hurry to get home. I had begun to get strange vibes from him — everything we talked about ended up in a discussion about sex. He told me all about his sexual experiences and wanted me to talk about mine. I was wearing jeans and an old top; when I hitchhike I dress as asexually as possible. So there was no way I was indicating my availability by the way I was dressed. Then he said we were going to stop whether I liked it or not and he was going to "make love" to me. I said, "I don't particularly want to make love to you." He pulled over to the side of the road and reached over me and put his elbow on the lock of the door and wouldn't let me out. He jumped on me. He ripped my clothes.

And then he raped her. Forced her into this act he called "making 2 love," and made believe that what he was recreating in the cramped space of the car's front seat was a lover's pleasure. She went to the police but never pressed charges. Instead she has spent the last year wrestling with her fears and her anger. She finally talked it all out into a tape recorder, partly as therapy and partly so that others would know and understand just what the experience of being raped is like.

3   He was no weirdo. He didn't prowl around neighborhoods and drool at passing women from behind bushes. He didn't have the kind of grizzled face and unfocused gaze of the dirty old men you see in subway cars and buses staring at women's thighs.

4   If you asked him about himself he would tell you he was just an ordinary guy. He had a good job, loved his mum, took girls to the movies and to bars, slept with the ones who let him. Hell, he'd say, most girls are *easy* these days. They all pretend at first that they are virgins or something and waiting for Mr. Right but, in the end, if you put a little pressure on them, and maybe get a little threatening, they almost always give in. Women want to be *persuaded,* roughed up a bit. You certainly don't have to take "no" as their final answer.

5   And if you asked him for his version of what went on in his car that night, this is what he might say: what do you expect a guy to think when he sees a chick all alone on the highway, hitchhiking? And when she turns out to be real friendly and dressed up like a hippie? I mean, come *on,* you'd have to be pretty dense not to figure out that she's on the make. So you can imagine how I felt when she suddenly got on her high horse and said, no, no!

6   No one, neither psychologists nor the police, rape counselors nor judges, seems to know just what pushes an "ordinary guy" over the line between courtship and rape. There is research available and theories have been formulated which attempt a description of *who* the rapist is, what his personal history is likely to be, what might go on in his mind during the attack and how he justifies himself. But precisely what it is that distinguishes a rapist from the rest of men who don't, in spite of frustration, humiliation, guilt or outrage, force sexual intercourse on a woman without her freely given consent, is a mystery. The rapist doesn't understand himself any better than we do. In fact, a rapist may not even be conscious he's done anything wrong. According to a recent study in Denver, Colorado, "most rapists can neither admit nor express the fact that they are a menace to society."

7   *I couldn't believe it was happening and that I could be so completely trapped. He was so much stronger than I was. When he was finished, I threw up and he got mad at me for messing up the interior of his car. I begged him to let me go. He said he couldn't because I would have to hitchhike home and suppose somebody picked me up and raped me! I thought, oh my God, he's insane.*

8   But, in all probability, he is *not* clinically insane. According to the Philadelphia criminologist, Menachim Amir, "studies indicate that sex offenders do not constitute a unique or psychopathological type; nor are they as a group invariably more disturbed than the control groups to

which they are compared." Most of us share the popular misconception that all rapists are "sexual psychopaths." And the average rapist shares this misconception with us. Since he knows he isn't a Jack the Ripper lurking in dark corners ready to pounce on an unsuspecting female and drag her away, he doesn't think of *himself* as a rapist. He sees rapes committed by others in the same way we do, as the behavior of perverted, *sick* individuals and not something that he, a normal, virile and assertive male does when he "makes love" to the protesting and revolted body of his victim.

He wouldn't, then, recognize himself in most of the psychological accounts of a rapist's motivations: "incestuous desires," "symbolic matricide," "latent homosexuality," "castration anxieties," etc. Even if he did, the information would not be very useful to him or to us: rape is an *act*, not a state of mind. The rapist has imposed his sexuality and his fantasies on someone who doesn't want to participate; he has violated another human being's right to self-determination and he has terrorized her through a show of power. For him to see this as lovemaking is the real sickness. And yet the rapist does operate within the spectrum of normal masculinity and male sexuality. Within that spectrum he is the extremist. 9

Amir's study (the only comprehensive one to date in North America) showed that the majority of rapists are between 15 to 24 years of age — the period of a man's life when he is most anxiously flexing his muscles in the new role of adult masculinity. Since the social messages he receives about manhood celebrate the mystique of aggressiveness and toughness, a young man who rapes may be covering up for his feelings of weakness, sexual inadequacy and dependence — feelings which he, as a man, is not supposed to have — and taking them out on a handy victim. Almost half of the rapists Amir studied had a previous criminal record and more than half were either unskilled labourers or unemployed. Debra Lewis, University of Toronto criminology student, points out that if you are angry, frustrated, humiliated and a man, you can often deflect your misery safely onto a woman. She's less likely to fight back than a man. 10

Other rapists Amir studied were employed or middle-class. The only theory that seems to explain their behavior is the psychological one — "shaky defenses." As one psychologist put it, "rapists show strong elements of misogyny and distrust toward the women they place in the position of sexual objects." 11

In 82% of the rapes studied, the victim and the rapist came from the same neighborhood and half the rapes originated in a meeting at the victim's or the rapist's house or at a party or a bar. Chances are the rapist knows his victim and moves in the same social circles. Chances are the rape will take place at the end of a social encounter. This makes it easier for him to see his behavior as "seduction" or "making love." That 71% 12 of the rapes were planned demolishes the myth that rape is the impulsive act of a loony who can't help himself. Eighty-five percent involved the use of force and the most excessive degrees of violence occurred in group rapes, suggesting that group rapists perform for each other to prove how "manly" they really are. It seems that the overpowering and humiliation of another person is as important as having sexual intercourse with her; that the event promises more than physical gratification for the rapist. Debra Lewis sees it in power terms. "If you're a person who doesn't feel very powerful or important, you're going to have the same attitude toward your body. The more degraded you can make your victim feel, the more you feed your own need. There is a large frequency of the rapist demanding the woman tell him she likes it, that she loves him, that she will go out with him after. It's a situation in which he has perfect control at last."

13   So, when a man rapes a woman, a lot more is going on than just non-consensual intercourse, more even than a "sexual power struggle," although that is certainly at the heart of it, as far as the victim is concerned. In the course of my research, it was pointed out time and again that rape is about *violence* and *power*. It is a measure of our social malaise that we group these things with sex.

14   *He said, "Give me one good reason why you should live because I want to kill you." I was terrified. I didn't want to die. I gave him what I considered to be a pretty good reason, that I was a human being and had as much right to live as anybody else. He said that wasn't good enough. He put his hands around my neck and told me to come up with something else. He told me I had no right to be alive.*

15   On the one hand, men are taught that women, being supposedly the softer and weaker sex, are in need of their gentlemanly protection; on the other hand, there are pervasive social messages in films, literature, music, television, that women are, in fact, venal, lascivious and masochistic. The rapist, as a product of this *generalized* hostility toward femaleness *and* the sentimentality around femininity, often makes what can be called the compromise of singling out certain *kinds* of women as rape victims. His mother and sister he'd defend to the death but that broad down the street in the tight sweater who went to bed with his buddy is fair game. Better still if she's non-white, unmarried, living on her own and working class. Amir writes that rapists are "more apt to view certain females as appropriate victims and certain situations as suggestive of, even opportune for, rape." This is not only because these women have low social status and therefore aren't considered "worth" so much, but also because forcible intercourse with them isn't even *perceived* as rape.

I thought about my parents and what a drag it was going to be for 16
them when my body was found. I got really angry about hurting them. I
said, "Look, if you don't get off me, I'm going to kill you." He looked
at me and said, "You're crazy, aren't you?" I was playing his game, and
it worked. He drove me back to the city. As we were driving, he said he
thought we could become good friends and he told me his address three
or four times. I think he was probably as scared as I was.

Although the police advise women *not* to resist an attack for fear of 17
provoking even more violence, the Denver study shows that a woman can
stop a rape (at the hands of a stranger) at stage one by refusing to be in-
timidated. "Above all, the rapist needs ordered and controlled behavior
from his victim." As women become more self-confident and aware of
their own strength, the incidence of rape may begin to decrease: the
Denver study pointed out that "resisters [of rape attempts] scored higher
on measures of dominance and sociability . . . were more self-accepting
and had a greater sense of well-being [than those who did not resist]."

And maybe fighting back is the only real deterrent there is. It is pretty 18
obvious to everyone that our legal system is no deterrent at all. It's
estimated that only one-third to one-tenth of all rapes committed are
reported to the police. Many women who do report attacks never even
get into a courtroom. They find the interrogation by the police to be such
a brutal process that they don't press charges.

The first thing the police detective said to me was, "What's the matter, 19
didn't he pay you enough money?" I couldn't believe it. He asked me if I
had enjoyed it, he said I must have enjoyed it, look at the way I dress, I
must be promiscuous. Then he told me that if I couldn't take this kind of
questioning now, I wouldn't be able to take it later in court. Did I really
want to press charges?

So the percentage of cases actually brought to court is small and only a 20
few of them actually result in conviction. In many cases, the conviction
that is finally obtained may not be for rape, but for a reduced charge of
indecent assault. It is important to note that the charge of rape (which
can be punished by a life sentence) applies only to forcible penetration of
the vagina (less than 50% of the cases examined in the Denver study involved vaginal rape).

For the victim, any kind of assault and sexual humiliation is horrible 21
and destructive. But it seems that to jurists and legislators, to police and
to the community at large, it is an attack on the vagina, the sacred highroad of marriage and maternity, that is the profoundest affront. Ontario
Crown Attorney John Kerr says he has been involved in cases "in which
the girl had been assaulted in a horrible manner but because no actual

vaginal intercourse took place the accused was liable only to a charge of indecent assault.'' Even though vaginal rape is obviously considered, in the eyes of the law, to be a most serious crime, Sergeant Robert Lynn of the Toronto police says he hasn't heard of a rapist in the last two years who's been sentenced even to 10 years. ''The average is four to five. If he had never been in trouble before, and if he's going to be getting psychiatric help, sometimes he'll only get two to three. Sometimes it makes you wonder.''

22   Kerr isn't encouraged by this trend to leniency among judges and juries. While no one is suggesting that we should go back to the old days and in a fury of vengeance castrate a rapist, or even whip him, Kerr worries that ''with our changing standards of morality, maybe juries aren't treating rape so seriously anymore.''

23   We know that rape statistics are rising drastically throughout North America. In part, this is because greater numbers of women are actually willing to press charges. But there are more pervasive reasons. The so-called Sexual Revolution of the Sixties ''liberated'' both men and women from the inhibiting restraints of a more puritanical sexual ethic. Then, with the women's movement of the Seventies, with the publicized strug-gle of women for independent status, many of the protective, Victorian devices surrounding women were withdrawn. A woman who insists on taking care of herself can no longer be an object of male solicitude. It was only when a woman was seen as fluffy, delicate and helpless that male protective ''instincts'' toward her seemed sensible. A woman on her own is fair game.

24   What, then, is to be done? How do we make our legal system a real deterrent to rapists? How do we make it capable of protecting the civil rights of women without resorting to extreme ''law and order'' measures? The prosecution of rape charges might be made easier by legislating different degrees of rape carrying different maximum sentences. Police departments should establish units such as New York's Sex Crimes Analysis Unit which is run by female detectives. The New York Unit, besides receiving and processing all cases of rape and at-tempted rape, also tries to reeducate male officers in their attitudes to sex crimes. As of this writing, no police department in Canada has tried to set up anything like it.

25   The legal profession has to realize that whatever the psycho-sexual transactions between a man and a woman during a rape, the physical in-timidation involved in the crime is a serious matter. Barbara Betcherman of Toronto's Rape Crisis Centre thinks that the way rape cases are handled now, particularly because of Section 142 of the Criminal Code (which requires a judge to instruct a jury that it is not safe to believe a woman on her word alone), they are *ipso facto* prejudicial.

Obviously, there is no single remedy that is going to eradicate sexual 26
assaults on women. Legislative changes are required; so are "rape
squads" in police departments. So are rape crisis centres and rap groups
and pamphlets. But these kinds of changes only deal with the aftermath
of a rape. If we want to *stop* rape, we have to figure out how to grow up
as human beings.

STRUCTURE:
1. Why does Myrna Kostash split the rape victim's tape-recorded story
   into five parts instead of presenting it all at once?
2. Point out at least five facts or opinions given by Kostash that develop
   her extended definition of what a rapist is or is not.
3. Kostash admits that in one important sense we are still unable to
   define a rapist. Describe the problem and point out where it appears in
   the essay.
4. Although this essay is an extended definition of a rapist, it also defines
   something else. What does the second definition explain and where
   does it occur?
5. Upon what form of argument is paragraph 23 based?
6. Upon what form of argument is the closing of this essay, paragraphs
   24-26, based? Why is this topic saved for last?

STYLE:
1. Why are paragraphs 3 to 5 so INFORMAL and even slangy, while most
   of the essay is more FORMAL in tone?
2. Discuss the IRONY of the rapist's warning to his victim: if he let her out
   of the car to hitchhike home, someone might pick her up and rape her
   (par. 7).

IDEAS:
1. Paragraphs 18 and 19 illustrate the blame that society tends to put on
   the *victim* of a rape. What are the motivations behind this blame?
2. If you have read "The 51-Per-Cent Minority," compare Doris
   Anderson's description of economic injustices against women with
   Kostash's description of sexual injustices against women. Do you
   think these problems are unrelated or do they stem from common
   causes?
3. Some anti-abortion groups want abortion to be illegal even after a
   rape. Do you agree or disagree with this point of view? Why?
4. Paragraph 18 describes how few rapes are reported and brought to
   court, and paragraph 21 describes the light sentences usually given for

this crime that, by law, can bring life imprisonment. How great a punishment do *you* think rapists deserve, and why? Might some rapes be worse than others and thus be cause for harsher punishment? Give reasons to support your answers.

5. Paragraph 17 states that it is self-confident women who are best at resisting rape. Has our society failed to encourage that confidence? If so, in what ways? As women gain power in society, will rape diminish?

6. Write a process analysis of what a woman can do to stop an attempted rape.

7. In essay form, write a profile of one of the following, giving enough examples and details to form an *extended definition:*

a vandal	a thief
a burglar	a prostitute
a bully	an arsonist
an embezzler	a pusher
a child molester	a tax evader
a terrorist	an extortionist

(Note: See also the Topics for Writing at the end of this chapter.)

Janice McEwen and the *Harrowsmith* staff

Thunderstrokes and Firebolts

Janice Burchell McEwen was born in Perth, Ontario. She holds a Journalism Newswriting Diploma from Algonquin College in Ottawa, and has worked as a freelance feature writer for Ottawa Valley newspapers. She is also a riding instructor and a professional rider of show quarter horses. "Thunderstrokes and Firebolts" appeared in Harrowsmith, *Canada's national magazine for gardeners, homesteaders and farmers, and in 1978 was anthologized in* The Harrowsmith Reader. *McEwen's interest in her subject is a family matter: her father is a lightning protection contractor.*

Imagine the chagrin of a Renfrew, Ontario farmer who pulled on the handle of a recently repaired barn door one morning following a thunderstorm only to have the door crumble into a heap of individual boards at his feet. 1

The man was left sheepishly wondering about his carpentry skills until a local lightning protection contractor examined the door and explained that, unknown to the farmer, a bolt of lightning had hit the barn during the storm. Leapfrogging from nail-to-nail along the Z-shaped bracing boards that supported the door, the lightning made its way to the ground. In the process the heat produced by the bolt reduced the nails to dust. 2

For the 118 passengers aboard an Air Canada DC-8 jetliner, lightning had much more serious consequences: the ill-fated plane crashed in a swampy field shortly after take-off from Montreal in November, 1963. When investigators finished sifting through the rubble of what is still Canada's worst airplane disaster, lightning was high on the list of probable causes. 3

Lightning is the most awesome of nature's weather phenomena — a single stroke of lightning produces more electricity than the combined output of all electrical power plants in the United States. The average cloud-to-ground lightning bolt averages only six inches in diameter, but attains a core temperature of about 50,000 degrees Fahrenheit — five times the temperature at the surface of the sun. 4

Each day some 44,000 thunderstorms break out around the globe, the greatest concentration of them within the belt extending 30 degrees north and south of the equator. As you read this there are 1,800 electrical storms raging throughout the world, and by the time you finish this sentence, lightning will have struck earth 100 times. 5

Too frequently, lightning strikes spell disaster. Each year several hundred North Americans are killed by lightning, and others die in the fires 6 that follow in the wake of electrical storms. Ten thousand forest fires and more than 30,000 building blazes are caused by lightning. Damages to property and loss of timber are estimated at more than 50 million dollars annually.

7   Yet the scientific study of lightning is still in pioneering stages, leaving unexplained many aspects of the complicated series of events that take place in the five thousandths of a second required for the average lightning bolt to strike.

8   Scientists are, for example, at a loss to explain "ball" lightning, a rare occurrence in which an orb about 20 centimetres in diameter forms at the lightning impact point. This blinding ball of energy is able to move around at a speed of several metres per second and is said to be accompanied by a hissing sound. Ball lightning is able to pass through closed windowpanes and often disappears with an explosion.

9   Little wonder that this astounding natural force has always aroused man's curiosity and fear.

10   For our ancient forefathers, there was no doubt about what caused lightning: various gods were flamboyantly expressing their disapproval of somebody's actions.

11   Zeus, as legend would have it, was particularly keen to use a handy supply of lightning bolts to express his frequent outbursts of rage. Unfortunate were the troops that attacked friends of this surly deity — Zeus would often step in when his side was losing and tip the tides of battle with a few well-placed bolts among the enemy ranks.

12   But recent findings by Nobel Prize winner Dr. Harold Urey suggest that the ancients may not have underestimated the nearly divine role lightning plays in terrestrial life.

13   Through laboratory reconstruction of the atmosphere of the young, lifeless earth — an atmosphere composed of ammonia, methane, hydrogen and water — students of Urey found that when electrical sparks, much like lightning, were passed through this medium, amino acids were created — the first building blocks in the evolution of life.

14   Recent findings also suggest that we can thank lightning (at least partially) for giving the world plants. Although nitrogen makes up 80 per cent of the earth's atmosphere, in its pure state it is useless to plants.

15   It has been found that lightning causes atmospheric nitrogen to combine with oxygen, forming nitric-oxide gas. This gas dissolves in rain and falls to the earth as usable nitrates. Some scientists estimate that hundreds of millions of tons of these nitrates are produced by lightning each year. It's enough to make a purveyor of bagged 20-20-20 weep.

16   Benjamin Franklin, that portly Renaissance man of the eighteenth century, made the first real breakthrough in man's understanding of lightning by determining that it was, indeed, a huge electrical spark. But it is ironic (in light of his factual discoveries) that one of the most prevalent

schoolboy myths still surrounding lightning features Mr. Franklin as its main character.

Everyone has heard about Franklin's kite flying antics. What few people realize is that his kite was never struck by lightning. Had it been, either the string would have burned and Mr. Franklin would have lost his kite, or the experimenter himself would have been struck, and the world would have lost an able scholar and statesman. 17

What happened during this famous flight was that there was enough difference in the electrical charge between the earth and the air at the level of the kite to create a small finger-tingling flow of electrical current through Mr. Franklin's string. 18

Today we know that conditions leading to electrical storms begin when a strong negative charge builds in rain (cumulo-nimbus) clouds. How this charge develops is still a matter of scientific debate, but an accepted theory is that air turbulence in the clouds creates a build-up of negatively-charged electrons. 19

Free electrons on the earth directly below the cloud are repelled by the huge numbers of electrons above, and therefore the charge of the earth becomes more positive. 20

Because opposing charges are attracted to each other, the electrons in the cloud yearn to get to the positive earth. 21

Air, however, is a poor conductor of electricity. As the cloud matures, the charge continues to build until pressure becomes great enough to permit the electrons to leap through the insulative layer of air. 22

The first tentative electrons probe toward the earth in a series of steps that gives a lightning bolt its irregular shape. These first electrons clear a path for those in the cloud, and as soon as the first electrons connect with the ground, an avalanche of electricity surges from the sky. 23

Lightning has struck. 24

Lightning bolts range from 1,000 to 9,000 feet long, and can attain speeds over 60,000 miles per second. 25

A lightning bolt seeks the route offering the least electrical resistance in its journey from cloud to ground. Almost any solid object offers an easier path for electricity than air: it could be a tree, a utility pole, a high patch of ground; it could also be your barn, one of your outbuildings — or your house. 26

Lightning is a hazard deserving special attention from rural dwellers. Grim statistics show that nine out of ten lightning-caused deaths occur outside city limits. Fire authorities estimate that lightning causes up to 37 per cent of all rural building fires. 27

G.A. Pelletier, chief of technical services in the Ontario Fire Marshall's Office and one of Canada's foremost authorities on lightning, attributes part of this phenomenal loss of life and property in rural areas to people being misinformed about this frightening natural force. 28

29   "Most people are totally unaware of what lightning is, how it behaves and what it can do," he said. "Take the old wives' tale about lightning never hitting the same place twice — a common enough belief. It's totally false. As a matter of fact, if a place has been hit once, it shows that it is a prime site for future strikes."

30   Pelletier also says that many people believe their homes to be safe from lightning because of the proximity of tall trees or a high television aerial. Neither is necessarily true.

31   We can thank Ben Franklin's inquisitive (and financially long-sighted) mind for the protection we now have against destruction of property caused by lightning.

32   "It has pleased God in His goodness to mankind, at length to discover to them the means of securing their habitations and other buildings from mischief by thunder and lightning," wrote Franklin in the 1753 edition of *Poor Richard's Almanack*. He went on to outline a system that not only worked, but which remains, almost unchanged, as the most efficient form of lightning protection.

33   The heart of a lightning protection system is a series of rods extending at least 12 inches above a structure at lightning vulnerable places: peaks, gable ends, chimneys, etc.

34   These lightning rods (or "air terminals" in the jargon of lightning experts) are connected to each other by a woven copper cable roughly one-half inch thick. The cable, in turn, is grounded on at least two sides of the building to rods driven 10 feet into the earth, although the depth will vary somewhat in accordance with soil conditions. It is often said that a lightning rod gives protection within a circle whose radius is the height of the tip of the rod from the ground. Unfortunately, lightning does not always adhere to this rule, but the Canadian Standards Association says that "a properly installed lightning rod system, if not 100 per cent effective, will ensure that in nearly all cases of lightning strikes to buildings, little or no damage will result."

35   Fire statistics support these claims: in 1975, the most recent year for which figures are available, only 91 of the 2,559 structural fires started by lightning in Ontario occurred in buildings protected by lightning rod systems.

36   Pelletier explains that a properly working lightning rod system creates an easy route for the electrical charges to follow, diverting them away from the building and allowing them to dissipate harmlessly in the ground.

37   This, of course, is preferable to the unprotected alternative — where the bolt strikes the roof of the building and passes through the structure itself, leaping through walls, appliances, plumbing fixtures, radiators (and in some cases human beings) en route to the earth. . . .

Your chances of being killed by lightning this summer are roughly one 38
in a million — certainly no reason to cancel plans for boating, picnics
and hiking during the warm season, but reason enough to implement
precautions.

An electrical storm that swept the New York City area took a typical 39
toll of human victims. A golfer whose foursome had sought refuge from
the rain beneath a tree (a common mistake that accounts for one-third of
thunderstorm fatalities) died when lightning slammed into the tree. His
companions were unharmed. The storm's next victim was a fisherman
holding a metal casting rod. Lightning leapt from the rod to his jacket
zipper. His single companion was injured but recovered. The final victim, a young man, died while standing near a beachhouse.

All of these deaths could have been prevented had the victims followed 40
commonsense safety measures.

A car is perhaps the safest place to be during an electrical storm. There 41
have been few, if any, substantiated cases of lightning striking an automobile, but laboratory experiments show that the charge would pass
harmlessly over the metal shell of the car and then leap from the under-
carriage to the pavement.

Second only to a car (and virtually 100 per cent safe) is a dry building 42
protected by lightning rods. When the first signs of thunder make
themselves manifest, the sensible thing to do is go straight to the shelter
of a protected building. Two-thirds of lightning-caused deaths occur outdoors.

When you are caught by a storm in an open area, do not, under any 43
circumstances, take shelter under an isolated tree. If you cannot reach a
protected building, seek a low-lying area of open land.

Trees are favourite targets for lightning, and electrical charges that 44
surge from the base of a struck tree can kill for a considerable distance.
In one instance, a single bolt of lightning struck a tree in a Utah pasture
and killed 500 sheep. There are recorded cases of cattle being killed while
standing 100 yards from a struck tree.

Few people are killed by direct lightning strikes. If someone were 45
directly hit, he would be severely burned. In most cases, the lightning victim is not burned but dies because currents cast off from a nearby lightning strike pass through his body, stopping his breathing and heartbeat.

Lightning frequently strikes water and electrical charges travel freely 46
through this medium. Boats are high on the list of undesirable places to
be when there is an approaching electrical storm. If you are in a boat, get
to shore immediately and move some distance inland; shoreline trees are
prime candidates for lightning strikes.

Swimmers, too, are in danger of being injured or killed by electrical 47
charges that surge through water as a result of lightning.

48   If you find yourself in a protected house at the outbreak of a thunderstorm, take heart; you are safe.

49   Still, it is wise to stay away from sinks and bathtubs — your plumbing system is connected to a metal vent pipe protruding through the roof and is a potential lightning target.

50   Avoid touching refrigerators, stoves and other large metal objects. Do not use telephones or other electrical appliances, and stay away from stovepipes, chimneys and fireplaces. Windows and doors should be closed.

51   If your home or one of your outbuildings is struck by lightning, an immediate check-over is due to insure that no hidden fires have started. (Old-timers often referred to hot and cold lightning — the former causing fires and the latter merely hitting with one explosive bolt.) When lightning fells a human, it is often possible to revive him with prolonged artificial respiration. Many victims have recovered fully, while others were left with sight or hearing impairments.

52   But even when nestled in the security of a snug, lightning-protected house, there are still some people who find themselves quivering under the bed with the dog at the faintest rumble of thunder. This unfortunate segment of the population might consider moving to the Arctic or Antarctic — areas which see only one thunderstorm per decade.

53   If relocation does not fit your plans, we can only offer the slim comfort of words spoken by one lightning protection expert: "If you heard the thunder, the lightning did not strike you. If you saw the lightning, it missed you; and if it did strike you, you would not have known it."

STRUCTURE:
1. Is "Thunderstrokes and Firebolts" a good title? Why or why not?
2. What technique does Janice McEwen use, in paragraphs 1-3, to introduce her topic?
3. What is McEwen's THESIS STATEMENT?
4. Which paragraphs are based mainly on statistics? What is the effect of all the statistics?
5. With its extensive use of examples, statistics and quotations, "Thunderstrokes and Firebolts" obviously took some research to write. Would you call this a research essay? Why or why not?
6. What form of development underlies paragraphs 19-24?
7. What forms of development underly paragraphs 40-53?

STYLE:

1. How ABSTRACT or CONCRETE is the style of this selection?
2. In paragraph 5, McEwen writes, ''As you read this there are 1,800 electrical storms raging throughout the world, and by the time you finish this sentence, lightning will have struck earth 100 times.'' Analyze all the ways in which this passage creates interest in its subject.
3. Why is paragraph 24 so short?
4. How does repetition contribute to the effect of the final paragraph?

IDEAS:

1. McEwen states in paragraph 4 that ''Lightning is the most awesome of nature's weather phenomena . . . .'' Do you agree? Have you ever experienced another that is more ''awesome''?
2. In paragraph 51, McEwen refers to ''old-timers'' who spoke of ''hot and cold lightning . . . .'' Do the oldest people you know talk more about the weather than do the rest of us? Are we less concerned with weather than people used to be? If so, what might be the reasons?
3. In the past, most people were able to predict the weather by noting the shape of cloud formations, the colour of sunset or sunrise, and the direction of the wind. Describe any of these signs that you can read.
4. In either written or spoken form, describe the most violent thunderstorm you have ever seen.
5. Write an extended definition of one of these:
   A tornado
   A hurricane
   A blizzard
   Hail
   A rainbow
   The northern lights

(Note: See also the Topics for Writing at the end of this chapter.)

Topics for Writing
Chapter 9: Extended Definition

(Note also the topics for writing that appear after each selection in this chapter.)

Write an extended definition of one of these:

1. Extrasensory perception
2. Burn-out
3. Anorexia nervosa
4. A good citizen
5. An education
6. Feminism
7. Determinism
8. Death
9. Continentalism
10. Communism
11. Patriotism
12. A Canadian
13. Good taste in clothes
14. Cybernetics
15. Gravity
16. Electricity
17. A great book
18. A good (or bad) marriage
19. Recreation
20. Good sportsmanship
21. Planned obsolescence
22. Organic gardening
23. "Appropriate technology"
24. Conservation
25. Infinity

GLOSSARY

ABSTRACT Theoretical, relying more on generalities than on specific facts. Abstract writing tends to lack interest and force because it is difficult to understand and difficult to apply. *See also* the opposite of abstract, CONCRETE.

ALLUSION An indirect reference to a passage in literature or scripture, to an event, a person, or anything else with which the reader is thought to be familiar. An allusion is a device of compression in language, for in a few words it summons up the meaning of the thing to which it refers, and applies that meaning to the subject at hand. Critics of big government, for example, will often allude to Big Brother, the personification of governmental tyranny in George Orwell's novel *1984.*

ANECDOTE A short account of an interesting and amusing incident. An anecdote can be a joke or a true story about others or oneself, and is often used as an example to introduce an essay, close an essay or illustrate points within an essay.

CLICHÉ A worn-out expression that takes the place of original thought: "to make a long story short," "sadder but wiser," "bite the bullet," "hustle and bustle," "by hook or by crook," "as different as night and day" and "hit the nail on the head." Most clichés were once effective, but like last year's fad in clothing or music, have lost their appeal and may even annoy.

CLIMAX In an essay, the point at which the argument reaches its culmination, its point of greatest intensity or importance. The closing of an essay tends to be most effective if it is a climax; if it is not, it may give the impression of trailing feebly off into nothingness.

COLLOQUIAL Speech-like. Colloquial expressions like "cop," "guy," "kid," "nitty gritty" and "okay" are often used in conversation but are best avoided in essays, especially FORMAL essays. Although they are lively, colloquialisms are often inexact: "guy," for example, can refer to a person or a rope, and "kid" can refer to a child or a goat. *See also* SLANG.

CONCISENESS The art of conveying the most meaning in the fewest words. A concise essay does not explain its topic less fully than a wordy one; it just uses words more efficiently. Concise writers get straight to the point and stay on topic. They are well enough organized to avoid repeating themselves. They give CONCRETE examples rather than pages of ABSTRACT argument. They use a short word unless a long one is more exact. And most concise writers, to achieve these goals, revise extensively.

CONCRETE   Factual and specific, relying more on particular examples than on abstract theory. Concrete language makes writing more forceful, interesting and convincing by recreating vividly for the reader what the writer has experienced or thought. SENSE IMAGES, ANECDOTES, FIGURES OF SPEECH and CONCISENESS all play a part in concrete language, and are generally lacking in its opposite, ABSTRACT language.

DIALOGUE   The quoted conversation of two or more people. Normally a new paragraph begins with each change of speaker, to avoid confusion as to who says what. A certain amount of dialogue can lend colour to an essay, but heavy use of it is normally reserved for fiction and drama.

ECONOMY   *See* CONCISENESS.

EPIGRAM   A short, clever and often wise saying. The best-known epigrams are proverbs, such as "What can't be cured must be endured" and "To know all is to forgive all."

ESSAY   Derived from the French term *essai,* meaning a "try" or "attempt," the word "essay" refers to a short composition in which a point is made usually through analysis and example. While most essays are alike in being limited to one topic, they may vary widely in other ways. The *formal essay,* for example, is objective and stylistically dignified, while the *familiar essay* is subjective, anecdotal and colloquial.

EUPHEMISM   A polite expression that softens or even conceals the truth: "pass away" for "die," "senior citizens" for "old people," "low-income neighbourhood" for "slum," "gosh darn" for "God damn," "perspire" for "sweat," "eliminate" for "kill," and "de-hire" or "select out" for "fire." Euphemisms are becoming more and more common in uses ranging from personal kindness to advertising to political repression.

FICTION   Imaginative literature written in PROSE. Consisting mainly of novels and short stories, fiction uses invented characters and plots to create a dramatic story; most essays, by contrast, rely on literal fact and analysis to create an argument. There is of course an area of overlap: some fiction is very factual and some essays are very imaginative.

FIGURES OF SPEECH   Descriptive and often poetic devices in which meaning is concentrated and heightened, usually through comparisons.
A. SIMILE: A figure of speech in which one thing is said to be like another. ("With its high buildings on all sides, Bay Street is like a canyon.")
B. METAPHOR: A figure of speech, literally false but poetically true, in which one thing is said to *be* another. ("Bay Street is a canyon walled by cliffs of concrete.")

C. HYPERBOLE: Exaggeration. ("The office buildings rise miles above the city.")

D. PERSONIFICATION: A figure of speech in which a non-human object is described as human. ("At night the empty buildings stare from their windows at the street.")

FORMAL   Formal writing is deliberate and dignified. It avoids partial sentences, most contractions, colloquial expressions and slang. Instead its vocabulary is standard and its sentences are often long and qualified with dependent clauses. In general it follows the accepted rules of grammar and principles of style. *See also* INFORMAL.

HYPERBOLE   *See* FIGURES OF SPEECH.

INFORMAL   Informal writing resembles speech and, in fact, is often a representation of speech in writing. It may contain partial sentences, many short sentences, contractions, COLLOQUIAL expressions and sometimes SLANG. *See also* FORMAL.

IRONY   A manner of expression in which a statement that seems literally to mean one thing in fact means another. "That's just great!" is a literal statement when said by a dinner guest enjoying the fondue, but is an ironic complaint when said by a driver who has backed into a tree. In a larger sense, *irony of situation* is a contrast between what is expected to happen and what does happen. It is this that creates our interest in the national leader who is impeached, the orphan who becomes a millionaire or the preacher convicted of tax fraud. Irony is a powerful tool of argument, and especially of SATIRE.

JARGON   Technical language or language that seeks to impress by appearing difficult or technical. Specialized terms can hardly be avoided in technical explanations: how could two electricians discuss a radio without words like "capacitor," "diode" and "transistor"? But these same words may need definition if they are used in an essay for the general reader. Other jargon uses technical-sounding or otherwise difficult words to seem important. An honest essayist will try to avoid "input," "output," "feedback," "interface," "knowledgeable," "parameters" and other ugly words of this sort when writing for the general reader.

METAPHOR   *See* FIGURES OF SPEECH.

NEOLOGISM   A newly invented word. Some new terms are accepted into our standard vocabulary. For example, a word like "laser" tends to become standard because it is needed to label a new and important invention. Most newly minted words are nuisances, though, for they are meaningless to the great majority of readers who do not know them.

OBJECTIVE   The opposite of SUBJECTIVE. In objective writing the author relies more on hard evidence and logical proof than on intuitions, prejudices or interpretations.

ONOMATOPOEIA   A poetical device in which language sound like what it means. Some onomatopoetic words, such as "boom," "bang" and "crash," are out-and-out sound effects; others, such as "slither," "ooze" and "clatter," are more subtle. Onomatopoeia can be achieved not only through word choice but also through larger aspects of style. A series of short sentences, for example, gives an impression of tenseness and rapidity.

PARADOX   A statement that seems illogical but that in some unexpected way may be true. The Bible is full of paradoxes, as in "Blessed are the meek: for they shall inherit the earth."

PERSONIFICATION   *See* FIGURES OF SPEECH.

PROSE   Spoken or written language without the metrical structure that characterizes poetry. Conversations, letters, short stories, novels and essays are all prose.

PUN   A play on words. A pun is based either on two meanings of one word or on two words that sound alike but have different meanings. Often called the lowest form of humour, the pun is the basis of many jokes. (Why did the fly fly? Because the spider spider.)

QUOTATION   The words of one person reproduced exactly in the writing or speech of another person. A well-chosen quotation can add force to an argument by conveying the opinion of an authority or by presenting an idea in words so exact or memorable that they could hardly be improved upon. Quotations should be reproduced exactly, and of course should be placed in quotation marks and attributed to their source.

SATIRE   Humorous criticism meant to improve an individual or society by exposing abuses. In TONE, satire can range from light humour to bitter criticism. Its chief tools are wit, IRONY, exaggeration, and sometimes sarcasm and ridicule.

SENSE IMAGES   Descriptive appeals to one or more of the reader's five senses: sight, hearing, touch, taste and smell. Sense images are vital in helping the reader to experience, at second hand, what the writer has experienced in person. CONCRETE language has many sense images; ABSTRACT language does not.

SIMILE   *See* FIGURES OF SPEECH.

SLANG   Racy, unconventional language often limited to a certain time, place or group. Slang is the extreme of colloquial language, terminology used in conversation but hardly ever in an essay except for dialogue or special effects. One reason to avoid a slang term is that not everyone will know it: expressions like "swell," "square" and "far out" have gone out of use, while expressions like "bug juice," "croaker," "jointman" and "rounder" are known to only one group — in this case, convicts. *See also* COLLOQUIAL.

STEREOTYPE   An established mental image of something. Most stereotypes are of people, and are based on their sex, race, colour, size or shape, economic or social class, or profession. Jokes about mothers-in-law, "Newfies," absent-minded professors, women drivers or short people are all examples of stereotyping. While they may provoke humour, stereotypes are anything but harmless: they hinder recognition of people's individuality and they encourage prejudices which, at their extreme, can result in persecution like that of the Jews in Nazi Germany.

STYLE   In general, the way something is written, as opposed to what it is written about. Style is to some extent a matter of TONE — light or serious, INFORMAL or FORMAL, ironic or literal. It is also a matter of technique. Word choice, FIGURES OF SPEECH, level of CONCISENESS, and characteristics of sentence structure and paragraphing are all ingredients of style. Although a writer should pay close attention to these matters, the idea that one deliberately seeks out "a style" is a mistake that only encourages imitation. An individual style emerges naturally as the sum of the writer's temperament, skills and experience.

SUBJECTIVE   The opposite of OBJECTIVE. In subjective writing the author relies more on intuitions, prejudices or interpretations than on hard evidence and logical proof.

SYMBOL   One thing that stands for another, as in a flag representing a country, the cross representing Christianity, or a logo representing a company. Symbols appear frequently in poetry, drama, fiction and also essays. For example the wall, in Austin Clarke's "Old Year's Night," physically separates the islanders from the tourists; at the same time it symbolizes the separation of the two groups by race, culture and economic class. Many symbols, like the wall, are tangible things that represent intangible things.

THESIS STATEMENT   The sentence or sentences, usually in the introduction, which first state the main point and restrict the focus of an essay.

TONE   The manner of a writer toward the subject and reader. The tone of an essay can be light or serious, INFORMAL or FORMAL, ironic or literal. Tone is often determined by subject matter; for example, an essay about cocktail parties is likely to be lighter and less formal than one about funerals. An innovative writer, though, could reverse these treatments to give each of the essays an ironic tone. The identity of the reader also influences tone. An essay for specialists to read in a technical journal will tend to be more OBJECTIVE and serious than one written for the general reader. The main point for the writer is to choose the tone most appropriate to a particular essay, then maintain it throughout.